W9-ALV-321

Issues in World Politics

Issues in World Politics

Third edition

**Edited by Brian White,
Richard Little
and
Michael Smith**

First published 2005 by
PALGRAVE MACMILLAN
Houndmills, Basingstoke, Hampshire RG21 6XS and
175 Fifth Avenue, New York, N.Y. 10010
Companies and representatives throughout the world

PALGRAVE MACMILLAN is the global academic imprint of the Palgrave
Macmillan division of St. Martin's Press, LLC and of Palgrave Macmillan Ltd.
Macmillan is a registered trademark in the United States, United Kingdom
and other countries. Palgrave is a registered trademark in the European
Union and other countries.

ISBN-13: 978–1–4039–4610–2   hardback
ISBN-10: 1–4039–4610–8   hardback
ISBN-13: 978–1–4039–4611–9   paperback
ISBN-10: 1–4039–4611–6   paperback

This book is printed on paper suitable for recycling and
made from fully managed and sustained forest sources.

A catalogue record for this book is available from the British Library.

A catalog record for this book is available from the
Library of Congress.
Library of Congress Catalogue Card Number: 2005048846

10   9   8   7   6   5   4   3
14 13 12 11 10 09 08 07 06

Printed in China

Contents

List of Figures, Tables, Boxes and Maps

Figures

Tables

Boxes

Map

Preface

This is the third edition of a book that attempts to meet the challenge of introducing students to world politics. It does so by adopting as its focus the range of issues that are at the heart of the agenda of contemporary world politics. The working assumption is that issues that are often the subject of topical debate and media coverage provide an important point of access to world politics for a large number of students. The book therefore seeks to build upon some knowledge and an existing interest not only by providing relevant information and a context for making sense of particular issues but also by explicitly addressing the question of what these issues collectively tell us about the nature of world politics at the beginning of the twenty-first century.

Once again, producing a third edition was only possible with the cooperation of a number of people. Steven Kennedy, our publisher at Palgrave Macmillan, supported and chivvied us with his characteristic enthusiasm and hands-on involvement. The editors were again delighted to receive the willing support of experts on various issues who rose to the challenge of writing for non-specialist as well as specialist students. Both old and new contributors made the editors' job manageable, and even pleasurable, for which many thanks to them.

Figures 3.1 and 4.1 are copyright of the World Trade Organization. Figure 12.1 is copyright of Mark D. Alleyne and is reproduced by permission of Palgrave Macmillan. Every effort has been made to contact all the copyright holders of third party material included but if any have been inadvertently omitted the publishers will be pleased to make the necessary arrangements at the earliest opportunity.

BRIAN WHITE
RICHARD LITTLE
MICHAEL SMITH

List of Abbreviations and Acronyms

ABM	anti-ballistic missile
AIDS	acquired immune deficiency syndrome
AOSIS	Alliance of Small Island States
APEC	Asia-Pacific Economic Cooperation
ASEAN	Association of Southeast Asian Nations
AU	African Union
BIS	Bank for International Settlements
BJP	Bharatiya Janata Party (India)
BTWC	Biological and Toxin Weapons Convention
CAFOD	Catholic Fund for Overseas Development
CBC	Christian Base Community
CBD	Convention on Biological Diversity (UN)
CBW	chemical and biological weapons
CCW	Convention on Conventional Weapons
CD	Committee on Disarmament
CEE	Central and Eastern Europe
CFCs	chlorofluorocarbons
CIA	Central Intelligence Agency
CIS	Commonwealth of Independent States
CITES	Convention on International Trade in Endangered Species
CMEA	Council for Mutual Economic Assistance (USSR)
CoCom	Coordinating Committee on Multilateral Export Controls
CSD	Commission for Sustainable Development (UN)
CTBT	Comprehensive Test Ban Treaty
CWC	Chemical Weapons Convention
DAC	Development Assistance Committee (OECD)
ECOWAS	Economic Community of West African States
ERM	Exchange Rate Mechanism
ETA	Euskadi ta Askatasuna
EU	European Union
FAO	Food and Agriculture Organization (UN)
FATF	Financial Action Task Force
FCCC	Framework Convention on Climate Change
FBI	Federal Bureau of Investigation (US)
FDI	foreign direct investment
FIS	Front Islamic de Salut (Algeria)
FSU	Former Soviet Union
G7	Group of Seven

G8	Group of Eight
GATT	General Agreement on Trade and Tariffs
GDO	grass-roots development organization
GDP	gross domestic product
GDR	German Democratic Republic
GEC	Global Environmental Change
GHG	greenhouse gas
GM	genetically modified
GNP	gross national product
HCFC	hydrochlorofluorocarbons
HIV	human immunodeficiency virus
IAEA	International Atomic Energy Agency
ICBM	inter-continental ballistic missile
ICC	International Criminal Court
ICES	International Council for the Exploration of the Seas
ICISS	International Commission on Intervention and State Sovereignty
ICMI	Ikatan Cendekiawan Muslin se-Indonesia (Association of Indonesian Muslin Intellectuals)
IFOR	Implementation Force (of NATO) in Bosnia-Herzegovina
IGO	inter-governmental organization
IIED	International Institute for Environment and Development
IMF	International Monetary Fund
INF	Intermediate Nuclear Forces Treaty
INGO	International Non-Governmental Organization
IPCC	Intergovernmental Panel on Climate Change
IPE	International Political Economy
IR	International Relations
IRA	Irish Republican Army
IUCN	International Union for the Conservation of Nature
JIT	just-in-time
KFOR	Kosovo Force (NATO)
LRTAP	Convention on Long-Range Transboundary Air Pollution
MDG	Millennium Development Goals
MERCOSUR	Mercado Comun del Cono Sur (Southern Common Market)
MNC	multinational corporation/company
MTCR	Missile Technology Control Regime
NAFTA	North American Free Trade Agreement
NATO	North Atlantic Treaty Organization
NGO	non-governmental organization
NIC	newly industrializing country
NIEO	new international economic order
NPT	Nuclear Non-Proliferation Treaty
NSG	Nuclear Suppliers' Group

NWICO	New World Information and Communication Order
OAS	Organization of American States
OCHA	Office for the Coordination of Humanitarian Affairs (UN)
OECD	Organization for Economic Co-operation and Development
OSCE	Organization for Security and Cooperation in Europe
PR	public relations
PRSP	Poverty Reduction Strategy Paper
PSI	Proliferation Security Initiative
PSO	peace support operations
RICO	Racketeering Influences and Corrupt Organizations Act
RPF	Rwandan Patriotic Front
SADC	Southern African Development Community
SALT	Strategic Arms Limitation Talks
SALW	small arms and light weapons
SAP	structural adjustment programme
SFOR	Stability Force
SIPRI	Stockholm International Peace Research Institute
SORT	Strategic Offensive Reduction Treaty
START	Strategic Arms Reduction Treaty
TNB	transnational bank
UK	United Kingdom
UN	United Nations
UNCED	United Nations Conference on Environment and Development
UNCTAD	United Nations Conference on Trade and Development
UNDP	United Nations Development Programme
UNEP	United Nations Environment Programme
UNHCR	United Nations High Commission for Refugees
UNICEF	United Nations International Children's Emergency Fund
UNIDO	United Nations Industrial Development Organization
UNMIK	United Nations Mission in Kosovo
US	United States
USSR	Union of Soviet Socialist Republics
VAT	value-added tax
WCED	World Commission on Environment and Development
WEU	Western European Union
WMD	weapons of mass destruction
WMO	World Meteorological Organization
WTO	World Trade Organization
WWF	World Wildlife Fund

Notes on the Contributors

Sita Bali is a Senior Lecturer in International Relations at Staffordshire University. Her doctoral research explored the international political implications of migration through an examination of the British Sikh community. Her specialist interests are Migration and Refugee Studies and South Asian Politics, and she has published articles and book chapters in these areas.

Susan Carruthers is an Associate Professor of History at Rutgers, the State University of New Jersey, where she teaches US foreign relations and international history. Her research focuses on the communicative dimensions of cross-cultural relations in the twentieth century. In addition to many articles, her books include *Winning Hearts and Minds: British Governments, the Media and Colonial Counterinsurgency* (1995) and *The Media at War: Communication and Conflict in the Twentieth Century* (2000).

Tim Dunne is Reader in International Relations and Head of the Department of Politics, University of Exeter. Previously, he worked for ten years in the Department of International Politics at Aberystwyth. He is author of *Inventing International Society* (1998) and was associate editor of the *Review of International Studies* from 1998 to 2002. He has edited six books including *Human Rights in Global Politics* (with Nicholas J. Wheeler, 1998) and *Worlds in Collision: Terror and the Future of Global Order* (with Ken Booth, 2002).

Jeff Haynes is Professor of Politics at London Guildhall University, where he teaches courses on international and third world politics. His most recent books include *Politics in the Developing World. A Concise Introduction* (2002), *Comparative Politics in a Globalizing World* (2005), *Palgrave Advances in Development Studies* (editor and contributor of three chapters) (2005), *The Politics of Religion* (2005), *Religion and International Relations* (forthcoming 2006).

Richard Little is Professor of International Politics at the University of Bristol. He has also taught at the Open University and Lancaster University and was the editor of the *Review of International Studies* from 1990 to 1994. He has written extensively on international relations theory and his publications include *The Logic of Anarchy* (with Barry Buzan and Charles Jones, 1993) and *International Systems in World History* (with Barry Buzan, 2000).

Michael Pugh is Professor of International Relations and Director of the International Studies Research Centre at the University of Plymouth. He is editor of the journal *International Peacekeeping* and of a book series on peacekeeping published by Frank Cass. His latest books are an edited volume, *The United Nations and Regional Security* (with W. P. S. Sidhu, 2004) and *War Economies in a Regional Context* (with Neil Cooper, 2004). He leads research on the post-conflict transformation of war-torn societies.

Melvyn Reader received his doctorate in international relations from the University of Southampton in 1998. His thesis was on 'The Rise of Protestant "Fundamentalism" in World Politics: A Case Study of Brazil'. He was Senior Research Manager at the Millennium Group, a research-based consultancy focused on the business consequences of the emerging network economy, and is now Policy Development Officer for Eastleigh Borough Council.

Alan Russell is a Principal Lecturer in International Relations at Staffordshire University. He teaches and publishes mainly in the area of technology and international political economy. He is the author of *The Biotechnology Revolution: An International Perspective* (1988). His most recent book is *The International Politics of Biotechnology* (with John Vogler as co-editor, 2000).

Stephen Ryan is a Senior Lecturer in Peace and Conflict Studies at Magee College, University of Ulster. He is the author of *Ethnic Conflict and International Relations* (1995) and *The United Nations and International Politics* (2000). He has also published widely elsewhere on the dynamics and the resolution of ethnic conflict and on UN peacekeeping. He is now working on a study of the transformation of violent inter-communal conflicts.

Michael Smith is Professor of European Politics and Jean Monnet Chair holder in the Department of Politics, International Relations and European Studies at Loughborough University. His publications include *Perspectives on World Politics* (with Richard Little as co-editor, 3rd edition, 2005), *Foreign Policy in a Transformed World* (with Mark Webber as co-editor, 2002) and *International Relations and the European Union* (with Christopher Hill as co-editor, 2005).

Joanna Spear is the Director of the US Foreign Policy Institute at the George Washington University, Washington, DC. She was previously a senior lecturer in the Department of War Studies, King's College London. Her current research encompasses a number of security issues including post-conflict peacebuilding, WMD proliferation, counter-insurgency and US defence policy.

Caroline Thomas is Professor of Global Politics at Southampton University. She has a long-standing interest in North–South relations. Her current research is on globalization and human security, with particular reference to inequality and health. Her publications include *Global Trade and Global Social Issues* (with Annie Taylor as co-editor, 1999), *Globalization, Human Security and the African Experience* (with Peter Wilkin as co-editor, 1999), *Global Governance, Development and Human Security* (2000), and articles in *Third World Quarterly*, *Global Governance* and the *British Journal of Politics and International Relations*.

John Vogler is Professor of International Relations at Keele University. Since 1990 he has been the Convener of the BISA Environment Group and a member of the Economic and Social Research Council Global Environment Change Programme Committee. His publications include *The Environment and International Relations* (with Mark Imber as co-editor, 1996), *The International Politics of Biotechnology* (with Alan Russell as co-editor, 2000) and *The Global Commons: Environmental and Technological Governance* (2000). Current research interests involve the role of the European Union in global environmental governance.

Mark Webber is Senior Lecturer in the Department of Politics, International Relations and European Studies (PIRES), Loughborough University. He is the author of *The International Politics of Russia and the Successor States* (1996), joint author of *The Enlargement of Europe* (1999), editor of *Russia and Europe: Confrontation or Cooperation* (2000), and co-editor (with Michael Smith) of *Foreign Policy in a Transformed World* (2002). His current research interests include European 'security governance', the transformation of NATO, and Russian foreign policy.

Brian White is currently a professor of International Relations at Warwick University and an associate professor in the Institut d'Etudes Politiques at the University of Toulouse. He teaches and researches mainly in the area of foreign policy analysis. His major publications include *Understanding Foreign Policy* (with Michael Clarke as co-editor, 1989), *Britain, Detente and Changing East–West Relations* (1992) and, most recently, *Understanding European Foreign Policy* (2001), and *Contemporary European Foreign Policy* (with Walter Carlsnaes and Helene Sjursen, 2004).

Phil Williams is Professor of International Security at the Graduate School of Public and International Affairs, the University of Pittsburgh. He is currently studying organized crime, terrorist finances, and intelligence for transnational threats. He has published extensively on national and international security issues and in the last ten years has focused his work on transnational threats to security.

Chapter 1

Issues in World Politics

BRIAN WHITE, RICHARD LITTLE
AND MICHAEL SMITH

When Zhou Enlai, the first Prime Minister and for 25 years the chief diplomat of communist China, was asked what he thought of the French Revolution, he is reputed to have said that it was too early to say. We are not taking this very long view of history. Instead, this book introduces the reader to world politics by providing an understanding of issues that are considered, at this moment, to be at the heart of the international agenda. Our assumption is that the identity of these issues, the general problems that they represent and the reasons for their location on the international agenda will tell us much about the nature of world politics at the beginning of the twenty-first century. To do this job effectively, however, it is also necessary to reflect on how and why the agenda has changed in the recent past and how it may change again in the future. The first two editions of this book were premised on the assumption that the end of the Cold War had a substantial effect on the international agenda. But it was also stressed that there are enduring problems that never disappear from this agenda. As we move through the first decade of the twenty-first century, this sense of continuity and change persists.

Two sets of images from this century, that have already acquired iconic status, reinforce the idea of change and continuity, but also highlight the difficulties of establishing whether and how dramatic events on the world stage will impact on the international agenda. The first set of images relates to the two planes, flown by members of Al Qaeda, that crashed into the World Trade Center on 11 September 2001 (9/11), causing the twin towers to collapse. The second set of images is of the giant tidal wave – a tsunami – rolling into the centre of a holiday resort, on 26 December 2004, followed over the subsequent week by innumerable images of villages and towns around the coastlines of Indonesia, Sri Lanka, Thailand, and Malaysia that had been utterly devastated by this natural disaster.

Both of these events seemed in some ways to come from nowhere; they were largely or completely unanticipated, and each of them took a form that seemed to be unprecedented in scale and destructiveness. In that sense, they can be seen (and were seen at the times they occurred) as sudden transformations with incalculable effects. But the reality is that they occurred within a context of previous incidents of terrorism and international conflict, or of natural disasters and their management, which gave them certain meanings and impacts. This is not to belittle the dramatic effects these events had on human lives and on whole societies when they did occur, rather it is to point out that even where events are at their most sudden and cataclysmic it is important to examine the context in which they happen, which often gives a new perspective on the quality of change and its consequences.

We already know some of the consequences of the Al Qaeda attack. It helped to precipitate a war on terror, led by the United States, and was used to justify in whole or in part invasions of Afghanistan and Iraq. The invasion of Afghanistan in 2001, however, deeply divided the international community; the invasion of Iraq in 2003 not only split the international community, but also threatened to destroy a consensus amongst leaders across the Western world on how to manage security issues that had held for over fifty years. So while there is no doubt that terrorism is high on the international agenda, there are deep divisions within the international community about how to assess and deal with this issue – divisions that do seem to mark a significant and enduring change in the political climate.

It is much more difficult to evaluate what the long-term consequences of the tsunami will be. At the time we wrote this chapter, only days after the tsunami, the full extent of the disaster was still not known, and the issue continued to occupy the top of the international agenda. But would it stay there? The evidence from the past is not encouraging. As natural disasters have slipped off the headlines, governments find it all too easy to forget their original verbal commitments and ignore the long-term consequences for countries struggling to deal with the aftermath of these disasters. A certain type of continuity is thus re-established, and the implications of changes and crisis are in some ways absorbed into the broader flow of political and social experience.

It is important, however, to recognise that neither the twin towers nor the tsunami disasters constitute international issues in themselves – rather, they are important and dramatic examples of broader issues linked with global conflict and cooperation, or with economic, social and environmental problems. Thus 9/11 unquestionably pushed the issue of terrorism up the agenda, and affected the management of global conflicts at least in the medium term, while it remains to be seen whether the Boxing Day tsunami fundamentally affects the ability of the international community to maintain sustained long-term humanitarian assistance. The immediate response by individuals and governments was unprecedented. But at an early stage there were concerns that this assistance would draw support away from other areas and issues. Although the death toll resulting from the tsunami was appalling, it does not begin to compare with the number of people around the world who are dying every year from malnutrition and preventable diseases.

This book, therefore, is designed to alert the reader to the ways in which current global issues have emerged, how they are handled and what their effects might be. There are, of course, other ways of writing an introductory textbook on world politics. We might, for example, have focused on the ways in which political activities at the global level have (or have not) changed in recent years, seen as a whole – as an interacting system of activity as it is often called – or, to use a different analogy, we might have concentrated on the foreign policy behaviour of the principal 'players' who participate in a game of world politics. Alternatively, we might have reviewed the main theories by which students of world politics try to make sense of the global political world in which we live. These are conventional approaches and there are several good examples of textbooks that employ one or a combination of them.

The approach adopted here is rather different, not in terms of the objective of understanding contemporary world politics, but in terms of the way we seek to achieve that objective. Without suggesting that our approach is superior, we would claim that an introductory textbook that focuses on global issues has the advantage of building upon a general interest in and knowledge of world politics that the reader may already have from exposure to the media – press, television and increasingly internet coverage of world politics. Of its nature, media coverage of world politics tends to focus on immediate, easily identifiable, often dramatic issues that will attract and hold the attention of its audience, rather than on longer-term trends or explanatory theories that are deemed to be less 'newsworthy' by producers/ editors who are preoccupied with sales or ratings. By using issues as our principal focus, we too hope to attract a more general reader who is intrigued by particular aspects of world politics, as well as the more specialized student of world politics for whom this will be a useful if rather unconventional introductory text.

The purpose of this first chapter is twofold: to put issues discussed in later chapters into both an historical and an analytical context and, more importantly, to establish a common framework for the discussion of those issues. Put in a more direct way, we are seeking here a preliminary answer to two deceptively simple questions: what are the most significant issues in contemporary world politics – and why?

The end of the Cold War and a new global agenda?

It should be stated clearly at the outset that there is no attempt here to cover all the major issues in contemporary world politics, if only because of limitations of space. But choosing to discuss certain issues rather than others does require making the criteria for selection explicit. An obvious starting point is to look critically at the idea that the world today is distinctively different from, say, the world of the 1970s or 1980s – because of the end of the Cold War. This new period is now well established though it is still often referred to rather unsatisfactorily as the post-Cold War period. It could be argued that events have overtaken the end of the Cold War and that it is 9/11 and the subsequent 'war on terror' that can be seen to be the more important turning point. If we take our cue from Zhou Enlai, however, it is probably still too early to say, but our betting is that in years to come it will be end of the Cold War that is seen to represent the more significant transformation point in world politics.

The alleged distinctiveness of the post-Cold War period rests upon the predominance of new issues. Not only have the operating structures changed – with world politics no longer defined essentially by an ideological–military struggle between two dominant centres of power controlled, respectively, by two 'Superpowers', the United States and the Soviet Union – but also, it is argued, the agenda of world politics has been transformed. The 'agenda' in this context may be defined as the cluster of issues around which political activity takes place. No longer is world politics dominated by issues arising from East–West relations – the threat of nuclear war, the ideological struggle between liberal democracy and Marxism–Leninism, crisis diplomacy, and so on. The international community is now preoccupied with other issues such as the search for a 'New World Order', the impact of terrorism, the disparities in wealth between developed and developing countries and environmental issues.

But as suggested earlier, the most cursory look at the world at the beginning of the twenty-first century suggests that an analysis that focuses exclusively on dramatic change, on the emergence of 'new' issues replacing 'old', understates important elements of continuity in world politics and lacks a sense of historical perspective. The period 1989–91 – from the dismantling of the Berlin Wall, through the removal from office of several Communist governments in Eastern Europe, to the demise of the Soviet Union – may well mark a watershed that will be compared by future historians to other key 'turning points' in history such as 1789–94, 1917–18, and 1945–7. But as the distinguished international historian, John Lewis Gaddis commented with respect to the end of the Cold War, 'precisely what has "turned" is much less certain' (quoted in Hogan, 1992, p. 22).

The short-lived euphoria of 1990–1, when a multinational military force headed by the United States and legitimized by UN resolutions defeated Saddam Hussein's Iraq and gave some substance to Western triumphalism, has long since given way to the painful realization that a 'New World Order', however defined, is still a long way from achievement. For all the immediate gains of post-Cold War world politics – and these must include the dissolution of apartheid in South Africa, a fragile peace in Northern Ireland and the extension of the European Union into Eastern Europe – we must also note the eruption of bloody armed conflict in such places as Bosnia, Angola, Kosovo, Congo, Chechnya and Sudan, genocide in Rwanda, nuclear proliferation (with India and Pakistan both acquiring nuclear weapons), and the persistence of conflict in the Middle East. The international community, far from being strengthened in its resolve or ability to solve problems, more often seems unwilling or incapable of dealing with these issues – although it is possible to view the outcome of the former Yugoslav conflict with a degree of satisfaction. Some at least of these problems appear to be either a product of the end of the Cold War or to have been exacerbated by these changes.

If we consider one of the so-called 'new' issues that has emerged in the wake of the Cold War, we may discover the limits of the 'everything has changed' hypothesis. A major issue that confronts the international community, already alluded to, is the military conflict between ethnic groups within, for example, the states that succeeded the former Yugoslavia and the former Soviet Union – Croat versus Muslim versus Serb; Azeri versus Armenian, Russian versus Chechen and so on. Clearly, the demise of the Soviet Union was directly or indirectly the catalyst for the emergence of open conflict in these areas. The sources of these and other conflicts, however, lie in a more complex struggle for national self-determination that has both a much longer historical explanation over time and a much wider spread geographically. Inter-ethnic conflict has emerged at different times and places and in different forms and posed different sorts of problems for the international community.

Whether an issue is 'old' or 'new' then appears to be less important than the factors that determine the form in which an issue appears on the international agenda. What we can suggest at this stage is that the prevailing international context provides one set of factors that determines the shape or form in which an issue appears. A different set of issues is likely to emerge at different times and (probably) in different forms – in part determined by the international context or situation. But there are other factors involved in determining why an issue emerges, when and in what form, and these need to be investigated.

Issues and problems

An issue in world politics attracts the attention of those who engage in that activity and requires the expenditure of resources in some form, if only the expenditure of diplomatic resources. Similarly, issues engage the attention of those who wish to understand world politics. But understanding an issue goes beyond knowing the facts and figures associated with it, however important that might be. It is necessary to put the issue into context. Part of that context has already been established – the international situation as it is at any point in history. The end of the Cold War has played a part in presenting issues in a particular form in contemporary world politics. Another, equally important context from an analytical perspective is to establish the problem area within which the issue resides and which gives meaning to that issue. The debt crisis, for example, was an issue that first attracted considerable attention from the international community in the

1980s. The fear was that many developing countries who were in considerable debt would default on their loans and create chaos in international economic relations. This issue was readdressed at the end of the 1990s with significant new attempts to remove debt. But it remains as a very significant item on the international agenda – indeed, pressure for debt forgiveness was one of the immediate consequences of the tsunami that struck a number of developing countries in South and Southeast Asia at the end of 2004.

The debt issue emerged from a specific international context. It was a product essentially of two developments. First, many developing countries borrowed heavily from abroad encouraged by the example of the oil-rich states who appeared to be successfully using 'commodity power' to change the terms of trade between developed and developing states. But, the recession that followed the dramatic rise in oil prices in the late 1970s/early 1980s ironically and equally dramatically eroded the ability of developing countries to repay the debts incurred.

The point being made here by reference to this illustration is not only that issues rise and fall on the international agenda for specific reasons but, more importantly, that they usually represent one 'face' of a more persistent problem or set of problems that confront world politics. In this case, the debt crisis was and is a particular manifestation of a problem that is usually known in a shorthand form as the 'rich–poor' or the 'North–South' problem. In general terms, this refers to the post-colonial situation in which a large number of new states (the 'South') find themselves forced to operate at a significant disadvantage in an international economic system controlled by and run for the benefit of a much smaller group of wealthy, developed states (the 'North'). This international context compounds the problems that developing states face from a host of domestic political, economic and social problems. From this inherently structural set of problems flow a number of inter-related issues that challenge the international community.

Issues, agendas and agenda-setting

If problems spawn issues in various forms, there is also an even more overtly political context that may determine whether or not an issue emerges on the international agenda and certainly helps to determine the form in which the issue appears. It can be assumed that the contents of the agenda of world politics at any point in time are not random. Those who participate in world politics (representatives of governments, various types of governmental and non-governmental organizations (NGOs), and so on) are essentially political actors, which means that they have interests to advance and defend. The resolution of these competing interests at the global level provides a simple definition of what world politics is all about. This is often presented rather snappily as 'who gets what, when and how'. Although theorists disagree about how that power is constructed, there is a structure of power and interests in world politics and we should not be surprised to see this reflected on the agenda, the range and type of issues located on that agenda and the form in which those issues appear.

This political context can be illustrated by reference to another issue that attracted much attention and debate, particularly after the end of the Cold War – the rise of what is called 'Islamic fundamentalism'. This issue can be described briefly as the resurgence of the Islamic world in religious and political terms, following a new confidence in indigenous social, cultural and political structures. Islam is clearly a global force of some significance, if only because some 20 per cent of the world population is Muslim, and Muslims constitute at least 50 per cent of the population in more than 30 countries. In terms of heightening awareness of the resurgence of Islam, an event of major significance for both the Muslim and the non-Muslim world was the Islamic revolution in Iran in 1979 which brought to power the Ayatollah Khomeini.

The wider problem from which this issue emerged also has a post-colonial context, though historians of Islam remind us that there have been several resurgences of Islam on an almost cyclical basis. After independence from colonial rule had been achieved, many leaders of Islamic countries took the view that the requirements of development necessitated the downgrading of traditional Islamic values and the enthusiastic embrace of what was variously called modernization, secularization and Westernization – adopting, in short, the liberal democratic social and political values of the West. For a number of reasons, however, including frustrated post-independence aspirations, rapid urbanization, population explosions and increasingly evident disparities in wealth, a popular disillusionment with Western values and materialism in particular began to set in. The result evident since the 1970s within and beyond Muslim states has been a continuing tension between very different sets of religious, cultural and political values.

Going beyond this simple description of an issue and a problem, however, we have to take note here of the political context which helps to present the issue in a particular form. The clue comes from the use in the West of the term 'fundamentalism' – rather than 'rise' or 'resurgence' – which has been commonly associated with Islam since the Iranian revolution. While the term 'Islamic fundamentalism' can refer to the growth of Islam as a religious force and a political ideology and, most accurately perhaps, to the desire to reinstate the Islamic legal code, the Sharia law, it has come to have rather different connotations in popular usage. For many in the West, 'Islamic fundamentalism' is synonymous with a form of religious bigotry and violence that poses not only a religious but also a political threat to Western values and institutions. Some even talk of an inevitable confrontation between Islam and the West (see, for example, Huntington, 1996). The use of suicide bombers by Al Qaeda and other Islamic groups helps to feed this manichean view of the world.

Clearly, the presentation of any issue in world politics in a particular form is likely to serve political interests. It is intended to evoke a particular sort of reaction from other players in the global political game. The student of world politics, whose prime concern is to understand what is going on, should take this political context into account. One way of doing this is to look critically at the assumptions that underpin the presentation of an issue and review the evidence that supports it. With reference to the resurgence of Islam, the question might simply be whether or not Islam constitutes a cohesive entity that is united in its determination to overthrow Western institutions. The answers may well cast doubt on the more lurid connotations associated with Islamic fundamentalism.

Types of issues

History has been said to consist of 'one damned thing after another'. And the same thing could be said of world politics. One of our tasks, however, is to help you to move away from such an assessment. There is nothing wrong with thinking of world politics as a continuous stream of events, but it becomes very difficult to analyze issues if they are always thought of in this way. Social scientists argue that it is necessary to classify issues so as to facilitate the task of comparing and contrasting them. The importance of this approach is now often taken for granted by social scientists because so many areas of the natural sciences seem to have reaped such enormous benefits from following it. Branches of the biological sciences, in particular, seem to have derived their initial impetus from analysts who displayed an interest in establishing typologies and taxonomies of living things.

It is dangerous, however, to draw too close a parallel between the natural and social sciences. The typologies established by natural scientists map onto an external reality which is left unaffected by the process of classification. In the social sciences, however, typologies can actually form part of the reality which is being analyzed. Because the typologies used by social scientists can be implicated in social reality, they can actually change the nature of social reality. Think, for example, of the various ways in which individuals get classified by the state, according to age, gender, class, race, religion and so on. The labels used in classifications can become very politically sensitive because closer inspection shows how the labels can become linked very directly to a political agenda. In former Yugoslavia, for example, it was the state that began to classify people according to religion. This was of no great consequence in Croatia, where the people were Catholic, or in Serbia, where the people were Orthodox Christians. But it did make a difference in Bosnia which had for centuries been a multicultural community made up of people who identified themselves first and foremost as Bosnian. Once the religious differences began to be accentuated, however, whereas the Muslims in the region continued to identify themselves as Bosnian, the Catholics in the area began to identify themselves more clearly as Croatian and the Orthodox Christian as Serbian. When tensions rose following the break-up of Yugoslavia, this development was to contribute to tragic consequences.

Ethnic identification is an issue that has risen rapidly up the world politics agenda in recent years. But for much of the Cold War, it was not a prominent issue. It is of interest, therefore, to look back on the classificatory schemes which prevailed during that period, not only because they illustrate that such schemes are a product of their time, but also because they help to reveal the origins of contemporary classification schemes. There were two dominant and inter-related typologies which prevailed in the early Cold War period. In retrospect, what is most apparent is how simplistic these typologies now appear. In the first instance, there appeared to be a neat and tidy as well as relatively uncontroversial distinction to be drawn between domestic and international issues. Because states were considered sovereign and autonomous entities, they were habitually identified, metaphorically, as billiard balls or chess pieces, moving within the arena of world politics. Issues arising within these impermeable entities were identified as domestic, while issues arising between them were considered to be international. On the basis of this initial distinction, international issues were then further distinguished in terms of high and low politics. The nature of this distinction, however, is not at all obvious and requires some elaboration.

It would be tempting, but only superficially accurate, to suggest that 'high politics' concerns important issues and 'low politics' concerns unimportant issues. But it would be closer to the truth to suggest that high politics involves issues that determine the nature of the environment within which low politics can take place. High politics, therefore, was seen to be concerned with the maintenance of state security and the management of the diplomatic environment within which states interact. High politics were conducted by officials from the foreign office and the defence department. By ensuring the security of the state and the stability of the international diplomatic environment, it was possible for officials concerned with low politics to undertake their tasks. They could negotiate the rules governing trade between states, establish rules that ensured that communications between states could take place, formulate rules that prevented pollution from entering the environment and all the other rules that enable states to interact freely and fruitfully. From this perspective, then, the Korean War, the Suez Crisis, the Test Ban Treaty and the Strategic Arms Limitations Talks (SALT) all involved high politics, whereas the negotiations over the General Agreement on Trade and Tariffs (GATT), the establishment of the Law of the Seas and the implementation of the Antarctic Treaty all involved low politics.

There are two important implications that can be seen to follow from this typology. The first is that high politics takes precedence over low politics. This is not to say that high politics is necessarily more important than low politics, although there is a very strong temptation for those involved in high politics to think in this way. But there is a presumption that low politics cannot take place in the absence of the framework established by the participants in high politics. The second implication is that academics studying world politics should focus on issues that emerge in the realm of high politics at the expense of issues identified in low politics. It then follows, if this typology is accepted, that the study of world politics must concentrate on security and diplomatic issues. And there is little doubt that in the early Cold War days, there would be some truth to the claim that it was issues in these areas that provided the main focus in most textbooks on world politics.

Both of these classificatory schemes, however, have been challenged. In the first place, it is argued that the distinction drawn between domestic and international issues reflects a false distinction. A wide array of issues has been identified which cannot be neatly classified as either 'international' or 'domestic'. The distinction presupposes that states really are hermetically sealed units. But the reality is that they are not. Frequently issues can be seen to have their origins within the state and their consequences beyond the boundary of the state. Problems related to the environment obviously fit into this category. But so too do a whole range of other issues, from refugees to terrorism. A glance at the list of issues dealt with in this book reveals that few of them can be neatly classified as 'international'. They form a type that has been somewhat inelegantly labelled 'intermestic', suggesting that they cannot be neatly located in either the international or the domestic category. These issues are essentially transnational rather than international in character and are regularly used to illustrate that it is simply not helpful to think of sovereign states possessing impermeable boundaries. This state of affairs is now more commonly associated with globalization – one of the most overworked terms in the language of world politics. In essence, globalization relates to the deterritorialization of society, economics and politics and the emergence of new actors and networks that operate alongside existing territorial ones. Non-governmental organizations, multi-national corporations and terrorist groups are all seen to be a product of globalization.

Once it is accepted that the distinction between domestic and international issues is inadequate, then it can come as no surprise that the distinction between high and low politics has also come under attack. Critics insist that it is simply not helpful to suggest that issues associated with military and diplomatic affairs fall into a distinctive category. The refugees who flooded out of Rwanda and Burundi into Zaire in 1994 posed just as much of a threat to this state as if they had been an invading military force. By 1996, this threat was already becoming a reality, and it remains a focus of instabilities in the region into the twenty-first century. And, by the same token, the radiation that escaped following the accident at the nuclear plant at Chernobyl in 1986 had environmental consequences that would have been no different from the explosion of a nuclear bomb. Moreover, the energy released by the 2004 tsunami was the equivalent of thousands of the nuclear weapons used against Hiroshima and Nagasaki. In contemporary world politics, economic collapse, environmental disaster or ethnic conflict are far more likely to bring about the demise of a state than an external war. The distinction between high and low politics, therefore, starts to appear increasingly dated.

There was, however, a very powerful logic that underpinned the distinction between high and low politics. There is no alternative typology that possesses the same level of coherence. In practice what has happened is that an ad hoc typology of issues has grown up, which is augmented as new types of issue come onto the agenda. This may not seem to be an entirely satisfactory state of affairs. On the other hand, it does represent an accurate reflection of the increasingly complex and diverse range of issues that are emerging in world politics. It is no longer possible – indeed, it never was – to think of world politics being defined in military and diplomatic terms. The distinction between high and low politics was always an artificial one. There is no alternative but to take account of the increasing number of issues that spill across the boundaries of states and have profound and long-lasting effects on the nature of world politics.

The significance of issues in world politics

It is clear from what has already been said that issues in world politics will inevitably vary in their salience or significance, and that this is related in quite complex ways to the interests of various groups and institutions operating in the world arena. What makes an issue 'significant' or 'insignificant' at any given time or for any given group? One straightforward definition would be that 'significance' is another word for drama or impact: the most significant issues are those which capture the attention of political leaders or the media at any particular time. But this can be a rather artificial way of defining what matters: the whims of news editors or the ability of groups to capture the headlines may give only a very misleading impression of significance.

It is therefore necessary to add to drama or impact an awareness of the attention paid or priority given to an issue by 'those who matter' – the political leaders or institutions that can make a difference through the kinds of decisions or action they take. This helps us to ask the question 'significant for whom?', which is important in framing an analysis of political action and interaction. A third way of refining our notion of significance is to ask about the long-term implications of an issue: whatever the short-term drama or salience of a particular issue, there needs to be some interpretation of the ways in which it contributes to broader processes of international change and development.

This gives us a set of three initial questions to ask about any issue. First, what is its short-term impact and salience? Second, what is its importance to 'those who matter'? Third, what are its longer-term implications? Seen in the light of these questions, an issue such as global environmental change can be seen to have varied on all three dimensions. In the first place, there have been periodic and often rather dramatic 'eruptions' of the issue – for example, when holes in the ozone layer are identified or their growth noted. At such points, speculation about future developments and 'doomsday scenarios' can proliferate, often fuelled by the media or by interest groups. But it is not apparent that such short-term attention translates into long-term salience for the issue. Such extended attention is likely to be given by the scientific community in particular, but increasingly also it is ensured by the fact that governments and other institutions have 'taken the issue on board' and have developed structures to monitor and analyse it. Thus, the existence of departments for environmental affairs and the associated growth of the environmental policy community ensures a more consistent evaluation – if not more consistent policy outcomes – in such areas as 'global warming'. In turn, this begins to build some awareness of the longer-term significance of the issue, exposing both the dangers of environmental degradation and the ways in which it can be handled through national or international policy-making. In this way, it could be argued that the 'environmental dimension' gets built into the world arena and cemented into the agendas of particular actors.

So far, the question of 'significance' has been assessed in a rather 'political' manner, with the emphasis on the ways in which issues enter the political arena and are noticed. There is a further set of more specific questions that can be asked about a given issue which helps to establish more clearly its location in the world arena. Often, these questions are asked more or less explicitly by political actors in framing their strategies and their responses to calls for action. Four such questions can be identified and used to classify issues:

1. What is the extent or scope of an issue? Does it affect large parts of the global arena, or can it be confined and contained? This, for example, is the kind of question often asked about civil wars and other limited conflicts. How far are they likely to spill over into the broader arena, and thus become of concern to a wide variety of actors?
2. What is the urgency or intensity of a particular issue? This, of course, is a rather subjective question, since it relates to the general question 'significant to whom?' To go back to the issue of global environmental change, it is quite clear that such an issue has different levels of urgency

for different political actors, who will as a result give it different degrees of priority, attention and resources.

3. What is the salience or visibility of a given issue? This question relates to a number of questions already raised in this chapter, and to the roles of the media or other groupings who confer urgency or intensity. It also relates to the ways in which a 'head of steam' can build up behind an issue to make it a fit subject for national or international action, whatever its objective impact.

4. What is the centrality or location of an issue? This is partly an objective issue of geography, implying that the closer an issue is to important actors the greater the attention and significance it will acquire. Perhaps the most famous or notorious expression of this quality is that of Neville Chamberlain when he described Czechoslovakia in 1938 as 'a faraway country of which we know little'. But this example also reveals the other dimension of centrality and location: they are expressions of sensitivity to the issue, and of its links to vital interests. Where these links are powerful, the constraints of geography are of little importance, and such links are enhanced by developments in the media and international communication.

The management of issues in world politics

Very often, when international issues are identified and given 'air-time', there is an implication that 'something must be done'. Sometimes this is expressed in terms of national action, or action by specific private groupings such as companies or pressure groups. But with many issues, there is also the feeling that national or private action is insufficient: the 'world community' should act, and establish some kind of management process to deal with the issue. The question of management is clearly inseparable from the analysis of many issues in world politics, but it is often unclear how the 'world community' or those acting in the world arena can get past the crude call for action and the feeling that if nothing is done things might get out of hand. The question of management is thus partly a matter of the mechanisms through which things can be handled and the interests of different groupings reconciled. At the same time, though, there are inescapable normative questions: about whether management itself is a desirable activity, and about what might be the most effective forms of management. Given that world issues are subject to conflicting assessments of significance and that they are often politically sensitive, these normative issues are likely to be among the most difficult to address and resolve.

A first question to ask about an issue is 'why should it be managed?' After all, the term 'management' itself has some overtones of conservatism and the desire to contain problems rather than to let them play themselves out. There is clearly a spectrum of ways in which the question can be answered.

At its crudest, the answer may be 'because if it is not managed we shall all be worse off', and this has often been applied to the issue of global environmental change. But there may well be those who feel that such an answer is just a way of suppressing legitimate demands for change. Who is to say that developing countries, who may need to pollute in order to achieve economic growth, should 'manage' the environment by standards set in the industrial world? The same often applies to international or internal conflicts: if they are not 'managed', they may get out of hand and have damaging effects on world order, but the same loss of control might enable specific groups to achieve their objectives. The question 'why manage' is thus not an open-and-shut one, and it is linked with some highly sensitive political issues.

Secondly, we can ask 'how can or should an issue be managed?' Again, the answer to this question is likely to be conditioned by differences of political values, aims and strategies. Perhaps the most obvious way in which this question expresses itself is through the tension between national action and action through international organizations. One of the most fundamental problems in world politics is the contradiction between national action and collective action, and this is made even more complex by the intrusion of non-state groupings calling for their own versions of management. Two dimensions of the problem stand out. First, there is the dimension of scale and participation. Should issues be managed unilaterally, bilaterally or multilaterally? This is a crucial question, for example, in the management of the world political economy: such matters as trade conflicts can be managed through unilateral measures such as trade protection, through bilateral agreements between concerned actors or through the development of international rules and agreements within the World Trade Organization (WTO). Very often, issues are managed through a rather uneasy combination of actions at different levels – the national, the regional and the global – and by a combination of different groups and organizations – governments, international organizations and a wide range of private commercial bodies.

The 'how to manage' issue has a second dimension: that of mechanisms. To stay with the example of world trade, it can be shown that an immense variety of mechanisms come into play in the attempt to manage. Some of these are linked to international institutions and the rules they set down for the conduct of international dealings. Others, though, are the reflection of a huge variety of national, international and transnational interactions. These can set up wide-ranging and complex mechanisms of conflict and cooperation, and they lead to a process of continuous and wide-ranging negotiation in the international trade system. Thus the WTO embodies a powerful set of legal mechanisms and procedures, but these can be put under pressure or even rendered redundant by negotiation at the regional level or in the context of large international corporations producing in many national jurisdictions. Alongside these international processes can go those of national economic and commercial management, which may in turn be at odds with the global or regional processes. As a result, members of the European Union (EU) find themselves dealing with and attempting to reconcile all levels of the world trading system whilst at the same time dealing with their own specifically national problems.

A final aspect of the 'management' problem is that of results and outcomes. In many ways, this links back to the 'why manage?' question, since it is apparent that the attempt to manage world political issues can create winners and losers as well as the more efficient handling of particular problems. At one level, it could be argued that the management of issues in world politics is for the common good: it could equally be argued that this is a 'winners' argument', reflecting the position of those who are satisfied with the current situation or management mechanisms. For the 'losers', the effective management of world issues may simply be another dimension of their subordination and the perpetuation of their losers' status. The result can sometimes be the rejection of management at the international level and the resort to unilateral action outside both the institutions and the rules of the 'world community'. Take, for example, the issue of nuclear weapons and their spread. There has emerged a powerful set of agreements sometimes known as the 'non-proliferation regime' and centred on the Non-Proliferation Treaty, which was renegotiated and extended in 1995. But for a number of states on the verge of acquiring nuclear weapons, and particularly those facing what they see as threats to their national existence, this regime appears far from natural or legitimate: the result for them is not an expression of neutral 'management', but it is rather a reflection of their containment and oppression. In the same way, although the WTO operates to increase world trade and the flows of goods and services, there is a widespread feeling in the developing world that it operates to widen the gap between them and the industrial countries. A final example can be found in the negotiation of peace agreements: these are an explicit case of 'management', it seems, but they can also be seen as a reflection of the underlying power balance and as a means of suppressing change. In other words, as in the cases of nuclear weapons and trade, we need to ask not only what the results are in tangible terms, but also what they tell us about the winners and losers in both tangible and intangible terms.

Selection of issues and key questions

Before moving on to begin our investigation of particular issues, the final part of this chapter provides a justification for the issues selected and describes the way in which each chapter will be organized in terms of key questions to be asked. It is worth repeating that there is no attempt here to offer a comprehensive set of issues that can be taken to encapsulate all the main features of contemporary world politics. What can be claimed, however, is that the selection here comprises an interesting and a representative sample that addresses some of the important analytical questions introduced in this first chapter. To merit inclusion in this book, an issue needed to meet certain criteria which remain unchanged in this new edition. First, the issue must be representative of the range of issues on the contemporary international agenda. Interestingly, several of the issues selected would not automatically have been included on the list if the first edition of this book had been written, say, 10 years earlier – migration and refugees, and transnational crime and corruption are obvious examples. Several of these issues are unlikely to have been included if this book had been written 20 or 30 years ago: the environment, religion, and possibly regions and regionalism are all examples. By the same token, certain issues – those relating to arms and the international economy, for example – would almost certainly have been included, though not necessarily in the form that they are presented here. In this third edition of the book we have added a chapter on terrorism, another issue that has acquired a new impact since the end of the Cold War.

While covering a selection of 'old' and 'new' issues, we were also concerned to provide a range of issues that, in terms of traditional typologies, were illustrative of 'low' as well as 'high' policy areas and that some, at least, were issues that crossed the boundary between domestic politics and world politics. In the event it would be difficult to argue that any of the issues analyzed here are simply 'international' issues. They form part of a set of issues that help to define the current state of world politics but, at the same time, they are also issues that contribute to the shaping of domestic political, economic and social agendas. Most if not all the issues covered here can be described as genuinely 'intermestic' in character.

More important criteria perhaps relate to the end of the Cold War. We have tried to select issues that appear to have been affected by the end of the Cold War, at least in the form in which they are presented on the international agenda. Among the questions we posed for planning purposes were: did a new period of world politics begin in the 1990s that could be characterized by a new agenda of issues? Or do 'new' issues simply represent 'old' problems presented in a new guise? Is contemporary world politics marked by change or continuity, or, more radically, by a total transformation? Following the end of the Cold War, has the international community devised new techniques or strategies for solving problems? Another criterion for selection was whether a particular issue promises to show novel forms of 'management' and control in terms of resolving problems or, at least, whether it illustrates the continuing dilemmas in trying to resolve problems at a global level in a post-Cold War era. As noted above, the impact of and responses to globalization are strongly related to this set of criteria.

Clearly, in an important sense, the appropriateness or otherwise of the issues selected can be judged only after the individual chapters have been presented. Therefore, the concluding chapter of this book critically reviews the issues selected and attempts to describe the picture of contemporary world politics that emerges from them. Meanwhile, to help the reader not only to understand the particular issues chosen but also to develop a more general understanding of world politics, all the contributors were asked to address a common set of questions. Although contributors could interpret these questions in ways that were consistent with their subject matter, it was felt to be necessary to establish as far as possible a common structure. The key questions posed that provided that structure were as follows:

1. What is the nature of the issue or set of issues to be discussed?
2. What type of issue or set of issues is it, and how significant is it?
3. What general problems does the issue represent?
4. Who or what is responsible for the location of the issue on the international agenda?
5. How has the end of the Cold War affected the form in which the issue is presented?
6. What institutional or other mechanisms have emerged to manage the issue at the international level?
7. What does the issue tell us about the nature and concerns of contemporary world politics, including the impact and management of globalization?

Chapter 2

States and Statehood

MARK WEBBER

The period since the end of the Second World War has witnessed a remarkable growth in the number of states, from around 50 in 1945 to some 190 in 2005 (see Figure 2.1). These range from the tiny city-states of Monaco and the Holy See all the way up to the Russian Federation and China, respectively the world's largest and most populous states (see Table 2.1). During the twentieth century, there were several great waves of 'state creation': in the period after the First World War, again after the Second World War and then in the 1960s. Most recently, the dissolution of Yugoslavia and the Soviet Union in the early 1990s led to claims of statehood on the part of a large number of subject peoples. In fact, the collapse of these two communist federations resulted in the emergence of over 20 new states on the international scene. In addition, several potential candidates exist for statehood: Chechnya, Kurdistan, Kashmir, Quebec and the Palestinian Authority, for instance. Statehood, to put it simply, is more popular and sought-after than it has ever been, but this raises important questions about the changing nature both of states and of statehood more generally.

Three central questions can be asked, all of which have evoked considerable disagreement. First, how is the state to be defined in terms of its constitutive features? Second, what are the purposes of the state – or, in other words, what is the state for? Third, how important is the state in relation to other actors in world politics?

The first of these questions has, in the study of International Relations, a rather straightforward answer. The accepted orthodoxy asserts that a state has common characteristics, of which a territory, a sovereign government and a subject population are the most important. These constitute the 'organization' of statehood and will be considered in greater detail in the next section. Suffice to say here that this rather legalistic definition is a far from satisfactory one. As we shall discover, most states do not and perhaps have never sustained these characteristics in full. Furthermore, some would argue that the definition is incomplete without mention of other allegedly requisite features of statehood from a list that may include, depending upon the persuasion of the author, the existence of a common culture, a sense of national identity, a minimum level of political stability and order and a

Figure 2.1 *Number of states belonging to the United Nations, 1945–2005*

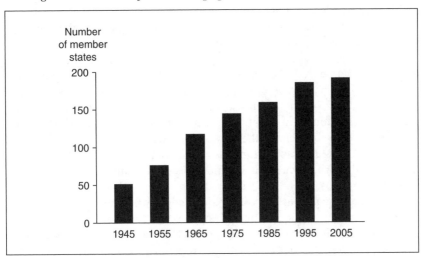

Source: Data from United Nations website.

Table 2.1 *The variety of states*

State	Territorial area (sq km)	Type of government	Population
Bhutan	47 000	monarchy	2 185 569
Brazil	8 511 965	federal republic	184 101 109
China	9 596 960	communist	1 298 847 624
Holy See	0.44	ecclesiastical	921
India	3 287 590	federal republic	1 065 070 607
Indonesia	1 919 440	republic	238 452 952
Japan	377 835	constitutional monarchy	127 333 002
Monaco	1.95	constitutional monarchy	32 270
Nigeria	938 768	republic in transition from military to civilian rule	137 253 133
Russian Federation	17 075 200	federation	143 782 338
Tuvalu	26	constitutional monarchy	11 468
United Kingdom	244 820	constitutional monarchy	60 270 708
United States	9 631 418	constitution-based federal republic	293 027 571

Source: Data from CIA (2004).

modicum of social and economic welfare (Jackson and James, 1993, p. 18; Del Rosso Jr, 1995, p. 178).

As for our second question, here opinion is particularly divided. In a far from exhaustive list, Mervyn Frost has identified four separate schools of thought. States can be seen as being motivated by: (i) the promotion of international order; (ii) their own survival, with a consequent emphasis on security; (iii) the protection of a particular form of political rule, democratic or otherwise; or (iv) the defence of dominant class interests and thus the regulation of a dominant economic form – capitalism. Yet, as Frost points out, despite their differences, these four approaches share a crucial common assumption: the state is important. It is conceived to be a piece of machinery geared to the achievement of certain ends. It is rational, powerful and pre-eminent (Frost, 1991, pp. 186–7).

As a cursory glance at any quality newspaper will confirm, the image of state supremacy is a popular one. Headlines that focus on state action and pronouncement in the form of phrases such as 'the United States issues a warning to Iraq' or 'Russian–Chinese relations are improving' certainly suggest that the state is paramount in world politics. Yet a more careful examination of our chosen newspaper can also reveal a slightly different image. References to the actions of say the EU (with regard to the conditions for beginning accession talks with aspirant member Turkey) and of the International Monetary Fund (IMF) (in relation to the terms and conditions of loans made to impoverished African states) reflect the fact that the state is by no means alone in world politics. It is accompanied by a host of other actors that include international inter-governmental organizations (IGOs) of which the United Nations (UN) and the EU are familiar examples; international non-governmental organizations (INGOs) such as Greenpeace and Amnesty International; and multinational companies (MNCs) such as Microsoft, General Motors and British Petroleum. It is the existence of these so-called 'non-state actors' that provides the context to our third question: how important is the state in relation to other actors in world politics?

To this, there is no simple answer. Few, however, would argue that the state enjoys an untrammelled supremacy. It interacts with other actors in myriad relationships. On certain issues this may affirm state dominance, but on others the role of the state is far less assured. To illustrate this, take the two examples cited above. The power of the EU to set the terms of negotiations for Turkey has had a far-reaching impact on the latter's domestic political and economic priorities even if, in some respects, the Turkish government has resented the degree of external meddling that this represents. Similarly, the ability of the IMF to link the provision of loans to economic and governmental performance reflects a presumption of authority on the part of this financial body that detracts from that of African states themselves.

The variety of answers to the three questions posed above indicates that the state is a contested concept (Navari, 1991). Its very meaning and purpose are the subjects of dispute and little approximating a consensus of views is apparent. This renders exploration of the nature of statehood especially problematic. In order to alleviate this problem, some narrowing of the focus of enquiry will be necessary. We make a start in this direction in the following section by examining further the orthodox definition of statehood noted above.

The nature of statehood: organization and practice

For all their great diversity states, if they are to qualify for the title, must possess the three common characteristics noted above: a territory, a sovereign government and a subject population. All three are important, yet it is the second that is crucial. The possession of sovereignty – commonly understood to mean the absence of any higher authority above the state both in domestic and external affairs – confers upon states a privileged position as the principal actor in international life. In numerous ways, it is a 'source of vitality' for the state, providing guarantees of formal equality and political independence, access to resources and connections, and an international identity or capacity that is unmatched (Miller, 1986). Sovereignty, however, requires practical organization; this is provided by governments. It is the personnel of government that represent the state and, by means of foreign policies, claim to act in defence of its interests.

To outline the three features of statehood is not, however, to suggest that states enjoy a placid or unchallenged life. Since the very inception of the international system of states (usually dated from the Treaty of Westphalia of 1648), these features have been the subject of regular violation and infringement.

Take first the quality of territoriality, the assumption that a delimited geographic area is the responsibility of a single state only. The obvious point to be made here is that historically speaking, territory has been the source of fierce dispute precisely because it has been claimed by more than one state. This may result in legal dispute conducted at a diplomatic level, state-sponsored subversion and, in certain cases, inter-state war. Both the First World War and the Second World War were precipitated at least partly by unresolved claims to territory on the part of major powers. The latter route to acquisition, it is true, has become something of a rarity, not least because of the expansion of legal restrictions on the use of force since 1945 and because the costs of war often outweigh any presumed benefits. This has, however, only changed the methods by which claims might be pursued, not the abundancy and potency of the claims themselves.

Even when the territorial integrity of a state is unchallenged (and this is a luxury European states, at least, have come to expect and enjoy since the end of the Second World War) territoriality can nonetheless be infringed in other ways. Stephen Krasner has highlighted the importance of 'authority structures that are not coterminous with geographic borders'. Examples include condominiums (for instance, that of Andorra, a co-principality of Spain and France); supranational organizations, notably the EU, which involve member states' submission to the binding decisions of extra-territorial bodies; and international regimes such as the Exclusive Economic Zone, which limits the jurisdiction of states over commercial shipping even within their own territorial waters (Krasner, 1995–6, p. 116).

Encroachments upon territoriality also entail a violation of sovereignty, the second core feature of statehood. In fact, sovereignty can be compromised in a number of different ways: through processes of domination, imposition, delegation, and intrusion. The first of these arises from imbalances of power between states. Here the legal equality embodied in the principle of sovereignty is not reflected in the possession of state capabilities (military structures, economic prowess, resource endowments and so on). Such an uneven distribution results in relationships between states that are far from equal and, in certain cases, the limitation by one state of another's freedom of action. Soviet influence over Eastern Europe during the period of communist rule and American oversight of much of the Caribbean and Central America are clear examples of such a pattern.

Imposition involves situations where a coalition of states force conditions upon a third party as a result either of the latter's defeat in war, or its transgression of accepted norms of behaviour. The peace treaties that Germany and Japan were forced to accept in 1945 are examples of the former, and economic sanctions directed against pariah states (for instance, apartheid South Africa) of the latter. In both cases, actions were taken from outside that either had a direct and obvious effect upon sovereignty (for instance, the supervision of Berlin by the Allied powers) or influenced the domestic political developments of a state to such a degree that sovereignty was severely undermined (as in the impact of sanctions on the removal of white-minority rule in South Africa).

Delegation is a less coercive form of infringement upon sovereignty. It is, however, no less important. Delegation has two dimensions. It can involve, first, states transferring sovereignty 'upward' to supranational organizations (as in the case of the EU noted above). This is a rare occurrence, but has, in Western Europe at least, progressed to a point where the sovereign status of the EU's member states has been questioned and the impression created that they are being absorbed into a larger, 'multi-level polity', an entity which itself has some of the features of a state (Caporaso, 1996). Second, delegation occurs 'downward', to regions within the state by means of granting them degrees of autonomy. In its more familiar guise this process is known as federalism and is the practice of states as diverse as the United

States, Switzerland and Brazil. While the scope for action open to the component parts of federal states is constitutionally delimited, their powers are often nonetheless fairly extensive. Moreover, federalism itself often presents real problems for state cohesion in that the internal administrative borders of a federated state can provide the basis of powerful claims of secession. As already noted, in the cases of communist federations such claims ultimately proved fatal to state survival.

As for intrusion, this entails challenges to sovereignty that arise from 'issues ... [and] relationships ... that dissolve the national–international divide' (Camilleri and Falk, 1992, p. 39). Take, for instance, economic issues. Here the ability of the sovereign state to pursue policies of its choosing has been fundamentally challenged in recent decades by the 'globalization' of trade, production and finance (see also Chapter 3). The subjection of national economies has occurred in several ways. The deepening of global markets results in borders that are more porous to unregulated economic activity, MNCs that are increasingly free of state control, and economically oriented international organizations (for instance, the IMF, the World Bank and the WTO) that are capable of an awesome influence (Camilleri and Falk, 1992, pp. 69–77).

Turning to the third feature of statehood, that of a subject population, here, too, qualification is necessary. This is not to say, of course, that states are without peoples over whom they rule; rather, that some populations have often felt compelled to escape the state in which they are contained. This is a problem that is at its most profound in states that are multi-ethnic and which simultaneously display a poor sense of overarching national identity. In these cases, an ethnic minority regards its usually subordinate position as demeaning and the only proper course of action that of self-determination – the construction of its own statehood. Such a situation is commonplace in the Third World. Here, decolonization created a large number of states whose borders, based on former lines of colonial administration, failed to conform to the patterns of population distributed both within and among them. This mismatch has not led to the creation of a large number of new states (Bangladesh, Eritrea and East Timor being rare cases in point). It has, however, resulted in battles for self-determination pursued with a force sufficient as to render whole areas effectively beyond state jurisdiction. This is a condition especially marked in Africa, where large swathes of Angola, Sudan and Zaire/Democratic Republic of Congo have been lost to central rule for much of the last two decades. Moving away from the Third World, the problem of self-determination has been no less acute. It has reared its head in Western Europe in the violence perpetrated by the Irish Republican Army (IRA) in Northern Ireland and by Euskadi ta Askatasuna (ETA) in the Basque region of Spain. More destructively, it has been apparent in the inability of the Russian Federation to offer sufficient voice to its small Chechen minority, a state of affairs that has resulted in two bitter civil wars since 1994.

Statehood as a problem in world politics

In reality challenges, both domestic and external, are by now the familiar experience of all states. In some instances, however, this need not be perceived as detrimental. Sovereignty may be willingly surrendered if some lasting benefit can be obtained. Hence, to return to an example cited above, Turkey's readiness to submit to the demands of the EU has been motivated by a realization that the infringements upon sovereignty are a price worth paying for the economic and political benefits of European integration. Moreover, there are many functions that the state can best achieve through collective action and this too requires a relinquishing of sovereignty. While the act of surrender is never stated in so many words – for purely political reasons the government of most states will rarely admit to presiding over a loss of sovereignty – in practice there is often no alternative. Few states, for instance, are capable of guaranteeing their own military defence and many consequently enter into alliances. Such an arrangement may involve a state binding itself to commitments that infringe upon its foreign policy and, in certain instances (the case of the North Atlantic Treaty Organization (NATO)) the subordination of its armed forces to a higher command structure. The resulting limitations to freedom of action are seen as tolerable if, through the acquisition of allies and arms, they offer a greater guarantee of the state's security. A similar logic can also apply in other areas, be this trade, transportation, communication or environmental protection, all of which have led states to recognize that constraint on individual action is a necessary cost of pursuing an otherwise unobtainable objective.

The norms of statehood

Many states, then, will tolerate, under certain circumstances some constraints on their own particular statehood. They are, however, extremely cautious when it comes to any revision of the concept of statehood in general and the norms of international behaviour which follow from it. States that, for instance, indulge in wilful acts of conquest are not just guilty of a resort to force but, equally important, of violating the territorial dimension of statehood. As such, they are the subject of condemnation and often find themselves up against a powerful coalition of states keen to restore the international order. Such was the fate of Nazi Germany and, more recently, Saddam Hussein's Iraq following its invasion of Kuwait in 1990. Of a slightly lesser order of gravity, there is a general predisposition against the notion of spheres of influence, owing to the gross undermining of the principle of sovereignty that it entails. Even those states that endeavour to dominate in such an arrangement have consequently felt the need to excuse their actions in some way. The Soviet-led military interventions in Hungary (1956) and in Czechoslovakia (1968), for example, were justified by reference to dubiously-based 'invitations' issued by the government of the violated state. More generally, despite Moscow's obvious oversight of the East European states at this time, it was still considered necessary to place inter-state relations within treaties of 'Friendship and Co-operation' that made ritualistic reference to mutual respect for sovereignty. The sham of this claim was, however, abundantly clear, such that when the Soviet Union under its last leader Mikhail Gorbachev reversed the policies of his predecessors this was trumpeted as amounting, in effect, to a welcome restoration of sovereignty for the subject states.

The bias of the international system toward respect for statehood can have perverse effects. True, respect for a principle may sometimes be the stimulus for action that is at once heroic and decisive (as in the case of the reaction to Nazism noted above), but it can also be a recipe for inertia and prevarication and, at worse, a passive acceptance of the intolerable. Take for instance, the case of what Robert Jackson refers to as 'quasi-states'. These enjoy the attributes of formal 'juridical' statehood (most importantly, external recognition) but lack its 'empirical' qualities; their governments are 'deficient in ... political will, institutional authority, and organized power'. Such states would seem unviable entities. They were created as a consequence of the recognized right of self-determination of ex-colonial territories. They have endured because of, first, the reluctance of established states to modify this recognition once given and, second, the existence of various forms of development assistance directed at improving their capacity for self-government. As a result, quasi-states that are often blighted by economic underdevelopment, political instability and even civil war have enjoyed a charmed existence, surviving when in a previous age the absence of a credible basis for statehood would have denied them membership of international society (R. H. Jackson, 1990, pp. 21, 31, 42).

In some cases respect for statehood takes a far more ambiguous form. It is widely accepted that sovereignty precludes outside interference in a state's domestic affairs (this is spelled out notably in Article II of the UN Charter). Even so, it has been argued that there are grounds on which the norm of non-intervention may be overridden (Berridge, 1992, pp. 164–5). These are:

- *Self-defence.* This can take two forms: the launch of a pre-emptive strike by one state upon another to forestall an attack, and a retaliatory strike against a state charged with aggression. An example of the former is the Israeli assault on the Arab states in 1967 (an operation welcomed in the West, but criticized by the Soviet bloc and many Third World states). An example of the latter is the American bombing of the Libyan capital Tripoli in 1986 (an event fully supported only by Britain and Israel).
- *Humanitarian intervention.* This may involve actions to rescue one's own nationals in a foreign country, as in the case of Israel's operation at Entebbe airport (Uganda) in 1976, and intercession to 'end human rights abuses'. Examples of the latter include Tanzania's 1979 overthrow of Idi Amin in Uganda and, more controversially, Vietnam's invasion of

Kampuchea in 1978–9. While the intervening state in both cases claimed a humanitarian motive, its actions were nonetheless seen by many as illegal encroachments upon the domestic affairs of others. Furthermore, as well as infringing upon sovereignty, the cause of humanitarian intervention has proven controversial because of inconsistent application. Intervention has not been forthcoming in cases of sustained human rights abuses if the offending state is powerful enough to resist or of sufficient value to the international community to be treated with sympathy. (Witness in this regard the lack of decisive action to correct Chinese abuses in Tibet.)

- *Civil war.* In this case intervention is considered justified if it is a response to a previous intervention by another state. Thus, the United States felt justified in arming anti-Marxist insurgents in Afghanistan, Nicaragua and Angola in the 1980s in opposition to what they saw as the seizure of power by Soviet-supported revolutionaries.

These examples notwithstanding, there is still no generally agreed *right* of intervention. Indeed, controversy arises precisely because the norm of non-intervention survives. To understand why this is so, simply consider what would happen if the norm did not exist at all. 'If it were regarded as normal that states *should* meddle in each other's domestic affairs the points of friction (already ample enough) would multiply hugely, all trust would dissolve, and civilized international relations would become impossible' (Berridge, 1992, p. 163).

The politics of statehood

As well as generating controversy at the level of general principles, issues pertaining to statehood can also stimulate debates, both within and between states, of a more expressly political nature. The existence of a perceived threat to statehood is a common charge in politics. Of particular interest are cases where the infringement of sovereignty is seen as a matter of choice; in these cases sovereignty issues are posed explicitly and debate ensues on possible alternatives. In Europe, such debate is commonplace owing to the pervasive influence of the EU. This debate has been particularly vexed within the United Kingdom. At one extreme, it has given rise to the UK Independence Party, a party which has called for withdrawal from the EU and which in June 2004 tapped an upsurge in anti-European sentiment sufficient to win twelve seats in elections to the European Parliament. In fact, since the 1960s the question of membership of the EU has proven one of the more divisive issues in British political life. Successive Prime Ministers from Harold Macmillan to Tony Blair have been forced to juggle dual demands. On the one hand, they have tried to keep sweet a British public and sections of their own parties appreciative of the unique features of the British system while, on the other, they have been sensitive to the imperative of integrating Britain carefully into a continental structure, absence from which is seen as economically and politically untenable. Managing this delicate balance has not been easy. The Conservative Party, the party of government during the 1980s and much of the 1990s, found itself at times paralysed over the issue, split between a leadership resigned to the inevitability of European involvement and a 'Euro-sceptic' wing, implacable in its opposition to the integrationist tendencies of the EU. The foreign policy consequences of this stance were also considerable. The championing of a specifically British interest resulted in isolation within the EU on issues ranging from monetary union to social protection. Similar dilemmas have also been faced by the Labour government elected in 1997. Under Prime Minister Blair, the United Kingdom has displayed a much more accommodating attitude toward the EU. Nonetheless, certain key components of the EU's integrationist agenda remain politically controversial. Thus, with an eye toward a sceptical British public, the Labour government has insisted that on issues of economic and monetary union, as well as the European constitution, British adherence would be dependent upon the holding of national referendums.

While the British position with regard to the EU may be characterized as ambiguous, for some states the threat of infringements to sovereignty has resulted in actions of a much more rejectionist character. Of the Soviet successor states, for example, several have kept a distance from the post-Soviet Commonwealth of Independent States, not because the organization has any great integrating momentum, but rather because it is seen as a vehicle for Russian influence. Estonia, Latvia and Lithuania all rejected membership upon exiting from the Soviet Union in 1991. Of the twelve successor states who did subsequently join the organization, only five were prepared to join Russia in developing a putative military arm, the Collective Security Treaty Organisation. Turning to a further case, the United States in 2002 withdrew from cooperation with the International Criminal Court (ICC). It did so despite having supported international criminal accountability for war crimes in Yugoslavia, Rwanda and Sierra Leone and did so on the grounds that accountability for crimes against humanity is best guaranteed by national judicial systems or, failing that, international tribunals established by the UN Security Council (where the United States holds a veto). In essence, the United Statess wished to preserve its sovereign right to try its own citizens. The US decision, while fully consistent with a traditional view of state prerogatives, nonetheless ran counter to a growing body of international opinion (in May 2004, there were 94 States Parties to the *Rome Statute* of the ICC) in favour of a strengthened international legal body 'with jurisdiction over the most serious crimes of concern to the international community as a whole' (*Rome Statute*, 1998)

By contrast with the above examples, debate in some states has occurred against a very different backdrop. These are cases where statehood is seen a actually being enhanced by membership of international organizations, even when this brings with it infringements upon sovereignty. This type of situation is especially pertinent in former communist Eastern Europe. Here, there has been an overwhelming desire among political elites (shared to varying degrees by wider publics) for entry into the EU and NATO. With the possible exception of Poland, none of these states entered the organizations in question with any expectation of being a major political player or with any illusions about the restrictions that membership would place upon political, economic and social priorities as well as foreign and security policy. Yet in each case membership was held to be a major prize, a route to net economic gains, security guarantees and, for some, affirmation of a future outside the Russian sphere of influence (Schimmelfennig, 2003, pp. 37–40, 52–4)

Statehood, the end of the Cold War and 9/11

World politics has in the last two decades been shaped by two fundamental turning points: (i) the end of the Cold War and of the bipolar rivalry between the West and the Soviet bloc, and (ii) the attacks on the US mainland on September 11th 2001. While these two developments are in many respects very different, both have had profound consequences for the institution of statehood. These can be considered under the following headings:

- state creation and viability;
- (non-)interference;
- economic power;
- states and international organizations.

State creation and viability

The end of the Cold War had mixed consequences for statehood. To begin on a positive note, one of its more visible effects was a massive proliferation in the number of states, a process, which for some, marked a 'springtime of nations' (Howard, 1989–90), or a 'renaissance of the nation state' (Brown, 1995, p. 2). The break-up of Yugoslavia, the Soviet Union and Czechoslovakia into their constituent, usually ethnically defined parts, and the due recognition granted to these nascent states by the international community, seemingly reinvigorated the idea of statehood based upon a defined population or nation. This process was coupled with a revival in the sovereign powers of previously dominated states. Client states which had formerly been subjected to the imposing influence of the Superpowers suddenly lost their utility to Washington and Moscow as the imperatives of East–West global competition diminished. Among the former Soviet satellites in Eastern Europe the consequent re-animation of sovereignty has not only seen the introduction of democratic political structures, but a wholesale reorientation of foreign policies. Poland, Hungary and the new Czech Republic, once firmly and forcibly contained within a Soviet sphere of influence, became members of the historically Western-oriented NATO in 1999. In 2004, Slovakia, Romania, and Bulgaria as well as three former Soviet Republics (Estonia, Latvia and Lithuania) and the erstwhile Yugoslav republic of Slovenia also joined the alliance, and that same year a major enlargement of the EU occurred embracing on this occasion eight former communist states.

The end of the Cold War also had less welcome consequences. The legitimacy given to nationalism proved a poisoned chalice in some new states which were themselves multi-ethnic. The vicious wars in Bosnia in the early 1990s, the secessionist struggle by the Chechens in Russia and the demands for greater autonomy on the part of Russian minorities in the Soviet successor states of Moldova, Ukraine and Kazakhstan are all testimony to this fact. Moreover, many of the new states are strongly redolent of the quasi-states described above. In the former Soviet Union, for instance, the successor states emerged at the end of 1991 with little preparation for self-government and, in the case of the five new states of Central Asia, no historical memory of statehood. All, moreover, had been weakened as a consequence of their removal from the once centralized Soviet economy, military and governmental administration, and thus faced problems of establishing and organizing political and civil order. More than a decade on not all of these issues have been resolved. Only a handful of the successor states (Estonia, Latvia, Lithuania, Ukraine and perhaps Moldova and Uzbekistan) could be said to possess the attributes of 'empirical' statehood. Most of the remainder are either still labouring under the weight of unresolved secessionist struggles (Azerbaijan and Georgia), Russian tutelage (Armenia, Belarus) or both (Tajikistan).

As for the more familiar quasi-states in the Third World, here too the end of the Cold War had its effect as states once propped up by Superpower patronage were forced to cope in a new austere climate. Central governments once reliant on an abundance of aid to prop up their economies and on free military hardware to fight their internal battles found themselves cast adrift. The resource-rich, for instance Angola, sought compensation in international arms markets. Others less fortunate, however, have gone to the wall, resulting in one case in state partition (Eritrea formally seceded from Ethiopia in 1993) and in others in international isolation (North Korea) or a further crumbling of empirical statehood (Zaire, for instance, collapsed into a condition of anarchy during 1996–7 with the removal from power of one-time US favourite President Mobutu Sese Seko). In fact, the plight of some in the Third World has become so catastrophic that they are now described as 'failed states' – entities totally deficient in internal order and 'utterly incapable of sustaining [themselves] as . . . member[s] of the international community' (Helman and Ratner, 1992–3, p. 3).

(Non)-interference

More ambiguous than the rise and fall of states have been the apparent modifications of principle that have gained ground since end of the Cold War. One important shift here has concerned the notion of non-interference derived from sovereignty. Matters previously excused as the purely domestic affair of a state have been the subject of increased international concern where they involve destabilizing external repercussions or gross human suffering (see Box 2.1). Ostensibly humanitarian operations inside Iraq, Somalia, Rwanda and elsewhere occurred during the 1990s without the clear consent of the state concerned and thus, strictly speaking, they amounted to infringements upon sovereignty. These actions were all the more notable in that they were multilateral, endorsed by the UN and, therefore, quite different from both the violations of sovereignty perpetrated by the Superpowers during the Cold War and other, unilateral cases of humanitarian intervention noted above (Ramsbotham, 1997, pp. 461–8). Equally far-reaching were the consequences of NATO's campaign of air strikes against Serbia/Yugoslavia in March–June 1999. Mounted with the professed humanitarian purpose of reversing Serbian attacks on Kosovar Albanians (but in the absence of an explicit UN mandate), this culminated in the emplacement in Kosovo of a peacekeeping mission (dubbed KFOR) and the establishment shortly after of a civilian administration overseen by the UN. These developments have had the effect of transforming Kosovo into a *de facto* NATO/UN protectorate despite the fact that it remains, in strictly legal terms, a province of Serbia and Montenegro

Interventions such as these have implications that take us back to the core qualities of statehood. The incidence of cases of humanitarian intervention in the post-Cold War period reflect two profound changes: a political one and, closely linked to this, a normative one. The first of these relates to the nature of the 'winning coalition' that emerged victorious at the end of the Cold War. Composed at its heart of the states of the West, this meant a victory of liberal democracy and *ipso facto* a discrediting of communism as a political force (Barkin and Cronin, 1994, p. 126; Buzan, 1995, p. 394). In that the dominant values within the international system have come to be increasingly associated with democracy, a normative context has been formed that renders intervention legitimate when it can be shown that certain states are in clear violation of its principles, specifically those that relate to human rights. In this sense sovereignty is a limited asset. To quote Stanley Hoffmann, 'the state that claims sovereignty deserves respect only as long as it protects the basic rights of its subjects ... When it violates them ... the state's claim to full sovereignty falls' (Hoffmann, 1995–6, p. 35).

Yet the degree to which these political and normative changes have resulted in a fairer, more just world can be far from gainsaid. In the first place, some would argue that actions based on a moral claim disguise a less worthy intent. Indeed, as Tony Blair's speech in Box 2.1 openly concedes,

Box 2.1 Humanitarian intervention

In April 1999 British Prime Minister Tony Blair made a speech in Chicago in which he addressed the issue of whether a general doctrine could be developed justifying humanitarian intervention. Blair argued that:

[t]he most pressing foreign policy problem we face is to identify the circumstances in which we should get involved in other people's conflicts. Non-interference has long been considered an important principle of international order. And it is not one we would want to jettison too readily ... but the principle of non-interference must be qualified in important respects. Acts of genocide can never be a purely internal matter. When oppression produces massive flows of refugees which unsettle neighbouring countries they can properly be described as 'threats to international peace and security'.

He then went on to outline some of the practical considerations that would determine whether an intervention should occur:

do we have national interests involved? The mass expulsion of ethnic Albanians from Kosovo demanded the notice of the rest of the world. But it does make a difference that this is taking place in such a combustible part of Europe.

Source: Tony Blair, 'Doctrine of the International Community', speech in Chicago, 22 April 1999, as cited in Roberts (1999, p. 119).

the NATO intervention in Kosovo was just as much the result of calculations of national interest as of a humanitarian impulse. Moreover, recent NATO or UN-endorsed operations have tended to be selective and sometimes temporary in nature. Only in rare cases (Bosnia and, latterly, Kosovo are cases in point) have determined efforts been undertaken to establish political order. Elsewhere amongst the failed states of the Third World concerted action has been much less forthcoming. Saving these states either through prolonged involvement or massive resource transfers is not top of the foreign policy agendas of either the European states or the United States. Take away the lucky coincidence of strategic interests, geographic importance and political prominence that motivated action in the Balkans and little of consequence will be forthcoming. Liberia, Sierra Leone, Somalia and Zaire/Democratic Republic of Congo are all cases where, in the post-Cold War period, Western-led efforts at a restitution of political order have proven to be both unconvincing and short-lived. Tackling these problems, rather, has been left to neighbouring states (Nigeria and Angola, for instance) who are themselves beset by their own problems of statehood.

Perhaps even more controversial than humanitarian intervention are cases where action has been taken on the pretext of self-defence. Controversy here might at first sight seem counter-intuitive. Article 51 of the UN Charter, for instance, is clear in recognizing the right to 'individual or collective self-defence' in the event of an armed attack. The circumstances and justifications used, however, are rarely straightforward. It was noted above that the use of force in self-defence can take two forms: pre-emption and retaliation. The latter is perhaps the most clear-cut – retaliation, by definition, presupposes prior evidence of attack and so the case for action is usually compelling. Thus in an almost immediate military response to the attacks of 9/11, the United States launched 'Operation Enduring Freedom' against the Taliban regime in Afghanistan, the pretext being that this regime was harbouring the leadership of Al Qaeda, the organization deemed responsible for the attacks on the American mainland. In this instance, the United States garnered widespread international support, including that of states such as Russia and China normally ill-disposed to expressions of US military power. Much more contentious are cases of pre-emption, especially where action occurs in the absence of an imminent threat. The US-led attack on Iraq in 2003 falls squarely into this category. As justified by Washington (and echoed in the case put by the UK government), military force was necessary in order to ensure the removal from Iraq of weapons of mass destruction (WMD). Pre-emption, in this case, was rationalized not as a matter of averting an imminent attack by Iraq but rather preventing a possible attack at some point in the future, either because WMD might be deployed by the Iraqi regime or such weapons might fall into the hands of terrorists. Yet such a rationale by its very nature begs certain questions, first on the credibility of evidence (if the threat to be averted is not imminent, how exactly is the possibility or probability of it to be judged?) and second on the scale of the response. Much more fundamentally, the Iraq operation called into question for some the very foundations of international order. As Gareth Evans has argued, the case put by the United States could as easily be put by any number of other states to justify preventive strikes in the world's more volatile regions. Infringing the norm of non-intervention in such a comprehensive fashion, he continues would mean 'living in a world where the unilateral use of force would be the rule, not the exception' (Evans, 2004, p. 66).

Economic power

More neutral in effect, but no less sweeping has been change flowing from economic forces. As well as a victory for liberal democracy, the end of the Cold War also witnessed the apparent triumph of market economics (Buzan, 1995, p. 393). The communist alternatives to the market in the form of central planning and state ownership were by the late 1980s thoroughly discredited and have since given way to market-oriented economies of varying forms throughout both the former communist countries and in China and Vietnam where communist parties remain in power. While this has not meant an unprecedented exposure to the global economy (the East

Europeans, for instance, were heavy borrowers during the 1970s and 1980s and the Soviet Union and China had become increasingly entwined in world markets), the extent of that involvement has undoubtedly deepened. The increased need for sources of external finance (to fund reform), coupled with trade reorientation and the encroachment of foreign equity have all opened up states formerly on the margins of the international capitalist system to those forces of economic globalization that intrude upon statehood.

Economics has made an impact in another sense: it has partly usurped military power as the crucial variable of status. The war in Iraq and the pre-eminence of US military power may have given continued credence to the argument that 'the threat and use of force are the ultimate instruments of international relations' (Slocombe, 2003, p. 118), however, as the rise of China to the rank of economic superpower has illustrated, growth and development remain fundamental bases of state strength. The emergence of economic powers, notably Germany and Japan, did, of course, occur while the Cold War was in progress. Yet there is a sense in which the ordering of capabilities has now fundamentally altered. The premium attached to military capability has been increasingly downgraded, at least among the states of the West (including Japan) in that the defence of territory has become a less pressing concern. Even allowing for the 'war on terror' and the consequent boost to military expenditure in the United States, as a percentage of GDP, only Turkey among NATO member states has spent more on defence in the 1990s and 2000s than was spent in the 1980s, the last decade of the Cold War (NATO, 2004). These sorts of trend have led some to argue that '[p]ower in world affairs is increasingly determined by economic success rather than military statistics' (Booth, 1991, p. 8). Statehood itself has not been altered by this change, but the relative importance of the indices that rank states one against the other certainly have.

States and international organizations

One further and much commented upon consequence of the Cold War's demise has been a process of adaptation on the part of international organizations. The UN and the Organization for Security and Cooperation in Europe (OSCE), for instance, have taken on board large numbers of new members from the Yugoslav and Soviet successor states. NATO and the EU, as already noted, have experienced significant post-Cold War enlargements.

Organizational development of this kind is part and parcel of a trend that has a far longer historical trajectory – a 'move to institutions' that in the twentieth century saw a proliferation and increase in the scope of international organizations and, linked to this, in the evolution of other areas of institutionalized behaviour – international law and international regimes.

The growing prominence of this dimension of international life has had significant consequences for states. At a surface level, it has actually reaffirmed statehood. International organizations, with rare exception, have only states as members, adhere in their documentation to the principles of sovereign domestic jurisdiction and generally are reliant on voluntary, as opposed to binding, compliance on the part of their members. Controversy arises, however, over two major issues: first, the relative importance of international organizations as non-state actors (something alluded to above) and second, the issue considered here – the degree to which international organizations can moderate state behaviour and encourage cooperation.

On the one hand there are those, usually referred to as 'neo-realists', who claim that organizations are empty vessels, existing only to the degree that they affirm state interests. Cooperation is not ruled out, but it occurs within a clearly delimited framework. Owing to the existence of a condition of anarchy (the absence of a world government above states), the international system is seen as insecure and characterized by distrust. Self-help becomes the order of the day and cooperation is inhibited by fears of cheating, dependency and 'relative gains' (the suspicion on the part of one state that collaboration benefits other states more than itself) (Grieco, 1988). This is clearly not a propitious environment for the operation of international organizations. Indeed, to the extent that they do carry out important roles, these are largely derivative of the international distribution of power between states. The more powerful create and shape organizations so that they might pursue selfish objectives, a state of affairs at its most obvious in the privileges enjoyed by the Permanent Five members of the UN Security Council. In short, organizations, of whatever type, will reflect only the balance of interests of their constituent parts (that is, states). When states are not in harmony, organizations will have to engage in negotiated compromise. When states disagree fundamentally, organizations will be rendered ineffective (Mearsheimer, 1994–5). Hence, the frequent impotence of the UN (illustrated, not least, by the breakdown of diplomacy in the Security Council in 2003 over the Iraq issue) and the somewhat limited success of internally divided bodies like the African Union and the Arab League.

Ranked against this rather pessimistic position are the arguments of the so-called 'neo-liberal institutionalists'. This view is willing to accept certain core neo-realist tenets (the position of states in a condition of anarchy and the subsequent pursuit of self-interest) but asserts that even the self-interested state will recognize the lasting benefits of cooperation. Following arguments derived from game theory models such as the Prisoners' Dilemma, it is argued that cooperation avoids outcomes which are 'suboptimal' – that is, situations in which states will be worse off owing to their neglect of mutual agreement. Organizations offer the means to formalize and facilitate such cooperation in world politics.

International organizations also address structural obstacles to coopera-tion. With regard to the problem of cheating, for instance, this can be deterred by, first, establishing punishment regimes for transgressors and rewards for cooperative states and, second, by creating expectations that the benefits of future cooperation will be jeopardized if a state seeks unilateral advantage. As for the 'relative gains' dilemma, organizations help to overcome this by facilitating an environment of security among states which encourages them to focus on 'absolute gains'. In such a setting, states measure success in terms of their own returns, and not whether their gains are greater or less than those of other states. This allows them to cooperate even in the knowledge that they will not be the only or the greatest beneficiary of cooperation (Stein, 1990, pp. 115–17). Moreover, in a world which has become increasingly interconnected, states are thrown together in an ever greater number of institutional arrangements. Some are entirely without controversy (the Universal Postal Union (UPU)), while some are rather more contentious (the IMF and the WTO). Membership creates a habit of institutionalized contact between states that leads to an awareness that their own interests need not be at odds with those of others. International organizations thus become the vehicles for the pursuit of common concerns and states learn to take the interests of others into account when framing their own policies; they become 'joint-maximizers rather than self-maximizers' (Stein, 1990, p. 53). In sum, states recognize the utility of international organizations and are prepared to invest substantial material resources in them. If not, how else would one explain the longevity and indeed the strengthening of bodies such as the EU, NATO and the WTO (Keohane and Anderson, 1995, p. 40)?

Despite the divergences of opinion within the debate on international organizations, both the neo-realist and the neo-liberal accounts are premised on a core assumption: that the state has an inherent usefulness, either as the vehicle of a self-defining interest or as the basic unit of international cooperation. The same cannot be said for a third, more radical view, the so-called 'global governance' perspective. This confronts the state head-on, arguing that it is an inadequate and even counterproductive tool for tackling a plethora of global problems ranging from AIDS, ecological catastrophe and mass poverty to nuclear proliferation and the population explosion. Since these problems cut across states, they can be resolved only through more directed international cooperation and a fundamental reallocation of state sovereignty and responsibilities. An effective structure of global governance is consequently seen as necessary. This should be anchored in international law and a strengthened UN system and ought gradually to 'displac[e] the state as central actor on the world political stage' (Falk, 1995, pp. 79–103).

Many have discounted the claims of global governance. States have proven extremely reluctant to hand over sovereignty under any guise. When it has occurred – for instance, in a limited form within the EU – it has been a luxury of the established, wealthy states. Governments of the weaker states, by contrast, regard sovereignty as virtually the only protection of their status and would be loath to surrender it to some remotely accountable global structure dominated by the established Western states (R. H. Jackson, 1990, pp. 175–6). Such criticisms are not to say that structures of global governance are totally absent (as well as the UN, one could point to other bodies with a global role, the IMF and the WTO), but these are deficient in view of the greater legitimacy that still attaches to the state.

Statehood and contemporary world politics

At a time of considerable turbulence in the international system it is hardly surprising that the state should be an object of some controversy. In this final section we will consider two perspectives on the future of the state. First, many have claimed that the state, if not dead, has at least reached the age of retirement (Mann, 1993, p. 115). In the face of urgent global problems and the influence of non-state actors, the state is seen as increasingly anachronistic and insufficient. In much of the Third World, statehood has either a 'quasi' nature or has failed entirely, while in the more economically developed areas of the globe it is becoming an increasingly irrelevant concept amid the interconnectedness of economic, cultural and political life, and the consequent drive toward tighter organized international cooperation. While none of these developments is entirely new, and the demise of the state has been heralded more than once before (Dyson, 1980, pp. 282–7) there is a perception that in recent years something of a different order has occurred. Rapid changes in the structure of the international economy, the dramatic pace of advances in technology and communication, the rise of nationalism, and the end of the Cold War – all have challenged the pre-eminence of the state (Horsman and Marshall, 1995, pp. ix–xx).

Yet amid this turmoil, the state continues to survive and even prosper. In contrast to a view of an embattled state, others have argued the case that it remains both a vital and essential part of the international system. Barry Buzan for one has claimed that '[f]or all its limitations, the sovereign territorial state seems to have no serious challengers as the organizing principle for the political life of humankind. Decolonization has made it virtually universal, and it remains the aspiration of almost every remaining group that is rebelling against the existing structure of power and authority' (Buzan, 1995, p. 392). Robert Jackson and Alan James have suggested similarly that sovereign statehood remains 'the fundamental way in which the world is politically organized' (Jackson and James, 1993, p. 6).

This more sanguine view is rooted in a perception that there exists no real alternative to the state, both as the ordering unit of the international system and as the framework for domestic governance. Most issues around the world tend to be considered in state terms. Granted, many do elicit an international involvement, but for every instance of this type, there are many more in which the state concerned is considered to be the primary agent for action. Squatter camps around Soweto are South Africa's problem, the pollution of Lake Baikal is Russia's problem, and the congestion on Britain's roads is Britain's problem (Murphy, 1994, p. 212).

The state, moreover, can be seen as something more than simply a passive onlooker of global transformation. States, it is argued, have proven adept at channelling many of the forces noted above and, in the process, have managed to adapt or 'reconstitute' their essential functions (Clark, 1998, pp. 489–91). Take, for instance, the manner in which states have reacted to economic globalization. While it would be true to say that in this regard their responsiveness may vary (there is a world of difference between the capacity of, say, the United States and the poor states of Africa), all are nonetheless privileged to some degree by virtue of the right to sovereign jurisdiction over their domestic sphere. This is not to argue that a state can totally resist the world outside or that it can operate with a limitless menu of policy choices. However, some scope for action still exists. States can tax, regulate, deny access, license; in sum, they can 'set the basic rules and define the environment' (Krasner, 1995, p. 279) in which transnational economic forces must operate. Indeed, when properly harnessed, many states can actually benefit from these forces. Consider two rather different examples. First, Angola, a state that was able to finance high levels of military expenditure during the 1980s and 1990s partly out of tax revenues collected from Western oil companies. And, second, Japan, a state that has exploited the desire of foreign companies to win access to its markets by requiring that they transfer valuable technologies to home firms, a stipulation that has helped in the development of world-beating, technologically advanced industries (Krasner, 1995, pp. 273–4).

The true picture of contemporary statehood is probably less clear-cut than the two alternatives outlined in this section suggest. Some have noted that trends in state development are not uniform and differ according to region, historical context and levels of economic, cultural and social development. The 'post-modern' states of Europe may have modified the principles of state sovereignty through involvement in EU processes of supranational governance (Sorensen, 2001, pp. 87–90), however, for the post-colonial states of Asia and Africa the tendency remains in the opposite direction with a continued premium attached to the construction of a strong nation state. Thus, according to Martin Jacques, the decline of the state 'is a regional [i.e. European] rather than a global phenomenon' (Jacques, 2004). Further, the complexity of forces that impact upon the state have had contradictory effects. It is entirely feasible to argue that the state has been 'both strengthened and weakened in complex ways since the end of World War Two' (Sorensen, 1998, p. 96). Its competencies have been fatally weakened in some areas, but in others it remains pre-eminent. To observe change in the former need not lead to the conclusion that the state in general is in decline. Similarly, one should not extrapolate a general crisis of statehood from specific cases of state failure and collapse. States rise and fall, but nowhere has the form itself been placed in abeyance as a preferred means of political organization. In sum, then, what appears crucial is the remarkable ability of the state as an institution to adapt and to survive (Jackson and James, 1993, p. 25).

Guide to further reading

Owing to its centrality in discussions of world politics, the concept of the state has given rise to an enormous and diverse literature. A good starting point is the collections edited by Navari (1991) and Jackson and James (1993). On the state system in international relations, the classic text is Hedley Bull's (1977). Berridge (1992, Chapters 1–4) and Hocking and Smith (1995, Chapters 4–5) also provide useful outlines. Discussions of statehood and sovereignty can be found in James (1987) and Krasner (1999). Hobson (2000) provides a detailed discussion of theoretical perspectives on the state and international relations.

An issue that has given rise to much recent debate is the position of the state in the post-Cold War order and in the context of globalization. These themes are treated at length in the collection edited by Sakamoto (1995), and the books by Horsman and Marshall (1995), Strange (1996) and Sorensen (2001, 2004). The state's relationship to international organizations is also the subject of controversy. The articles by Mearsheimer (1994–5), and Keohane and Anderson (1995) provide a flavour of the debate.

Chapter 3

Trade, Money and Markets

ALAN RUSSELL

After many years of escalating increases in the amount of money crossing national borders, the start of the new century has seen a reduction in the otherwise fearsome amounts involved. As the last century drew to a close the amount of foreign exchange dealing across national borders, around the world, peaked at some $1.5 trillion daily (BIS, 1999, 2002). In contrast, total government foreign reserve holdings – the money by which governments can enter the game of market speculation and intervention – has been but a tiny fraction of this enormous flow of money. The volatility of foreign exchange markets has on many occasions led to financial crises: a collapse of the dollar in 1987; the Mexican crisis and subsequent bail-out in 1995; the 1997 Asian Crisis, whereby one country after another in the region succumbed to financial meltdown; and more recently crises have centred on Russia (1998), Brazil (1999), Argentina and Turkey (2000). With ever increasing amounts of money crossing national borders the IMF enhanced its 'surveillance' role – watching and waiting. Then the upward trend stopped. The new century has seen the daily flow of currency fall back by some 19 per cent (BIS, 2002). However, it is undoubtedly too soon to relax because two things stand out. When it comes to international monetary issues, national economies are highly interdependent with each other and remain vulnerable to the foreign exchange market. Because of this, individual governments face a loss of control over the economic destiny of their countries.

In 1944, the world witnessed the birth of the so-called 'Bretton Woods' economic order, encompassing the IMF and the World Bank. Fear of a return to the economic disorder of the 1930s spurred internationally agreed action to address the issues of international currency management and post-war reconstruction. The subsequent Marshall Aid plan for Europe speeded these objectives along, and the success of these initiatives has long been recognized. But in one area there was dismal failure. The planned third organization, the International Trade Organization, was stillborn. Such is the political sensitivity of trade that it took until December 1993 to achieve agreement on a World Trade Organization (WTO). Again, two things stand out. As with international money, interdependence characterizes trade relations. From the perspective of governments, the very issue of economic control over trade gets to the heart of the politics of trade. However, at a crude nationalist level, governments might prefer to maximize their nation's gains from trade at the expense of their national competitors. Where competitiveness is insufficient the alternative may be deliberate intervention to distort markets.

Both trade and international monetary issues suggest interdependence between countries of the world – an interdependence generally considered to be increasing. Moreover, because stable monetary relations are designed to assist trade, and disruptions to trade can seriously affect exchange rates, money and trade are also interdependent. Taking the interplay of forces evident between economic and political systems and between domestic and international levels it is possible to identify a range of linked issues. The key to understanding these linkages is the concept of *interdependence*.

Economic interdependence: a set of issues

Interdependence is a difficult concept – but a very important one. It refers to the many types of connections between countries around the world. Such connections include: economic links of all kinds; the movement of people across borders; cultural linkages; almost all forms of communication; shared international concerns for issues like the environment, human rights, technological advance and health improvement; and the rapid growth in the number and range of international organizations. Connections between countries increased dramatically over the course of the twentieth century, largely owing to technological advance – with decreasing communication times heralding an associated image of a shrinking world. Yet, interdependence is more than simply the growth in connections, important as they are in themselves.

Interdependence means that economies, societies and governments are affected by events beyond national borders – events which may have origins within the borders of other countries. Strictly speaking, this would imply *dependence*. However, because such effects travel both ways we talk of interdependence. In other words all societies and economies are potentially influenced, in this fashion, by all others. In reality, it may be more sensible to confine images of interdependence to links among industrially developed states or regional groups of such states. There is a strong case for arguing that developing countries are *dependent* on the industrialized world. Here, the two-way street is not so evident. Another way of seeing interdependence, again suggesting its two-way nature, is by defining it as *mutual dependence* (Keohane and Nye, 1977, p. 8; Jones, 2000, pp. 100–2). The great merit of this latter definition is that it suggests that interdependence can entail national costs inasmuch as future destiny is shaped through external dependence. Although, of course, national influence may be extended internationally in issue areas where dependence is reversed.

Especially significant has been the growth of economic connections which generate interdependence. The chaos of the 1930s, when the Great Depression spread like a disease through the Western world, was a manifestation of *economic interdependence*. Lengthening dole queues and resurgent protectionism sent powerful signals to governments about how much their economic prosperity was intertwined. Where the then-new Keynesian economic theory advocated governments intervening in their domestic economies to manage them, it provided simultaneously a rationale to consider *collective* management of economic interdependence at the international level. The post-war Bretton Woods institutions were the pragmatic response. Growth and prosperity were recognized as dependent on international trade, and a suitable economic environment for trade was believed to require a stable international monetary order.

International monetary stability – eventually based on a fixed exchange rate system – was the cornerstone of Western post-war prosperity. But it came at a cost. Each government within the system was faced with a trade-off between having to abide by the rules of international stability at the cost of a loss of independence in the realm of domestic economic management. Collective management of interdependence was not politically neutral. When governments had to make efforts to ensure their balance of payments balanced, they found that this could compromise preferred economic policies at home. Reducing imports and increasing exports, to avoid a balance of payments deficit, usually meant a government taking measures to affect domestic economic prices, a move that could be unpopular at home if the intervention increased the cost of popular imports and lowered the cost of exports, perhaps with an associated rise in unemployment.

Governments have responded to the problems and potentialities of interdependence in a variety of ways. International institutional arrangements such as those of the Bretton Woods organizations are one response. Other responses which encourage interdependence included deregulating monetary movements, encouraging free trade and promoting cross-investment between economies. Despite such positive measures, which help foster economic interdependence, governments have shown willingness to manipulate circumstances of interdependence to their state's advantage and have rarely held back from using political influence for economic advantage.

The scope and intensity of economic interdependence

The scope and intensity of important issues derived from interdependence can now be considered. The first issue is judging the extent to which interdependence amongst a group of countries is equally reciprocal. If there is significant bias in the relationship then we can talk of *asymmetric* interdependence, a situation which can extend to the political relationships between nations. In the post-war example of the dominance, or even hegemony, of the United States in the Western world, there was clear asymmetry. At the end of the Second World War, the United States accounted for around 40 per cent of the world's total economic output (expressed as Gross National Product or GNP). It has remained between 20 and 25 per cent since the start of the 1970s to the present day when it is around 21 per cent (Strange, 1994, p. 238; CIA, 2004). In other words the world economy does not comprise a set of equally important economies.

Nevertheless, the concept of interdependence is still useful. The US economy may not be as dependent on the Mexican economy as the latter is on the US economy, but the US economy is dependent for markets on the other economies collectively. It is easy to fall into a trap of seeing interdependence as if it should apply only to pairs of states: the United States and Japan; France and Germany, and so on. The world economy has many national economies with economic connections creating a web of links across the globe. Yet, asymmetries do exist and often lead to political debate over particular bilateral links.

A second issue to consider is the extent to which economic interdependence is encouraging a process of globalization. In the words of the song: 'money makes the world go round.' Financial markets allowing the trading of currency and other capital assets have become global. Technology and policies of deregulation have enabled the traditionally important financial markets, such as those of London, New York and Tokyo, to become linked through information technologies, effectively allowing 24-hour 'real time', if impersonal, trading. This has heightened international concern over the stability of foreign exchange markets and led one author to succinctly identify the broad issue as one of 'mad money' (Strange, 1998). Tremors in one money market could spread rapidly to others, perhaps leading to volatility in national interest rate policies and volatility in business links across borders. The sheer size of the pool of liquid assets available to the private sector is constantly in the minds of national policy-makers. The consequence has been growing pressure for the world's leading economies to coordinate their economic policies in such a fashion that there is avoidance of excessive divergence in interest rates or inflation rates, bringing some measure of greater certainty in money markets. Unfortunately, as we shall see, the politics of reaching such agreements on coordination have dogged meetings of the Group of Seven industrial nations (G7). Yet, for Europe the establishment of the Euro has eased regional cross border trading in currency and partly accounts for the global decline of 19 per cent in the daily turnover indicated at the beginning of this chapter (BIS, 2002).

Globalization is also evident in the changing nature of production, with fundamental implications for the ways in which we view trade. One author has described a set of changes in the pattern of international production as a 'global shift' (Dicken, 2003). In the nineteenth century, the industrialization of much of the world proceeded with a corresponding growth in trade between national economies. Then, especially since the end of the Second World War, the world witnessed an immense growth in big firms setting up production operations outside their home economies (creating what is called foreign direct investment or FDI). Rather than produce goods at home and then export them, the economics of competition encouraged multinational corporations (MNCs) to take their expertise in production nearer to the foreign markets in which they sold. In particular, highly efficient US firms were in the vanguard (Vernon, 1971).

From the 1950s to the mid-1970s, US firms accounted for between 40 and 50 per cent of total FDI (Dicken, 2003, p. 54). In 1960 the United States and the United Kingdom between them accounted for two-thirds of the world total. The global shift has been to a new development on top of this. It is no longer just the big companies that operate with an international outlook. Globalization in production has brought even small firms to consider their operations in relation to selling in a global market rather than in a national one. Trade is decreasingly an 'arm's length' phenomenon between separate economies. Today it is effectively impossible to quantify real figures for trade as around half the trade for some industrial countries, and perhaps one-third of all trade, takes place within the operations of single firms – in other words subsidiaries of a single firm 'trade' with each other, across national borders, in an activity described as *intra-firm* trade. In addition some three-quarters of all trade by the mid-1980s was conducted within or by MNCs (Dicken, 2003, pp. 52–3; Dunning, 1993; Held *et al.,* 1999, pp. 236–8). Consequently, there has been a relative decline in the percentage of world FDI originating in the United States as the new production links become more global and others have jumped on the bandwagon, including the economies of South East Asia – vibrant and expanding until the setbacks of the Asian crisis. In 2000 the US share was down to 20.8 per cent of the total while the developing countries share had risen to 12 per cent (Dicken, 2003, pp. 56–7). Interestingly the share of the United Kingdom rallied from 10.6 per cent in 1995 to 15.1 per cent in 2000 putting it in a clear second place to the United States. In terms of the receipt of FDI, in recent years there has been a significant increase of FDI going to Southeast Asia, while China has become the world's leading recipient, overtaking the United States. In the same period it is notable that there has been a marked fall in that going to the former East and Central European countries (UNCTAD, 2004).

Once again, a significant driving force for the changes in the nature of production is technological innovation. Where Henry Ford's production line set the precedent for exploiting economies of scale through the mass production of near-identical units, in his case automobiles, technology is bringing a startling transformation. High technology and very adaptable production lines are allowing much smaller batches of units with differing characteristics to be produced, without expensive retooling. Information technologies guide the production process in an adaptive fashion. Ultimately car production is heading towards 'build to order' (*The Economist*, 2004a, p. 11) using 'just-in-time' (JIT) methods, whereby one day the customer will enter a showroom, choose the colour (old Henry Ford would have none of that!) and the specification, all of which the sales person will enter into a terminal and the car will be manufactured that afternoon.

Globalization can also be seen in the way many firms now market their goods around the world. Marketing strategies have begun to exploit the growing similarity of tastes in many nations. Brand images are used to achieve recognition and identity with a product the world over. Thus Coca-Cola and McDonald's are commonplace in many countries, irrespective of level of development (Gill and Law, 1988, p. 61). Automobile manufacturers have turned to using names for their cars that are either recognizable in many languages or invented and not found in any. Strange but partly familiar words like 'Mondeo', 'Vectra' or 'Laguna' have resulted. The entertainments industry sees the outpourings of Hollywood and the popular music industry eroding cultural differences. The push for common brands and marketing strategies is reinforced by what Robert Cox has described as an emerging transnational management class bonded by a shared image across borders of how business is done and how people train for this world – a culture promoted the world over by prestigious business schools and management training programmes (Cox, 1987, p. 359).

Thus we face a global economy of high interdependence in monetary, trade and production activities. Understanding the associated issues draws us into attempting to understand a changing environment of political and economic interactions. The impact of interdependence and globalization may ultimately be so far-reaching that the sovereign state may become increasingly anachronistic in the face of regional developments and new and powerful forces of transnational production and money movements. Ultimately it is differences in our perspectives or ideologies (see Box 3.1) that go to the heart of assessments of the role and dynamics of markets, and the ability of states to manipulate them. The former British Prime Minister Margaret Thatcher once said 'you can't buck the market'. Markets are undoubtedly viewed as powerful distributive phenomena. Two influential texts summarize the nature of international political economy in terms of 'states *and* markets' (Strange, 1994) or 'states *versus* markets' (Schwartz, 2000) [emphasis added]. Capitalism in the late twentieth century, with the collapse of the communist Eastern bloc, was all but supreme as the organizing mode of production the world over. However, capitalism and the global market are host to a range of influential actors: not least the state, the transnational corporations and national big businesses, international finance organizations, labour organizations and myriad small businesses. They span monetary, trade, production and investment activities. Whether intentionally or not, their actions also have political consequences.

General problems of economic interdependence

The analysis of economic interdependence is, not surprisingly, a source of disagreement between scholars and practitioners. Box 3.1 presents a number of the broad areas in which different schools of thought contend.

Box 3.1 Perspectives to help understand the global political economy

An important question to consider is how we go about understanding the way the global political economy works: this will involve utilizing theoretical approaches. Further, in our search for understanding it is necessary to realise that *the policy-makers of the world themselves are applying their own ideological bias* and this in turn affects our perspectives as analysts. Students of International Political Economy (IPE) have identified *three* broad analytical perspectives applicable to the study.

The most established and widespread view, often claimed as the guiding viewpoint in government policy circles and international economic institutions, is the *liberal* perspective. This centres on the ideals of open markets and pluralist democratic political systems. Markets, therefore, are seen to create and distribute economic wealth. Government intervention in markets is modest, with the state tending towards a hands-off approach. The liberal viewpoint in general welcomes the growth of economic interdependence.

A second perspective is associated with *Marxist* views of class conflicts and the spread of global dependence, whereby poorer states of the world are seen to be locked into a relationship with the industrial world characterized as dominance and dependence. The FDI activities of large firms have been a particular focus, with attention drawn to their ability to exploit poor economies and to repatriate profits to their home economies (Hymer, 1972). While few countries today operate Marxist policies, the analysis of Marxist and dependency theorists can still offer powerful critiques of the other two perspectives. However, a development of this form of analysis has highlighted the emergence of a hegemonic transnational managerial class – centred on global business and financial institutions – bound together by shared theory and ideology (liberalism as above), and supported by institutions (including state apparatuses) and material capability (Cox, 1987; Sklair, 2001).

The third perspective focuses on *economic nationalism* (Gilpin, 1987, 2001), whereby governments are seen to act to promote the interests of their home economies at the expense of others. Subtle and sometimes very unsubtle measures may be taken to protect areas of important economic activity, including the use of tariffs and quotas, orderly market arrangements, voluntary export restraints and restrictive national standards. Economic nationalism may at times better characterize government attitudes even when they profess to be following liberal principles. From a national perspective, it may be fortuitous if other countries follow policies of economic openness at a time when one's own country is able to avoid economic penetration by others – the basis of many complaints against Japan.

The specific form of issues of interdependence may change but they tend to be symptomatic both of these schools of thought and of a set of general problems. These can be examined under the headings: trade problems, international monetary problems, global production problems, and general problems.

Trade problems

Interdependence in trade has brought a set of general problems underlying many present issues. A fundamental problem is achieving international agreement on principles – the differing perspectives on international political economy can result in different sets of such principles. However, membership of the WTO implies a degree of acceptance that trade operates best with minimal governmental intervention, reciprocity and the gradual reduction of all barriers to trade. Such principles represent the dominant liberal perspective. Associated problems include ensuring compliance with these principles, the resolution of disputes over protectionist practices and the inclusion within the set of principles of controversial areas such as agricultural trade. Nevertheless, trade conflicts keep recurring.

Trade conflicts between the United States and Japan, for example, have often been the subject of media headlines, with the US Congress from time to time threatening economic retaliation against Japan because of the difficulties of penetrating the Japanese market while the United States appears open to Japanese trade and FDI. When the US trade deficit reached $160 billion in the 1980s, some 37 per cent of this was with Japan (Balaam and Veseth, 2000). Even the popular author Tom Clancy managed to weave a tale of military conflict between the United States and Japan with origins in trade and financial disputes (Clancy, 1994). The European Union has also found itself in trade disputes with the United States. Disputes have included the infamous 'banana wars', European resistance to importing GM soya protein, and European displeasure at US tariffs placed on steel imports.

International monetary problems

Once again there is a key problem of agreeing principles. International monetary stability, as a principle, may be agreed internationally but there are still disagreements regarding the relative merits of fixed or floating exchange rate systems and the means to manage or police any agreements. Fixed rates have often, in the past, been seen as preferable but with acknowledgement of a problem of a trade-off between the needs of international economic stability and domestic autonomy. Moreover, this trade-off did not apply equally to all states. In the post-war period the power of the US economy, supported by the role of the dollar as an international reserve currency, ensured that the United States could avoid many of the distasteful costs at the domestic level. Indeed, the United States deliberately ran a balance of payments deficit to encourage the spread of dollars around the world.

Ultimately the United States' trading partners objected to this US immunity from politically sensitive domestic costs – an immunity gained at their collective expense. Some writers, however, have argued that such a dominant economic and political leader – a *hegemon* – is necessary in order to ensure that all countries abide by the agreed principles and thus maintain stability (Gilpin, 1987, pp. 72–80). Provided the hegemon is seen as 'benign' then its leadership may be collectively recognized and supported. Misuse of its position, an accusation increasingly made against the United States by the early 1970s, may lead to a decline in authority. The whole issue of hegemonic leadership as a means of stabilizing the international economic environment has become quite controversial. Its continued relevance lies in the uncertainties and instabilities that have followed the collapse of post-war Bretton Woods arrangements with a move to floating exchange rates and high levels of market dealings in currencies, and the unipolar nature of the post-Cold War world. The problem has become one of what level of international management is now possible and who should undertake it – a question given added poignancy in the light of the Asian financial crisis of the late 1990s.

Global production problems

The globalization of production has added to the range of problems associated with economic interdependence. Trends towards production patterns associated with post-Fordist and JIT methods, which avoid the need for huge inventories (such as completed cars sitting in huge car parks awaiting purchase), has meant the 'networking' of component suppliers together. This networking does not stop at national borders. There has been a widespread increase in cross-border acquisitions and mergers since the 1980s which, combined with less formal links, is blurring the borders of firms as well as the borders of countries (Badaracco, 1991; Dunning, 1993). We thus witness a growing global interdependence between companies evident in intra-firm and intra-industry trade. Such developments of networked links between the businesses of the world, combined with innovations in decentralized decision-making – again cutting across borders – led Robert Reich (1990) to ask the pertinent question about the control of US domestic production activities: 'Who is US?' In other words, if a state is to take action to promote its national economic welfare, it may find itself encouraging foreign-owned firms that provide jobs and investment in its economy in preference to its nationally owned firms that may be more busy beyond its borders, thus assisting employment in foreign countries.

General problems

Taken together, there is a general trend towards increased economic interdependence across many areas of economic activity. This has raised complex issues in each case. The changes involved reflect some general problems. In particular, there is the question of the autonomy and independence of individual countries. If monetary stability requires high levels of policy coordination, trade arrangements require complex negotiations and agreements, and global production methods entail the opening of borders to cross-investment, then economic and political independence is severely challenged. The global context is emphasized with national borders being simply less important – leading to the popularization of images of a 'borderless world' of high technology communications. In the words of Peter Dicken:

> national boundaries no longer act as 'watertight' containers of the production process ... As a consequence, each of us is now more fully involved in a world economic system than were our parents or grandparents. Few, if any, economic activities now have much 'natural protection' from external competition whereas in the past, of course, geographical distance was a powerful insulator. Today, fewer and fewer activities are oriented towards local – or even national – markets. More and more have meaning only in a regional or global context. (Dicken, 2003, p. 9)

In sum, the most significant effect of this process of globalization is the loss of national independence for states. Governments simply cannot keep track of the complex web of cross-investment that has grown between developed countries and increasingly with developing countries. Intra-firm and intra-industry activities, the movement of financial resources globally and the general growth of economic uncertainty taxes the abilities of governments to respond. Such is the importance of this interdependence in the calculus of competitiveness that governments have been actively engaged in the liberalization of markets and, in Europe, governments compete to offer the best deals to encourage FDI from Japan and the Asian 'tigers'.

Putting issues of economic interdependence on the international agenda

Part of the character of a transnational, interdependent world political and economic system is the politics of agenda-setting itself. The complexity of economic interdependence gives rise to efforts by many actors to bring issues to international attention and to resolve politically a wide variety of problems. In this respect, Stopford and Strange have highlighted the 'new diplomacy' evident between states and firms (1991). The new diplomacy represents a growing recognition that governments must negotiate with firms as well as other governments and that firms have also adopted ways that 'become more statesmanlike as they seek corporate alliances, permanent, partial or temporary, to enhance their combined capacities to compete with others for world market shares' (Stopford and Strange, 1991, p. 2). The determination of items for the global agenda can be made under the following categories.

Government-to-government issues

Under this category there are high-profile issues such as reciprocity in trade, agricultural subsidies, trade protectionism, international intellectual property recognition, trade in services and strategic trade policies – all of these being key issues within the trade regime which is largely overseen by the WTO. Governments have also negotiated over mutually sensitive or coordinated monetary policies – a constant issue for G7 meetings and intergovernmental relations within the European Union. Governmental relations between the industrial world and less industrialized countries have in addition included issues of foreign aid, loans, credits and debt, regulation of MNC activity and access to and protection of resources. Such dialogue between countries is paralleled by traditional inter-state processes such as diplomacy and political negotiations. For the economic nationalist, the links between the political and economic areas may in any case be very close.

Government-to-firm issues

Under this heading, agenda issues include enticements to invest, commercial 'sweeteners', government contracts, subsidies, bribery, protection, technology transfers, transfer pricing, financial market activities, repatriation of profits, environmental sensitivity and development. However, government–firm relationships vary tremendously. Relations with the government of an MNC's home state can be quite different to a possibly more adversarial relationship with foreign host governments. Past activities of some multinationals brought considerable bad press to MNCs, eventually leading to the UN and the Organization for Economic Co-operation and Development (OECD) exploring means to set standards of acceptable behaviour for MNCs. Today the situation is less hostile with many governments competing to attract inward investment from MNCs.

In a similar fashion, governments are locked into a complex relationship with the international private sector in financial markets. While tumultuous events like the run on the dollar in 1987, the run on sterling during 'Black Wednesday' (1992) and the more recent Asian financial crisis bear witness to government failures, governments still have their influence (see also Chapter 2). At a minimum they have two significant weapons. The first is the ability to manipulate their national interest rates, at least in the short term – a normally powerful instrument given that it is interest rate differences that primarily encourage the trade in currencies in foreign exchange markets. However, this approach completely failed, in 1992, when the British Chancellor of the Exchequer authorized the spending of more than one-third of Britain's total foreign currency reserves in a rearguard action in the face of a market-led assault on the pound. By the end of what became known as 'Black Wednesday' the policy had failed and the Quantum fund run by George Soros was $1 billion in profit. If governments are reluctant to interfere with interest rates, they have a second weapon. They can themselves become players in the foreign exchange markets, buying and selling currencies, including their own, in order to influence relative prices. Both weapons tend to be reinforced by a psychological game of trying to influence the expectations of the market. It has to be said that the British government used both weapons to no avail on Black Wednesday, when the overriding objective was to hold sterling at a particular value commensurate with it remaining in the fixed European Exchange Rate Mechanism (ERM). The psychological game was also played and lost, as the Chancellor of the Exchequer threatened to raise interest rates by a total of 5 per cent and was simply not believed! Further witness to the difficulties were evident in the bond-market crash in industrial countries in 1994 and the Mexican bail-out of 1995. Recognition of the general problem of management led the liberal publication *The Economist* to ask in late 1995, 'Who's in the Driving Seat?', and to proclaim in 1999, following the Asian crisis, that it was 'time for a redesign'. By 2003 *The Economist* was using the metaphor of a 'cruel sea of capital' whereby financial integration could potentially lift countries up or sink them (*Economist*, 1995, 1999, 2003) – and noting that one of the hallmarks of recent financial stress has been the multinational character: 'One country gets into financial difficulties, then another and another' (2003, p. 18).

Firm-to-firm issues

Under this heading we see corporate alliances, mergers, acquisitions, market sharing and price-setting, subcontracting, and joint representations in dealing with governments. The global linkages between firms are changing as we have seen. With complex patterns of subcontracting and alliances within industries becoming more significant, linkages appear to ignore national borders. With this internationalizing of production, firms have demanded more sensitivity within governmental circles to their collective requirements.

One response to this was witnessed in the rush to deregulate in the 1980s. The apparent international agenda of liberalization and general removal of restrictions to trade and cross-investment over borders, with greater tolerance of intra-firm and intra-industry trade, was partly encouraged by the activities of large companies. In some respects the changes levelled the cross-border playing field for medium-sized and smaller firms which lacked the capacity for intra-firm trade displayed by the larger MNCs. The problem was that the big firms could avoid the constraints of national economic policies by their intra-firm activities where smaller firms could not (Gill and Law, 1988, p. 175). For example, if a country put its interest rates up, a small firm borrowing money to expand faced a higher cost of doing so. In contrast a big MNC could raise the money abroad at lower interest rates and transfer it to the country in which it wished to expand, by internal transfer pricing, thus avoiding the effects of the interest rate increase and in the process getting around national exchange controls. Of course, the reduction of restrictions and levelling of the playing field, in recognition of the growing demands of cross-investment and trading in global markets, has been at the expense of national economic autonomy.

Setting the international economic agenda is no longer something confined to governments (if ever it was), yet inter-governmental negotiations must never be underestimated. They have been of great importance in the likes of trade negotiating rounds, G7 meetings, forums such as the IMF and World Bank, and in more controversial organizations such as the United Nations Conference on Trade and Development (UNCTAD) and the United Nations Industrial Development Organization (UNIDO). However, inter-governmental agenda-setting is shaped within a broader environment of many economic actors clamouring for a say, either by pressurizing their home or host governments, or through the development of new and often unstoppable trends in their operations.

Unipolarity, globalization and economic interdependence

The late twentieth century saw the end of the Cold War, a process of reintegration of Eastern and Central Europe with the West, and the emergence of the United States as the only remaining true superpower – a transition from bipolar to unipolar world. Cold War politics gave way to Western efforts to assist the transformation into democratic market economies by encouraging linkages in trade, finance and production. Not least, large-scale loans were involved. At stake was the avoidance of a return to conflict with a potentially isolated Russia. A partial cause of the collapse in the East had undoubtedly been the inability of those countries to remain at high levels of economic isolation from the West. From the early 1970s, trading links and later financial links had grown steadily.

The issue of economic interdependence gained new momentum with the end of the Cold War. First, the relative decline of the high politics issues of security and East–West stability made more space on the international agenda for issues of international political economy. Second, the pattern of economic globalization itself extended eastwards, albeit in an uneven fashion. Third, there was an effort within Western governments and former Eastern bloc governments actively to encourage the fostering of economic interdependence as a basis to lock in the process of transformation and to avoid any return to Cold War politics. In this respect Russia received huge IMF loans for economic reform and was invited to join G7 meetings – invoking the label 'G8'. Since 1998 it has been a full-member of G8, although G7 continues to meet separately to discuss economic and financial matters. Fourth, the Central European countries saw economic interdependence as a basis for joining the general European process of integration centred on the European Union and its subsequent enlargement. Fifth, with the decline of a Cold War focus on Europe, more attention came to rest on other parts of the world, such as Southeast Asia and China – with China obtaining membership of the WTO and thus becoming even more fully integrated into the global economy. In 2004 it was also invited to attend an informal meeting with G7.

Nevertheless, post-9/11, we have witnessed the United States returning to a more traditional flexing of its muscle – through protracted military activity. Its position within a uni-polar world has seen it bring security issues back to the fore – where the new terrorist threat itself is a product of globalization and transnational interaction. Thus while globalization is today running alongside the growth of economic interdependence, there are profound contradictions between the autonomy of the state, especially for militarily powerful states, and the challenges brought by globalization – leading one author to talk of a 'world turned upside down' (Jones, 2000). Jones gets to the nub of the problem in observing that a 'central paradox informs contemporary concerns: that, on the one hand, the state seems to be under threat from economic, technical and cultural developments, while on the other hand, the military capabilities of states have never been greater and the concentration of military strength in the hands of the United States of America – has never been exceeded' (Jones, 2000, p. 3). Thus the growth of economic interdependence, and the many attendant transformations associated with globalization, appear to have emerged alongside a concentration of power in one hegemonic superpower. In this respect the debates about US hegemony will continue.

However, the focus on US military dominance and contrasting images of globalization, in some respects, can be brought together. An alternative view of hegemony sees the United States, not just as a dominant state *per se* in a world of territorial states, but as an economy and polity at the centre of global networks of influence – embracing production, finance, knowledge and security, with an imperative to engage in constructive leadership (Strange, 1994). Others go further and suggest a hegemony or dominance is focused on a transnational managerial class, taking account of the range of interdependencies (Cox, 1987; Sklair, 2001). US businesses, banks, organizations and government, one could argue, are central elements in this more amorphous dominance. While acknowledging the dominance of the United States such a view is less focused on hard images of polarity, maintains emphasis on globalization and interdependence, and offers a clearly *political economy* insight (see Box 3.1).

Managing global economic interdependence

As there is no single issue involved in economic interdependence various international institutions are active. The established institutions of the Bretton Woods system (the IMF and World Bank) have been joined by the new WTO (which subsumes GATT). Often accused of dominance by the industrially developed (predominantly Western) states, these organizations coexist with others such as UNCTAD and UNIDO where the developing states have more voting influence. Despite this, the key organizations remain those associated with Bretton Woods (including the WTO). In addition, G7/G8 and the OECD play significant roles.

The IMF and the World Bank

The Bretton Woods institutions were established with the express purpose of attempting to facilitate the management of economic interdependence at a time when prevalent economic theories justified interventionism. Many of the principles of Bretton Woods were abandoned in the early 1970s, leaving a period of great uncertainty. Notably the IMF lost its main role as guardian of the fixed exchange rate system, as currencies were allowed to float and find their own value against each other. This effectively encouraged the huge growth in foreign exchange markets, producing figures such as those cited in the opening paragraph of this chapter. The World Bank had long ago turned its attention to the needs of developing countries following the post-war rush to independence from former colonisers. The irony is that in carving out a new role for itself, the IMF has found its activities overlapping with the World Bank. As many developing states went further into debt with Northern banks, a crisis grew which threatened the financial system. In 1982 the crisis came to a head when Mexico announced it could no longer service its debts. Many banks were faced with the possibility of collapse. In other words, the interdependence of the situation threatened both the lenders and the creditors. The IMF stepped in with assistance designed to enable developing states heavily in debt to continue to make repayments – often by providing new loans. In return, as it also moved further into debt-related issues in the 1980s, the World Bank began to apply conditions on loans comparable to those required by the IMF. Both institutions moved to centre-stage in dealings with developing states (see also Chapter 5). For the IMF, dealing with financial crises in general has now become one of its main responsibilities (see Box 3.2).

Box 3.2 Surveillance, fire-fighting and financial crises

The IMF has gradually found a new lease of life in the wake of a spate of financial crises that occurred at the end of the twentieth century. Tasked in some measure by G7 to respond to the threat of destabilizing crises in the global money system, the watchword has become 'surveillance' (IMF, 2003). The very expensive (\$40 billion) US-led Mexico bail-out in 1995 was in retrospect viewed as something that should have cost much less had they seen it coming. 'Surveillance' calls for a continuous look-out for signs of trouble. On its own this is not enough. Rapid response with all alarms ringing – the 'fire-fighting' metaphor – is also needed. Like water poured early on the base of a fire, bail-out money timely poured into a troubled financial system might stop the conflagration.

The Asian financial crisis, bad as it was, could have been much worse. IMF money, from the tender of its liquid assets, flowed into the region, supported by other sources of loan. As the initial bush-fire spread across national borders, bail-out packages were rapidly deployed. The IMF pledged \$21.1 billion as part of a \$58 billion dollar rescue package for South Korea; it pledged \$15 billion to Indonesia as part of an overall package of \$49.7 billion; and it pledged \$4 billion to Thailand towards its package of \$17 billion. Soon after the start of the Asian crisis, an IMF support package of \$41 billion for Brazil was announced, along with the by-now tough conditions placed on the borrowers. This latter effort was compromised by Brazil's failure to deliver on promised fiscal reforms (*Economist*, 1999, p. 15).

Ultimately, as *The Economist* notes, the problem is that:

Today's currency crises differ from those of the 1970s and 1980s in four crucial ways. They spread more quickly; they involve bigger sums of money; they are often caused by private rather than government profligacy; and they are devilishly difficult to diagnose. (*Economist*, 1999, p. 15)

The Group of Seven (G7)

G7 was viewed with some optimism in the late 1980s. With the end of the Bretton Woods order based on fixed exchange rates, new issues of interdependence were eventually recognized as requiring 'management'. The growth in foreign exchange markets, within a floating exchange rate environment, created the potential for instability in monetary relations. Following the 1985 Plaza agreement, G7 formally established procedures for policy coordination between them. In particular, there was concern over the, by then, massive US trade and budget deficits. The dollar was seen to be valued too highly by the market and hindering US export potential. G7 planned to monitor their respective economic performances and was prepared to intervene collectively in currency markets to stabilize exchange rates. It offered something of a return to the spirit of Bretton Woods, with national discipline being needed for the good of international economic order. The 1987 stock market collapse and the run on the dollar shattered confidence for a time. Ironically, one contributing cause of this was the apparent lack of consensus in G7, at its Paris summit earlier that year, on how much it should intervene in order to lower the value of the dollar, and by what amount. A sharp lesson was learned and the incentive to achieve real policy coordination was temporarily renewed. Following a new Mexican collapse in 1995, it was all but recognized that policy coordination was dead in the water and there was considerable talk in G7 meetings and elsewhere of the intention to strengthen the Bretton Woods institutions. Complacency was then shattered with the Asian crisis that unfolded in 1997, further encouraging the new role of the IMF (see Box 3.2).

Trade organizations

The WTO oversees trade issues and ensures implementation of the Uruguay Round agreement. Most significantly it has extensive dispute-settlement provisions which extend into controversial areas newly established under the Uruguay agreement. These include much greater coverage of agriculture (previously a major weakness), intellectual property protection, trade in services and foreign investment. Unlike the IMF, which weights voting in accordance with economic power and allocated quotas, the WTO operates on one vote per member. This opens interesting possibilities for the developing states *vis-à-vis* the developed world, while the United States keenly watches out for any apparent anti-US bias in decisions and dispute settlements. It has become the host organization for future trade Rounds, although the inauspicious failure in Seattle to begin work on the successor to the Uruguay Round merely provided further testimony to the politically charged atmosphere of all trade negotiations. In Seattle the interesting development was that immense pressure on the process came from a wide gamut of transnational NGOs, who in no small measure hi-jacked the headlines from the official trade representatives. After this set-back the progress of the current Doha Round has been bumpy. However, further complexity is evident in the interdependence of trade with the global finance system. As Figure 3.1 shows there was a marked fall-off in the growth of world trade following the Asian financial crisis. The WTO laid much of the blame on the events in Asia and their repercussions beyond the region (WTO, 1999). Management of money and trade are therefore not divorced from each other. In all this older organizations such as UNCTAD, a focus in the past for many calls from the developing countries for a new international economic order (NIEO), can be expected to lose further ground against the institutions favoured by the developed world.

At the regional level there are many organizations around the world that have issues of economic interdependence as part of, or the whole of, their brief (see Chapter 4). These include the EU, the North American Free Trade

Figure 3.1   *Real GDP and merchandise exports, 1995–2003*

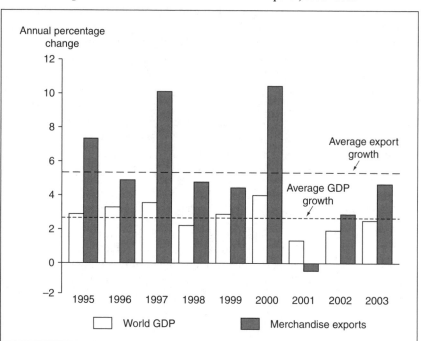

Source: WTO (2004).

Agreement (NAFTA), the Asia-Pacific Economic Cooperation (APEC), and the Organization of American States (OAS) amongst others. The most established of these, the EU, acted collectively in the negotiations leading to the Uruguay Round.

Whether regional or global, monetary or trade-oriented, a key issue in any organizational effort to manage aspects of interdependence is the extent to which the big economies might dominate the decision-making. The United States is no stranger to accusations of dominance and bias. It is worth noting that NAFTA, APEC and the OAS all include the United States. The influence of Japan and Germany must also be considered as very important in various organizations. What may be most significant is that the many organizations could simply be host to growing economic rivalries if policy coordination should fail.

Economic interdependence and contemporary world politics

The set of issues involved in economic interdependence raises serious questions about state sovereignty and the predominance of state-centred international politics. The activities of many other actors have encouraged the growth of interdependence and in turn have themselves been influenced by the continued increase in interdependence. Governments attempting to achieve economic and political objectives (domestically and internationally) have to give more attention to the activities and objectives of other agents: other governments; international organizations; transnational companies; banks; finance houses; and the behaviour of individuals aggregated through markets (Held *et al.*, 1999, pp. 49–62).

Economic interdependence as part of the process of globalization has given rise to a much greater complexity of linkage between societies, affecting all aspects of life, including ideology, culture, entertainment, environment, technology, wealth creation and distribution, and implicit in all of this is a growing interdependence in security questions (themselves defined more broadly than in the past). In this context politics is also becoming more transnational or globalized (Luard, 1990).

Concepts such as 'interdependence' and 'dependence' help us to identify issues and attempt to understand their underlying causes. Metaphors such as 'globalization' give us images of an uncertain, but no doubt exciting future. It is a future of benefits as well as costs to most of the main actors, states included. It is a future where politics and economics at domestic and international levels will be increasingly hard to separate. It is a future where the movement of money, the globalization of production and the complexity of trade issues will remain high on the international agenda – alongside other issues such as the environment, security, human rights, religion and poverty.

Guide to further reading

Balaam and Veseth (2000) have produced an excellent introduction to all aspects of economic interdependence and the international political economy, covering money, trade and production as well as issues such as energy, the environment and food. Spero and Hart's (2003) text is well established as a narrative covering the politics of the post-war development of the international economy. Most aspects of globalization are dealt with excellently by Held *et al.* (1999) and Jones (2000) while more detail on the globalization of production is provided by Dicken (2003). More advanced IPE texts include Woods (2000), Gilpin (2001), Gill and Law (1988) and Schwartz (2000).

Chapter 4

Regions and Regionalism

MICHAEL SMITH

From the early 1990s onwards, there has been a notable surge of interest and activity in both regions and regionalism. One manifestation of this has been the renewed salience of regional conflicts such as those in the Balkans and the Persian Gulf, or in the former Soviet Union. At the same time, there has been a sharpened awareness of the possibilities of regional cooperation and institution-building. For example, a WTO study published in 1995 listed over one hundred regional trade arrangements, ranging from the highly-developed institutional framework of the EU to limited and often specialized agreements between three or four countries (WTO, 1995, pp. 77–91). Figure 4.1 summarises the position in 2002; by late 2004, a World Bank Report was able to identify almost 230 such arrangements, with a further 60 or so being negotiated (*Economist*, 2004b). There has also been an increasing tendency in all parts of the world to search for mechanisms of cooperation in the political and security fields: for instance, in the case of Southeast Asia, the Association of Southeast Asian Nations (ASEAN) developed in the 1990s from a loose association of countries with rather

Figure 4.1 *Evolution of regional trade agreements in the world, 1948–2002*

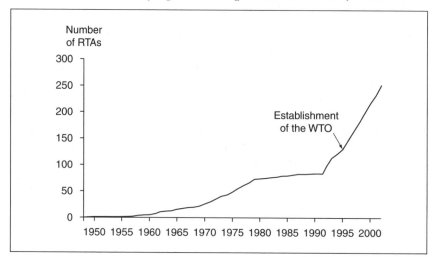

Source: WTO website.

unclear regional objectives into a more elaborate and focused set of institutions with explicit aims in the political and security fields. In Latin America, there has also been a revival of the search for regional identity in both the economic and the security fields (Hurrell, 1992).

Concern with regional patterns and with regionalism did not suddenly begin in the 1990s: it has been a focus of study and political action since the beginning of the twentieth century, and some would argue for even longer than that (Mattli, 1999; Fawcett, 2004). Why, then, has the concern with regionalism fluctuated, and why has it re-emerged with such force in the post-Cold War era? As already noted, regionalism is often linked very strongly with regional organization and institutions. Why do these institutions arise, how have they developed, and how do they relate to other, more global institutions? Not only this, but how do they relate to that most pervasive, if debatable institution, the national state? Does regionalism imply the coming together of states and their interests, or does it reflect broader forces of integration which may eventually at the level of the region undermine the predominance of the state itself? How does the uneasy combination of economic globalization with the apparent dominance of one military superpower – the United States – affect regionalism in the new millennium?

It can be seen from this set of questions that regions and regionalism can act as a kind of 'lens' through which central issues of world politics are refracted and given particular shape. For instance, it is often argued that processes of cooperation and integration are easier at the regional level; but this can be paralleled by the awareness that regional conflicts can have a peculiar intensity and violence. Equally, it is argued by some that regionalism contributes to the broader development of global order, and in the economic sense that it can be seen as a reflection of globalization; but alongside this is often the fear that regional groupings can become introspective and protectionist in their leanings, closing themselves off from the world economy. By focusing attention on such questions at the regional level, it is possible to explore key issues in some detail, whilst still preserving an awareness of the national and the global pictures.

Regions and regionalism: characteristics and driving forces

Many scholars have attempted to define the essential characteristics both of regions and of regionalism in world politics. The 1960s and 1970s saw a first wave of analysis, focused particularly by the regional impact of the Cold War and by the emergence of regional institutions both in Europe and in the Third World (Russett, 1967; Cantori and Spiegel, 1970; Nye, 1971). During the 1990s, as noted above, there was renewed interest because of what has been termed 'the new regionalism' of the post-Cold War era, and this has led to further attempts at definition (Fawcett and Hurrell, 1995; Hurrell, 1995; Gamble and Payne, 1996; Hettne, Inotai and Sunkel, 1999; Mattli, 1999; Teló, 2001; Breslin *et al.*, 2002). One of the most concise of these attempts has been made by Stubbs and Underhill (2000, pp. 231–4), who identify three central elements to regionalism. First, there is a common historical experience and sense of shared problems among a geographically distinct group of countries or societies: this effectively gives a definition of 'region'. Second, there are close linkages of a distinct kind between those countries and societies; in other words, there is a 'boundary' to the region within which interactions are more intense than those with the outside world: this intensification of interactions has been termed 'regionalization'. Finally, there is the emergence of organization, giving shape to the region in a legal and institutional sense and providing some 'rules of the game' within the region: this element of design and conscious policy is central to 'regionalism'. Although Stubbs and Underhill are concerned particularly with the political economy of regions and regionalism, their criteria can be extended to cater for all areas of interest and activity. Notably, the criteria do not make judgements about the outcomes of regional activity and organization: these outcomes can as easily take the form of an intensification of frictions as an intensification of cooperation or integration. The key element is proximity and intensity of relationships. Thus, the extent of 'common historical experience and sense of shared problems' could be said to be at its peak in areas such as the Balkans where there has been a history of destructive conflict, as much as in areas where there is a long tradition of cooperation, such as Scandinavia. Both areas also show evidence of strong tendencies towards regionalization, with concentration of attention and activity within the boundaries of a certain group of countries. Not everyone would agree, however, that the Balkans and Scandinavia show equivalent levels of regionalism.

A brief examination of the contemporary world arena confirms this initial impression: there are strong elements of region and regionalization, but not always of regionalism. Regionalism is widespread, but it is also diverse. The most formal and wide-ranging expression of regional interactions is undoubtedly the EU: a highly-developed set of institutions expressing not only the economic but also increasingly the political integration of the western European region, with recent extension both into central and eastern Europe and into the field of security and defence, or to other parts of Europe. Some have argued that this implies ultimately the construction of a kind of 'regional state', in which the traditional roles of national state authorities are transferred to the European level (for a review see Laffan *et al.*, 2000, Part 1). This possibility, of course, has also been the focus of intense political debate and often open dissent within the EU itself. At the other end of the spectrum, there is a wide range of regional agreements which focus on a limited number of states or societies and often on very specific problem areas: for example, agreements between landlocked African countries for transit by land or air to the outside world, or between countries in the Middle East over the supply and use of water from rivers running through several countries (see Mattli, 1999, Chapter 5).

In dealing with this variety, three particular elements seem important. First, there is the spatial dimension of regionalism: how large is the area covered, and how is that area defined or redefined as conditions change? As an example, one can examine one of the most highly developed regional security arrangements, NATO, which was established in the late 1940s and early 1950s. Even then, there was a difficulty in defining the 'North Atlantic area' and adjusting membership to reflect it. By the early 1950s, Greece and Turkey were members of the organization, but no-one would argue that this was because of their presence in the North Atlantic: it was a reflection rather of the (equally regional) concern to surround and contain the Soviet Union. The disappearance of the Soviet Union with the end of the Cold War posed an equally demanding question of definition, if purely geographical criteria were to be used. By 2004, Poland and other major central and east European countries were members of NATO, and it was clear that political change had impacted again on the geopolitical definition of the 'NATO area'. This also demonstrates that regional boundaries can overlap or interpenetrate: many European countries can be considered as parts of several regions or 'sub-regions' depending upon the criteria used, and of several regionalisms according to their involvement in different organizations and institutions (Bremner and Bailes, 1998). Figure 4.2 shows the way in which this has affected the regional security organizations of Europe, with NATO, the EU and the OSCE forming a complex jigsaw of membership and exclusion.

A second key feature in the variety of regionalism is its scope: in other words, the tasks or areas of interaction covered by the region or by regional organization. Here, the variety is, if anything, even more bewildering. NATO, at least, is centred on defence and security; but these have changed their meaning markedly in the 1990s. The EU began (in the form of the European Economic Community (EEC) during the 1950s) as a predominantly economic organization and expression of regionalism, but has developed towards political and security activities; by 2004, it had established a Common Foreign and Security Policy and a Common European Security and Defence Policy. Other expressions of regionalism can take cultural forms, for example in the awareness of shared heritage between Muslim countries in the Middle East, or in the notion of Nordic regionalism which has been present for centuries. It is often noted that African nations have a well-developed sense of Africanness, but that for a number of reasons they are not very closely tied economically. Africanness – and the establishment of organizations such as the African Union – has also

Figure 4.2   *Organizational membership in Europe, 2005*

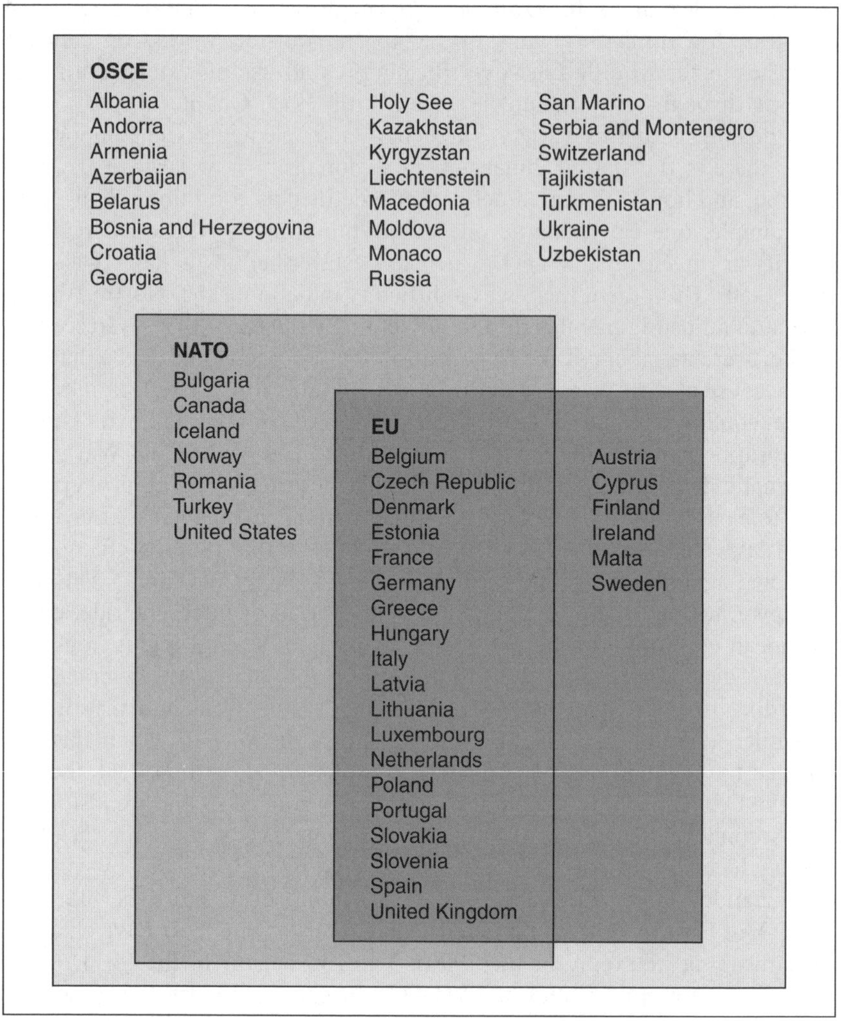

OSCE

Albania	Holy See	San Marino
Andorra	Kazakhstan	Serbia and Montenegro
Armenia	Kyrgyzstan	Switzerland
Azerbaijan	Liechtenstein	Tajikistan
Belarus	Macedonia	Turkmenistan
Bosnia and Herzegovina	Moldova	Ukraine
Croatia	Monaco	Uzbekistan
Georgia	Russia	

NATO

Bulgaria
Canada
Iceland
Norway
Romania
Turkey
United States

EU

Belgium	Austria
Czech Republic	Cyprus
Denmark	Finland
Estonia	Ireland
France	Malta
Germany	Sweden
Greece	
Hungary	
Italy	
Latvia	
Lithuania	
Luxembourg	
Netherlands	
Poland	
Portugal	
Slovakia	
Slovenia	
Spain	
United Kingdom	

not prevented large numbers of regional conflicts among the states of the continent. One of the problems entailed in trying to capture the variety of regionalism is thus the need to cater for overlapping tasks and functions. As with the geographical boundaries of regions, so do the functional boundaries shift and overlap or merge.

A third feature of the variety of regionalism is the level and extent of regional organization. It is clear that although the overall level of regional organization has risen over the decades, and particularly in the post-Cold War period, it remains uneven and fluctuating. Some regional organizations are tightly structured, permanent and impose important constraints on their members: this is most true of regional organizations in Europe: not only the EU, but also NATO and the OSCE. Others are much looser, depending on the shifting political or economic needs of their members and on the broader political climate in the world arena. The example already cited of ASEAN is a case in point. For many years, this grouping existed as a largely defensive political club designed to express its members' interest in steering between China, Japan and the United States. During the 1990s, it increased and deepened its organizational structure, both in the economic and in the security domains, but it remains essentially a club of national governments rather than an integrated set of structures and roles. For some of the more extensive and general-purpose organizations, such as the OAS or the African Union (AU) there are complex bureaucratic and administrative structures, but it is not always clear how much they express the common interests of very diverse memberships.

The three criteria suggested by Stubbs and Underhill, therefore, are useful as much because they expose the variety and unevenness of regionalism as because they define its essential features. They also demonstrate that, in the same way as 'interdependence' and 'development', regionalism is a set of issues rather than a single problem area for the analysis of world politics. Such an impression is further borne out by a study of some of the major patterns of regional interaction as they have been studied in the literature of world politics. Three such varieties can be identified here: regional integration, regional transnationalism, and regional security complexes.

Perhaps the most salient form of regionalism in the contemporary world arena is that of regional integration. Predominantly based on the intensification and organization of economic interdependence, this form of regionalism has become part of the economic orthodoxy of the new millennium. Although it is often identified primarily with the EU and with the EEC first established in the late 1950s, there is now a wide range of attempts to organize and to institutionalize economic integration in all regions of the world (Coleman and Underhill, 1998, Part 1; Hocking and McGuire, 2004, Part I). One of the most notable efforts has been the creation of NAFTA between Canada, Mexico and the United States; this has established elaborate mechanisms for furthering trade, investment and other economic relationships between the three members, and may over time extend to other countries in the western hemisphere. APEC, established in the early 1990s, has developed not only a permanent organizational structure, but also plans to create free trade in its region by the year 2020. In Latin America, MERCOSUR, composed of Argentina, Brazil, Paraguay and Uruguay (with Chile as an associate member), promises to establish a full customs union and some of the features characteristic of the EU; in 2004, it unveiled plans to establish a wider regional trade organization with the states of the Andean Group, in the form of the South American Community of Nations. ASEAN, as noted above, has developed plans for economic cooperation and the reduction of trade barriers as well as a regional security forum.

Regional integration is also closely linked with a second form of regionalism, regional transnationalism. Much of the activity directed towards regional integration has not unnaturally been led by states and their governments, but it has been accompanied in every case by an awareness that many of the regional interests and processes on which it focuses are transnational in their scope. They spill over borders, involving contacts between groups who are located in different national societies but who are linked by economic, cultural or political needs. Sometimes these groupings are directed towards private commercial or other objectives: this is clearly the case for major MNCs, which are often organized on a regional or continental basis for reasons of efficiency or because of the dictates of the market. Other transnational groupings at the regional level are less concerned with private profit than they are with political influence: they may wish to achieve results in areas such as environmental protection, human rights and other areas which demand governmental action at the national or the regional level. In such areas, there is an intimate relationship between organizations such as Greenpeace, Friends of the Earth or Amnesty International and the regional bodies with responsibility for the specific issue areas in question, such as the EU or the European Commission for Human Rights. More subversive and sometimes more dramatic are the groupings operating transnationally in specific regions to attack the 'established order': liberation movements or movements for regional autonomy within national states can often take action across national boundaries to destabilize their 'home' governments, as have the Basques in France and Spain, the contending forces in Afghanistan during the 1980s and 1990s, or the various movements in post-Soviet Russia, most dramatically in the case of Chechnya. In turn, this can lead to the development of regional structures to try and control such groupings, through military or police collaboration at the regional level. Since the attacks on the United States on 11 September 2001, the 'war against terror' has often engaged such measures and reflected the broader impact of regional conflicts.

This concern for transnational public order within regions links with the third type of regionalism to be explored here: regional security. One of the longest standing focuses, both of regionalism in general and of regional organization in particular, has been the concern with regional security and stability (Nye, 1971). Traditional analysis of international politics very often focused on the problem of the regional balance of power, and of the ways in which regional stability linked with the broader world order (Bull, 1977, Chapter 5). More recently, Barry Buzan has developed the notion of 'regional security complexes' (Buzan, 1991, Chapter 5). These complexes are seen as expressing distinctive regional security dynamics, which exist between the national and the global levels; in particular, they reflect three key forces, those of proximity, of power relations and of 'amity and enmity', operating between the states within a given region. An example furnished by Buzan is that of South and Southeast Asia: each region contains often intense security interactions, but there are very clear boundaries between them, and a clear climate of indifference. Thus, the tensions between India and Pakistan are of intense interest to powers in the South Asian complex, but of little direct concern to those in Southeast Asia, whilst the conflicts involving Vietnam, Cambodia and Laos over the years have had little direct effect in the South Asian sphere. In neither case is it clear that regional organization has developed in such a way as to handle more effectively the underlying conflicts: there is no 'South Asian security community' which might set out rules of the game or apply them to disputes, for example.

Problems of regionalism

Perhaps the most significant problem posed by regionalism in world politics centres on the relationship between intra-regional relations and the broader world arena. As noted above, one of the key tensions exposed by the study of regionalism is between what goes on within a given regional arena and what goes on between that arena and the outside world. In this section, the focus is on these two dimensions.

Intra-regional relations

The most immediate problem posed by the study of intra-regional relations concerns the role of states. It has already been noted that in many regional arenas and regional organizations, the role of states is either constrained or in extreme cases thrown into fundamental doubt. But national governments often see it rather differently. By entering into regional agreements and organizations, they may be better placed to achieve their national objectives, whether these focus on prosperity or security. Thus, while the EU undoubtedly limits the freedom of its members to pursue their own independent courses of action, there is no doubt that in economic and political terms participation in the EU adds to the strength of each of its members, and this is particularly clear in the case of those countries from the former Soviet bloc that entered the EU in 2004. From a purely rational national perspective, therefore, the gains can very easily outweigh the losses. Likewise, in the case of NATO, there is no doubt that collective regional defence adds to the ability of each of the members to defend itself.

Often, these generalized benefits of active regional participation on the part of states are underlined by specific gains to individual countries. For example, in the Americas, one of the perennial problems for all countries apart from the United States is the United States itself: a dominant power in both economic and security terms, whose actions if unconstrained can have unpredictable effects on the rest of the hemisphere. From the point of view of countries such as Canada and Mexico, therefore, it makes sense to construct regional arrangements which set out some rules of the game for the conduct of relations with and by the United States, and it is well worth sacrificing some independence in order to achieve this. From the point of view of the United States, this can also have specific benefits, if it forestalls the possibility of defensive actions on the part of its partners and opens their markets to US goods. This example also underlines the fact that in many cases, regionalism arises from the positive adoption of state policies, and from agreements between national governments. In other words, whilst what is going on in such agreements as NAFTA may look like the sacrifice of national independence, it can also be seen as the exercise of national choice – an expression of sovereignty as well as a sacrifice of national freedom (Leyton-Brown, 2000; Breslin *et al.*, 2002, Chapter 5; Hocking and McGuire, 2004, Chapter 4).

Regionalism therefore expresses a constant tension between the demands of statehood and the pressures for collective action or adjustment to regional realities. One of the key realities is the distribution of power between major regional actors, usually but not always states. As noted above, for all states in the western hemisphere, the dominance of the United States is an inescapable fact of life, all the more telling because of its regional expression. In the EU, the actual or potential predominance of a united Germany was one of the underlying themes of the 1990s, conditioning all efforts at EU reform and enlargement and shifting perceptions of the long-established Franco–German alliance at the centre of the 'European project'. Not surprisingly, other regional systems also demonstrate the importance of the regional distribution of power. Thus, in South Asia, the centrality of India and of its conflicts with its neighbours has been a relatively permanent aspect of the regional economic and political orders (Buzan and Rizvi, 1986). In other cases, sudden or radical change in the regional distribution of power can have important catalytic effects: thus, in 1979, the deposition of the Shah of Iran and the installation of a radical Muslim regime reverberated throughout the region and beyond. Likewise, in Afghanistan, Soviet intervention in 1980 had important effects on the regional order, whilst the prospect of a radical Muslim regime there in 1996 led to significant new efforts at regional collaboration among the states of central Asia. These efforts were in turn given greater emphasis by the tensions in the former Soviet Union after the end of the Cold War, and by the impact of the 'war on terror' after 2001, which focused in large part on the replacement of the Taliban regime in Afghanistan and American penetration into the central Asian region.

Arising from the interaction of states and regions, and expressing in part the shifting distribution of power within regions, is the broader problem of regional order. As Robert Cox has argued, international orders express a combination of forces including the distribution of power, the role of institutions and the existence of identities and ideologies (Cox, 1986). From what has been said, it is apparent that these are important at the regional as well as at the global level. Where there is a close 'fit' between the three elements of power, institutions and ideas, there is at least superficially a settled regional order. This could be said, for example, of western Europe for long periods during the 1950s, 1960s and 1970s or of Latin America during the same periods. Where there is no close 'fit' between the elements, or there are radical shifts in the balance between them, then there ceases to be a settled order (Smith, 1993; Laffan *et al.*, 2000, Chapter 3). Such conditions arguably prevailed in Southeast Asia for much of the Cold War period, and can be seen in central Asia or the Balkans during the post-Cold War era. In the new millennium, they are also accompanied by growing sensitivity to the ways in which the US 'hyperpower' can penetrate into any region of the world and affect intra-regional balances of forces.

A further problem at the intra-regional level is the relationship between economics and security. It has been seen already that this is one of the ways in which regionalism can be defined or described, but it is also apparent that it has significant impacts on the functioning of regions and regional orders. For example, the rise of protectionism and exclusive economic agreements during the 1930s was seen as a strong force in the approach of the Second World War (and, incidentally, conditioned the post-1945 desire for European economic integration). During the Cold War, one of the underpinnings of the Soviet bloc was the establishment of regionalized economic processes in central and eastern Europe through the agency of the Council for Mutual Economic Assistance (CMEA). Whilst the USSR retained its military and political dominance of the region, it was possible to maintain some semblance of a regional division of labour economically. But the decay of Soviet power in the 1980s and its collapse in the 1990s was paralleled by the decay and collapse of the purported regional economic order. Outside Europe, part of the debate about the emergence of a potential East Asian bloc as a competitor for the United States and the EU has been centred on the apparent growth of a regional economic system, but this has been qualified by the frictions between Japan, Southeast Asia and other regional actors arising from the uneven distribution of economic power and prosperity (Cable and Henderson, 1994; Gibb and Michalak, 1994; Coleman and Underhill, 1998, Part I; Breslin *et al.*, 2002, Chapters 7–8).

Not surprisingly, it is not always clear to observers that the growth of regionalism is a 'good thing'. This is essentially a normative question, about the way things ought to be as well as the way they are in world politics, and regionalism is not the only issue which raises it: for instance, one could ask whether statehood itself is a good or desirable thing, or whether globalization and certain models of development are to be desired (see Chapters 2, 3 and 5). As in other cases, though, regionalism focuses the question in a distinctive way, because it combines the demand for specific policies or institutions with broader demands of change in the world arena. Thus it mattered greatly to Americans whether NAFTA was going to bring them benefits or whether they would lose business and their jobs to Mexico or Canada. In the same way, the intense arguments about British membership of the EU have not simply been generalized arguments about world order: they are arguments about jobs, living and working conditions and about local and regional democracy. In Southeast Asia, it matters intensely what rules are developed for the regional management of resources such as those of the Mekong River, and it matters not just to governments but also to local and regional interests. Regionalism, it might be said, reaches parts that other issues do not always reach.

Regionalism and the world arena

Many of the problems described above as intra-regional intersect with problems in the broader world arena. In a sense, the two arenas are inseparable, but by dealing with them separately one becomes more aware of the linkages and tensions between them. Three particular problems can be identified here: the problem of inter-regional relations; the problem of relations between regionalism and globalism; and the problem of relations between regional orders and world order.

Inter-regional competition and collaboration between regions is an important dynamic in the world politics of the 1990s, and will remain one into the new millennium. The most obvious formal manifestation of this process centres on the EU. At one and the same time, the EU can be seen – and is seen both in Europe and outside – as a formidable competitor in the world political economy and as an attractive partner for other regions of the world. In the first of these guises, the EU has sometimes been presented as a 'fortress Europe' in the making, taking every opportunity to protect its own and to attack the entrenched positions of the Americans and the Japanese (Rosecrance, 1991; Katzenstein, 1993). This fits with the idea that inter-regional relations may give rise to a world of competing blocs, not just in the economic but also in the military spheres (see below). On the other hand, the EU itself often presents itself as a 'world partner', constructing agreements and initiating dialogue with other regions; in this guise, it has developed a web of inter-regional agreements with groupings such as ASEAN, MERCOSUR, the Andean Pact and (more loosely) with a wide range of Mediterranean countries. In their turn, many other regional groupings have initiated a search for inter-regional partnerships, partly as a defensive measure to maintain access to potential 'fortresses' and partly as a conscious attempt to build new forms of world order (Edwards and Regelsberger, 1990; Teló 2001; Aggarwal and Fogarty, 2004; De Flers and Regelsberger, 2005).

Attempts to build ambitious inter-regional arrangements thus have a certain ambiguity to them, and this ambiguity is underlined when it is related to a second problem: the relationship between regionalism and globalism. As can be seen in Chapter 3, there are very strong pressures in the world political economy towards globalization of processes of production and exchange; these run alongside the awareness of global problems such as those of development, of the environment or of peacekeeping in the post-Cold War world (see Chapters 5, 7 and 11 in particular). Given the strength of regionalism in the new millennium, how can these forces be reconciled? In a sense, this is again not a new problem: during the 1950s, the tensions between the search for security in Europe and the broader demands of world order were apparent, and there is a continuing tension between regional economic integration and the multilateral rules of the world trading system (see Chapter 3; Anderson and Blackhurst, 1993; Aggarwal and Fogarty, 2004).

The pressures of regionalism after the Cold War and after 9/11, though, put a new gloss on these tensions, giving new point to the question once posed by Robert Lawrence: are regional organizations 'building blocks or stumbling blocks' when it comes to the search for world order? In particular, the frictions can be seen in two areas: those of institutions and rules, and of identity. Many regional organizations have developed elaborate systems of rules and accompanying institutions, and it is sometimes unclear how these relate to global institutions and rules. The most obvious example here is the WTO (see Chapter 3; WTO, 1995), which has to pay a great deal of attention to the ways in which regional rules match up to its global multilateral framework. But the problem is not absent in the sphere of security: the development of elaborate codes for regional conflict resolution has posed a challenge to the UN and other bodies in their attempts to manage regional conflicts. More intangible is the tension created by the search in some regions for a 'regional identity', which affects expectations and habits in distinctive ways. A case in point is that of differing attitudes towards Burma (Myanmar) during the mid-1990s and after. The EU and other 'western' groupings saw the human rights policies of the Burmese government as an outrage, and demanded that the regime be ostracized and subject to sanctions. ASEAN countries saw the issue differently, and as a grouping were able to resist the demands of the 'outsiders', which were expressed in terms of world order and universal rights. Although ASEAN was aware of the offences committed by the Burmese regime, they concluded that there were different and more regionally appropriate ways of dealing with the problem.

Regions, regionalism and the international agenda

One explanation for the fluctuating salience of regions and regionalism as an issue on the international agenda is that it reflects in large measure the fluctuating preferences of states. For large states, there is something to be said for regionalism if it can be used as a vehicle for their influence in the international arena: as a result, it may be promoted as a means of extending and consolidating influence. The clearest examples of this are regional efforts sponsored by dominant or hegemonic powers, such as the United States and the USSR during the Cold War. During the 1950s and 1960s, the United States in particular attempted to extend its influence – or sometimes to legitimize the influence it already had – in many regions of the world, particularly through regional alliances. Outside the military sphere, organizations such as the EEC were also viewed as the expression of US desires to shape western Europe. It is not always predominant or hegemonic powers that instigate regional cooperation, however. As already noted in the case of ASEAN, it can be argued that regionalism gives weaker countries an outlet, enabling them to avoid either domination by predominant powers or marginalization by them (see also Chapter 5; Gibb and Michalak 1994; Gamble and Payne, 1996; Breslin *et al.*, 2002, Chapter 1).

Implicit in this discussion of regionalism on the international agenda is the question 'who benefits?' We have already seen a range of potential beneficiaries from the processes and products of regionalism: hegemonic states, weaker states, MNCs and others. It is sometimes also argued, for example, that the real beneficiaries of regionalism are domestic political and economic elites in the countries concerned. Rather than having to account directly to their populations for their decisions and any damage that may arise, they can effectively cover their tracks by operating at and through the regional level. Christopher Hill, in studying the foreign and security policies of the EU, has pointed to the 'cover function' whereby responsibility for awkward decisions can be shifted to the European level (Hill, 1983, 1996; see also Manners and Whitman, 2000); others have pointed to the ways in which this can be used to justify unpopular policies, or escape the blame for them, at the national level. Other beneficiaries from regionalism may include military leaders who can point to regional commitments as the justification for increased defence budgets, pressure groups who can bypass national administrations to try and achieve their aims at the regional level, and commercial or industrial interests who can organize and influence more effectively through regional bodies than through the national process or at the multilateral level.

An evaluation of the place occupied by regionalism on the international agenda thus depends partly on the significance given to the needs and preferences of states, and partly on the significance allotted to the wider range of beneficiaries who can participate and influence processes of regionalization. It is also important to point out that the salience of regionalism has a direct and significant connection with the development and structure of the global arena itself. Where that arena is highly polarized and dominated by major states or groupings, it is likely that regionalism will be subordinated to the dictates of the global balance. Equally, if globalized processes of production and exchange are the dominant patterns of relations in the world political economy, it might be expected that regionalism and regional organization would be effectively a transmission belt for those patterns. In the new millennium, what we have is in fact a rather uneasy blend of these two qualities: uneven globalization, accompanied by the dominance of the United States in areas of military security. The consequences for regionalism are likely to be profound.

Regionalism in the contemporary world

How has regionalism been affected by the uneasy balance noted above, between globalization and American dominance? As noted earlier, the recent upsurge of interest in regions and regionalism clearly has strong links with the collapse of the USSR and of the Soviet bloc, the emergence of many new states and of many new potential focuses for conflict and cooperation – in other words, the globalization of security concerns. But it would be misleading to trace the upsurge in regionalism solely to this set of events, in particular because the direction and pace of change in different areas of world politics have been markedly different. To put it simply, the onset of economic interdependence and associated issues leading to the focus on regionalism and globalization is not simply a product of the 1990s and 2000s: nor are the problems of development and inequality which have beset regionalist efforts in the developing areas of the world; whereas the new forms and focuses of regional conflict or of nationalist tensions in Europe and Eurasia in very large part are. This is an important point for the analysis of world politics as a whole: there are different 'timetables' for change and for the onset of novel trends depending upon the particular issues under examination (Fawcett and Hurrell, 1995, Chapter 1; Breslin *et al.*, 2002, Chapter 1; Fawcett, 2004).

This said, there can be no doubt that the collapse of the Soviet 'empire' and the radical changes in the global distribution of power associated with it are a profound influence in the 'new regionalism' of the 1990s. Barry Buzan has referred to this as the removal of the 'Superpower overlay' which affected almost all areas of the world and which had the effect of suppressing or distorting processes of regional interaction (Buzan, 1991, Chapter 5). Apart from this, the newly-recognised dominance of the United States in the realm of 'hard security', and the implications for intervention and what some saw as a 'new imperialism' are key to the nature of the contemporary world arena. Initially, and most dramatically, this process removed the once seemingly permanent division of Europe, throwing into question the tidiness of the regional divisions that accompanied it. At one and the same time, the EU was catapulted into a wider Europe and the countries of central and eastern Europe were left without the (admittedly uncomfortable) certainties of Soviet domination. In this situation, it was not clear what the 'region' was: 'western Europe' and 'eastern Europe' were contrivances of the Cold War, but they had gained a certain reality because of the adjustment of policies and institutions to the East–West divide (Wallace, 1990; Laffan *et al.*, 2000, Chapter 3).

The result of this transformation was not felt only in Europe, nor only as the consequence of the Soviet collapse. Reference has already been made to the fact that processes of globalization had made themselves apparent during the 1980s, as had the possibilities of intensified competition between regions surrounding the EU, the United States and Japan. What the changes in Europe added was a major element of uncertainty about regional alignments and about the relationships between regionalism and the broader world order. As noted in Chapter 7, the UN was widely seen as the solution to many of the new areas of conflict which emerged during the late 1980s and early 1990s, but it rapidly became apparent that the UN was ill suited and poorly resourced to deal with the demands of regional conflict management. As a result, the UN Secretary-General, Boutros Boutros-Ghali, was led to call for a new division of labour between the UN and regional organizations in conflict management and peacekeeping, a call followed up and reinforced by his successor, Kofi Annan. In some cases regional bodies and their major members were eager to take over the task, but in many cases – for example, in former Yugoslavia, the former Soviet Union or a range of African conflicts – they proved unequal to it or were ignored by regional and other powers (Chayes and Chayes, 1996). As a result, there was confusion and uncertainty about the roles of different global or regional institutions.

There is thus a strong argument to be made that the end of the Cold War 'took the lid off' a number of intractable regional problems, with an ethnic as well as a national security dimension (see Chapter 8), whilst at the same time increasing the likelihood of intervention by the dominant global power – the United States – and its allies. On the one hand, this may well have led to a stronger emphasis on processes of regionalization and on regionalism as an issue, but on the other hand it also underlined some of the limitations of regional institutions in dealing with new challenges. Even the strongest of regional institutions, such as the EU and NATO, found themselves often in uncharted territory; NATO planners had spent the 1970s and 1980s planning for what happened when Yugoslavia collapsed, but they had not at all foreseen the prior collapse of the Soviet bloc. Outside Europe, there were also new challenges, or at least familiar challenges in new conditions, such as those in Somalia or – most dramatically – in the Persian Gulf. Following the Iraqi invasion of Kuwait in 1990, intervention by a multinational coalition led to a regional war and then to an extended period of economic and military sanctions; in 2003, in what might be seen as the follow-up to the war of 1991, an American-led invasion with at best indirect support from UN resolutions toppled the regime of Saddam Hussein, with uncertain consequences. Here, the predominance of the United States led some to expect that it would become a global and a regional police force, and thus either that it would supplant regionalism or encourage a resurgence of 'defensive regionalism'. In contrast, when regional tensions in Southeast Asia led to open conflict about the status of East Timor during the late 1990s, a novel 'coalition of the willing' of regional states led by Australia was able to deal with the peacekeeping task, but despite some similar attempts in West Africa this remained an isolated success.

In the security domain, then, the post-Cold War world provides a very patchy picture of regional challenges and regional responses, perhaps because it was in security matters that the Cold War 'overlay' had been most pervasive and the shift in power balance towards the United States most dramatic. Economically, the post-Cold War period saw less of a new world than a continuation of marked trends in the old one. As noted earlier, the growth of new regional trading and regulatory arrangements had been going on apace during the 1980s, and major international trade negotiations under GATT had since 1986 been wrestling with the coexisting tendencies towards globalization and regionalization (Anderson and Blackhurst, 1993; Cable and Henderson, 1994; Gibb and Michalak, 1994; Coleman and Underhill, 1998). There were, though, some major changes in the problems confronted as these processes moved into the 1990s and beyond. In the first place, the nature of regional arrangements and of economic processes had changed, with the rise of trade in services and the increased emphasis on regulatory policies which reached 'behind the border' (see Chapter 3). One major question which arose from this set of challenges was whether global or regional institutions were best suited to handle the emerging problems and to provide what has become known as 'governance' in the global political economy; the result was an often uneasy coexistence of the two, with regional organizations such as the EU or NAFTA introducing new regulatory mechanisms alongside, and sometimes in conflict with, attempts at global agreement (Coleman and Underhill, 1998; Hocking and McGuire, 2004).

It therefore seems that the post-Cold War – and post-9/11 – world has created both fertile new ground for regionalism and a whole set of new challenges. Importantly, these challenges often cut across the national/ regional/global divide, creating tensions between different levels of government and administration. This is as true of problems in the sphere of security as it is of those connected with economic and social questions. Sometimes, these questions come together in new and particularly demanding ways: thus, the conflicts in former Yugoslavia exacerbated problems of migration and employment in a number of European countries as large numbers of refugees looked for a safe haven (Waever *et al.*, 1993). This again was not an unprecedented regional problem; the end of the Vietnam war in the 1970s had led to an exodus of large numbers of 'boat people' whose presence imposed heavy burdens on a number of regional actors. But the coming together of post-Cold War conflicts with new economic and social demands certainly gave a new twist to the process, which was rendered even more distinctive by the challenges arising from the 'war on terror' and associated problems after 11 September 2001.

The most important question arising from this confusion of regional and global processes concerns regional and world order. Is there evidence that in the contemporary global arena, regionalism has assisted in the maintenance of stability, the containment of conflict and the maximization of prosperity? There has been a rash of new regional organizations and agreements, particularly in the economic field, but it is open to question whether they have yet generated (or can generate) a settled set of regional orders within a stable world order, or indeed whether this sort of order is more reliable than one underpinned by unilateral US power. If one returns to the earlier discussion of international orders based around the three criteria of power, institutions and ideas, it could be argued that there is still an absence of settled regional orders, most particularly in Central Asia and the Middle East, and that world order has proved much more difficult to sustain given the absence of the Superpower 'overlay' for security matters and the presence on the one hand of US dominance and on the other of globalization for economic problems.

Managing regionalism

At the beginning of this chapter, one of the central focuses was on the variety of regionalism and of regional organizations. Reference has been made at many points to regionalism at a number of different levels, centred on a wide range of different activities. In terms of management processes, this variety and range can be seen both as a problem and as a source of potential solutions. When viewed as a problem, it can easily seem that regionalism is a mess of competing tendencies and organizations, often getting in each other's way and sometimes coming into open conflict, with clashing claims to authority and influence. When viewed as a source of potential solutions, it can be argued that the variety of regionalisms is a reflection of the variety and complexities of world politics, and that without a wide range of organizations the world would be short of ways to address important questions about security and economic development.

Not surprisingly, this diversity and untidiness has spawned many different images of regionalism and its management in the twenty-first century. On one level, regionalism itself can be seen as a mechanism through which states and other groupings attempt to manage their involvement in the international arena. The test of effective management, as suggested earlier, is thus the extent to which regionalism expresses and channels the needs of the actors involved in it. At another level, regionalism can be seen as a means by which authority is transferred away from states and other groupings to regional bodies better able to manage the problems that confront them. Often, this transfer is strongly contested, but the test of effectiveness is the extent to which security and prosperity can be achieved through collective action at the regional level. At a third level, regionalism appears either as a contributor to or as an obstacle to world order and the management or governance of the changing international arena – a building block or a stumbling block. During the past decade, there has been a considerable debate about the relative merits of so-called 'open regionalism' and 'closed regionalism': the first implies an openness to the needs of the broader world order and a readiness to adapt to it, whilst the second implies an attempt to build a fortress and to manage by using regionalism as an insulator against the broader challenges of world politics. On the whole, the evidence gives a good deal of support to the building of 'open regionalism' both in economic and security questions, but it is not impossible that adverse economic or security conditions could lead to a reversal of this tendency (Rosecrance, 1991; Katzenstein, 1993; Hettne, Inotai and Sunkel, 1999).

The effective management of regionalism in world politics thus depends to a large degree on how management is attempted through regionalism: the one is in many respects the flip-side of the other. Depending on the extent to which regionalism reflects state strategies as opposed to integrative forces, or is problem-centred as opposed to legalistic in style, it has the potential to be both a bridge and a barrier to the achievement of order. What it does express is the emergence of a multilayered policy environment characterized by the multiplicity of institutions and the need for political action to take account of linkages and complexities in novel ways.

Regions and regionalism: implications for world politics

The implications of regionalism for world politics are as diverse as the forms and features of regionalism itself, but three central strands can be isolated from the discussion in this chapter:

- First, regionalism can be seen both as a force for integration and as a force for disintegration in world politics. At one and the same time, it expresses the desire for collective action and identity and the desire for difference and distinctiveness in the world arena. In doing so, it has some of the properties of other issues dealt with in this book, such as nationalism and statehood. The tension is ultimately unresolvable, since it is built into the foundations of the drive to regional awareness and regional organization.
- Second, regionalism has profound implications both for statehood and for world order as focuses of aspirations and activity in the world arena. It can be seen as both promoting and dissolving statehood; it can be seen as a bridge and a barrier to world order. It has two faces, inevitably as a result of its place at the intersection of the national and the global

systems. The pursuit of regionalism as a goal thus brings about some very challenging situations for policy-makers, and these have multiplied as the result of the spread of regionalism in the 1990s and after. The disappearance of such moderating devices as the Superpower 'overlay' has meant that the 'new regionalism' has to be constructed in a new context, and that its implications have not yet been fully recognized.

- Third, there is no one model of regionalism, nor one predominant theoretical framework for the analysis of regionalism. Andrew Hurrell, in one of the most wide-ranging treatments of the subject, identifies three major theoretical tendencies in the study of regionalism: systemic theories which see regionalism as a response to outside pressures and forces; theories focused on the development of regional interconnectedness and interdependence; and domestic-level theories which stress the impact of changes such as democratization on the tendency to regionalization and regional cooperation (Hurrell, 1995). It is clear from the discussion in this chapter that any full analysis of regionalism requires the deployment of all three types of theory. Not only this, but it must recognize that theories of regionalism are themselves part of the debate about the merits and demerits of regionalism itself as a phenomenon in world politics.

In the final analysis, a study of regionalism as an issue in world politics is a way of taking a perspective on virtually all of the major questions of our time. It encapsulates the paradoxes of a world more united yet also in some ways more divided than ever before, and it raises important questions about the future both of the state and of world order.

Guide to further reading

The best general collection dealing with regionalism, both in its historical context and as it has re-emerged in the 1990s, is Fawcett and Hurrell (1995); it covers both the theoretical aspects of the issue and a series of comparative case-studies. The article by Hurrell (1995) is the best short treatment of concepts and theories, and Fawcett (2004) provides an up to date historical review. Another good treatment is Gamble and Payne (1996), which focuses particularly on state strategies and has a set of regional case studies. Classical treatments of regionalism include Cantori and Spiegel (1970), Russett (1967). Issues of regional security are well covered in Buzan (1991) and in Nye (1971). On regionalism in the world political economy, see Stubbs and Underhill (2000, especially Part III), and Hocking and McGuire (2004, Part I). The relationship between regionalism and the world trading system up to the mid-1990s is described in detail in WTO (1995), which has a wealth of data and looks at the institutional arrangements. For more conceptual analyses of the economic and political issues, see Anderson and Blackhurst (1993), Hettne, Inotai and Sunkel (1999) and Breslin *et al.*

(2002). The specific problems of regional economic blocs are best handled by Cable and Henderson (1994) and Gibb and Michalak (1994), whilst Teló (2001) and Aggarwal and Fogarty (2004) provide a good range of studies focused on EU relationships with other regional organizations.

Many regional organizations (or global organizations relevant to regional issues) have useful websites. Among the most significant are the European Commission http://www.europa.eu.int/index_en.htm; the World Trade Organization http://www.wto.org; NATO http://www.nato.int; the EU Institute for Security Studies (originally the WEU institute) http://www.iss-eu.org; the NAFTA Secretariat http://www.nafta-sec-alena.org; and APEC http://www.apecsec.org.sg.

Chapter 5

Development and Inequality

CAROLINE THOMAS AND
MELVYN READER

A consideration of development and inequality raises a crucial paradox. At the dawn of the twenty-first century, despite 50 years of official development policies and despite huge advances in science and technology, inequalities between and within states are growing, and almost a third of humanity continue to live in poverty. Moreover, the rapid technological advances under way have the potential to decrease or increase existing inequalities, depending on how they are used and what rules determine the distribution of the benefits. The associated inter-related challenges for all of us in the new century are immense: the reduction of global poverty; the reduction of inequality between states and between human beings; the harnessing of scientific advancement for the benefit of the majority of humankind. These challenges will require a fundamental shift in how we think about development.

Over the last half-century, a particular way of thinking about development gained credence with international institutions like the IMF and the World Bank, and with the majority of governments. Under this approach, development referred to the change from a traditional subsistence economy (agrarian, unscientific, economically unproductive) to a modern economy (industrial, scientific, economically productive, engaged in mass consumption). This would be achieved by an elite-driven or 'top-down' approach relying on the application of modern science and technology, and 'expert knowledge' held outside of the society to which it was to be applied. The aim was to replicate in the South the social and economic changes that had occurred in the North following the scientific and industrial revolutions of the seventeenth and eighteenth centuries. Through the application of modern science and technology on a grand scale, nature would be tamed and harnessed to serve humankind. A core idea in this approach was the possibility of unlimited economic growth, which would trickle down through societies and ultimately benefit everyone. While this approach remained rooted in the thinking of the Western capitalist world, several features were also shared by the conception of development held by socialist countries of the Eastern bloc. For the latter, the transformation of societies into modern industrial economies by the application of scientific knowledge and the exploitation of nature were central to the development project. Opinions on the process by which this was to be achieved, however, differed.

The preferred policies for achieving the end state of development differed according to the ideological orientation of the state involved. For the states of the former Eastern bloc, central planning was the key to development. The newly independent states of the South accepted the centrality of the state sector to promote development. In the Western bloc, the state played an important role, but increasingly the private sector was given more emphasis as the vehicle for achieving development. International institutions such as the IMF and World Bank promoted policies acceptable to their major funders, the Western powers, particularly the United States. In the 1980s, those institutions were heavily influenced by the neo-liberal ideas which Presidents Reagan and Bush and Prime Minister Thatcher advocated. After the demise of the communist bloc, the IMF and World Bank universalized a particular view of how to achieve development which stressed the role of the market and diminished the role of the state. This approach came to be known as the 'Washington consensus'. This remains the dominant approach, albeit in a modified form known as the 'post Washington consensus'.

Apart from the mainstream view of what constitutes development, outlined above, other ideas have been put forward by various individuals, community groups, UN organizations and private foundations. We can refer to these broadly as a critical alternative approach. Core elements of this essentially 'bottom-up' approach include: equitable satisfaction of basic material and non-material needs, self-sufficiency, self-reliance, diversity, appropriate (often local) knowledge, community participation, local ownership and control of policies and projects which are predominantly small-scale, and cultural, economic and environmental sustainability.

To date, the mainstream approach has absorbed some of the terminology of the critical alternative approach, such as sustainability concerns and poverty reduction, but advocates of the alternative approach question the ability of current policies of international institutions and governments to deliver positive results. This can be seen in the recognition by the mainstream of the need for development policies to address global poverty more directly. For example, central to the UN's Millennium Development Goals 2000 was the setting of a target date of 2015 for a 50 per cent reduction in the number of absolute poor, and those suffering from hunger. The IMF and the World Bank expect these results to be achieved through modifications to the neo-liberal approach to development, rather than its replacement. Advocates of the critical alternative approach, while applauding the goal of poverty reduction, are sceptical of the ability of current development policies, based on the market, to deliver the required results. The evidence in Sub Saharan Africa bears them out (Sahn and Stifel, 2003).

Issues of development and inequality

In recent years there has been a flurry of scholarly debate as to whether the global situation regarding inequality is improving (Dollar and Kraay, 2000; Wade, 2001; Milanovic, 2003). Whatever one's position in this debate, it is the case that the scope of development and inequality issues is global. The UNDP noted in 2002 that incomes were distributed more unequally across the world's people than within the most unequal countries. Since the early 1980s the economic differentiation which characterized world regions has been replaced by polarization between world regions, within regions and within states. This calls for a more sophisticated analysis than the exclusive categorization of 'rich' and 'poor' states which has dominated the International Relations (IR) discipline for so long.

Nevertheless, the traditional categorization of rich and poor states is still important, and 'the countries with the highest per capita incomes in the early 1800s are still today's richest countries' (UNDP, 2003, p. 39). The overwhelming majority of poor people after all live in Third World countries. Even within the 'New Globalisers' (the World Bank's term for countries which have integrated successfully in the global economy and made significant economic gains – such as China, India and Mexico), economic and social gaps are widening as certain groups fail to enjoy the benefits of economic growth. Moreover, many of the states of the former Eastern bloc have joined the Third rather than the First World. In Russia, the number of people in poverty increased from 2 million to well over 60 million during the 1990s – that is, to 20 per cent of the population. Central and Eastern Europe (CEE) and the Commonwealth of Independent States (CIS) ended the 1990s with lower average incomes than Latin America and the Caribbean. However, huge variations exist between the CIS states – Armenia, Azerbaijan, Georgia, Kyrgystan, Moldova, Tajikistan and Uzbekistan – which have incomes on a par with least developed countries, and some of the CEE states such as Czech Republic and Poland, which showed a strong economic performance in late 1990s. Sub Saharan Africa saw significant reversals in the 1990s; the figure in extreme poverty is expected to rise to 404 million by 2015 (World Bank, 2003). If the region continues on its current course, it will take another 150 years to reach the Millennium Development Goals (MDG) target of halving poverty, and the hunger situation continues to worsen there (UNDP, 2003).

The distribution of global income, resources and wealth between the highest- and lowest-income countries may be exacerbated rather than offset by technological advance and the associated communications revolution which play a crucial role in global wealth generation. The digital divide is intensifying, and increasing disparities between states and between people (see also Chapter 12). In Africa, for example, while the number of telephone subscribers has more than doubled over the period 2000–2003, less than

6 per cent of the population has access to any kind of telecommunications (AfricaFocus, 2004).

Over the 1980s and 1990s, deepening inequality within a society was as much a feature of the developed First World states as of the Third World states. Over that period, all OECD countries except Italy and Germany experienced an increase in wage inequalities, and this was worst in the United Kingdom, the United States, and Sweden. In the United Kingdom, the number of families below the poverty line increased by 60 per cent from the early 1980s to early 1990s (UNDP, 1999, p. 37). The situation is improving in the UK, but in the US inequality continues to rise and threatens the democratic process (APSA Task Force, 2004).

In terms of visibility, the issues of development and inequality receive relatively little attention. One reason for this is that subjects such as routine poverty and hunger do not generally make very 'newsworthy' items for the global media industry, largely because they are ever-present, difficult to resolve and are unresponsive to the 'sound-bite' treatment. Neither viewers nor advertisers want to see images of poverty constantly projected on to the television screen. Those brought up in a 'modern' secularized culture feel uncomfortable when reminded of their own mortality. Development matters capture the media's attention only when they are perceived as sudden, dramatic or catastrophic, and sometimes not even then. Major catastrophes such as HIV/AIDS receive scant attention. Cases of the disease – for which there is still no cure – have increased from 10 million in 1990, to 38 million in 2003 (UNAIDS, 2004). While 70 per cent (approximately 25 million) of current cases are experienced in Sub Saharan Africa – the continent least equipped infrastructurally and economically to deal with the challenge – by 2025 it is expected that there will be 70 million cases in China, 110 million in India and 13 million in Russia. (UNDP, 2003, p. 43). In Sub Saharan Africa, the social fabric is being decimated by the disease which is creating millions of orphans, halving life expectancy in some countries, and crippling economic productivity.

Meeting the general challenge of development and inequality and particular problems such as HIV/AIDS requires a fundamental change in social structures globally as well as nationally and locally. Unfortunately, the media in general seem less able to focus on development-related issues at this sort of depth. Therefore, as students of world politics, it is necessary for us to realize that:

Behind the blaring headlines of the world's many conflicts and emergencies, there lies a silent crisis – a crisis of underdevelopment, of global poverty, of ever-mounting population pressures, of thoughtless degradation of the environment. This is not a crisis that will respond to emergency relief. Or to fitful policy interventions. It requires a long, quiet process of sustainable human development. (UNDP, 1994, p. iii)

The general problem of development and inequality

The crisis of development and deepening inequality highlights two key general problems in the contemporary international system. The first is the problem of the rules which govern access to resources and which account for the skewed nature of distribution of food, shelter, education, employment and so forth. The second is the problem of trust, or lack thereof, within the international system. The result is that pledges are made by states who are happy to sign up to them, but then often fail to implement them. Let us consider each of these factors in turn.

The development perspective which was universalized in the 1980s and 1990s elevated the importance of the market in determining access to resources, and diminished the role of the state. Former World Bank President, Barber Conable, speaking of the 1980s, asserted that:

> If I were to characterize the past decade, the most remarkable thing was the generation of a global consensus that market forces and economic efficiency were the best way to achieve the kind of growth which is the best antidote to poverty. (Quoted in Cavanagh *et al.*, 1994, p. 3)

This statement reflects the powerful influence that the political and economic philosophy known as 'neo-liberalism' came to have upon the policies advocated by the world's governing elites during the 1980s and even more so in the 1990s. It is important to understand the essential components of 'neo-liberal' thinking which also came to be referred to as the 'Washington consensus'. The name reflects the fact that such thinking was accepted and promoted by opinion leaders in Washington: the IMF and the World Bank, independent think-tanks, the US government policy community, investment bankers and so forth.

In essence the 'neo-liberalism' of the 1980s and 1990s argued that the production, distribution and consumption of almost all goods and services should be determined by market forces, and that the free functioning of the market should not be distorted by government interference. Consequently advocates of neo-liberalism favoured minimum government and 'laissez-faire' economics. This harked back to the views of the nineteenth-century 'Manchester School' liberals, but owed much of its more recent popularity to the writings of 'neo-classical' economic thinkers such as F. A. Hayek and Milton Friedman. The ideas of these thinkers gained many adherents among professional economists in the late 1970s, and subsequently came to have an important effect upon the policies of the New Right-influenced governments of the United States and the United Kingdom. The World Bank and the IMF were also profoundly affected by neo-liberalism via their US-trained economic advisors and the strong role exerted by the US government in their management.

At the beginning of the twenty-first century, even though it has become fashionable to advocate growth with poverty reduction, in reality the dominant approach to development is more rooted in these neo-liberal values and policies than ever before. The key to the reduction of global poverty and hunger is identified as global economic integration via free trade; this is expected to achieve the greatest possible global economic growth which, in turn, is expected to result in the greatest possible contribution to global economic welfare. The key problem with this, of course, is that it does not secure an equitable distribution of the benefits of increased global economic welfare.

Critics of neo-liberalism argue that its policy prescriptions have helped create the highest levels of global inequality seen in the post-war period (Adams, 1993, p. vii). Such changes provide a potent illustration of the historian Eric Hobsbawm's observation that:

> [t]he belief, following neoclassical economics, that unrestricted international trade would allow the poorer countries to come closer to the rich, runs counter to historical experience as well as common sense. (Hobsbawm, 1995, p. 570)

Even supporters of the free-market model have had to admit its failure to assist the world's poor, and even its ability to erode development progress. By the late 1990s, the voices calling for 'a human face' to this economic approach were growing, as it became very clear that some countries which had applied its prescriptions intensely were in fact going backwards. Also, the potential ill effects of capital liberalization were experienced in the late 1990s and beyond, as a series of financial crises rocked Southeast Asia, Russia and Argentina and eroded human development. Senior staff within the IMF and World Bank realised that without greater attention to equity concerns, the globalization project might be derailed.

Contemporary advocates of the critical alternative view of development therefore believe that the continuation of global development-related problems, such as poverty and inequality, is inevitable while neo-liberalism informs the mainstream approach to development. For them, until the issue of entrenched global economic structures is addressed, it will remain true that although 'humanity shares one planet, it is a planet on which there are two worlds, the world of the rich and the world of the poor' (Raanan Weitz quoted in Todaro, 1989, p. 3).

Let us turn to the general problem of trust in international relations. Trust is an essential component of inter-state relations, as it is of all human relations. A key problem regarding development is that many promises have been made by the governments of rich countries, and by the governments of developing countries, but they have failed to deliver on them. There has been a breach of trust between North and South, and within the South between governments and citizens.

The breach between North and South is clear in relation to aid. Over many decades a number of commitments have been made or reaffirmed. Most notable among these is the target set by the OECD's Development

Assistance Committee (DAC) in 1969 of 0.7 per cent of GNP of rich donor countries to be dedicated to overseas development assistance. Very few developed countries have reached this target, yet they have repeatedly reaffirmed their commitment to it even in the context of declining volumes of aid. For example, in June 1997, DAC countries (with the exception of the United States) reaffirmed their commitment to this target at the UN General Assembly Special Session (Development Initiatives, 1997, p. 9). To the countries of the developing world, such affirmations appear completely hollow in the context of their experience of very reduced aid flows.

In 2000, the developed countries endorsed the Millennium Development Goals, which listed significant targets across a range of social issues. This was followed in 2002 by the 'Monterrey Consensus: A Compact for Development'. At the UN's International Conference for Financing for Development, held in Monterrey, the governments of North and South recognized their specific roles and responsibilities for promoting development. The North would provide more financial assistance and better access to their markets, and the South agreed to strengthen the rule of law, reduce corruption, and improve the environment for private sector growth.

These goals are laudable. However, without dedicated effort to meet them, their mere existence undermines trust and confidence in North–South relations and between governments and their people. Moreover, improved efforts to ensure that a greater proportion of aid goes to poverty eradication remain totally inadequate in the face of the burden of debt repayments, declining terms of trade and so on of the least developed countries, and the routine protectionism and dumping practised by the developed Northern states. There is little point in giving with one hand and taking away with the other.

Development and inequality on the international agenda

For most of the post-war period, the status and handling of the issue of development at the international level has been determined by Northern governments, especially through the G7 Summits, and the intergovernmental organizations which they dominate, primarily the IMF and the World Bank. This is particularly so since the late 1970s, when the fairly open multilateralism through the UN system, which had previously enabled discussion of development issues such as a New International Economic Order, gave way to narrow managerialism by the G7-dominated IMF and World Bank. As Table 5.1 demonstrates, the G7 is not very representative in terms of global population or number of states. This is striking when compared with the G77 of developing countries.

From the beginning of the 1980s, the policies of the IMF and World Bank actors were all strongly influenced by the neo-liberal agenda, and this

Table 5.1   *Global economic governance, 1997*

Title	Institutional grouping	Membership	% world GDP	% world population
G7	Western economic powers	Canada, France, Germany, Italy, Japan, United Kingdom, United States	64.0	11.8
G77	Developing and some transition countries (not Russian Fed. or Poland)	143 members	16.9	76.0

Source: Adapted from UNDP (1999), p. 109.

line-up was reinforced in 1995 with the creation of the WTO. One manifestation of this at the international level has been the Structural Adjustment Programmes (SAPs) supported by the IMF and the World Bank. These programmes have similar aims and components for all countries to which they are applied: a reduction in government expenditure through the removal of subsidies, the cutback of welfare spending and the privatization of government-owned industries and services; the removal of restrictions on the import and export of goods; the deregulation of the economy; the promotion of foreign investment; and the devaluation of the exchange rate in order to encourage exports and reduce imports. The IMF and the World Bank have claimed that such policies are essentially apolitical in nature and simply reflect the 'value-free' principles uncovered by 'positive economics'. However, such a claim is questionable, since SAPs clearly adhere to the neo-liberal political agenda of minimal government, a laissez-faire free-market economy, international free trade, and the promotion of private business interests. Indeed, the IMF and the World Bank must be regarded as the principal instruments through which the doctrine of neo-liberalism has obtained its current hegemony in the global order (Broad and Landi, 1996, p. 15).

The IMF and the World Bank believe that, although SAPs may in the short term have a deleterious effect on the economies to which they are applied, they will eventually secure long-term prosperity for Southern countries. In support of this view, they cite the cases of the economic 'tigers' of Southeast Asia, such as Hong Kong, Taiwan, South Korea and Singapore, which secured high economic growth rates during the 1980s on the basis of their export-oriented policies. However, these countries – which represent only 2 per cent of the total population of the South – should be regarded as the exception rather than the rule. Furthermore the policies of these newly industrializing countries (NICs) in Asia placed heavy reliance upon state intervention and investment in targeted sectors of their economies and cannot be regarded as models of free-market orthodoxy. Moreover, the financial liberalization of their economies in the 1990s, at the behest of the United States, the G7, the IMF and so forth, contributed to the East Asian crisis in 1997–8, the human impact of which continues to reverberate throughout the region. Certainly, for much of the rest of the South, SAPs have had detrimental consequences for the poor and socially marginalized. In 1990, for example, the Report of the South Commission noted that,

> the complete disregard of equity in prescriptions for structural adjustments ... had devastating effects on vital public services like health and education, with especially harmful consequences for the most vulnerable social groups. (South Commission, 1990, p. 67)

Consequently, while development defined according to the orthodox perspective – the generation of economic growth through the promotion of free-market principles – has occupied a relatively high location on the international agenda, the view of development held by the critical alternative perspective – the promotion of human welfare – has, until recently, been hardly considered at all.

Another set of actors that influence the way development is treated at the international level is MNCs. These, along with transnational banks (TNBs), grew in significance throughout the 1980s and 1990s. Given current trends, it is probable that in the future their activities will become even more important in determining the course of development. In large part this can be attributed to the success of the G7/8, IMF and World Bank in promoting the development of a neo-liberal global order in which the role of the state is minimized and that of the market is maximized. Indeed, some analysts go so far as to suggest that, rather than assisting countries to achieve higher living standards for their poor, '[t]he main role of the IMF and the World Bank is the construction, regulation and support of a world system where multinational corporations trade and move capital without restrictions from nation states' (Laurence Harris, quoted in Vallely, 1990, p. 185).

The rise of MNCs has undoubtedly been a key aspect of the latest phase of economic globalization. In the late 1960s there were only about 7000 MNCs, whereas in 1992 there were over 37 000 of them and they were responsible for 5.8 trillion dollars worth of sales – more than the value of all the world's trade exports put together (*Newsweek*, 26 June 1995, p. 35). Table 5.2 reveals that many MNCs have enjoyed greater annual sales than the GDP of individual countries.

In the 1990s, investments by MNCs and private international banks in the South became much more significant in monetary terms than official development aid (which for most Northern governments has never reached the UN target figure of 0.7 per cent of their GNP). At the end of the twentieth century, aid was at its lowest level in 50 years. In 1998, public

Table 5.2 *Top corporations' sales and countries' GDP, 1997*

Country or corporation	GDP or total sales (US $ billions)
General Motors	164
Thailand	154
Norway	153
Ford Motor Company	147
Mitsui and Co	145
Saudi Arabia	140
Mitsubishi	140
Poland	136
Itochu	136
South Africa	129
Royal Dutch/Shell Group	128
Marubeni	124
Greece	123
Sumitomo	119
Exxon	117
Toyota Motor	109
Wal-Mart Stores	105
Malaysia	98
Israel	98
Colombia	96
Venezuela	87
Philippines	82

Source: Data from *Forbes magazine* (1998); UNDP (1999), p. 32.

overseas development assistance stood at $33 billion, 40 per cent down on 1990, and equivalent to 0.25 per cent of the GDP of the rich countries. Within one decade, the balance between public and private finance had switched. As public finance has dwindled, private lending through banks and other new instruments, and company investing, has soared. Unfortunately, the investment has been concentrated in a handful of 12 'emerging market' countries, such as Brazil, Russia and Indonesia. The rest of the Third World has been unable to attract private funds. Moreover, much of the investment is short-term and speculative, contributing nothing to the long-term development of the recipient countries.

The declining importance of foreign aid relative to foreign investment is set to continue in this millennium for two main reasons. First, government-to-government aid is regarded by the prevailing neo-liberal orthodoxy as a form of state intervention in the market which is undesirable (it is noteworthy that the World Bank increasingly prefers to channel funds to private organizations rather than to states). Secondly, the adoption of neo-liberal-inspired privatization programmes by Southern governments is providing further opportunities for MNCs to expand their sphere of operations. This has happened for example in the water sector.

While MNCs are generally welcomed by the governments of the South because of the financial capital, technology, managerial skills and elite career opportunities that they introduce into the economy, there has been increasing concern on the part of local and Northern civil society groups about the consequences of their activities. The profit-maximizing objectives of MNCs, if not restrained by ethical concerns, can have highly deleterious social and environmental consequences in Southern states (Madeley, 1999). Examples include: the extraction of natural resources in a manner which causes local environmental degradation, destroys livelihoods of local communities and undermines human rights – witness the extraction of oil in the Niger Delta by Shell; and the export of unsafe commodities, such as pesticides, cigarettes, and pharmaceutical products, which have been banned in the North.

The activities of MNCs have encouraged the emergence of a worldwide affluent, consumption-oriented class, so that the lifestyle of elites in the South has far more in common with their North American and European counterparts than with most of those living in the South. Too often in the past, MNCs have represented both the products and agents of a materialistic culture which encourages the pursuit of self-gratification and the wasteful consumption of global resources. Certainly, the adoption of ethical mission statements and community involvement programmes on the part of some MNCs is a hopeful sign of change and, if widely implemented, could significantly alter the impact that MNCs are having in the South.

Developmental NGOs and grass-roots development organizations (GDOs – these are distinguished from NGOs by being made up of the poor themselves) represent another set of non-governmental actors that in recent decades have attempted to influence the international agenda with regard to development. While most MNCs are headquartered in the North (with the exception of a few based in NICs, such as Daewoo of South Korea), there are now many NGOs headquartered in the South, as well as in the North. Prominent Northern NGOs with developmental concerns include Oxfam, the Save the Children Fund, the Catholic Fund for Overseas Development (CAFOD), World Vision and Christian Aid. Examples of Southern NGOs include the Malaysian-based Third World Network, the Campaign against Hunger in Brazil, the Sarvodaya Shramadana Movement in Sri Lanka, the Grameen Bank of Bangladesh and the Freedom from Debt Coalition in the Philippines. Southern GDOs include landless peasants' movements, rural workers' unions (such as the rubber-tappers' union founded by Chico Mendes), tribal peoples' rights groups, food cooperatives, credit and savings groups and the Christian base communities (CBCs) associated with the Roman Catholic Church. These groups have access to considerably fewer resources than those available to MNCs, Northern governments or multilateral development banks, yet they have made important contributions to meeting the needs of poor people around the world. They have also played an important role in campaigning for change in the policies of the World Bank. It is chiefly from among NGOs and GDOs that the critical alternative perspective on development has arisen and although, as we will see in the next section, this perspective has yet to make major inroads on the development orthodoxy, there have been some successes.

Development and inequality in the post-Cold War era: the impact of unipolarity on the presentation of the issue

The end of the Cold War had a number of important repercussions on the presentation of development and inequality. At the time of the destruction of the Berlin Wall in 1989 there was much talk of a 'peace dividend' and the possibility was voiced that funds previously assigned to military budgets could be diverted to provide a larger source of funds for development-oriented projects in the world's poorer countries. This has proved illusory. Before the Cold War ended, some Southern governments had certainly become 'Accustomed to an age where conflict provided a magnet for ... foreign policy attention'. Since the competition between the two Super-powers to secure allies in the South has ended, it should not be surprising that the latter 'now fears falling off the North's agenda' (Kegley and Wittkopf, 1993, p. 263). Indeed, the South has faced competition from the former Eastern bloc for a diminishing pool of inter-governmental aid. Consequently, Southern governments have had to turn to other sources, primarily private foreign investors and foreign-owned MNCs and increasingly Northern and Southern NGOs.

The changes associated with the end of the Cold War mean that the special development needs of the South have increasingly been ignored by the North which is putting forward an essentially Western, localized worldview as a universal truth. This is clear in the words of Francis Fukuyama, who has claimed that we are witnessing:

> not just the end of the Cold War ... but the end of history as such: that is, the end point of mankind's ideological evolution and the universalization of Western liberal democracy. (Fukuyama, 1989, p. 4)

According to Fukuyama, the collapse of the state-controlled, centrally planned economies of the former Eastern Bloc symbolized 'the triumph of the West ... an unabashed victory of economic and political liberalism ... [and] the total exhaustion of viable systematic alternatives to Western [neo-]liberalism' (1989, p. 3). The arrogance of this claim is astonishing, as is the ignorance of other possible modes of social and economic organization that may better serve humanity.

Post-Cold War, the dominant development discourse goes largely unchallenged. Indeed, since the mid-1990s an ever-more coordinated grouping of unelected global governance institutions – both public and private – has reinforced the orthodoxy, and laid the blame for development problems squarely within the poorer countries rather than within the structures of the global economy or even a balanced combination of both.

Post-9/11 this approach has had a boost. Rather than questioning the appropriateness of a neo-liberal development model to deliver progress for the majority of people in the South, the model is being further reinforced by a coordinated set of unelected public and private institutions. Poverty is now seen as a key threat to global peace, and the route to poverty reduction is deeper global economic integration. In an increasingly coordinated fashion, donors line up behind the model, and the possibility of alternative sources of funding for different development paths is virtually non-existent. Nationally developed 'Poverty Reduction Strategy Papers' (PRSPs) now form the basis for loans to each country. Through the linking of new funds and debt relief to the acceptance of a country's PRSP, donors are vetting entire national development strategies. Thus the potential for conditionality goes far deeper even than with the SAPs of the 1980s and 1990s. These strategies are presented as national plans and nationally owned; yet the World Bank has published a voluminous sourcebook on how to write the plans. Borrowing governments know very well that unless plans are in keeping with the model they will not be acceptable to the funders.

In the South, the adverse effects of the prevailing market-oriented development model have stimulated the generation of a critical alternative model of development among grass-roots communities who have been obliged to engage in cooperative 'self-help' practices to secure their access to basic resources. We have already examined some of the main elements of this alternative model and mentioned some of the groups involved. In the next section we will see the role that this alternative perspective on development has played in the institutional management of development-related issues at the international level during the post-Cold War era.

Managing issues of development and inequality

In the 1990s, one of the most important institutional mechanisms for dealing with development-related matters was the convening of global summits under the auspices of the UN. Most noteworthy for the broad framework they provided for understanding development have been the United Nations Conference on Environment and Development (UNCED) or 'Earth Summit' held at Rio de Janeiro, Brazil, in June 1992, and the United Nations World Summit on Social Development held at Copenhagen in March 1995. Others include the 1995 International Conference on Population and Development in Cairo, the 1995 World Conference on Women in Beijing, the 1996 Human Settlements Conference in Istanbul and, in the same year, the Rome Food Summit.

The Earth Summit was important for familiarizing a wider audience with the concept of 'sustainable development'. This concept had first come to public attention in the early 1980s in an International Union for the Conservation of Nature (IUCN) document. It received further emphasis in the influential *Brundtland Report* of the World Commission on Environment and Development (WCED) in 1987, which defined sustainable development as a process that 'meets the needs of the present without compromising the ability of future generations to meet their own needs' (WCED, 1987, p. 8). Embracing the new terminology of sustainable development, the official inter-state UNCED gathering gave public acknowledgement to the idea that the environment and development are inextricably linked, and it encouraged important actors such as the World Bank to assert their commitment to a 'new environmentalism, which recognizes that economic development and environmental sustainability are partners' (World Bank, 1995, p. ii). However, most significantly, the conference gave further legitimation to market-dominated development policies. The UNCED linked environment and development in name only and the agenda of the conference was dominated by the entrenched interests of Northern and Southern elites (see also Chapter 11).

Consequently, the inter-state conference failed to identify the global environmental crisis as part of a larger developmental crisis. It ignored the major issues of debt, terms of trade, aid and the consumption of resources, which formed a central part of the discussions conducted at the parallel NGO summit at Rio. Some critics have therefore concluded that, despite the apparent 'mainstreaming' of environmental concerns that occurred at UNCED, 'the old thinking about economic growth [still] prevails' and 'the old establishment that had made a living out of such economic growth has [merely] repackaged itself in green' (Chatterjee and Finger, 1994, p. 162).

The task of the 1995 Copenhagen Summit was to address continuing and widespread poverty, inequality and unemployment. However, despite the dissent voiced earlier by some Southern governments, the inter-governmental *Summit Declaration and Programme of Action* concluded that the best method for alleviating development-related problems is the pursuit of economic growth through the continued promotion of free-market policies and individual initiative. Effectively the declaration called for a further extension of the neo-liberal model of development, and while there were a few very watered-down references to structural adjustment, debt and the need for dialogue between the UN and the IMF/World Bank, no mention was made of the social responsibilities of MNCs or the possibility of new transfers of finance from the North to the South.

In contrast to the inter-governmental deliberations, the *Alternative Declaration*, produced by the parallel NGO Forum at the Copenhagen Summit, severely criticized the prevailing neo-liberal development model for aggravating rather than alleviating the global social crisis, and put forward its own alternative model of development based on the principles of environmental sustainability, social equity and community participation and empowerment. The NGOs specifically identified the policies of government privatization and trade liberalization as being responsible for growing global inequality, and called for the immediate cancellation of debt, improved terms of trade, greater transparency and accountability of the IMF and the World Bank, and international regulation of the activities of MNCs.

UNCED and the Copenhagen Summit highlight two major shortcomings in current strategies to manage development problems. Both managed to incorporate some of the language of the alternative development model into the development orthodoxy. By so doing, opposition to the orthodoxy was effectively neutralized. But there was a complete failure to address the underlying cause of the continuing development/environment crisis and so no appropriate ways out of the crisis were put forward. Secondly, the global scope of the development crisis requires a response which transcends the limitations of inter-state agreements. The state is simultaneously too small to deal with some development concerns, and too large to deal with others. The global nature of the crisis requires the involvement of a whole range of non-state actors, not simply in pre-conference discussion groups, as happened prior to the Rio Summit, but also at the decision-making, implementation and monitoring stages. The NGO community received a massive impetus in the run-up to the Rio and Copenhagen summits. However their role in implementation is negligible. For example, the Commission for Sustainable Development (CSD), created to monitor the implementation of the UNCED output, is composed of state representatives; NGOs can speak at meetings only at the discretion of the chairperson. And local governments, on whom so much depends in terms of implementation of sustainable development policies, do not get a voice there at all.

The pattern of neutralizing criticisms of the development orthodoxy by incorporating their vocabulary – but not their values – into the mainstream orthodoxy continues today, with the focus on growth with poverty reduction.

Before closing this section it is important to mention the efforts of the United Nations Development Programme (UNDP) to legitimize a different set of indicators of development. In 1990 the UNDP published its Human Development Index, and every year since it has developed the ideas contained in this concept. Recognizing a need to move away from conventional indicators of development based on measuring the rate of economic growth, *per capita* income and industrialization, the UNDP set itself apart from the World Bank and IMF and suggested measuring life expectancy, adult literacy, and local purchasing power (see UNDP, 1994). As an institutional mechanism, this yardstick is gaining ground within the

UN system, but until it is accepted by the IMF and World Bank, its impact on altering the fundamental parameters of the development experience of the poor will be very limited.

Since the mid-1990s the UNDP has also been influential in developing the idea of human security. This approach explores the entire spectrum of threats to vulnerable people (that is, the majority of contemporary humankind), ranging from socio-economic to civil and political. UN Secretary-General Kofi Annan has been influenced by this approach and has become a champion of its use as a vehicle for understanding people's needs and the range of factors and actors – including governments, international institutions, transnational corporations, markets – which can undermine them.

Development, inequality and world politics

Consideration of the topic of development raises a number of important challenges to some prevailing conceptions of world politics. The dominant state-centric approach has focused on external military threats to a state's territorial boundaries. Scant attention has been paid to the activities of non-state actors and to issues such as poverty, hunger, and environmental degradation.

Chapter 1 pointed out that practitioners of world politics have traditionally categorized issues relating to the security of the state as matters of 'high politics', while issues relating to the economic and social welfare of its citizens have been consigned to the relatively less important realm of 'low politics'. Development-related matters have therefore, unless they have implications for state security, been placed into the relatively marginalized 'low politics' category. Furthermore, since the most influential practitioners and analysts of world politics have tended to be residents in the 'developed' North, the issue of development has generally not been high on the agenda even when 'low politics' has been considered. Consequently, students of world politics have tended to give low priority to the issue of development.

To put into perspective the relative importance that traditional security concerns and development-related matters represent to global humanity, it is worth noting that the total number of people killed during the First and Second World Wars is estimated to have been about 30 million, while the number of people who currently die of hunger-related causes each year is nearly 15 million. Consequently we can say that every 2 years the number of people who die of hunger is roughly equivalent to the number killed in 11 years of world war.

The expansion of the market into all areas of human life means that global resources are increasingly channelled to meet the wants of the relatively wealthy while the needs of the relatively poor are ignored. In other words, human security is being eroded. The ability of the world's poor to secure their families and communities in terms of basic needs is diminishing. Economic globalization is narrowing choice and opportunity for the vulnerable. In response to this disempowerment, a new type of politics is evolving – a participatory, emancipatory politics of empowerment. The range of examples is increasing daily, and this trend cannot be encapsulated neatly. However, our inability to formulate neat categories should not blind us to the significance of such protest. The successful campaign against the Multilateral Agreement on Investment (1999), which would have increased the rights but not the obligations of investors, the demonstrations at the WTO meeting in Seattle in November–December 1999, the Chiapas uprising in Mexico in 1994, and the peasant Intercontinental Caravan in 1999 are high-profile examples of protest against the orthodox neo-liberal model of development. Well-organized opposition is even emerging at inter-governmental level: for example, at the WTO Ministerial meeting in Cancun, in September 2003, a newly emerging group of 22 Third World governments, including Brazil, China and India, articulated a common position on agriculture and stood up to the North; the negotiations were halted. But there are very many other local protests which never hit the global headlines, nor often the national ones. But they represent a discontent with the current order, and a rich ground of alternative ideas about how best society – from the local to the global – might be organized. Most importantly, they demonstrate that the end of history is certainly not here. As we enter the new millennium, the challenge of development is as great as ever, and the evidence suggests that the recipe in place to meet that challenge is inadequate, even inappropriate. The greatest development challenge for the early twenty-first century is to recognize the limitations of grand solutions, whether rooted in neo-liberal orthodoxy or central planning.

Finally, as students of world politics it is important for us to realize that we have a duty to contribute to the development debate. In the words of David Korten:

> being among the world's privileged, you and I have a special obligation to think and act as a global citizen, to be a steward of whatever power we hold, to contribute to the transforming forces that are reshaping the world. The future of human society, of our children, depends on each of us. (Korten, 1990, p. 216)

We can contribute in a number of important ways. We can support an open environment in which the aims, the processes and the outcomes of development policies are never assumed, but held up for scrutiny. We can keep asking the critical central question: In whose interest is development operating?

Guide to further reading

An excellent starting point for beginners is B. Jackson (1990). This is a straightforward, lucid and compelling account of the problems of poverty and underdevelopment. Building on this, readers can move on to John Rapley (1996) *Understanding Development* (Boulder, Col.: Lynne Rienner), which provides an accessible account of changing approaches to development since 1945. Students interested in a challenging, critical perspective on the meaning of development should consult the collection edited by M. Rahnema and V. Bawtree (1997). For those interested in increasing their empirical knowledge of the development experience in different parts of the world, Angkie Hoogevelt (2001) *Globalisation and the Post Colonial World* (Basingstoke: Macmillan) provides a historically and theoretically well-informed comparison of the impacts of globalization and the responses to it in Sub Saharan Africa, the Middle East, East Asia and Latin America.

Chapter 6

Arms and Arms Control

*JOANNA SPEAR**

The problem of achieving state insecurity was traditionally solved by the acquisition of weapons. However, during the twentieth century it was increasingly realized that the arms racing that resulted from this search for security was in itself sometimes destabilizing and that there needed to be a mechanism for regulating arms competition. Arms control was one of the solutions used to try and solve this problem. During the Cold War arms control became a major tool for managing insecurity, preventing conflicts from escalating and providing channels of communication between states. In twenty-first-century world politics the prime issue concerning arms control is whether it can still aid conflict management, provide reassurance and reinforce security.

Two main categories of weapons are discussed in this chapter; so-called *weapons of mass destruction* (nuclear, chemical and biological weapons) and *conventional weapons*. In each case the weapons are discussed in the context of security, economic and ethical issues. What quickly becomes apparent is that conventional weapons are the 'odd man out'. Weapons of mass destruction (WMD) have traditionally been the targets of national and international arms control efforts because they are regarded as having important implications for international security. WMD have consequently been subject to export controls and are a focus of considerable ethical concern. By contrast, conventional weapons have rarely elicited such attention. This is particularly ironic as major insurgencies in Iraq and Afghanistan have been fuelled by conventional weapons, mainly small arms and light weapons (SALW), the control of which the United States – while battling these insurgencies – has consistently opposed. With respect to both WMD and conventional weapons, there are tensions between the economic benefits of sales and the security problems that may result from such transfers. However, whereas in the realm of WMD the balance is firmly weighted towards controls, with conventional weapons there is much less consideration of the security implications of sales and a greater focus on the economic advantages that result. Although the profits from the sales of SALW are not huge compared to those on fighter aircraft, there is nevertheless a substantial constituency favouring continued sales, with

* The author would like to thank Dr Neil Cooper of the University of Bradford for his helpful suggestions on this chapter.

35 per cent of all small arms companies based in the United States (Small Arms Survey, 2004, table 4.1 pp. 103–6). This neglect of the long-term security implications of conventional arms transfers is potentially problematic.

WMD have long been subject to debate on ethical grounds. The manner and scale of their operation differentiates them from other weapons, and these ethical concerns in part account for the significant number of initiatives aiming to control or eliminate these weapons. By contrast, much less attention has been paid to the ethical consequences of conventional weapons deployment and use. However, that is now beginning to change.

The significance of arms and arms control issues

Weapons of mass destruction

Fear of nuclear war dominated security planning during the Cold War, and enhanced security was sought through arms control agreements between the two Superpowers (see Box 6.1).

The end of the Cold War has led to a decrease in concern about the dangers of thermonuclear war between the Superpowers. This is paradoxical because the majority of the nuclear weapons that were perceived to cause the problem still exist (Gottemoeller, 2003). If planning is done on the basis of capabilities (as Realists claim it should be) then this is an urgent problem. Nevertheless, because of the benign relationship between the United States and Russia there is less inclination to invest in destroying these nuclear arsenals. The 'new arms control' of the SORT Treaty is seen by US policy-makers as having largely solved the problem. This means that those interested in arms control and disarmament are having a hard time convincing governments and publics that *existing* nuclear arsenals are an issue that needs to be tackled.

If the perceived danger of nuclear war between the Superpowers has declined dramatically, other nuclear issues have increased in importance. In the post-Cold War period there is greater concern about nuclear proliferation – that is, the spread of nuclear weapons themselves and the technology and knowledge required to build them. This was a less significant issue on the security agenda during the Cold War when there were two different perspectives on nuclear proliferation. First, those states who were already acknowledged as possessing nuclear weapons (the United States, the Soviet Union, Britain, France and China) were concerned to prevent other states from obtaining nuclear weapons, thus preventing what is called *horizontal* proliferation. A different perspective was taken by non-nuclear states such as India, Indonesia and Egypt who were concerned about the build-up in the arsenals of the five nuclear powers, and particularly about the nuclear arms race between the Superpowers. They

Box 6.1 Major bilateral arms control treaties

1972 Strategic Arms Limitation Talks (SALT) produced an interim agreement on the limitation of strategic nuclear weapons and included the Anti-Ballistic Missile (ABM) Treaty.

1972 Anti-Ballistic Missile (ABM) Treaty restricted the number of ABM launchers and systems. The United States withdrew from this treaty in 2002 in order to move forward with plans for Ballistic Missile Defences (BMD). Subsequently Russia also announced plans for an ambitious new BMD system (Finn, 2004, p. A25).

1979 SALT II slowed down the arms race by placing a limit on certain categories of strategic arms.

1987 Intermediate Nuclear Forces Treaty (INF) was the first treaty which sought to reduce the number of arms rather than to limit their increase. It removed all intermediate range nuclear weapons in Europe.

1991 Strategic Arms Reduction Treaty (START) sought to reduce the number of nuclear warheads and delivery systems.

1993 START II further reduced the number of nuclear warheads and also eliminated certain categories including multiple warheads on land-based intercontinental ballistic missiles (ICBMs).

START III talks began in Moscow in 1999 but were stymied by disagreements over a possible renegotiation of the ABM treaty.

2002 Strategic Offensive Reduction Treaty (SORT) is a change from traditional arms control agreements, being less than three pages long and containing no verification measures. It focuses on a reduction in *deployed* US and Russian warheads, permitting each state to hold between 1700 and 2200. The remaining warheads are to be put into storage, rather than destroyed and either party can withdraw from the treaty at three months notice, leading to concerns about the reversibility of this form of arms control by 'gentleman's agreement'.

were more concerned about what is called *vertical* proliferation. Reflecting the power positions of the nuclear weapons states, however, the concerns about horizontal proliferation always received much greater attention. This is illustrated by the Nuclear Non-Proliferation Treaty (NPT) of 1968, which placed great emphasis on stemming horizontal proliferation with barely a mention of vertical proliferation. (Other examples of multilateral arms control agreements are listed in Box 6.2.)

The 2003 Proliferation Security Initiative (PSI) is another example of 'new arms control'; a flexible agreement among seafaring nations which have agreed to interdict shipments of dangerous technologies on their territories. This is a controversial measure as it includes interdiction in international territorial waters. The end of the Cold War has not diminished the significance attached to nuclear weapons, as many had hoped (Woollacott, 1996). Indeed, the incentives for states to acquire nuclear

---

Box 6.2 Major multilateral treaties pertaining to WMD

1963 Limited Test Ban Treaty restricted nuclear tests to underground.

1968 Nuclear Non-Proliferation Treaty (NPT) is the key treaty covering nuclear proliferation. The Treaty was extended indefinitely in 1995. Almost all states have signed the NPT with the notable exceptions of India, Israel and Pakistan.

1972 Biological and Toxin Weapons Convention (BTWC) seeks to eliminate the entire class of biological and toxin weapons.

1987 Missile Control Regime seeks to control the export and production of missile technology capable of carrying chemical, biological and nuclear weapons.

1993 Chemical Weapons Convention (CWC) requires the destruction of stockpiles of chemical weapons. It came into force in 1997.

1996 Comprehensive Test Ban Treaty (CTBT) seeks to ban all nuclear explosions. It has been negotiated on and off since the late 1950s. It finally opened for signatures in 1996, but is yet to be ratified by the states necessary to bring it into operation. In 1999 the US Senate refused to ratify the Treaty, condemning it to waiting in 'limbo' for a change in the geo-strategic environment.

---

weapons would appear to have increased in the post-Cold War period (Carpenter, 1992, pp. 64–5, 71). Four comments are relevant here. First, the fact that nuclear weapons states have substantially maintained their nuclear arsenals shows that they consider that nuclear weapons play some positive role in providing security. US discussions about creating a new generation of low-yield 'mini-nukes' (making them potentially 'usable' and not just a deterrent) and British plans for a follow-on to the Trident nuclear system also point to the continued importance of nuclear weapons. Moreover, the continued reliance on nuclear deterrence and the rhetoric of deterrence sends a signal to the rest of the international community that nuclear weapons are still useful. This contradicts the explicit message that these same states are pushing, that horizontal proliferation should be prevented.

Second, there are now greater incentives to acquire nuclear weapons for those non-nuclear states who have lost the guarantee of extended deterrence previously provided by the Superpowers. Extended deterrence, or the 'nuclear umbrella', exists when a nuclear weapons state promises to come to the aid of a non-nuclear state should it be attacked. With the retreat from extended deterrence these states feel vulnerable. For example, even Japan has suggested that should the United States withdraw its nuclear umbrella, she would feel obliged to become a nuclear weapons state (Rafferty, 1996).

Third, the combination of the loss of extended deterrence with regional dynamics appears to have increased the incentives to proliferate. For example, Pakistan now perceives itself to be vulnerable to attack from India because the United States has scaled back its support. India, which has lost the backing of the Soviet Union, in turn feels vulnerable to both Pakistan and China. In such situations, the instability caused by the breakdown of Cold War alliances can be seen as an incentive to states to acquire a nuclear deterrent. In 1998 both India and Pakistan tested nuclear devices and joined the 'nuclear club'.

Fourth, the contrasting experiences of Iraq and North Korea suggest strong incentives to proliferate *fast* and establish deterrence. The 2003 US-led invasion of Iraq was explicitly justified in terms of Iraqi nuclear, chemical and biological weapons capabilities; Iraq's potential for a programme made it vulnerable. After the invasion it became clear that – despite Saddam Hussein's rhetoric to the contrary – although Iraq had begun to reconstitute its WMD programme demolished by UN inspectors after the 1991 war, it had made little progress due to UN sanctions (Orton and Cirincione, 2004, pp. 31–4). By contrast, in the case of North Korea, the state is judged to have made *too much* progress in creating nuclear weapons for an attack to be feasible; North Korea has deterrence. In 2005 North Korea announced that it has nuclear weapons, ending years of speculation. It is thought that Iran has not been slow to learn from these contrasting experiences. Thus, in summary, not only have the incentives to proliferate increased, but speed and stealth have become more important to success, creating further problems for the international community.

Four events have increased fears about horizontal nuclear proliferation since the end of the Cold War. First, to go back in time, in the aftermath of the 1991 Gulf War, UN Weapons Inspection Teams discovered alarming evidence of the extent of the Iraqi nuclear programme. It was found that Iraq had made significant progress towards a nuclear weapons capability (and had also developed chemical and biological weapons) and had been assisted in this by the purchase of equipment and technologies from both Eastern and Western states (Zimmerman, 1994). This led to the recognition that existing non-proliferation strategies had failed because Iraq – a signatory of the NPT since 1968 – was covertly developing nuclear weapons (Kay, 1994). Without Saddam Hussein's miscalculation over Kuwait, the world would not have known about the Iraqi nuclear programme. For the international community the key question was 'who else might be cheating?'

Second, the threat of horizontal proliferation was, ironically, heightened by one of the consequences of the end of the Cold War; the demise of the Soviet Union. The emergence of a clutch of new states which retain sectors of the Soviet military industrial complex and which face severe economic problems, led to increased fears that their nuclear technologies, fissile (radioactive) materials and scientific knowledge will be sold off to the highest bidders (Potter, 1995). These fears are heightened because many of these new states had and still have very rudimentary or non-existent export controls. There have been several instances of attempts to sell fissile materials on the international black market, and there is mounting concern about the ability of intelligence agencies in the East to prevent these transfers (van Ham, 1994, p. 54). With greater opportunities for obtaining weapons and fissile materials there are also fears about 'nuclear terrorism', a term that describes the possibility of state-sponsored or non-state terrorist groups obtaining nuclear weapons and holding the world to ransom (Potter, 1995, pp. 13–14) The proliferation activities of radical Islamist networks such as Al Qaeda have been a great cause of concern since they came to international prominence with the (conventional) attacks on US targets on 11 September 2001.

Third, a nuclear arms race began in South Asia after nuclear tests by India and Pakistan in May 1998 (Box 6.3). India first exploded a 'peaceful' nuclear device in 1974, and Pakistan made little secret of its attempts to 'balance' India's nuclear programme. Until 1998, however, neither power had openly declared their nuclear capabilities and had a policy of 'nuclear ambiguity'. In May 1998, however, India conducted a set of nuclear tests and despite intense diplomatic pressure to prevent retaliatory tests, Pakistan followed suit. Fears are heightened because the two states have a history of hostility and are engaged in a protracted conflict over Kashmir. Furthermore, both states have missiles capable of carrying nuclear weapons within range of each other's capital cities (Walker, 1998). The two powers successfully managed a conventional confrontation over Kashmir in 2001 without any escalation to nuclear war. However, this was after intense diplomatic pressure from the international community, repeated visits from diplomats and politicians and even then the behaviour of the two sides was not wholly reassuring. For example, the two capitals had installed a 'hot line' for use in times of emergencies, but according to the BBC at the time, both sides took delight in refusing to answer the phone!

Fourth, in 2003 the International Atomic Energy Agency (IAEA, the inspection arm of the NPT) uncovered an illicit supply network. The investigation had been triggered by US-led concerns that Iran had an illicit nuclear weapons programme, not the civil nuclear programme it claimed. Iran, keen to clear its name, invited IAEA inspectors to the facilities. What they found led to new proliferation concerns that spread far beyond Iran. The IAEA was startled to discover that Iran's fissile material enrichment programme used modern technological approaches and was closely modelled on that of Pakistan. This started off a chain of allegations concerning clandestine proliferation activities by the popular 'father of the Pakistani bomb', Dr Abdul Qadeer (A.Q.) Khan, according to which Dr Khan had played a pivotal role in bringing stolen centrifuge designs, contacts with Western firms willing to act as illicit channels for goods, and significant know-how to the Pakistani nuclear project. Once that had succeeded, he was further alleged to have used his status in Pakistan – and those same assets – to help others to proliferate, creating between 1987 and 2003 an extensive nuclear supply network able to provide designs, precision machine-tooled parts and possibly even fissile materials for nascent nuclear programmes. Khan was said to have developed contacts with a 'who's who'

Box 6.3 Nuclear status of states

Declared nuclear powers	Until 1998 the world's declared nuclear powers (those states which openly admit to their nuclear capability) were the five Permanent Members of the UN Security Council – United States, Russia, Britain, France and China.
	In 1998, after carrying out a series of nuclear tests, India and Pakistan joined the club of declared nuclear powers.
	In 2005 North Korea ended years of speculation and declared itself a nuclear power.
Opaque nuclear states	'Opaque nuclear states' are those states which, although generally believed to be developing nuclear weapons, conceal their nuclear programmes. This list includes Israel, Iran, and possibly Algeria
Former nuclear states	Brazil, Argentina and South Africa are former opaque nuclear states who have voluntarily abandoned their nuclear programmes and renounced nuclear weapons.
	The Ukraine, Belarus and Kazakstan inherited nuclear weapons after the break-up of the Soviet Union. The weapons were returned to Russia in exchange for US economic aid.
	Iraq did not voluntarily give up its nuclear capability, rather it was eliminated by the International Atomic Agency (IAA) along with its chemical and biological weapons and missiles as part of a treaty which ended the Gulf War.
	Libya voluntarily gave up all WMD programmes in 2003, after nine months of secret negotiations with UK and US officials. In return for this promise and, it is said, intelligence that enabled A.Q. Khan to be exposed (see above) sanctions against Libya were ended and new trade agreements initiated.
Potential nuclear states	Certain states have the technological capability to become nuclear powers within a matter of weeks. These include Australia, Canada, Germany, Japan, South Africa, South Korea and Ukraine.

list of potential proliferators: Iran, Iraq, Libya, Syria and Saudi Arabia (Clary, 2004, pp. 33–42). The consequences are still being calculated but it is clear that Pakistani know-how significantly advanced a number of states' nuclear programmes. Khan was a difficult domestic problem for President Musharraf as the scientist was venerated for his role in the Pakistani nuclear programme. He was also a difficult international problem as the President risked losing the support of his major backer, the United States, and many states were keen to know just whether Khan was a 'lone wolf' or part of a state-sanctioned proliferation network. When evidence of Khan's activities could no longer be ignored, President Musharraf moved to close the scandal down. Within weeks Khan was reported to have been interrogated, proved guilty and pardoned by Pakistan! As President Musharraf is a key figure in the US's 'Global War on Terror' the matter has been officially dropped and the argument that Khan acted alone has been accepted. This is, however, extremely unlikely.

To turn briefly to other WMD, chemical and biological weapons (CBW) were always considered to be illegitimate weapons of war. Indeed, in the aftermath of the First World War, it was agreed – in the 1925 Gas Protocol of the Geneva Convention – that nerve gas would not be used in the future because the injuries and suffering it caused were unacceptable (Best, 1994, p. 296). During the Cold War, attention centred primarily on the CBW of the Superpowers, but in fact, more ominous developments occurred outside the Superpower relationship. Chemical weapons were used in the war between Iran and Iraq in the 1980s, and Iraq employed nerve gas against Kurdish villages in 1988 (Black and Pearson, 1993). Although some of the inhibitions on the development and use of CBW remain, these events indicated that existing control measures were inadequate.

Concerns about CBW proliferation have increased since the early 1990s. There were fears that Iraq would use CBW against the United States and her allies in 1991 and 2003. Thankfully, this did not materialize. However, after the first Gulf War the international community successfully negotiated the Chemical Weapons Convention (CWC) to try and ward off future threats. Over the last decade there have also been efforts to strengthen the 1972 Biological and Toxin Weapons Convention (BTWC), which currently has no verification measures that can reassure others that a state is not secretly making biological weapons. To date, these efforts have been unsuccessful, blocked by the United States, which is sceptical that adequate verification can ever be achieved.

Although there have been some successes in stopping potential state-based CBW programmes, the post-Cold War era has highlighted a new threat: non-state actors developing and using CBW. The most surprising example comes from Japan, where in 1995 a millennial cult, previously perceived as benign, released deadly Sarin gas on the Tokyo metro system. In subsequent investigations it was discovered that the cult had across-the-board programmes for chemical and biological weapons, that it had been trying out biological weapons such as Anthrax for some time (luckily with limited effects; many dogs in a neighbourhood it targeted had died, but humans were unaffected) and that in 1992 forty followers had gone as far as Zaire (now the Democratic Republic of Congo) – posing as humanitarian workers – in search of the Ebola virus (US Senate, 1995, Section IV).

Several subsequent incidents have led to even higher concerns about biological weapons threats. The discovery of the deadly toxin Ricin in the possession of Algerian terror suspects in Britain and the empty phials with traces of Ricin found in a Paris railway station point to an Islamic network experimenting with some forms of biological weapon. The known interest of Al Qaeda in chemical and biological weapons is also of great concern. Also, the source of Anthrax attacks on the US Congress and a national magazine that used the US postal service as a delivery system remains undetected, although the incidents are being defined as domestic terrorism rather than international terrorism (Shea, 2004).

It was concerns about biological weapons threats that led the Pentagon to advocate a more proactive approach to dealing with such proliferation concerns. The 1993 Defense Counterproliferation Initiative was the Clinton Administration's attempt to increase the options it had for dealing with such threats. However, the Initiative was extremely controversial because of the suggestion that the United States might *pre-emptively* deal with potential threats (Spear, 2003 pp. 216–17). The first US example of its implementation was the 1998 missile attack on what was thought to be a chemical weapons facility in Sudan (later shown to be a pharmaceutical factory built with aid and technical support from Ireland). By the second Clinton Administration such language had been dropped – along with the incendiary phrase 'rogue state' – only to re-appear with the Presidency of George Bush. Under Bush the United States moved to pre-emptively deal with WMD threats from Iraq. The subsequent discovery that Iraq's WMD programmes were in tatters has called into question the intelligence used to justify that attack and made it more difficult for the United States to make the same claims about Iran (Cirincione, 2004, pp. 3–10; Pullinger, 2004, pp. 10–17.)

Conventional weapons

The fact that the proliferation of conventional weapons has rarely received great attention in world politics reflects the fact that, unlike WMD, they are considered legitimate tools of defence and statehood. During the Cold War, conventional weapons were regarded as a premier tool of Superpower diplomacy and supplied freely to key allies and neutral states. The Cold War has bequeathed two important legacies in the realm of conventional arms. The first is the vast amount of weapons which were stored up by the two alliances in anticipation of war between East and West. The end of the Cold War has meant that many countries are left with large arsenals of weapons which are both more numerous and more sophisticated than required for the types of security threats that they now face. Many states – but particularly those formerly part of the Soviet bloc – have been selling off what are now regarded as 'surplus weapons' from their arsenals. These sales are considered a necessity to obtain hard currency. Although these states may consider their weapons surplus or obsolete, they can nevertheless have a significant impact upon security when supplied to states or non-state groups further down the arms hierarchy.

The second legacy is the economies of the two alliance blocs, geared towards military production. During the Cold War, conventional arms transfers were justified in geo-strategic and political terms, with little attention paid to the economic side of the equation. However, supplier states became dependent on arms transfers abroad for maintaining their defence production-oriented economies. With the end of the Cold War there has been a sharp decrease in national military procurement in both East and West. This means there is now even greater pressure to sell abroad to maintain defence industries (and therefore prosperity and employment) at home. The key point here is that, in the aftermath of the Cold War, the trade in conventional weapons has been largely depoliticized and is now regarded primarily as a commercial venture.

Together these trends of continued production and the selling off of surplus weapons have led to significant changes in the international conventional arms market, which is now characterized by overcapacity. This move to a 'buyers' market' is having important effects upon the international trade in conventional weapons. First, the increasing commercialization of the trade – and its consequent deregulation – has brought in a whole new range of players, both individuals and companies, legitimate and illegitimate, all involved in trying to secure conventional weapons sales.

Second, a consequence of the permissive market and the desperation to secure sales is that existing (minimal) ethical standards governing weapons sales are being eroded This is particularly true for European supplier states whose market positions are being squeezed from above (by US sales of high-technology systems) and below (by supplier states with surplus weapons and old designs sold at bargain prices). The major markets left to them are the disputed 'grey zones' where the rules of the game are flexible. The commercialization and depoliticization means that issues such as human rights are being increasingly marginalized in the search for sales opportunities. For example, British Aerospace (BAe) has been engaged in selling Hawk aircraft to Indonesia. The human rights record of the Indonesian government is very poor and the sales have been criticized as 'an outrageous deal' supporting a repressive regime (CAAT, 1996). BAe and the British government justified the deal by saying that the aircraft could not be used against local populations. However, this is disputable, as reports suggest that Hawks were used in counter-insurgency activities in East Timor, an island which, until 1999, was illegally occupied by Indonesia. The fact that BAe and the British government went ahead with this ethically controversial sale is an indication of the commercial importance of sales abroad. This pattern of the primacy of economic over ethical considerations is repeated in many other supplier states.

Third, the buyers' market has led to an erosion of the convention that weapons are to be sold only by states to states. Although not completely adhered to, this norm did inform commercial arms transfers made during the Cold War. Now, however, sales to non-state actors are actively sought (because higher prices can be charged for black market transactions) and such groups are able to obtain weapons with apparent ease. Increasing supplies of weapons are now reaching sub-state groups involved in battles against their governments or involved in inter-ethnic conflicts (Spear, 1996, pp. 383–4). A good example of the primacy of commercial considerations comes from Russia, where in 1995 the Chechen rebels obtained weapons from *Russian* manufacturers more interested in earning money than supporting their government (Agence France-Presse International News, 1995).

Finally, during the Cold War, supplier states did not provide weapons to states engaged in conflict unless they had a direct strategic interest in the outcome of the conflict. In the post-Cold War period there seems to be confusion among suppliers. For example, in Rwanda, after the Rwandan Patriotic Front (RPF – the Tutsi-dominated group) began an insurgency against the Hutu government, the Belgians banned all weapons supplies to Rwanda (even though it was their client state). By contrast, the French government stepped up its transfers in support of the Hutu government (Goose and Smyth, 1994). Today potential conflicts are regarded as a *sales opportunity*. For example, in 2001 as the international community was trying to defuse the Kashmir conflict between India and Pakistan, many of the politicians who visited India were also 'pitching' their states' fighter aircraft in the same meetings that they were urging restraint in the Kashmir confrontation.

Although considered non-controversial during the Cold War, conventional weapons issues are now forcing their way onto the international agenda. There are three areas of concern. First, there is increasing concern about ballistic missiles as delivery systems for WMD payloads. Ballistic missiles are conventional weapons, but their importance stems from the fact that they can be armed with nuclear, chemical or biological warheads. Worse; it is impossible to tell what the payload is, so policy-makers must plan for the worst. The advantage of ballistic missiles is that they can deliver payloads to distant targets relatively cheaply and they are hard to detect and destroy in flight (unlike most bomber aircraft). Concerns about ballistic missiles in the hands of Third World states were first raised in 1988 when Iran and Iraq used these weapons to terrorize each other's civilian populations in the 'war of the cities' (Bowen and Dunn, 1996, p. 117). However, it was not until the Gulf conflict that fears about the combination of ballistic missiles and WMD payloads became acute. Missile proliferation is now considered a key security threat by many states, and one which will only worsen over the next two decades. In the United States, for example, this perceived threat has led to the decision to deploy anti-ballistic missile defences.

Second, conventional weapons proliferation is being recognized as one of the factors fuelling inter-ethnic conflicts (see also Chapter 8). Although rarely the sole cause of such conflicts, the transfer of conventional weapons – and particularly the easy availability of light weapons – has prolonged and intensified existing inter-ethnic conflicts and helped to ignite new conflicts (Goose and Smyth, 1994; Hartung, 1995; Spear, 1996). One connection which is not receiving sufficient attention in the United States (a dominant player in setting arms control agendas) is that their counter-insurgency operations in Iraq and Afghanistan are facing insurgents mostly armed with SALW. To date the United States has opposed any real action on the problem of SALW proliferation for a mix of domestic concerns (the power of the National Rifle Association that fears international regulation coming to impinge on US domestic practices) and pragmatic reasons (how would you actually stem the trade?). Other states both working with the United States on counter-insurgency operations and interested in SALW control are Britain and Australia. As yet, they have not persuaded the United States to try and reduce the military challenge they face in the field through systemic activity to curb SALW proliferation.

Third, an ethical debate about conventional weapons has re-ignited with a focus on 'inhumane' weapons. 'Inhumane weapons' seems an odd term as the whole point of weapons is to debilitate enemies by inflicting pain, suffering and death. It is nevertheless the case that at several points in modern history, particular weapons have been outlawed – by mutual agreement – because the suffering they cause is considered unacceptable. During the First World War, for example, so-called 'dumdum bullets' (soft-nosed bullets which spread out into the victim's flesh doing massive internal damage) were outlawed by common agreement. During the Second World War, in addition to the ban on dumdum bullets, the 1925 Nerve Gas Protocol was observed.

During the Cold War, the attention given to the question of inhumane weapons was minimal. The demands of establishing and maintaining nuclear deterrence were thought to override such minor considerations. Nevertheless, as the Cold War thawed, interest in this category of weapons increased and there have been attempts to extend the category of weapons internationally acknowledged as 'inhumane'. In the 1990s, fairly successful campaigns were mounted to eliminate two types of weapons: anti-personnel landmines and blinding laser weapons (Leahy, 1995). Since the Mine Ban Treaty came into force in 1999 more than 100 countries have destroyed more than 62 million stockpiled mines and cleared 425 square miles of territory (*Washington Post*, 2004, p. A28).

Despite the higher profile of conventional weapons for the reasons outlined above, one proliferation issue that has arisen since the end of the Cold War remains largely unacknowledged: that global spending on weapons is once again going up, increasing by 18 per cent in real terms since 1994. According to the Stockholm International Peace Research Institute (SIPRI), in 2003 global military expenditure was $956 billion, equal to 2.7 per cent of global GDP and costing every person on earth $152 (Sköns *et al.*, 2004, pp. 305–39).

General problems of arms and weapons-related issues

The continuing significance of arms and weapons-related issues points to several deep-rooted problems which continue to drive the production and trade in both WMD and conventional weapons and the consequent security, economic and ethical dilemmas examined in this chapter. To deal first with the question of security, the fact that states continue to seek both WMD and conventional weapons points to the fact that they feel insecure. The search for security has for centuries involved the acquisition of weapons. However, as Robert Jervis has noted, getting weapons does not always bring security as it can have unanticipated consequences. To illustrate, State A acquires weapons (through production or transfer) in order to ensure its security. However, what State A regards as a defensive action may not be perceived in that way by State B, which feels threatened by State A's weapons and decides that it requires more firepower itself. Jervis calls this the 'security dilemma' and notes that it has often resulted in arms races (Jervis, 1978).

It is clear that some states regard the acquisition of WMD as a means of escaping the security dilemma because they would then be protected by nuclear deterrence or by possession of the 'poor man's bomb', as chemical weapons are often called. However, as the Cold War arms race between the Superpowers illustrated and the India–Pakistan arms dynamic shows, getting WMD is not an end to the problem, but an upward ratchet in the arms race. The key question remains then, how to escape the security dilemma? One answer would seem to lie in arms control initiatives.

The international community – dominated by a few great powers – is willing to tackle these proliferation issues only by attempting to cut off supply. There is a general unwillingness to deal with the demand side of the equation – that is, to look at the problems that lead states to seek WMD and advanced conventional weapons. This unwillingness to look at the causes of the security dilemma is a traditional approach to security in an anarchic, self-help-based international system. However, it means that responses to the proliferation problem are inevitably one-sided and will at best control the problem, rather than solve it.

Turning to the interaction between economics and security in the realm of arms, it is in debates over export controls that the tensions between the two become most obvious. The problem arises because many of the technologies and techniques necessary for the creation of WMD and conventional weapons also have civil (non-military) uses. These 'dual-use technologies' are regarded by would-be recipients as necessary for the development of various industries (such as nuclear power, pharmaceuticals, satellite launch facilities, electronics and bio-technology) which in turn are regarded as essential to economic development. There are also potentially profitable transfers which supplier states are unwilling to forgo.

During the Cold War, the Western allies were fairly unified in a desire to avoid technology transfers that would aid the Communist bloc in developing WMD and advanced conventional weapons. Export controls were agreed through an organization called the Coordinating Committee on Multilateral Export Controls (CoCom) founded in 1949. However, as the Cold War thawed, there were increasing disputes within CoCom over the desire of European states to tilt the balance in favour of greater trade. The extent of the disputes was such that the allies were unwilling to retain the CoCom structure, but neither were they able to negotiate a follow-on export control regime for over two years.

The post-Cold War forum for export controls is called the Wassenaar Arrangement on Export Controls for Conventional Arms and Dual-Use Goods and Technologies. The regime is not East–West focused and states such as Russia are included as full partners. However, this creates problems. It has proved very difficult to gain agreement among the 33 member governments as to the balance to be struck between economic and security issues. Also, recipients object that the regime has a North–South focus. One of the few concrete successes attributable to the Wassenaar Arrangement is a ban on the sale and supply of Man Portable Air Defence Systems (MANPADS, the type of shoulder-fired systems that have been used in attempts to bring down commercial aircraft, for example in Kenya in 1998).

When looking at the issue of export controls the question arises as to whether states in the South are being kept in an economically subservient position – though justified on the basis of security – by being denied access to key technologies. This is certainly the perspective of many Southern states. The example of satellite launch facilities will serve to illustrate this. There is a very close relationship between the civil technologies necessary for launching satellites into space and the technologies that provide a ballistic missile capability. The 1987 Missile Technology Control Regime is designed to prevent the spread of technologies that would aid the development of ballistic missiles. However, this agreement is regarded by many Southern states, particularly India, as also being designed to prevent them from gaining access to the lucrative satellite launch market, keeping them dependent upon Western launch facilities and therefore stunting their economic development.

Arms and arms control on the international agenda

The United States is certainly in an 'agenda-setting' position on issues of security through its seat on the UN Security Council, its leadership of NATO, the security guarantees it still extends to many important states (for example, Japan) and its economic and political connections to other key states. The United States and its allies are also very influential within the international fora at which specific issues are addressed, for example, the Committee on Disarmament (CD), NPT and Convention on Conventional Weapons (CCW) review conferences, and the negotiations over chemical and biological weapons. In all these fora, the United States is able to play a prominent role in proceedings both because of the resources it can invest in preparing for meetings and the alliances upon which it is able to draw. The United States is also one of the few states able to invest the resources required for action on these issues.

The United States can be described as a 'unipolar power', indicating that its defence capabilities are now unchallenged. This unipolar position allows the United States a determining role in global security issues. Due to this dominance, US security priorities, such as the threats posed by 'rogue' states, the leakage of fissile materials from the former Soviet Union, the horizontal proliferation of WMD, and ballistic missile proliferation, are the issues that the United States raises and the issues that become the major global security issues addressed by the international community. This is in part because many of these issues are a general threat to international security, but they are also, importantly, those issues that could threaten US pre-eminence.

The obverse is that the United States is in a position to undermine initiatives of which it does not approve and since the 1990s it has been increasingly willing to do so, on the grounds of protecting US security. This is not just due to the advent of the George W. Bush Administration, it was true of the Clinton years too. For example, the Clinton Administration refused to invest political capital in getting the Senate to ratify the CTBT and therefore condemned the Treaty to oblivion, and it was the Clinton team that slowed progress on landmines in the CD. The Bush Administration has pursued more extreme and blatant forms of the same policy, stymieing efforts to add a verification system to the BTWC and seeking to halt initiatives within the UN for global controls on SALW proliferation.

What we have seen in the last five years is the United States taking proliferation and arms control issues out of the traditional international fora (the UN, treaty negotiations, international regimes etc.) and putting them into fora where they have more control, including the G8 meetings. For example, it was in the G8 that the United States negotiated the 'Partnership Against the Spread of Weapons and Materials of Mass Destruction', not the UN Security Council or the NPT. It has also worked to create 'coalitions of the willing' on particular arms control problems, for example, the PSI. These are both attempts to achieve 'effective multi-lateralism' and a recognition that in the traditional fora the United States does not always get its own way, but it is more likely to do so in organizations over which it has greater control.

It is very difficult for a state that lacks the military and political power of the United States to get issues onto the international security agenda. Even potentially influential organizations such as the EU do not have sufficient 'clout' in the security field to set the agenda. Fora such as the UN General Assembly (where all states have equal representation) are not very effective in this context. The UN Security Council is much more influential, but even here the fact that permanent members have the power of veto means that initiatives can easily be derailed.

Nevertheless, despite the power of the United States and its allies, Third World states can on occasion influence, if not set, the international security agenda. Examples of this are the moves towards the establishment of nuclear weapons-free zones (see Box 6.4). These are an attempt by non-nuclear weapons states both to increase their security and to question the legitimacy of nuclear weapons as a tool of state power (Davis, 1996). In this way they can be seen as aiding the fight against horizontal proliferation, but they are also a challenge to existing nuclear weapons states because they question the legitimacy of *all* nuclear weapons. They are therefore a source of some discomfort to nuclear weapons states.

Another example of agenda-setting concerns the case of landmines which shows that, on occasion, weak actors can influence the security agenda. In this case the weak actors are NGOs. Globally, landmines are thought to kill 10 000 civilians per year and maim a further 20 000. Landmines were being sown in the 1990s at a rate of 2–3 million per year and are a tremendous problem in countries such as Cambodia, Laos, Angola, Mozambique, The Falklands Islands and the states of the former Yugoslavia (HRW/Arms Project and Physicians for Human Rights, 1993). As noted earlier, a campaign was launched in the 1990s to ban the production, trade and deployment of antipersonnel landmines. The campaign was initiated by a group of US NGOs headed by the Vietnam Veterans of America Foundation and including Human Rights Watch/Arms Project and Physicians for Human Rights. These groups were concerned about the human, economic and environmental costs of the millions of landmines sown around the world. These NGOs gathered the support of other groups such as Oxfam and the International Red Cross and together they lobbied governments to ban landmines.

Box 6.4 Nuclear-free zones

There are five treaties establishing nuclear weapons-free zones

- Antarctic Treaty (1959) was the first to establish a nuclear weapons-free zone
- The Treaty of Tlatelolco (1967) covered Latin America and the Caribbean
- The Treaty of Rarotonga (1985) established a nuclear-free zone in the South Pacific
- The Treaty of Pelindaba (1996) declared Africa to be a zone free of nuclear weapons and nuclear testing
- The Bangkok Treaty (1997) created a nuclear-free zone in Southeast Asia.

As a result of these five treaties, most of the Southern hemisphere is now a nuclear-free zone

When efforts to use the CCW – the route that defines weapons as 'inhumane' under international law – were blocked by China and Russia, and progress in the CD was regarded as glacial, Canada moved outside the established international fora by inviting delegations from states and NGOs to a conference in Ottawa. Out of this was born the 'Ottawa Process' which, although boycotted by a number of major powers, resulted in the Ottawa Treaty which bans landmines. This was signed by around 100 states in Ottawa in December 1997, and came into force in 1999 despite being boycotted by some of the key landmine supplier and recipient states (Russia, United States, India). The momentum which this issue has gathered indicates that it is possible to get issues onto the international security agenda. Three lessons can be noted. First, that there can be arms control 'from below', with smaller states and NGOs collaborating to bring an issue onto the agenda and scoring some successes despite the opposition of the major powers. Although an imperfect regime in terms of membership, the Ottawa Treaty is having a positive impact on human security. Secondly, one of the keys to success on landmines was defining the issue as a public health issue (due to high death rates and the suffering of amputees) that allowed NGOs a legitimate say in an issue that – when defined in security terms – they were not able to participate in. Finally, it is important to note that the UN played an important role in legitimating the role of NGOs, as did states such as France and Canada, through including them in negotiations as 'experts'.

Nevertheless, two salutary facts are worth noting. First, the anti-landmine campaign was primarily a Western campaign with Western support: by contrast, in non-democratic states, its success has been limited. Second, as indicated above, the campaign has yet to succeed in drawing in all supplier states, indicating the primacy of economic and security issues over ethical concerns.

International control mechanisms

The international control mechanisms which exist are dedicated to limiting the horizontal proliferation of WMD and conventional weapons through a variety of means. To date, there has been no comprehensive approach to these issues, despite the urging of arms control advocates. This reflects the fact that security agreements are very difficult to negotiate. Suspicions about other states' motives make it very hard to entrust a state's security to an international arrangement, so the agreements that do exist are limited in scope. This means that the coverage that these various mechanisms provide is incomplete. In the aftermath of the Gulf War, there were efforts to close gaps between the various regimes to inhibit horizontal proliferation more effectively. However, as shown below, this aim was not achieved before the momentum behind the moves was lost, leaving a patchwork of initiatives which are not stitched firmly together. Three types of initiatives are briefly discussed here in the context of both WMD and conventional weapons: export control regimes, treaties and conventions and, finally, confidence and security-building measures.

Export controls

There is a strong tradition of export controls over WMD and their components, and a much weaker thread of controls over conventional weapons exports. In the realm of WMD two export regimes are particularly important. The Nuclear Suppliers' Group (NSG, also known as the 'London Club') was established in 1975 and provides the guidelines that underpin the inter-state trade in nuclear materials and technology. In the aftermath of the 1991 Gulf War the NSG expanded the list of materials and technology that could not be transferred. The Australia Group of supplier states was also formed in 1975 and monitors and restricts exports of chemicals and dual-use equipment. In addition, the 1987 Missile Technology Control Regime (MTCR) has proved an important inhibitor of transfers of both complete missiles and missile technologies and components.

Several export control regimes have covered both WMD and conventional weapons, and the key Cold War organization here was CoCom (1949–94), which instituted export controls over nuclear equipment, munitions and dual-use equipment. As noted above, CoCom was unable to survive the end of the Cold War. Its successor regime, the Wassenaar Arrangement, is designed to cover much the same range of goods as CoCom, but is directed against a limited number of 'rogue' states and has been much more active on preventing transfers of WMD components to these states, but has done relatively little on conventional arms transfer issues.

All of these export regimes have limitations which inhibit their effectiveness. Three limitations are particularly noteworthy. First, these export control arrangements do not include every supplier state and therefore the coverage they provide is incomplete. For example, the refusal of China to participate in the NSG, the Australia Group and the Wassenaar Arrangement means that this key supplier is free to make transfers (with implications for the security of all) while all the others have agreed to forgo them.

Second, each of these export control regimes relies upon national interpretation and implementation of the rules, and as van Ham noted when examining the NSG:

the level of enforcement of the export controls differs markedly among the various countries ... [and] non-proliferation concerns regularly take a back seat to commercial and foreign policy goals. (van Ham, 1994, p. 17)

National interpretation of export controls can also lead to disputes over whether or not a transfer is breaking a regime's guidelines. Thus, there have been disputes between China and the United States over Chinese missile sales to Pakistan which the United States claims break MTCR guidelines. There have been similar disputes between the United States and France over missile sales.

A final limitation of export controls is that, because they are supplier-led, they tackle the symptoms and not the causes of insecurity. Nor are they designed to gain the support and acquiescence of recipient states. Rather, recipient states are treated as targets, not partners, and this gives an adversarial air to export control regimes.

There are a number of examples of arms control 'from below' that involve export controls and, in contrast to those discussed above, were initiated by recipients. The most longstanding inter-state effort has occurred in West Africa. It was initiated in 1993 by Mali and has resulted in a number of agreements to halt the flow of weapons into the region, including a moratorium on purchases, combined with some disarmament. Other efforts include a Southern African Development Community (SADC) protocol on the control of firearms, ammunition and other related materials (Lombard, 2000, p. 29). In April 2004 eleven nations from the Great Lakes and Horn of Africa regions signed the Nairobi Protocol for the Prevention, Control and Reduction of Small Arms and Light Weapons, the first binding agreement in this part of Africa. Amongst the measures that the state parties will implement are legislation to ban civilian ownership of automatic and semi-automatic rifles, sanctions for unlicensed gun possession and uniform minimum standards for the manufacture, control, possession, import, export, transit, transport and transfers of small arms and light weapons (Spear, 2004).

Treaties and conventions

Treaties and conventions are the international legal arrangements designed to limit proliferation. The key treaty covering nuclear proliferation is the 1968 NPT. As noted above, there have always been concerns about the discrimination inherent within the Treaty which prioritized horizontal over vertical proliferation and was perceived to give all the duties to the non-nuclear states and all the rights to the nuclear weapons states. In 1995 these concerns were given a new prominence because a collective decision had to be taken by the NPT state signatories on whether to end the Treaty, extend it for a limited amount of time, or extend it indefinitely. Whereas the nuclear weapons states wanted the Treaty to be indefinitely extended (without any alteration of the balance established between horizontal and vertical proliferation and the clear prioritization of the former), some states wanted the Treaty extended for no more than 25 years (with future renewal dependent upon the nuclear weapons states instituting deep cuts in their nuclear arsenals), while a minority wanted the Treaty to be abandoned altogether (Simpson, 1995).

Reflecting the influence of the United States and its allies, some confusion in the ranks of the Treaty's sceptics and the constructive diplomatic role of the South African delegation, the NPT was indefinitely extended at the 1995 conference. Following this the diplomatic battleground shifted to the negotiations in Geneva over a Comprehensive Test Ban Treaty (CTBT), with key non-nuclear states again attempting to tie any progress on this issue to vertical disarmament by the existing nuclear weapons states. Forty-four named nuclear-capable states have to ratify the Treaty for it to come into force. As of December 2004, 120 states have ratified the treaty, including 33 of the named states (including Britain), but there are key nuclear-capable dissenters who have not signed or ratified, including India and Pakistan. Moreover, the US Senate's failure to approve ratification in 1999, particularly because the United States is a named state, creates great doubt over the Treaty's future.

The CWC, reflecting concerns about chemical weapons elicited by the Gulf War, came into force in 1997. The treaty bans an entire class of weapons and has been signed by 167 states (as of November 2004). The CWC contains an extensive verification regime which works through both routine and challenge inspections of both states and chemical industries (this is significant because non-state actors have not previously been brought into arms control treaties). Nevertheless, critics remain sceptical of the CWC's deterrent abilities. In the case of biological weapons, there is a convention, the BTWC which opened for signature in 1972. As of December 2004 153 states had become parties to the Convention. The BTWC has important shortcomings, most notably that it does not have a verification regime – that is, provisions for inspection and investigation designed to verify that biological weapons are not being manufactured. Because of these short-comings, it is recognized that the CWC and BTWC are in themselves insufficient to deal with the chemical and biological weapons threat. However, they do gain strength from being paralleled by the export controls discussed above, and from moves towards intrusive verification regimes (Pearson, 1993). Furthermore, the issue of verification is the subject of further (apparently never-ending) negotiation in the BTWC.

The CCW came into force in 1983 and is designed to ensure that certain types of weaponry are not employed on the battlefield. Since the end of the Cold War there has been increasing interest in the CCW as a means to rid the world of certain types of weapons which do great damage to the human person. A new protocol, Protocol II, places certain limits on the use of fragmentation weapons, landmines, booby traps and incendiary weapons. The CCW also banned the use of weapons which deliberately aimed to blind the enemy, in an attempt to pre-empt the use of a new class of weapons.

Confidence and security-building measures

Notable initiatives here are the multilateral agreements to establish nuclear weapons-free zones (see Box 6.4, p. 111). These fulfil several purposes. First, they are confidence-building measures designed to prevent the operation of the security dilemma by showing that no state in the region will destabilize the situation by seeking nuclear weapons. Second, they are designed to safeguard the region from the nuclear weapons of outside powers (who are invited to become signatories). Third, they are intended to boost efforts towards nuclear disarmament by questioning the legitimacy and desirability of nuclear weapons.

One of the few surviving initiatives in the realm of conventional weapons is the United Nations Register of Conventional Weapons. The Register was established in the aftermath of the Gulf War on the crest of a wave of concern about the proliferation of conventional weapons. Plans for the Register came from the UN General Assembly and pre-dated the Gulf War, but up until that time the idea had received little support from the crucial supplier states who were also members of the UN Security Council. The Register was intended to begin to tackle 'excessive and destabilizing' accumulations of conventional weapons. The Register is a transparency regime designed to throw light on the murky world of the arms trade and performs several functions: to increase the confidence and security of states by showing them (through openness) that the military procurements of their neighbours are not threatening; to increase the degree of difficulty experienced by black marketeers trading in illicit weapons and the difficulty and costs to recipients of illegally procuring these weapons; and to provide information on conventional arms transfers in order to initiate debate about the security, commercial and ethical consequences of such sales (Laurance, 1993). The Register currently requests transfer data on seven categories of weapons: Battle Tanks; Armoured Combat Vehicles; Large Calibre Artillery Systems; Combat Aircraft; Attack Helicopters; Warships; and Missiles and Missile Launchers.

By the mid-1990s, adherence to this (entirely voluntary) regime was not complete, with only approximately 80–90 states returning details of their sales and acquisitions each year (Chalmers and Greene, 1995) and this figure has since fallen. Importantly, many of the major recipients of weapons have steadfastly refused to participate, for example, Saudi Arabia. Adherence to the regime has been particularly poor in the Middle East which is, ironically, the region the Register was designed to help.

Like the NPT, the Register has been criticized as discriminatory. It demands information about exports and imports but makes no mention of domestic procurement (that is, weapons indigenously produced) and hence discriminates against states without their own defence industries. In an attempt to blunt this criticism, states are now offered the opportunity to report domestic procurement in their submissions to the Register. To date, few states with large defence industries have chosen to do this, though a number of states such as Canada are providing this information in an attempt to increase the utility of the Register.

Arms, arms control and contemporary world politics

The international community is sending out mixed signals about the utility of nuclear weapons in the post-Cold War world. On the one hand, states such as the United States are championing the cause of non-proliferation and seeking to strengthen the regimes that deal with these issues. On the other hand, however, the declared nuclear weapons states are largely maintaining their nuclear arsenals, and still talk in terms of deterrence. In this situation, actions speak louder than words and horizontal WMD proliferation remains a problem.

It is clear that, although the era of global tensions may be over, the security dilemma is still a reality for many states. The regional arms races in Southeast Asia, the Korean Peninsula and the Middle East are evidence of this. The eternal question seems to be, how to break the cycle of the security dilemma? The existing institutional mechanisms designed to build confidence and enhance security are very weak compared to the security problems that they are designed to overcome.

For the future the biggest arms control problem may not be the behaviour of states, but the fact that the major proliferators are not states at all, but non-state actors beyond the reach of traditional tools of diplomacy. It is not clear that the international community is equipped or ready to face this challenge.

Guide to further reading

For readers interested in keeping up with current developments in this field, the best reference sources are the yearbooks produced by the Stockholm International Peace Research Institute, for example, SIPRI Yearbook (2004). In addition, SIPRI has a very useful website which is regularly updated, http://www.sipri.org. SIPRI also has a free on-line reference system http://first.sipri.org. Other useful websites include that of the US Center for Defense Information, http://www.cdi.org/, the Anglo-American British American Security information Council (BASIC), http://www.basicint.org, and The Arms Control Association, http://www.armscontrol.org.

Three books on WMD proliferation are recommended. The problems of the existing arms control regimes and how they might be righted are considered in Cirincione (2000), while issues of intelligence on threats and how to respond are considered in Cirincione, Wolfsthal and Rajkumar (2002). A useful book that brings together in debate the two major thinkers on proliferation, the nuclear 'optimist' Kenneth Waltz and the nuclear 'pessimist' Scott Sagan combines theory and practice in important ways (Sagan and Waltz, 2003).

Chapter 7

Peacekeeping and Humanitarian Intervention

MICHAEL PUGH

Political and media attention is frequently drawn to crises in which international actors get involved in conflicts that are said to threaten international peace and security, or which expose brutality and extensive human suffering. There are many levels and types of response to such crises, from those of individual aid workers and NGOs, to forcible intervention by states and groups of states, to international peacekeeping by the United Nations. This chapter focuses on the relationship between these responses and the power structures of world politics, and the way that 'peacekeeping' and 'humanitarian interventions' have been affected by the strategic goals of powerful states.

Peace support measures in world politics

The main contention in this chapter is that issues of peacekeeping and humanitarian intervention reflect failures in world politics and a perceived need to deal with the manifestations of problems. Intervenors claim to be putting right what has gone wrong. At the same time, there has been increasing recognition, especially since the attacks in the United States in September 2001, that economic instability and lack of economic development in poor parts of the world can lead to political unrest and perhaps state failure. The problem requires new development strategies and well-targeted development aid, rather than reliance on military force (Center for Global Development, 2004). Furthermore, weak states can become 'breeding grounds' for international political violence. But the roles played by the chief actors mirror the way they visualize and structure the international system. Much of the impetus for peacekeeping and humanitarian relief comes from parts of the world that benefit from the maintenance of global inequalities. By contrast, the actors in civil conflicts and disasters – those immediately affected – are overwhelmingly from poor parts of the world. They are often inadequately portrayed in the discourse of peacekeeping and humanitarianism as victims of authoritarian politics or primeval ethnic tensions. But it is no coincidence that the 'targets' of intervention are people who have been marginalized in the world economy and who are now to be rescued or policed by those who organize the intervening.

Whether the activities (defined in Box 7.1) genuinely support peace is open to question. Interventions can increase instability, to the extent that, as in Iraq, the invasion in 2003 by the United States and its allies turned that country into a recruiting ground for groups engaged in political violence. Going to war to save lives also implies a contradiction. The notion of Just War has a long-standing legal and political pedigree to resolve this. The term 'Grotian' doctrine, based on criteria for determining the justice and

---

Box 7.1 Definitions of peacekeeping terms

Intervention can be used to mean either any kind of involvement (such as beaming a media broadcast to another state) or, in the stricter sense used here, the use of armed forces to interfere in another state. This can take the form of collective action under Chapter VII of the UN Charter, which allows states to go to war in order 'to maintain or restore international peace and security', as a coalition of states did to remove Iraqi forces from Kuwait. It may also mean a limited war without a UN mandate for reasons that are said to have a 'humanitarian' purpose, such as NATO's bombing of Kosovo and Yugoslavia in 1999.

Humanitarianism is an ideal that the International Committee of the Red Cross and many NGOs promote – a neutral, impartial and non-coercive alleviation of human suffering according to need. Controversially, the concept has been stretched by intervenors to mean abandoning neutrality to take sides with groups who are being brutally suppressed in a dispute.

Peacekeeping is activity, mostly by military units to patrol and observe. They generally only use force in self-defence, operating as impartially as possible with the consent of the parties to disputes. Increasingly, peacekeeping has been broadened to include police and civilian units performing a range of new tasks such as crime control, demilitarization and the demobilization of combatants.

Peace enforcement is a mutation of peacekeeping that allows the use of force against bandits and militias to protect relief supplies and/or against militarized political factions to induce them to abide by peace agreements.

Preventive deployment has occurred in one instance, when a UN deterrent force (UNPREDEP, 1992–9) was located in Northern Macedonia to deter conflict spilling over from Bosnia and Herzegovina and Albania.

Peacebuilding refers to measures taken, mostly in the aftermath of violence, to support political, social and economic processes and structures in a war-torn society with the purpose of minimizing the risk of a return to war. It can encompass election organization to promote democracy, civil administration to restore state functions and de-mining to increase freedom of movement.

Peace support operations (PSOs) is a general phrase used to cover military and police involvement in the above types of activity.

legitimacy of forceful interventions, as refined by the seventeenth-century jurist, Hugo Grotius, includes provision for humanitarianism. Nevertheless, Grotian principles are open to interpretation and the issue has generated a great deal of intellectual argument, for example about whether non-forceful peacekeeping remains relevant in situations where civilians need protection, and whether humanitarian intervention is justified by ethics and outcomes (Bellamy and Williams, 2004). The external use of force to stop genocide is certainly allowed under international law (UN Chapter VII), but lack of strategic interest in the Rwandan case led the United States and others to avoid interpreting the situation there as genocide (defined as attempts to eliminate certain groups or part of a group of people).

The international deployment of forces has fluctuated over time (see Figure 7.1). Whereas only 13 UN peacekeeping missions were started between 1948 and 1987, in the period 1988–2004 there were 46 new operations. At a peak in 1994, UN peacekeeping operations involved nearly 80 000 military personnel and civilian police around the world, seven times the figure for 1990. This had fallen to 14 500 by December 1998, but thereafter the commitments rose again. In September 2004 there were over 60 000 military personnel and civilian police engaged in 16 UN operations (including six that were started after 2000) (see Map 7.1). To these figures we can add a number of military and police personnel in non-UN peacekeeping

Figure 7.1   *Fluctuations in UN peacekeeping force deployments, military personnel and civilian police in UN missions, 1990–2004*

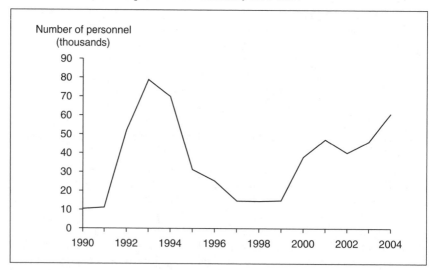

Note: The figures are at 31 December for each year, except 1990 (30 June), 1993 (31 July), 1998 (30 November), 1999 (30 November) and 2004 (31 August).

Source: Jakobsen (1998, p. 4) and UN Department of Public Information.

Map 7.1 *Map of UN operations, 2004*

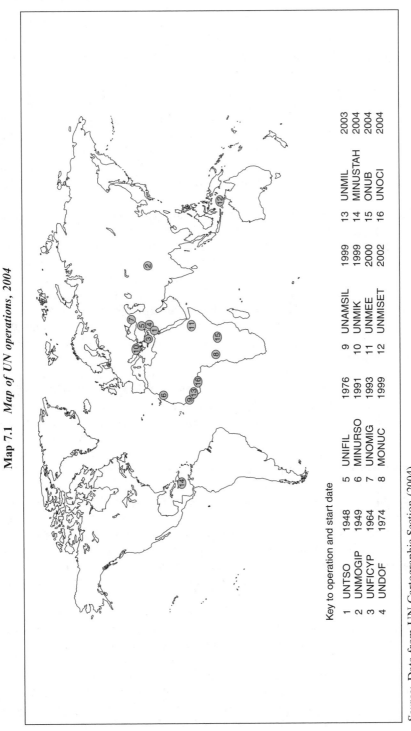

Key to operation and start date

1	UNTSO	1948	5	UNIFIL	1976	9	UNAMSIL	1999	13	UNMIL	2003
2	UNMOGIP	1949	6	MINURSO	1991	10	UNMIK	1999	14	MINUSTAH	2004
3	UNFICYP	1964	7	UNOMIG	1993	11	UNMEE	2000	15	ONUB	2004
4	UNDOF	1974	8	MONUC	1999	12	UNMISET	2002	16	UNOCI	2004

Source: Data from UN Cartographic Section (2004).

operations, such as the NATO-led Kosovo Force (KFOR) and the EU forces in Bosnia and Herzegovina (EUFOR) and Afghanistan (EUCORPS). In addition, thousands of civilians were attached to missions, and there were many more thousands of humanitarian relief workers. With the notable exception of the Congo operation in 1960–64, Cold War peacekeeping was mainly limited to observation and interposition along ceasefire lines between states. Operations since 1989 have involved many more sorts of activities, usually attempting to address conflicts within states (Durch, 1994). All but three of the 58 major conflicts in the period 1990–2002 were internal.

International actors of all kinds have devoted considerable attention to peace support measures. but have also neglected certain crises and under-resourced multilateral operations. This reflects two main factors. First, there has been a continued failure by international organizations to address underlying structural problems in the global system. Accordingly, states intervene in order to contain problems that would adversely affect their interests. Second, states have undertaken humanitarian intervention in response to moral concerns that have agitated their own populations and become domestic political issues. At first sight these two developments may seem contradictory. How can the 'international community' foster, ignore or wrongly diagnose the causes of civil conflict, and yet also assume that some conflicts are internationally significant requiring energy and resources to fix them?

The failure to prevent, and the pressure to fix, may both stem from processes of globalization. On the one hand, the global spread of capitalism, of Western cultural and media influences may have fostered economic and social injustice and political tensions to the point where the governments are confronted by social and economic collapse and insurgency (Chua, 2002). This has been referred to as 'structural violence': the built-in disparities which ensure that peripheral areas of the world economy are forced to struggle for bare survival. In some cases, where external interest is negligible, the crisis area is treated as being beyond global integration and isolated. By contrast, a potent interventionist mix comprising the strategic interests of states and their technological power, a sense of obligation to relieve distress, and a perceived need to improve access to economic resources has resulted in efforts to integrate some areas into a 'liberal peace', comprising democracy, capitalism and economic integration (Duffield, 2001).

Peace support operations and humanitarian issues have sometimes had high visibility in the popular media in Western states, though overshadowed by counter-terrorism operations after 2001. Television coverage of the outflow of refugees from Kosovo in 1999 probably influenced public opinion and policy to intervene on humanitarian grounds. Conversely, another illegal war and occupation, partially represented by the United States and the United Kingdom as liberating Iraqis from tyranny, led to widespread public opposition around the world. The attention of policy-makers, the media and the public is further heightened when the lives of peacekeepers and aid workers are at risk or deaths occur. Television pictures of a US soldier being dragged through the streets of Mogadishu and UN soldiers held hostage in Bosnia and Herzegovina caused a flurry of diplomatic activity, media coverage and public debate which led to changes in policy.

Agendas after the Cold War

The responsibility for peace support measures and humanitarian assistance being placed high on the international agenda does not lie with any single event, person or school of thought. Structural violence has been a long-standing feature of the international system which is promoted, ignored or denied by policy-makers in the wealthy parts of the world until confronted by a crisis which affects them, such as the international debt crisis. The end of the Cold War increased the sense that barriers to improving global security were being lifted but also increased the system's exposure to the problems of insecurity in areas that had been economically and politically marginalized by the former preoccupation with the strategic balance between the capitalist and socialist systems.

In this climate, the UN Secretary-General, Boutros Boutros-Ghali, seized the chance to promote the UN's standing in his report, *An Agenda for Peace* (1992). It did not present many new ideas; it was rather a repackaging of old ones, many of which had been around since the UN's problematic intervention in the Congo in the 1960s. It was realist in assuming that the UN could do only as much as the member states allowed it to, but also liberal internationalist in recognizing the problems of structural violence and attempting to foster management and budgetary reforms in the UN. Traditional peacekeeping had often been presented as the maximum that states engaged in the Cold War could agree upon in terms of collective military intervention. Now, it seemed, a lot more was possible. The near-universal response to the challenge posed by Iraq's invasion of Kuwait and the military victory of the UN-authorised Coalition in 1990 also placed multinational operations high on the agendas of defence establishments.

However, the UN's main purpose – conflict prevention – was also its greatest weakness. The collapse of Yugoslavia indicated that no amount of early warning could substitute for the political will to act. Subsequently, in various reassessments, including a *Supplement to an Agenda for Peace* (1995), Boutros-Ghali and his successor Kofi Annan scaled down the UN's ambitions. Enforcement operations were hardly mentioned, except as something that should be delegated to regional organizations. Thus the UN's presentation of the issue fluctuated from near euphoria in early 1992 to despondency by mid-1995 as the operational problems of peace support measures overwhelmed the intervening agencies.

Nevertheless, reforms were effected, such as opening a 24-hour operations centre (when previously UN commanders in the field could contact the officials in New York only during office hours). A 'Lessons Learned Unit' was established in the UN Department of Peacekeeping Operations in 1995 (later renamed Best Practices Unit). Various incisive reports were issued by panels on Rwanda and Srebrenica, on peacekeeping in general (Brahimi Report, 2000) and on the responsibility to protect populations in danger (ICISS, 2001). As well as generating reforms to the policy-making and mechanics of peacekeeping, the Brahimi Report called for forceful measures to uphold UN mandates, requiring the abandonment of impartiality in the face of aggressors. A conflation of peacekeeping and peace enforcement, repackaged as 'peace support operations', had already been under way hesitantly in the mid-1990s, reflecting the increased militarization of peacekeeping within states believed necessary by the five permanent members of the security council who contributed to UN and non-UN operations. Although the UN itself was not provided with the means or the political backing to undertake outright enforcement, this did not spell the end of UN operations altogether. Indeed, they increased, as testified by the 15 000-strong deployment to Liberia in 2003.

The primary concerns of peacekeepers were not fundamentally altered by the 2001 attacks in the United States. Their role was to build peace between parties to a dispute, not to hunt out terrorists. Only in so far as they could help to sustain a ceasefire, stabilize a peace and start to re-engineer societies, through elections, democratic policing and legal systems, might they be contributing to counter-terrorism (Tardy, 2004). However, one of the main effects of the post-9/11 counter-offensive was to switch the priorities of the most fearful governments to an open-ended commitment to eradicate terrorism around the world. This not only drew huge resources into tracking and attacking the so-called sources of terrorism, it also involved subsidizing 'front-line' undemocratic regimes in Pakistan and Uzbekistan. Although some governments may have regarded UN peace-keeping as a contribution to stabilizing those environments which terrorist groups might find attractive for operations against 'Western' interests, the Bush Administration initially considered that peacekeeping might be killed off. Certainly, US involvement in it was inappropriate for a superpower whose main security task was to exert its global military power to eradicate threats such as terrorism (Fleitz, 2002). Nor was the Bush Administration initially interested in nation building. However, flaws in the stability programme in Afghanistan and the gaping political vacuum after the Iraq invasion, dictated that this policy could hardly last. Nor did the UN's legitimating function cease with the counter-terrorism offensives and the invasion of Iraq (Berdal, 2003). Indeed, the UN was harnessed by the United States to promote anti-terrorism and democracy in post-war Iraq and Afghanistan.

Nevertheless, divergence in the European and US agendas had became more evident by 2004. A collective drive by the EU to develop a common foreign and security policy following tensions with the United States in the Kosovo war, and to counterbalance US security policies, led to various initiatives, including two small and short-lived military operations in Macedonia and the Democratic Republic of the Congo in 2003 (Bono and Ulriksen, 2004). A European Security Strategy adopted at the end of 2003 placed far more emphasis than US policy on preventive engagement and multilateralism, though there was little consensus about how it should be implemented. For the UK Prime Minister, Tony Blair, it still spelt conservative military thinking in the form of rapidly deployable 'battle groups' to be sent beyond Europe (Traynor, 2004). For others, the European Security Strategy presented an opportunity to engage in peace operations and humanitarianism of a different kind. Rather than a multilateral imitation of US militarism, and indeed rather than a familiar UN peacekeeping agenda, the EU High Representative for Common Foreign and Security Policy, Javier Solana, was urged to establish a 'human security response force' of military and civilian elements to protect abused civilians. Dialogue and consultation with local populations would facilitate early warning and local backing for implementing and sustaining deployments (EU Study Group, 2004). Whether or not Solana and national leaders will adopt such a cosmopolitan agenda, closer to the ideals of the UN than to the foreign policy of the United States, it represents a new 'human security' initiative to cope with future Srebrenicas.

Critical issues in peace support operations

In addition to the fundamental structural issue discussed above, quandaries posed by peace support operations can be considered under five headings: conceptual issues, legal provisions, operational problems, the accountability deficit and world order hegemony.

Conceptual issues

The first set of problems relates to the concepts of collective security and peacekeeping. Originally, the UN founders envisaged that the financial benefits of pooling defence resources and the political benefits of having a global security structure to maintain world peace, would work in accordance with Chapter VII of the UN Charter. This specifies that member states will make arrangements to provide the UN with a large armed force that could be used against an aggressor. The provision of a veto power to the United States, the United Kingdom, France, Russia and China (the permanent members of the Security Council) meant that collective security could never be directed against one of themselves since they would veto it. One of the major difficulties with such a collective security arrangement is that without a predetermined enemy, participants cannot readily make advance commitments to use force against any aggressor declared by the Security Council. The aggressor could turn out to be an important trading partner, a close ally or capable of mustering so much military force that to join a fight against it would be national suicide. A system of collective security is therefore inherently unreliable. Moreover, a global system carries the risk of turning local disputes into much larger ones.

The concept of peacekeeping, by contrast, is based on the idea that there is no enemy except conflict itself. Peacekeeping is not even mentioned in the UN Charter; it was invented as an ad hoc response to the need for international supervision of troop withdrawals at the end of the Suez War in 1956. The principles, devised at the time by the Canadian Minister of Foreign Affairs, Lester Pearson, and the UN Secretary-General, Dag Hammarskjöld, emphasize that peacekeepers are impartial towards the parties in a dispute and indifferent as to the outcome of a dispute. Because the consent of the parties has generally been a minimum requirement, UN peacekeeping operations during the Cold War tended to deal with relatively small-scale problems and had no effect on the big picture, except to insulate problems from becoming part of Superpower rivalry. Furthermore, it is a long-standing criticism that peacekeeping freezes hostilities rather than resolves them. There may be an incentive for sides in a dispute to agree to a ceasefire, perhaps because they are militarily exhausted, but, as in the case of Cyprus, no real incentive to reach a long-term solution to their dispute. Therefore, peacekeeping could be conceived in a more active way, linking it to conflict resolution and helping in the recovery of war-torn societies (Woodhouse and Ramsbotham, 2000).

In the 1990s, a different sort of criticism emerged: that peacekeeping was inadequate to meet the problems encountered when civil wars are still in progress and where consent for a peacekeeping presence is fragile and parties to a dispute see peacekeepers as biased against them (Jakobsen, 1998). A lively debate raged in the 1990s about whether peacekeeping within states rather than between them was a 'dead end' (James, 1994), and whether the answer was to enable peacekeepers to be more forceful in dealing with bandits and paramilitary forces – not to win a war but to act as a kind of tough police force (Roberts, 1995–6; Ruggie, 1996). More cautious commentators believed that peacekeeping forces could use coercion only to sustain peace agreements (Goulding, 1996). Still others regarded 'robust peacekeeping' as potentially counter-productive, likely to become part of the crisis itself and to jeopardize humanitarian activities (Berdal, 1993). Commentators argued that it was a grave mistake to use the wrong kind of force in the wrong situation, to send lightly armed peacekeepers to defend an area under siege, or to extend a mandate so that ill-equipped peacekeepers became involved in combat (Berdal, 1995). The use of soldiers in civil emergencies, such as earthquakes, where there is no political unrest, is perfectly viable. But switching between roles, from the modestly armed and transparent peacekeeper to the camouflaged combat soldier was problematic. It raised the question as to whether a new type of force was needed for situations where local consent was fragile or unreliable (Kinloch Pichat, 2004). UN members have been averse to spending money on such a force, and have opted, instead, to increase the presence and role of civilian police and to strengthen non-UN bodies, so-called 'regional organizations' (Holm and Eide, 2000).

Legal provisions and predicaments

Of the new UN operations set up between January 1992 and January 2005, all but two (on the Iraq/Kuwait and Ethiopia/Eritrea borders) dealt with internal conflicts, often between sub-state actors within and across state boundaries. Modern peace support operations that contravene the principle of host consent involve trespassing on the internal affairs of states. This challenges the foundations of a state-centred international order that intervenors as well as those intervened against are reluctant to abandon. The doctrine of non-intervention is upheld in Article 2(7) of the UN Charter, which says that nothing authorizes the UN to intervene 'in matters which are essentially within the domestic jurisdiction of any state', except when authorized by the Security Council or General Assembly under Chapter VII of the UN Charter. Chapter VII allows international intervention with force in cases that are determined by the UN as threats to international peace and security. UN member states have therefore attempted to keep two conflicting norms of international relations in balance: respect for the non-intervention principle, set against responding to the human needs of those exposed to abuse by states or sub-state factions. This balancing act has led to an ambiguous situation in international law and the customary behaviour of states. As one might expect, governments most likely to be the objects of intervention have been vociferous about maintaining the non-intervention principle. In deference to nervousness in the developing world about establishing a trend, Resolution 794 (3 December 1992) which authorized intervention in Somalia, referred to 'the unique character' of the situation and its 'complex and extraordinary nature'. The uneasy balance between the international community doing nothing and intervening with force was reflected in efforts to gain consent for assistance in the case of East Timor when Indonesia's consent for international involvement was sought and eventually obtained.

Over several decades, UN declarations on strengthening humanitarian assistance have stressed the principle that states are sovereign, though of course they can give consent for outside involvement. But the Grotian view justifies forcible intervention to protect people from genocide or other outrages against humanity (Wheeler, 2001). The French doctor, Bernard

Kouchner, who witnessed the Nigerian civil war in the 1960s and set up the aid organization, Médecins sans Frontières, argued that it was nonsensical for governments to have the right to do whatever they like to their own populations. From this cosmopolitan perspective, interventions should show 'solidarity' with people being abused (Kaldor, 2000, p. 185; Wheeler, 2001). However, this gives rise to several problems in addition to challenging state sovereignty.

First, the contradiction in trying to preserve human life by going to war is mitigated only by the highly speculative risk that greater evil would be done by not using force. It is not at all self-evident, despite political rhetoric to the contrary, that the world was made safer by the invasion of Iraq.

Second, if two or more groups are engaged in mutual oppression, deciding which is the more guilty and the more deserving of support can be problematic and can dissolve into demonizing one of the parties. When the international forces in Kosovo stood aside in March 2004 while the Albanian 'victims' of 1999 engaged in a bout of ethnic cleansing against the former, but now demonized, Serb 'aggressors', it seemed that moral certainties were beyond adjustment (HRW, 2004). It also suited the peace enforcing states to idly witness a step towards ethnic homogeneity that would bring Kosovo's independence, Serbia's break-up, and their own disengagement closer.

Third, delivering relief with the barrel of a gun is often unwelcome to humanitarian aid workers because it threatens to damage their intention to work independently among all who need help. In particular, the International Committee of the Red Cross depends on the cooperation of signatories to the Geneva Convention for protecting the rights of all people in war, including those being attacked by an international intervention force. Restrictions on NGOs in Kosovo and the US military's delivery of both bombs and relief supplies over Afghanistan drew heavy criticism. A declaration by the USAID Administrator, Andrew Natsios, that NGOs should act as an arm of the US government, generated strong resistance to the likely impact such politicization would have on building trust with local communities (InterAction, 2003).

Fourth, it can involve abuse of the humanitarian principle to disguise ulterior motives based on national interest. As the Kosovo war demonstrated, the absence of a UN Security Council mandate was an embarrassment to the quest for legitimacy by the intervenors who were probably impelled mainly by the need to reassert NATO's credibility (Ali, 2000). Subsequently, an International Commission on Intervention and State Sovereignty explored the whole of issue of non-intervention doctrine in environments where widespread human rights abuse was occurring. It acknowledged that a new legal doctrine would be unlikely to gain universal acceptance, but contended that legitimation increasingly depended on an emerging recognition of new international norms in favour of humanitarian intervention and the protection of populations at risk. However, since the

Clinton Administration announced in May 1994 that the United States would support only UN operations that advanced US interests, it is hardly surprising that states are extremely concerned about any development of international law and practice in this direction. After 2001, in an international context dominated by the US drive to intervene militarily for other reasons (such as counter-terrorism or securing oil reserves), the conflation of morality and national interest simply meant that power politics would decide who got 'protected', with or without UN approval (Chandler, 2004). In effect the new norms would give rich and powerful states a green light to evade international law and impose a liberal peace under the guise of humanitarian legitimacy.

Operational problems

The absence of a common doctrine of peace support measures has operational as well as legal significance: the risk that confusion would add to the political and social causes of the problem. The participation of relatively new and inexperienced actors has led to tensions. Some of the militarily powerful states, such as the United States, France, Russia and the United Kingdom, have entered the arena with a history of warfare and counter-insurgency against defined enemies (though the United Kingdom did have previous peacekeeping experience in Cyprus, as did France in Lebanon). Confusion and lack of understanding about the concepts of peacekeeping were reflected in Somalia when US forces launched attacks against General Aideed's forces for killing Pakistani peacekeepers, ignoring the fact that the international community was not trying to win a war.

Germany and Japan were also new to peacekeeping and they gradually overturned legal constraints and historical legacies to send military forces abroad. Germany sent troops to Kosovo, for example, and Japan to East Timor. In the post-9/11 panic, and under US pressure, Japan's legal framework was changed to allow its Self Defence Force to participate with services and logistic support in counter-terrorism and peacekeeping operations. It could also use force, not only for self-protection, but also to protect civilians and soldiers under its control (Ishizuka, 2005). Other novices have pursued strategic goals, too. Italy led an intervention to provide relief in Albania in 1997, essentially to limit the number of Albanian refugees entering Italy. Others have participated for the income which it brings in. Sometimes, participants have been poorly equipped or ill-disciplined (abusing local women in Somalia, Cambodia and Namibia, for example). But misbehaviour is not confined to novices. Canada, with its considerable experience and a national culture which accords peacekeeping a high status, had to disband an airborne division after some of its members committed murder in Somalia.

Clearly soldiers have to conduct certain duties, such as demilitarizing armed factions and removing mines. But civilian administrators, relief organizations and development agencies should be the principal agents in fostering economic recovery, rebuilding services, refugee protection, psychological counselling and the rehabilitation of health, education and legal systems. However, relations between military and civilian personnel in responding to emergencies can be tense and suspicious. The two groups have contrasting cultures and traditions of discipline; they draw their authority from different sources and the work of NGOs can be politically tainted by being too close to military operations. Whereas soldiers are sent by governments, civilian workers in NGOs attempt to remain independent of governments (even when governments supply them with funds). Moreover, coordination of effort among the many and varied actors who participate in peace support measures is fraught with difficulty, largely because each organization involved has its own mandate, ethos, funding and political 'turf' to protect (Vaux, 2001). Although the UN created an Office for the Coordination of Humanitarian Affairs (OCHA) in 1997, it has no power to direct operations, merely to facilitate cooperation between those involved.

Three other problems at the operational level need to be mentioned. First, women are seriously under-represented in peacekeeping, both as civilian personnel (where they account for 10–30 per cent of staff according to the mission) and as soldiers (a mere 2–5 per cent). Yet the absence of females and the inadequacy of gender training for men is damaging to the effectiveness of peacekeeping. It has led to failures in protecting women from sexual violence, insensitivities in dealing with the needs of women in war-torn societies, and their exploitation and abuse by peacekeeping troops. Moreover, as the UN's Windhoek Declaration on Mainstreaming Gender emphasized in 2000, women can make distinctive contributions to peace processes, as mediators, for example. The UN has a formal commitment to gender equality in the representation of women in peacekeeping, and women have been given more responsibility, notably in Kosovo. But implementing the gender mainstreaming and training programmes has a long way to go and has to compete with other programmes and agendas (Olsson and Tryggestad, 2001).

Second, just as charities and agencies are reluctant to submerge their identities and power within a centralized system, so states have been reluctant to relinquish control over their armed forces and to make commitments to multinational operations. Command and control of UN forces has become an issue, especially when operations are likely to involve combat. The UN does not have a large military staff of its own, and some states, especially the United States, have refused to put their troops under a non-US commander. This problem came to the fore in Somalia, when US marines took orders from their own headquarters in the United States (Ruggie, 1996). States supplying troops for enforcement are concerned about costs, about deflection from other commitments and about casualties. While no soldier was killed by enemy action in Europe during the Cold War, about 600 UN peacekeepers lost their lives through hostile acts between

1948 and mid-2004. NATO's high-level bombing strategy against Yugoslavia in 1999 and US bombing raids against insurgents in Afghanistan and Iraq were generally ineffective, but designed to limit the number of US body bags, though not local civilian casualties.

Third, delays in sending troops that were blamed for allowing human tragedies to unfold, notably in Rwanda in 1994 and East Timor in 1999, led to a series of reforms. Efforts by the UN to establish a data base of commitments for stand-by forces, the creation of SHIRBRIG (a multi-national stand-by headquarters unit based in Denmark) and mechanisms proposed by the Brahimi report for financing the initiation of a force even before its mandate is agreed, have had a modest impact. Slowness in reaction and problems over who commands the force reflect the general problem in world politics that states are reluctant to share control over their military forces.

The accountability deficit

Finally, the issue of peace support measures and humanitarian activity illustrates problems of international accountability. To whom are peace-keepers and humanitarian workers accountable and responsible, and how is accountability implemented? Military peacekeepers are, of course, responsible to their commanders and governments, but there is no mechanism for accountability to the Security Council, which ultimately decides the mandate, the budget and the force structure. Humanitarian workers are accountable to their agency committees, donors, contractors and governing boards that are often driven by the need to raise funds for their own survival. Relief aid is big business. Moreover, performance is often measured by the numbers of blankets issued, people fed, water wells provided – and not by whether the activity fulfils a mandate.

In some 'host' countries, notably Rwanda, Burundi and the Sudan, there has been a reaction against the 'invasions' of NGOs and journalists and an attempt to regulate their activities, especially as aid workers may publicize continued abuse of human rights and have a distorting impact on local economies. However, many prominent NGOs have signed up to codes of conduct, such as that elaborated by the International Committee of the Red Cross, and for many years have continued to gain access, albeit restricted, to Darfur in Sudan where 150 Afrian Union monitors and 300 supporting troops were only deployed in 2004.

Usually the last people in a crisis to be consulted about their future are those being protected or assisted. Yet local communities usually know what measures work best for their own survival and can offer rational assessments of their needs. Médecins sans Frontières now sends personnel to a crisis in order to discover the requirements of local communities. This is not as simple as it sounds. Survivors may no longer have a functioning decision-making structure, their spokespersons may be unrepresentative, and they may include war criminals and human rights abusers. Nevertheless, the most highly-praised relief organizations are often those that listen to local advice and which, like the UN International Children's Emergency Fund (UNICEF), try to employ as many local people as possible.

The accountability deficit has been particularly acute where peacebuilding has been reinforced by international civil administration. In East Timor, Bosnia and Herzegovina and Kosovo, international administrators have directed recovery strategies, law and order programmes and state building, but often without consultation with local communities or concern for their employment and welfare needs (Chopra, 2000; Suhrke, 2001; Chesterman, 2004; Paris, 2004). In Kosovo, the secretive 'Quint' (the United Kingdom, United States, Germany, France and Italy), though influential in drawing up the territory's constitutional framework, is unaccountable. The Dayton Peace Implementation Council is also unaccountable, and the Office of the High Representative in Bosnia and Herzegovina offers the extraordinary spectacle of a former 'centrist' British Member of Parliament, Paddy Ashdown, and his American economic advisor, rubbing salt into the war wounds of impoverished Bosnians by dictating an aggressive free-market capitalism to the detriment of economic recovery and social justice (Pugh and Cooper, 2004, pp. 157–85).

World order hegemony

The Security Council is heavily dependent on the foreign policies of its permanent members, who can each veto decisions according to interpretations of their interests. The Security Council has determined that some issues are a 'threat to peace, breach of the peace, or act of aggression', while others are not. For example, the United States persuaded the Security Council to consider the government of Haiti to be a threat to international peace and security and to permit the United States to invade in 1994. Hitherto, US administrations had ignored the human rights abuses of the Duvalier regime and had sustained it economically for decades, until it lost control in the mid-1980s. Only when an exodus of refugees headed for the US and Caribbean coasts after 1994 did the Clinton Administration regard Haiti as a threat requiring military intervention (Jakobsen, 1998). But reduced interest in resolving conflicts through the UN afflicted the United States in particular. The Clinton Administration adopted an increasingly hostile view towards the UN, and in May 1994 issued Presidential Decision Directive 25 (PDD 25) which laid down criteria for US involvement in UN operations, including the need for clear US interests to be at stake and a limited period for each engagement. The United States also decided unilaterally to reduce its assessed share of peacekeeping costs from just over 30 per cent to 25 per cent of the global cost. This is not to say that the United States actually paid its dues. On the contrary, it continued a habit of refusing to pay up until a deal was reached with Congress in 1999. The effect was to weaken the UN's ability to continue with existing tasks. Yet the UN peacekeeping budget for 2004–05, about $2.8 billion, was less than the annual expenditure of the New York fire and police departments. The estimated total costs of all operations 1948–2004 was $31.54 billion, compared to $800 billion spent on armaments by governments worldwide in 2002 alone.

The United States exercises a quadruple veto: its Security Council veto, its ability to deny political leadership, its ability to deny intelligence or material assistance for operations and its financial veto through refusal to pay contributions. The United States and the United Kingdom went ahead with the invasion of Iraq after failing to secure Security Council agreement. This suggested to many observers that the UN was in terminal decline. But the Bush Administration's appeals to UN support for counter-terrorism and for peacebuilding in Iraq demonstrates that US policy-makers prefer to manipulate the UN than ignore it altogether (Mingst, 2003). Moreover, opposition in the Security Council to the Iraq invasion also shows that there are limits to the extent that other states are willing to play along with the manipulation. Although selectivity on the basis of national political interests may guard against the UN becoming overstretched, it also leads to inconsistency and reinforces the security interests of states with dominant power in world politics.

International management

The fluctuating quantity and changing quality of international peace support measures have put international management mechanisms under great strain. The main organization involved, because it has unrivalled legitimacy, has been the UN. Management responsibility lies with the Secretary-General for supervising the implementation of Security Council mandates. He is assisted by an Executive Committee for Peace and Security, which represents three key UN departments: the Department of Political Affairs, Department of Peace-Keeping Operations and the OCHA. The Committee aims to ensure that officials are following coherent policies. Ultimately, however, the UN's management abilities depend on what the member states, especially the Security Council members, permit and what they are willing to fund. They can undermine the management of peace support measures by failing to provide the means to accomplish tasks and by circumventing UN authority.

The reluctance of states to provide the necessary back-up to Security Council mandates has contributed to damaging the UN's credibility as a management mechanism and paved the way for peace support measures to be farmed out to other bodies. Decentralization of responsibilities has been an important trend favoured by UN Secretary-General, Kofi Annan. Regional bodies or coalitions are encouraged to engage in crisis management under Chapter VIII of the UN Charter, provided it is done in a way that is compatible with the Charter's spirit. Given that the UN is itself under-resourced it can make practical sense to delegate responsibility to groups of states willing and able to undertake peace support missions, much as New Zealand and Australia took on the burden of unarmed peacekeeping in Bougainville in 1998 and Australia led the protection force in East Timor in 1999 (Fawcett, 2003).

Various options exist for Europe. One of the issues on which all NATO partners can readily agree is peace support operations. This is relatively uncontroversial and places limited demands on the neglected military capabilities of the new members from East–Central Europe. Consequently NATO has devoted attention to planning, joint training, the development of common approaches, and initially commanded military operations in Southeast Europe. However, in the Kosovo crisis, NATO states side-stepped the UN, damaged relations with Russia and betrayed internal disunity – over negotiations with Yugoslavia, over the aerial bombing strategy and over command and control issues (Ali, 2000, pp. 356–7). NATO was subsequently bypassed by the United States in the Afghanistan campaign and, as noted above, the EU pushed further towards developing its own military capability with plans to create a force for sending into crisis zones. It took over from NATO in Bosnia and Herzegovina and in Kosovo. The OSCE has provided negotiators and ceasefire observers in the Caucasus region of the former Soviet Union, such as Nagorno-Karabakh. It has the great advantage over the other European organizations of being a pan-European body, including Russia, in which all members are equal partners. However, it has a small bureaucracy and no muscle to back up its decisions.

Outside Europe, severe limitations and the lack of managerial expertise and military capacity mean that few regional organizations are adequately equipped to be partners. In 2004 Asian states were only just debating the idea of a joint peacekeeping training centre. In Africa, the Economic Community of West African States (ECOWAS) had already authorized a stand-by peacekeeping force of 6500 for rapid deployment in West Africa. The African Union had provided peacekeepers to Burundi in 2002, established a Peace and Security Council, and in 2004 was preparing to send monitors to Darfur in the Sudan. External powers, notably the United Kingdom, France and the United States were supporting these African capabilities, in part to avoid committing their own ground troops. In effect, delegation of responsibility is not a panacea for global security, and it is worth noting that coalitions of the willing have not necessarily been any more effective than the UN.

More attention needs to be given to managing the relationship between the UN and the regional organization concerned. If the UN delegates authority, it loses control over an operation or coordination becomes highly problematic. A dual-management system was made for the UN Protection Force in Bosnia, but produced debilitating controversies between the UN and NATO over the use of air support to ground troops. In Kosovo, the four pillar structure of the UN Mission in Kosovo (UNMIK), in which NATO, the OSCE, the EU and UN pursued their comparative advantages, was poorly coordinated. Finally, unless UN management is strengthened, particularly in managing relations with regional and coalition groups, peace support measures will be little more than part of the control mechanism exercised by the rich and powerful states over the poorer states (Pugh, 2003). The richer states already provide the best equipment and soldiers who are generally prepared and trained. A peacekeeping apartheid can occur if regions are only entitled to the level of peacekeeping their organisations can provide (Goulding, 2002, p. 218).

Peacekeeping and contemporary world politics

Peace support measures do not address the root causes of social, economic and political problems which are embedded in the state-oriented and capitalist-dominated structure of the international system. Peace support measures merely deal with the manifestations of problems and mark the extent to which international cooperation has failed to provide security for large parts of the world. States and intergovernmental organizations like the UN can even become part of the problem because of their lack of accountability to recipients of intervention and the lack of attention they give to achieving lasting political solutions to disputes.

To many theorists, the end of the Cold War and the 'war on terror' has made little difference to the way the international system works. The deployment of multinational forces depends upon a coincidence of interests among the rich and powerful states. Liberal humanitarianism and counter-terrorism have become part of the packaging in which interventions are wrapped (Chomsky, 1999; Pugh, 2004). Invasions such as the removal of the Taliban government from Afghanistan and the Ba'athist government from Iraq are military responses to problems that do not address root causes, including the role of powerful states (and the international organizations that reflect their influence) in pursuing policies and maintaining structures that foster social unrest.

At the same time, the issue of peace support reflects a major concern of contemporary world politics: the fact that people are often abused by state elites and that humanitarian needs are a global concern. The concepts of peacekeeping, forceful intervention and humanitarian aid are having to adapt to this situation and to the fact that states are inadequate to deal with many international security issues. The UN's operations have been a relative success in some instances (Central America and Cambodia), and a relative failure in others (Somalia, Southeast Europe) largely because peacekeeping could not easily be adapted to internal conflicts and especially to the protection of populations at risk. Finally, what is the answer to the question: who benefits from peace support measures? Many communities have benefited in the short term from protection, relief assistance and a transfer of resources from rich to poor. There is little doubt that shattered communities are assisted, but they may pay a price for that assistance in their weakened voice in global politics. The imperfections of global security mean that peace support measures underpin the dependency of poorer parts of the world on decisions made in the richer parts of the world. In so far as the rich and powerful states and organizations of the world control the major decisions affecting peace support operations and humanitarian assistance, these measures can also be seen as mechanisms for attempting, not always successfully, to police disorderly parts of the world to the benefit of the existing hierarchy.

Guide to further reading

Useful starting points are works by Bellamy and Williams (2004), Bellamy, Williams and Griffin (2004), Ramsbotham and Woodhouse (1996, 2000) and Vaux (2001). *International Peacekeeping* (London: Cass) and the *Journal of Humanitarian Assistance* on-line at www.jha.ac carry relevant articles. The following websites should also be consulted: UN at www.un.org; UN Foundation at www.unfoundation.org; and OCHA, http://www.reliefweb.org.

Chapter 8

Nationalism and Ethnic Conflict

STEPHEN RYAN

Ever since the start of the age of nationalism at the end of the eighteenth century, there have been tensions between the concepts of the *state* and the *nation*. Where the political borders of the state and the cultural boundaries of the nation do not coincide, as is the case with the vast majority of so-called *nation-states*, friction develops between the principles of territorial integrity and national self-determination. For 200 years these competing claims have introduced a basic fault line into world politics and there is every indication that the consequences of this tension will continue to bedevil world society. Thus the 'new world order' and the 'new Europe' are still confronting this old problem for the international community.

However, the significance attached to this matter has varied considerably. When the discipline of International Relations emerged in 1919, 'national, religious and linguistic' minorities were considered to be of major importance. The Versailles settlement had identified their status as a key issue for post-war reconstruction. Two approaches were forced on the defeated German, Austrian and Russian empires. First, it was proposed that the principle of national self-determination should be applied in a systematic manner in Central and Eastern Europe (CEE). Second, where national, linguistic or religious minorities remained, the newly created states were legally bound, under League of Nations' supervision, to protect individuals who belonged to them. In the inter-war period, therefore, interest in what we now call 'ethnic conflict' was high on the agenda of international relations (Claude, 1955).

This was not the case after 1945. In Western Europe, recovering from a world war that some blamed on nationalism, the ideology could be condemned as dangerous and reactionary. This was not the view in colonized states, many of which were ruled by Western powers. Here nationalism was still seen as a progressive force capable of mobilizing peoples to resist imperialism. In retrospect, though, leaders only supported the principle of self-determination until independence, thereafter they tended to regard claims for self-determination from groups in their own sovereign state as illegitimate. But in 1945, Western voices tended to dominate the study of world politics even more than they do today. In the developed world, the major global conflict formation was based around two ideologies that did not attribute high significance to ethnic and national groups. Indeed, between 1945 and the late 1970s, in a world dominated by the conflict between capitalist individualism and Marxist class analysis, there were only a handful of studies that examined ethnic conflict in international relations, and one can look in vain in the textbooks of the period for any reference to ethnic issues.

Although specific ethnic conflicts did receive attention between 1945 and 1989, a distinct analytical category called 'ethnic conflict' comes into its own only after the end of the Cold War. The 1990s witnessed a phenomenal growth of interest in this form of conflict, provoked by the break-ups of Yugoslavia and the USSR, though Harff and Gurr show that the 'explosion' of ethnopolitical conflicts, usually attributed to the end of the Cold War, was, in fact, 'a continuation of a trend that began as early as the 1960s' (Harff and Gurr, 2004, p. 17). As ethnic conflicts increased, traditional inter-state conflicts appeared to be in decline. Indeed, according to Wallensteen and Sollenberg (1999) of the 108 armed conflicts from 1989 to 1998, only seven were inter-state wars.

However, it might now be the case that we are moving to a period where the emphasis on ethnic conflict in international politics might start to decline, even if it will never again experience the outright neglect of the Cold War era. In part this is because after 9/11 other issues have emerged to push ethnic conflict lower down the agenda. However, it also appears that the incidence of such conflicts has declined since its peak in 1989–91. This is certainly the authoritative conclusion of the Minorities at Risk project that has identified a worldwide 'short peace' and a 'global recession' of serious ethnopolitical conflicts after 1992, which is a reversal of a forty-year trend. Evidence suggests that, of the 59 armed ethnic conflicts under way in 1998, de-escalating conflicts outnumbered escalating ones by 23 to 7. The number of new ethnopolitical protest campaigns is declining and 16 secessionist wars were settled and 11 checked between 1991 and 1999 (Gurr, 2000, pp. 276–7). By 1997 the number of refugees from internal conflicts that were being repatriated substantially exceeded the outflow of new refugees (Gurr, 2000, p. 35–6).

Before we can go any further, however, we need to define what we mean by the concepts 'ethnic' and 'nation'. Smith (1991) makes an important distinction between 'ethnicity' and 'nationalism'. The former is a way of thinking about the world that is evident throughout recorded history. It is based on the attachment we feel for people who share the same culture as us, though Smith claims that there is more to an 'ethnie' than a group's awareness of cultural difference. It also needs a myth of common descent, a shared history, a sense of solidarity and an association with a specific territory.

Nationalism, on the other hand, is a modern idea and it turns ethnic difference into a major political principle. Nationalism 'is a very distinctive species of patriotism, and one which becomes pervasive and dominant only under certain social conditions, which in fact prevail in the modern world, and nowhere else' (Gellner, 1983, p. 138). According to Smith (1991) the core doctrine of nationalism is based on the following set of assumptions: the world is divided into nations; the nation is the source of all political and social power and loyalty to the nation over-rides all other allegiances; human beings must identify with a nation if they want to be free and realize themselves; and nations must be free and secure if peace and justice are to prevail in the world.

The relationship between ethnicity and nationalism is, however, complex, especially since many of us seem to carry multiple identities. Research suggests that the majority in Scotland see themselves as both Scottish and British, that over three-quarters of Catalans identify with both Spain and Catalonia, and about half of the people in Brittany feel themselves to be both Breton and French. Both 'identity' and 'culture' are complicated concepts, and we should be careful to avoid oversimplifications when we use them.

There is another reason to be cautious about the use of the term 'ethnic conflict', because it may promote mistaken preconceptions. It seems to imply that the main causes of such conflict are internal to that society and that it arises out of the inability of two or more cultural groups to live together. External factors, such as colonial practice, and structural factors, like bad governance or social injustice, may therefore be ignored or undervalued.

Many Bosnian Muslims, for example, resented the way that their conflict was characterized as 'ethnic'. They argued that the 'Muslim' side contained Catholic Croats and Orthodox Serbs and that it would have been more accurate to describe the war as a multi-ethnic society under attack from the forces working for a Greater Serbia. Shaw argues that to describe the Bosnian conflict as 'ethnic means an implicit acceptance of the ethno-nationalist description of events'. However, this merely assumes what has to be explained, which is the 'disintegration of a largely multiethnic and in some sense pluralist society into ethnic fragments' (Shaw, 1994, pp. 102–3).

Some African writers also argue that the label 'ethnic' oversimplifies and misdirects. Khiddu-Makubuya (1994), for example, while not denying that violence in Uganda has an ethnic aspect, argues that there are other factors that have to be taken into account. These include the colonial legacy, religion, different levels of development, poor leadership, militarism and foreign interests and the external debt burden. The Rwandan case, in particular, raises issues of misrepresented conflict. It is clear that many policy-makers in the United States were willing to label this an 'ethnic' or 'tribal' conflict rather than a genocide, and this could have undermined attempts to mobilize international action (Power, 2003)

Because of the problems associated with the label 'ethnic conflict' it is important to stress that the term is used here only to refer to the form a conflict takes. It does not say anything about the origins of a particular conflict, which will be the result of a complex interplay of factors. The term really tells us very little about the causes of inter-communal violence. To understand these we have to look at factors such as political inclusion and exclusion, social injustice, insecurity and respect for cultural difference. In explaining why some situations give rise to serious violence but others do not we also have to be sensitive to what Stavenhagen (1996), in an attempt to downplay the 'ancient tribal hatreds' idea, has termed 'triggering mechanisms of conflict emergence'. These will vary from case to case but might include the break-up of states, the unwillingness of a dominant group to share power, and intra-elite rivalry.

Ethnicity as an issue

Although ethnic tensions are found throughout world politics, their impact will vary in scope, urgency, intensity and visibility. One reason for this is that the context within which such conflicts are played out varies from region to region. In the developed West, serious inter-ethnic violence has been rare since 1945, confined mainly to Northern Ireland and the Basque region of Spain, although there have been problems elsewhere (Corsica, South Tyrol, Brittany, Quebec) and there is the ongoing problem of racism in all Western societies. Nonetheless, the success of states in the West in responding to the 'ethnic challenge' is significant and could be related to a number of factors, including wealth, the presence of democratic cultures, a willingness to decentralize power, the creation of a stable and peaceful regional environment and the existence of strong states prior to the age of nationalism. Other regions have not been as fortunate. Gurr (2000, p. 8), in the most significant empirical analysis of global minorities, reveals that at the turn of the century there were 275 ethnic or communal groups included in his Minorities at Risk study because they were 'disadvantaged by comparison with other groups in their society'. These make up 17.7 per cent of the world's population. In Sub Saharan Africa the percentage of the population at risk is as high as 35.7 per cent, though this is an improvement on the 42.3 per cent at risk in the 1980s (Gurr, 2000, p. 12).

One indication of the contemporary significance of ethnic conflict is the way that international organizations have become involved with this issue. Many of the recent major international military deployments have been to situations of protracted inter-communal violence: most notably Bosnia, East Timor, Kosovo, Liberia, Sierra Leone and the Democratic Republic of Congo. Other, more traditional, peacekeeping operations are still deployed in ethnic conflicts in Cyprus and Lebanon. The UN has also established Ad Hoc War Crimes Tribunals to investigate and punish those responsible for breaches of the laws of war and the Genocide Convention in the former Yugoslavia and Rwanda. In Europe, the OSCE has made several declarations about the rights of national minorities and also created a

High Commissioner on National Minorities in 1993 to provide early warning and early action in regard to tensions involving national minority issues. It has also sent monitors to various ethnic trouble spots, including Kosovo, the Baltic states, Chechnya, the Ukraine, Georgia and Slovakia.

With the creation of IFOR in Bosnia and KFOR in Kosovo, NATO has also become deeply involved in ethnic conflicts. It has also expanded its area of responsibility to include Afghanistan, something that would have been inconceivable a decade ago. The extent of the international involvement in rebuilding societies decimated by ethnic conflict can be seen in Kosovo. Here several major international organizations are now working under the umbrella of UNMIK in an attempt to rebuild the region and promote better inter-communal relations there. There are four pillars, all under the general responsibility of the UN Secretary-General's Special Representative. Pillars one and two are led by the UN directly and cover Police and Justice and Civil Administration (www.unmikonline.org). Pillar three is led by the OSCE, and covers democratization and institution building. To this end it has primary responsibility for election management, human rights promotion and monitoring, and for supporting democracy. It has set up a number of bodies to train and support individuals who might require human rights education, including the Kosovo Judicial Institute, the Criminal Defence Resource Centre, and the Kosovo Police Service School. It is also trying to strengthen civil society through the creation of Community Centres and through support for NGOs and an independent media (www.osce.org/kosovo). The fourth pillar, Economic Reconstruction and Development, is led by the European Union (www.euinkosovo.org). It has held donors conferences, helped create a number of financial institutions and systems and is acting as a mentor to key ministries in its area of work. In fact the euro is the legal currency in Kosovo.

International mechanisms of response to ethnic conflicts continue. The decision of the EU summit in December 1999 to establish a European rapid reaction force for humanitarian and peace purposes indicates that there is an expectation that other interventions may be ordered in the future. Nor is this sort of work confined to Europe. In 2002 the African Union established a Peace and Security Council, which is meant to strengthen this organization's capacity for conflict prevention, peacebuilding and peace-making activities. It has also established a Continental Early Warning System linked to sub-regional organizations and hopes to create an African Standby Force for peacekeeping and preventive deployments.

General problems of nationalism and ethnic conflict

Although the Treaty of Westphalia (1648) is regarded as the starting point of the sovereign state system it is easy to forget how, about 150 years later, the ideology of nationalism introduced an important qualification. Thereafter, it was not enough for international politics to be based around sovereign states. These sovereign states, nationalists believed, had to be nation-states if they were to be truly legitimate. Yet as Gurr (1993) points out, although there are only about 180 states in the world, there are between 3000 and 5000 'nations' and 575 'potential' nation-states. The world political system, therefore, retains a high potential for ethno-nationalist conflict.

These conflicts impact on world politics in a number of ways. First, there is the problem of how to respond to secessionist movements. The inter-state system, fearing 'Balkanization', has been reluctant to accept such claims when they are resisted by the states concerned. This is one reason why so many secessionist attempts have ended in failure, including those in Katanga, Biafra, Punjab, the Tamil areas of Sri Lanka and the Southern Sudan. Indeed, between 1945 and the end of the Cold War, Bangladesh was the only state to obtain general recognition after Indian assistance allowed it to break away from Pakistan in 1971. Despite the international recognition of some of the former Yugoslav republics against the wishes of the government of Yugoslavia there are still no signs that the general opposition to secession has weakened since the end of the Cold War. There has been a reluctance, despite human rights concerns, to support independence claims from the Kurdish areas of Turkey or Iraq, Chechnya and Kosovo. Of course this bias against secession does not mean that individual states may not attempt to aid particular secessionist movements, either because of an affective link or because they wish to obtain a strategic advantage.

Sometimes governments themselves are motivated by irredentist claims, where one state wants to reclaim fellow nationals living in neighbouring states. Most of the serious irredentist movements during the Cold War were based in the Third World, but the rapid rise of nationalism in the former USSR and Eastern Europe provoked its increase in parts of the post-communist world (Ambrosio, 2001). There has been a bloody war between Armenia and Azerbaijan over possession of Nagorno-Karabakh and attempts by Serbia and Croatia to dismember Bosnia. Dissatisfaction with existing political boundaries may give rise to irredentism in Russia (over 20 million Russians live outside of Russia in the 'near abroad'), Hungary (about 20 per cent of Magyars live outside Hungary in Vojvodina, Ukraine, Transylvania and Slovakia) and parts of the former Yugoslavia. Will the Dayton Agreement be respected or will the shadow of Greater Serbia re-emerge to haunt the Balkans? In the same region, Macedonia is threatened by possible irredentist claims from Albania, Serbia, Bulgaria and Greece.

Ethnic conflicts can cause major human rights abuses including genocide (East Timor, Rwanda, Burundi, Sudan and Bosnia), forced assimilation (Tibet, Iraqi Kurdistan until the Gulf War, the Chittagong Hill Tribes of Bangladesh) and a wide variety of other actions that provoke international concern. Many serious ethnic conflicts also create major refugee problems and what are now termed 'complex humanitarian emergencies'. One interesting development here is the growing awareness of the way ethnic conflicts impact on certain groups. The past decade has seen the growth of research into the impact of wars on both women (Kumar, 2001) and on children (Machel, 2001) .

Given the significance of all these issues it is not surprising that Rupesinghe (1990) has noted the 'disappearing boundaries' between internal and international conflict. A collection of papers by Lake and Rothchild develops this theme by examining two ways that such conflicts can spill over into the wider international system. The first of these is diffusion, when 'a conflict in one state increases the probability of conflict in a second' (Lake and Rothchild, 1999, p. 23). In Central Africa, for example, the violence in Rwanda spilled over into neighbouring Burundi and the Democratic Republic of the Congo. The second way ethnic conflict can spread is through escalation, when ethnic violence sucks in foreign belligerents. So Israel and Syria have both intervened in Lebanon and Turkish interventions in Cyprus have complicated inter-communal relations there. The violence in the Democratic Republic of the Congo in 1999 dragged in seven surrounding states to support one or other of the opposing parties.

Putting ethno-nationalist conflict on the international agenda

For reasons already discussed, ethnic and nationalist conflicts have become increasingly visible in world politics. But we have also noted that the extent of the internationalization varies considerably from conflict to conflict. We should remember that ethnic groups, because they are not states, do not have an automatic right of access to international bodies like the UN, and can, therefore, find it difficult to bring their grievances before world opinion. This has been a major problem for many indigenous peoples and for the Roma. It has also been an handicap for the Kurds, who are a minority in four states in the Middle East (Turkey, Iraq, Iran and Syria) but lack the support of states willing to champion their cause at the international level.

Several factors are likely to determine the location of the ethnic question on the agenda of world politics. First, affective links – where one or more of the parties has cultural links to groups in other states – can contribute to the international significance of a particular case of ethnic conflict. In the former Yugoslavia, outside involvement was linked to such sympathies. Thus many Muslim states sided with the Bosnia Muslims, the Russians tended to support the Orthodox Serbs and some of the Catholic states of Europe identified most with the Croat cause. The Cyprus conflict offers another case of affective intervention, with Turkey supporting the Turkish Cypriots and Greece supporting the Greek Cypriots. The Tamils of India have played an important role in supporting the minority Tamil population in Sri Lanka. The role of diasporas is also of interest here. The literature on the influence of 'hyphenated Americans' on US foreign policy, for example, shows how Jewish-Americans, Irish-Americans and Greek-Americans have had an important role to play in influencing US attitudes to Israel, Ireland and Cyprus, respectively.

Second, the geo-strategic and economic interests of states, and especially the permanent members of the UN Security Council, can affect the salience of ethnic conflicts. After the Indonesian invasion of East Timor in 1975, powerful Western states refused to put pressure on Jakarta because it was both an important market and an ally against communism in a strategic part of the world. A strong response did not come until the Cold War was over. For similar reasons many states are reluctant to put pressure on China over its policies towards Tibet and on Russia for its military actions in Chechnya. Both Moscow and Beijing have made clear statements defending the principles of sovereignty and non-intervention in their internal affairs and such attitudes from two permanent members of the Security Council could constrain the UN from developing a stronger interventionist role in world politics. The lack of unanimity on the Security Council was a major reason why the UN was sidelined in the case of Kosovo in 1999, where NATO conducted the military action in the name of humanitarianism.

Third, the geographical location of a conflict is also an important factor. The high profile given to the conflict in the former Yugoslavia is in part owing to the fact that this occurred on the margins of Western Europe. The security and refugee problems this raised had to be taken seriously by the EU. Premdas (1991) points out how a location close to a major metropolitan centre will make it more likely that the global media will pay attention to a conflict. On the other hand, 'orphaned conflicts' such as those in Fiji, Irian Jaya and Abkhazia, are likely to pass unnoticed by those not directly affected.

Fourth, some NGOs can bring specific cases to the attention of the international community. Aid and charity bodies, human rights' organizations and church groups may investigate and publicize abuses during intercommunal conflict. Some of these bodies may also have consultative status at the UN, where they can take up the cause of communal groups that may not otherwise have an international voice.

How has unipolarity and globalization affected the form in which the issue is presented?

We have already noted that there may be a declining interest in ethnic conflict in the study of international politics. One reason for this is the new security agenda post-9/11. The 'Bush Doctrine', as set out in the National Security Strategy of the United States of America of September 2002 (www.whitehouse.gov/nsc/nss.html) identifies the key threats to international security as the spread of WMD, rogue states and international terrorism.

The emphasis here is on inter-state relations. Even international terrorist networks, which on the surface seem to be non-state actors, only become a real threat, the document argues, when states provide them with 'sponsorship, support and sanctuary'. The language is one of rogue states and terrorist clients. Through pre-emption, free trade, democratization, economic assistance and military might the United States will be able to assist in the defusion of regional conflicts and the strenthening of allies

There is nothing in the document that would give heart to those scholars who have been calling for a greater awarness of ethnic groups and other non-state actors in the analysis of world politics. In one sense this is understandable. Ethnic conflicts in distant states do not appear to be a serious threat to US security. Most such conflicts, it appears, can be safely ignored. As Lake and Rothchild point out, the 'international diffusion of ethnic conflict is a compelling political problem that must be recognised and understood, but it is limited in nature' (Lake and Rothchild, 1999, p. 341). Hoffmann reflects this by noting the 'collective non-intervention' that arises when such conflicts appear to be 'safely forgettable' (Hoffmann, 1998, p. 217). There is a danger here because, as Rieff has pointed out, 'America may not be obsessed with the rest of the world, but the rest of the world is obsessed by America' (Rieff, 2002, p. 17). It is also interesting to note where the Bush doctrine has led us. In both Iraq and Afghanistan the international community is now faced with the problem of 'post-war' reconstruction where cultural differences have complicated the peace process and have challenged simplistic ideas about 'democratization'. In Iraq there is the prospect of serious violence between the Kurds, the Sunni and the Shia, which could suck in Turkey and Iran. In Afghanistan there are serious tensions between *inter alia* the Pushtuns, Tajiks, Hazaras and Uzbeks.

For more than a century there has been the 'liberal expectancy' that ethnicity would not survive for very long. For a generation after the Second World War, the most obvious example of this expectancy was the nation-building idea. Today, the prophets of ethnic decline tend to emphasis globalization. From this perspective the blinkered parochialism of ethnic identity seems an unsatisfactory and inappropriate response to a world of MNCs, satellite television and the internet. In such a context ethnicity can seem outdated, a reactionary and negative force in the contemporary world.

There are several possible responses to these claims. The first is to ask what are the alternatives to nationalism as the basis for group identity in world society? No convincing candidates present themselves at present, with the possible exception of strong religious attachment (see Chapter 9). Of course individuals do identify themselves in other ways – gender, class, region, city, even the human race – but none of these appears to exert as strong a pull as the nation (Smith, 1995).

Another response to the claim that globalization will erode ethnic attachment is to point out that its effects are not spread equally throughout world society. There will be winners and losers. Where the divisions between those who do and do not benefit coincide with cultural differences, ethnic particularism may be reinforced and mobilization on the basis of nationalism may appear to be a rational option in the contest for resources. A final response is that globalization is not a neutral process. It is, in fact, closely linked to a specific worldview that is 'Western'. It involves the diffusion of a certain culture (Hollywood, Disneyland, McDonald's, MTV), a certain form of economic organization (capitalist) and a European conception of human rights (individualistic rather than collective). Such globalization can threaten groups whose culture does not fit in with dominant values and may, in fact, promote rather than reduce ethnic tensions.

Belgium presents an interesting case study of the contradictory nature of globalization. Here is a state which is at the heart of the integration process in the EU. Indeed, it is difficult to think of any other society where the impact of globalization has been so significant. Yet Belgium is a state which has split into two separate linguistic communities (three, if we include the small German-speaking community) and where Brussels – the 'capital' of the European Union – sits uneasily across the communal divide.

Increased globalization is undermining the effectiveness and legitimacy of the nation-state, but one of the major consequences of this might be an increasing identification with an ethnic community which may lead, though this is not inevitable, to the development of even more groups seeking national self-determination. To complicate matters even further, the internationalization of ethnic conflict is part of the process of globalization. This is one reason why Kaldor (1999) has referred to the 'new wars' of the late twentieth century. She argues that we cannot understand the nature of contemporary ethnic violence outside the context of globalization. In particular, she points to factors such as the role of international media, the presence of intergovernmental agencies and NGOs, the involvement of co-nationals living overseas, and the globalized war economy where local groups may be linked to international black markets in arms and drugs and may obtain funding through the expropriation of international humanitarian assistance.

Managing ethnic conflict

Much of the analysis of the impact of ethnic conflict on world politics has centred on the issue of intervention in complex emergencies. This is understandable given that between 80 and 90 per cent of the victims of inter-ethnic conflicts are non-combatants and that civil war contributes to a wide range of problems that include hunger and displacement. Furthermore, bitter ethnic violence can result in the collapse of the state and the paralysis of effective government. In such circumstances there is a greater need for outside help. We should not forget, however, that humanitarian intervention is a short-term, technical response that deals only with the symptoms of ethnic conflict. Indeed, the need for such action is a sign that international community has failed to respond adequately to the causes of such conflict (see also Chapter 7).

Gurr (2000, p. 56) suggests that one reason for the decline in ethnic conflicts in recent years is 'due mainly to an increase in civil and international capacities for managing ethnopolitical conflict'. A number of mechanisms have been developed to deal with underlying causes. First there have been attempts to develop new international legal norms, including the legal protection of individuals belonging to ethnic minorities. In December 1992, for example, the UN General Assembly finally adopted a Declaration on the Rights of Persons Belonging to National or Ethnic, Religious and Linguistic Minorities (UNGA Resolution 47/135). Ironically, the first draft of this Declaration was introduced by Yugoslavia in 1978. It expects states to adopt appropriate legislative and other measures to protect the existence of minorities within their territories and to encourage conditions for the promotion of their identity. It also recognizes the right of persons belonging to minorities to participate fully in decisions which affect them. Nonetheless the Declaration has several weaknesses. The most obvious one is that it is not a legally binding document: it has only moral force. Furthermore its inability to define what it means by 'minority' and the use of imprecise language such as 'appropriate measures', 'wherever possible' or 'where required' makes it easier for states to evade its proposals. It is not surprising, then, that Henrard (2004, p. 50) has noted that despite some significant progress in the area of minority rights, especially in Europe, 'in several respects the current minority rights standards and practices are deficient and disappointing'.

Another promising move to promote the legal protection of ethnic minorities concerns the 1948 Genocide Convention. This makes it illegal to undertake actions with the intent to destroy, in whole or in part, a national, ethnical, racial or religious group. The problem, however, has been implementing this Convention. Experts point out that, although there have been several examples of genocide since 1948 (see Table 8.1), the Genocide Convention was never invoked to punish those responsible. This led to a withering attack on the UN's record in this area (see, for example, Kuper, 1985, p. 10). In the mid-1990s, however, the UN Security Council established ad hoc war crimes tribunals for Yugoslavia and Rwanda. Both were mandated to investigate accusations of genocidal activity and to indict individuals who may have had a case to answer. However, both have been criticized for their low conviction rate, slow pace, lack of resources and their inaccessibility to local people. There have been serious tensions between the Ad Hoc Tribunal for Rwanda and the Rwandan government, in part

Table 8.1   *Major cases of genocide since the adoption of the 1948 Genocide Convention*

Date	State	Victims	Deaths
1943–57	USSR	Chechens, Ingushi Karachai	230 000
1944–68	USSR	Crimean Tartars, Meskhetians	57 000–175 000
1950–77	China	Tibetans	Not available
1959–75	Iraq	Kurds	Not available
1962–72	Paraguay	Ache Indians	90 000
1963–64	Rwanda	Tutsis	5000–14 000
1963	Laos	Meo Tribesmen	18 000–20 000
1965–66	Indonesia	Chinese	500 000–1 million
1965–73	Burundi	Hutus	103 000–205 000
1966	Nigeria	Ibos in North	9000–30 000
1966–84	Guatemala	Indians	30 000–63 000
1968–85	Philippines	Moros	10 000–100 000
1969–79	Equatorial Guinea	Bubi Tribe	1000–50 000
1971	Pakistan	Bengalis of Eastern Pakistan	1.25–3 million
1971–9	Uganda	Karamajong, Acholi, Lango	100 000–500 000
1975–79	Cambodia	Muslim Cham	90 000
1975–98	Indonesia	East Timorese	60 000–200 000
1978–	Burma	Muslims in border regions	Not available
1979–86	Uganda	Karamanjong, Nilotic Tribes, Bagandans	50 000–100 000
1981	Iran	Kurds, Bahais	10 000–20 000
1983–7	Sri Lanka	Tamils	2000–10 000
1992–5	Bosnia-Herzegovina	Mainly Bosnian	200 000 Muslims
1994	Rwanda	Tutsis	500 000–1 million

Source: Compiled from Harff (1992) and Kiernan (2003).

because the international court is not allowed to pass a death penalty on those found guilty of genocide.

The issue of the inconsistency that is a consequence of an ad hoc approach may be overcome by the International Criminal Court (ICC), established in 2003 at the Hague. However, although the Clinton Administration signed the Rome Statute that created this body, there was never a realistic chance that it would be ratified by Congress. In fact, the United States 'unsigned' the Statute in 2002, and actively set out to undermine the ICC by trying to persuade other states to sign bilateral agreements that would exempt American citizens from the jurisdiction of the Court when working abroad. The Court is not part of the UN system, and so its work is not subject to veto by the Security Council. The United States is not the only state not to have either signed or ratified the Rome Statute, but the opposition to the Court in Washington is, perhaps, the greatest threat to its effectiveness.

Two other proposals have concentrated on the need to amend the state-centric bias of international norms. The first concerns the right of national self-determination. The present position in international law is that there is such a right, but it is restricted in its applicability. Thus 'nations' have a right of self-determination if they are an oppressed group ruled by a colonial or racist power, but once independence is achieved the principles of sovereignty and territorial integrity become more important. So, for example, Nigeria had a right to self-determination when it was part of the British Empire, but the Ibo people in the newly independent state had no right of independence from Nigeria. The only possible exception may be where a state commits gross violations of human rights. In such circumstances, some commentators seem willing to argue that the principle of territorial integrity can be violated. However, there is no consensus on this issue.

The second suggestion is meant to reduce the need for 'external self-determination' and concerns the role of autonomy, sometimes referred to as 'internal self-determination'. This offers a middle path between the conflict-promoting options of secession and forced integration. Hannum, who has written an influential study of this idea, points out that the principle of autonomy 'recognizes the right of minority and indigenous communities to exercise meaningful internal self-determination and control over their own affairs in a manner that is not inconsistent with the ultimate sovereignty . . . of the state' (Hannum, 1990, p. 473). Sisk claims that there is 'an urgent need to discover and refine practices that contain the inherent fissiparous tendencies that can tear multiethnic states apart, that foster tolerant and beneficial cultural diversity, and that [ideally] do so within a democratic framework' (Sisk, 1996, p. 3). Evidence from places like the South Tyrol (German-speaking area of Italy) and the Åland Islands (Swedish population living in Finland) suggests that, when minorities are offered such internal self-determination, ethnic conflict declines.

Yet the concerns of states are clear. There is a fear that nations may be unhappy with the status of 'minority' and will insist on their own state. Or the willingness to make concessions to minorities might be viewed as a sign of weakness. One reason why the Russian government has taken such a tough line against Chechnya is that Moscow fears that if it grants autonomy to this part of Russia it may provoke similar demands from other regions.

Ethnic conflicts are notoriously difficult to resolve. This is due to a number of factors that include the asymmetries introduced where the conflicts are between a state and a minority group, the non-negotiable nature of identity and security needs and the difficulties of achieving a settlement through geographical separation based on recognized boundaries – which is how inter-state conflicts are often ended. Yet, despite the inherent problems in attempting ethnic conflict resolution, it may be that the lack of success may also be a consequence of the inadequacies of the methods used.

There is a vast academic literature on mediation, much of it suspicious of what is called 'traditional' or 'track-1' diplomacy. Critics claim that it is too rigid and unimaginative to be a consistently effective mechanism. In some circumstances unofficial, 'track-2' approaches, undertaken by private individuals or groups, may be more successful. Such initiatives often focus on interests rather than positions. Their informal and private nature may encourage the parties to be more relaxed and forthcoming and because they are not official initiatives they cannot confer formal legitimacy on any group, which makes it easier to move between the parties in asymmetric conflicts. The role played by private Norwegian facilitators in the Israeli–Palestinian conflict and the activities of the US-based Carter Center have raised the profile of this sort of intervention in ethnic conflict.

The work of Burton (1997) has been especially influential in the development of innovative approaches to conflict resolution. He has offered both a theory and a technique of ethnic conflict resolution. The theory calls for a paradigm shift in the way we think about the resolution and prevention of conflict away from interventions based on power towards analysis based on universal human needs. From this perspective, protracted ethnic conflicts are not really about sovereignty, which is a zero-sum issue. This emphasis is a symptom of a deeper problem, which is that one or more of the parties is not allowed to have its human needs fulfilled. Since basic human needs do not exist in a zero-sum situation – in recognizing my identity you do not have to renounce your identity – this approach to conflict resolution creates the possibility of 'win-win' outcomes. The technique which allows these insights to be introduced into a conflict is called the 'problem-solving' workshop, where academic facilitators attempt to get the parties to engage in joint analysis of the problems they face.

The existence of a growing number of multi-ethnic societies coming out of conflict has stimulated research into what Boutros-Ghali (1992) called 'post-conflict peacebuilding'. What he means, of course, is *post-violent* conflict peacebuilding. There is a mild form of post-conflict peacebuilding which concentrates on the reconstruction of war-torn societies (see Box 8.1). Here the emphasis is on economic reconstruction and foreign aid (Esman and Herring, 2001), the promotion of mutual understanding and the development of new constitutional structures which accept ethnic differences as the basis for a new society. On the other hand, there is a more radical form that concentrates on conflict transformation through grass-roots social movements and the deconstruction of conflicting identities and narrow ethnic identity.

At the other end of the conflict cycle there is also a growing interest in the prevention of ethnic conflict (Rupesinghe, 1998; Scherrer, 2003). Suggestions here include: confidence-building measures, including arms control (see Chapter 6); fact-finding; global monitoring and early warning; preventive deployment, such as the dispatch of UNPROFOR personnel to Macedonia; and the creation of demilitarized zones. The problem here is not the lack of ideas or information, but the unwillingness of states to use the available measures. So the solution has to be long-term. It will involve 'creating a climate of opinion, or ethos' within the international community in which the norm will be for states to accept UN involvement (Boutros-Ghali, 1995, para. 28).

Box 8.1 Major peacebuilding strategies for world society in the aftermath of protracted and violent ethnic conflict

- Restoration of basic services (water, power, health care, etc.) and government functions
- Assisting with return of refugees and internally displaced persons
- De-mining and mine-awareness training
- De-militarization – includes demobilization, decommissioning of weapons, reintegration of combatants into society
- Changes to administration of justice and improvements to judicial systems – includes the de-militarization and the reform and retraining of police
- Electoral reform and election monitoring
- Social and economic development
- Promoting respect for human rights through education, training and monitoring (includes protection of minorities and other social groups)
- Creating a culture of peace through education, prejudice reduction, peace museums, etc.
- Promoting reconciliation through dialogue; may involve truth commisions and/or other investigative bodies
- Creation of a free and fair media
- Capacity-building and community development to empower all sections of society

Nationalism, ethnic conflict and contemporary world politics

The fault line between the state and the nation is likely to be a basic feature of world politics for the foreseeable future since many states are never going to be able to eradicate the ethnic challenge to their legitimacy and not all nations are going to be able to obtain their own state. So Mayall has pointed out that

> First, the primacy of the national ideal amongst contemporary political principles has modified the traditional conception of an international society but has not replaced it. Second, there is no immediate prospect of transcending the national idea, either as the principle of legitimation or as the basis of political organisation for the modern state. (Mayall, 1990, p. 145)

Yet although the fact of ethnic difference and the ideology of nationalism will present a major challenge to the territorial integrity, or even the survival, of certain states, they cannot be seen as a fundamental challenge to the sovereign state system as a whole. The state is important to the nation. It is a sign of self-worth and allows a nation to have a stronger role in protecting its interests and culture. Indeed, we should note that a consequence of recent ethnic conflicts has been the creation of more not fewer sovereign states: 22 new sovereign states have been established because of the break-up of the USSR, Yugoslavia and Czechoslovakia, though none of them is really a nation-state either. In fact, it is difficult to think of any group that is more tightly wedded to territory than ethnic and national groups. So although many commentators have referred to the crisis of the nation-state, nationalists appear to be unimpressed by such claims.

However, a state-centric bias is unlikely to facilitate constructive responses to the ethnic issue, for several reasons. The anarchic nature of inter-state politics breeds a sense of insecurity which tends to make governments suspicious of minorities. Furthermore, the sovereign state system means that international responses to particular ethnic conflicts and national self-determination claims will be filtered through the self-centred interests of states. This can lead to hypocrisy and inconsistencies. Serbia, for example, supported the right of the Croatian and Bosnian Serbs to self-determination at the same time as they were denying it to the Albanian majority in Kosovo. Turkey invaded Cyprus in 1974 to uphold the right of Turkish Cypriots to self-determination, but have denied such a right to their Kurdish minority. Also, since most states feel threatened by ethnic groups they have a mutual interest in not extending them too many rights. The temptation in inter-state politics, therefore, is to support the status quo.

It is, therefore, interesting to note that all of the methods of managing the ethnic challenge mentioned in the previous section require some modification of the state-centric view of world politics. The development of legal norms will involve a more intrusive role for international organizations and will strengthen the notion that the international legitimacy of states should be made conditional on their human rights record. The idea of the international protection of minorities also challenges the norm that it is only states and individuals that are the main subjects and objects of international law. Effective conflict resolution may also involve a move away from the realist paradigm to the world society approach favoured by the 'Burton school', which recognizes the significance of non-state actors and of human needs analysis.

The complex nature of identity means that we should avoid over-simplistic analysis. Perhaps, in the short run, all we can hope is that self-determination will be informed by a desire not for separation but for autonomy within a broader, pluralist community. We are witnessing this to some extent in Western Europe, where groups like the Scots and the Catalans, inspired by the vision of a 'Europe of the regions', now seem to prefer the idea of autonomy within the EU. This phenomenon has been examined by Keating (1998), who makes the intriguing claim that the regions of the EU should be seen as new political arenas since they have become a part of European international politics yet do not want to recreate the nation-state.

One major task for the international community should be to make the less exclusive and more pluralist choice an attractive option for individuals belonging to ethnic groups. This means promoting good governance in multi-ethnic societies. Indeed, Harff and Gurr show that in the 1990s nearly 80 per cent of politically active ethnic groups were 'disadvantaged because of historical or contemporary economic discrimination' (Harff and Gurr, 2004, p. 4). As long as the sovereign state is the principal unit of organization in world politics the key determinant of the extent of ethnic conflict will be the policies adopted by individual states. There is, however, a considerable literature to guide states on good governance in multi-ethnic societies (McGarry and O'Leary, 1993; Horowitz, 2000). Perhaps the most influential contribution has been Lijphart's concept of 'consociational democracy' (see Box 8.2).

Yet this does not mean that there is no role for the international community as a whole, and some of the most important contributions that the international community can make have been explored in this chapter. Recent international interventions in ethnic conflicts and the increased interest in minority rights demonstrated by a number of international organizations seem to indicate that the promotion of good governance is also now an international responsibility, though the extent of the obligation is still debated. If this commitment is to become a serious one then it is crucial that mechanisms and institutions are developed that can enable the international community to respond more constructively and more efficiently to ethnic conflict. There is still an urgent need for a range of options between neglect and armed intervention.

Box 8.2 Principles of consociational democracy

Lijphart believes that stable, democratic government is *possible* in multi-ethnic societies, but argues that for this to happen elites should reject majoritarian principles and adopt four key consociational ideas. These are:

- *Grand coalition.*   Governments should be composed of representatives from all the major ethnic groups. Lijphart argues that this is the most important of the four principles.
- *Proportionality.*   A certain number of seats in Parliament and public office should be allocated to minority ethnic groups on the basis of their population numbers.
- *Mutual veto.*   All major ethnic groups should be able to stop or delay legislation that they believe will seriously affect their interests.
- *Segmental autonomy.*   Wherever possible power should be devolved so that those regions of a state where an ethnic minority is in fact the majority can have considerable local autonomy. This would include federal arrangements.

Source: Lijphart (1977).

Guide to further reading

The edited books by Hutchinson and Smith on ethnicity (1996) and nationalism (1994) contain good sets of readings on these topics. Ozkirimli (2000) is a fine overview of competing theories of nationalism and Mayall (1990) explores the relationships between nationalism and international society. For general studies of ethnic conflict, see Horowitz (2000), Rupesinghe (1998) and Ignatieff (1998). Taras and Ganguly (2002) and Harff and Gurr (2004) concentrate on international aspects of ethnic conflict. Miall *et al.* (1999) provide a concise and comprehensive guide to conflict resolution theory with a special emphasis on internal conflicts and there is a useful collection of essays on ethnic conflict settlement in Schneckener and Wolff (2004). Maynard (1999) is a good introduction to post-conflict peacebuilding. The Minorities at Risk web page at www.cidcm. umd.edu/inscr/mar/ will provide updates on the empirical work of Gurr and his colleagues. A comprehensive guide to websites related to ethnic conflict can be found at www.incore.ulster.ac.uk/services/cds.

Chapter 9

Religion

JEFF HAYNES

The early twenty-first century is an era of fundamental political, social and economic change at the global level. Much of the change stemmed from, or at least was galvanized by, the ending of the Cold War and the consequent development of globalization. Now a truly global economy is being consolidated and, some would argue, a 'global culture' – based on 'American values' – is slowly emerging. During the 1990s in particular there was a steady, if uneven, advance of democracy – from Latin America to Eastern and Central Europe, Asia and Africa. In addition, there are many examples of the political involvement of religious actors around the world. This development led an American commentator, George Weigel, to identify a global religious revitalization that he refers to as the 'unsecularization of the world' (quoted in Huntington, 1993, p. 26). This expression does not imply that the respiritualization of world politics is *apolitical*, but denotes, on the contrary, a new and widespread interaction between religion and politics. This chapter examines the nature and the extent of the interaction between religion and politics, assessing its significance both domestically and internationally for the twenty-first century.

The impact of religion on world politics

Many recent events support Weigel's contention that the impact of religion on politics is occurring in areas where it was long thought to have left the public domain. This trend has not been confined to one or two countries, but is a prevalent feature of contemporary world politics. In Europe, a region frequently presumed to be inexorably secularizing, civil war in the early 1990s in Bosnia-Herzegovina among Croats, Serbs and Bosnians degenerated into a *de facto* religious conflict. Most combatants identified themselves in religious and cultural terms and, rather than finding ideological allies, they consolidated religious and cultural ties with, respectively, Germany, Russia and the Arab–Muslim world. In the late 1990s, the civil war in Kosovo between ethnic Albanians and Serbs could also be defined in terms of a conflict between Muslims and Christians. In Poland, Catholic prelates achieved considerable political importance in the post-communist order. Pope John Paul II, a Pole, involved himself in political and social issues, including fierce denunciations of birth control.

His aim was to stem the tide of what he saw as a serious 'moral decline' and the rise of 'evil'. In Russia, the Orthodox Church emerged from communism as an actor of major social and political significance. Islamist radicals subjected various constituent republics, including Chechnya and Dagestan, to serious attempts at Islamicization. More generally, a rise of Islamic militancy was widely noted in various parts of the world, a development linked in many people's minds to the events of 9/11, when the Twin Towers and the Pentagon were subjected to terrorist attacks and nearly 3000 people died. In the United States, sustained attempts by Christian fundamentalists to mould and drive the political agenda have also underlined the growing socio-political significance of religion. At the same time, in Israel, the political influence of Jewish fundamentalist groups was marked by their membership of several governing coalitions in the 1990s and early 2000s.

In the developing world, religious actors with political goals appeared to be on the increase. Perhaps the most visible, encouraged by the 1978–9 Islamic revolution in Iran, was the widespread Islamic militancy in the Middle East and beyond. There was also the attempt by 'secular–socialist–nationalist' Iraq to play the Islamic 'card' in both its conflicts with the West, in 1991 and 2003. In addition, an explosion of militant Hinduism in officially secular India, focused on but not confined to the Babri Masjid mosque incident at Ayodhya in 1992, helped to transform that country's political landscape. Henceforward Hindu fundamentalists, located in the Bharatiya Janata Party (BJP), became politically important, as they helped to govern the country in several coalition governments. Following the 2004 elections, however, the BJP lost power.

In Africa, Nigeria seemed polarized between Muslim and Christian forces, and Somalia appeared to be lurching towards an Islamist government. Sudan was divided politically on religious grounds between Muslims and non-Muslims to the extent that there was renewed civil war, especially in the beleagured Darfur province. Algeria endured a dozen years of civil war from 1992, with Islamic militants fighting the government forces; more than 120 000 people were killed in the conflict. In Thailand, new Buddhist groups and parties emerged with their own political agenda, although they failed to make a sigificant impact upon the country's political scene. The list of examples can be extended, but hopefully the point is clear: in the early twenty-first century it is difficult to find any country, especially in the developing world, where religion is not somewhere near the top of the political agenda, even in states that have long experienced secular principles and practices (Haynes, 1993, 1998).

Religion and globalization

Many observers have argued that globalization and the renaissance of religion in world politics are strongly connected. McGrew suggests that globalization is the product of multiple 'linkages and interconnections between the states and societies which make up the modern world system' (McGrew, 1992, p. 23). Although global interconnections have existed for centuries, their impact in the past has been comparatively minor, amounting to little more than 'trade routes or select military and naval operations' that only affected 'certain towns, rural centres and territories' (Held, 1993, p. 38).

Religion, of course, did have political consequences in the past. For example, Christianity and Islam grew to become world religions, conveying their associated civilizations around the world via colonization, conquest and the expansion of global trade. In the sixteenth and seventeenth centuries, during a period of sustained expansion of the international system, contending religious beliefs provided the chief motor for international conflicts and the main threat to international peace and security. But the development of the global state system after the Treaty of Westphalia in 1648 (which ended the religious wars in Europe between Catholics and Protestants) has largely reflected the history of clashing nationalisms, with each national group desiring its own state.

Before the rise of the European empires, Muslims had spearheaded religious globalization. For hundreds of years, prior to the late fifteenth century, Islam expanded from its Arabian heartland in all directions. The consequence was that vast territories in Africa and Asia and smaller areas of Europe (primarily parts of the Balkans and much of the Iberian peninsular) were Islamicized. The Moors' capital, for example, was Cordoba in Andalusia in southern Spain. But the demise of the Islamic European empire in the late fifteenth century was swift, a consequence of the rise of centralized European states with superior firepower and organizational skills.

Contemporaneous with the end of Islam as a cultural force in Western Europe was the beginning of the expansion of European influence across the globe. The search for gold in the Americas led in the early sixteenth century to the formation of European colonies there, and colonies were also established in the Caribbean and Asia. Between the fifteenth and nineteenth centuries, the spread of Christianity to Africa, accompanied by the extraction of millions of slaves, and to the Middle East and the Americas added to the emerging web of global interactions. Despite this global expansion of Christian Europeans, the social and cultural systems defined by Islam survived across Eurasia and the worldwide influence of Islamic beliefs persisted.

In the early years of the twentieth century, communism and fascism appeared as universal, secular ideologies with the propensity to attract converts across state boundaries. There was a process of global ideological differentiation, deepening after the Second World War, when the defeat of fascism led to the emergence of liberal democracy as the dominant but not yet global ideology. During the Cold War, one set of ideas – communism – was pitched against another – liberal democracy and its economic counterpart, capitalism – in a struggle for dominance that culminated in the defeat of Soviet-style communism at the end of the 1980s.

It is widely believed that the fall of the Soviet empire was due, in part, to the processes of globalization which ended the country's self-imposed isolation from the non-communist world. These processes have been immeasurably facilitated by easy, widely available methods of interpersonal communications, such as the telegraph, telephone, the internet, email, and fax. As Beyer puts it, we live in 'a globalizing social reality, one in which previously effective barriers to communication no longer exist' (Beyer, 1994, p. 1). The development of *transnational* in conjunction with *national* religious communities has been greatly enhanced by the explosion of inter-personal and inter-group communications. Ease of communications has helped these communities to spread their message and to link up with like-minded groups. Links between religious and political actors both *in* and *between* countries have multiplied, as the contributors to Rudolph and Piscatori (1997) make clear. Primarily concerned with investigating the political consequences of cross-border interactions between Muslims and Christians, one of the book's findings is that transnational networks of religious groups feed off each other's ideas, often aid each other with funds, and form geographically extensive organizational bodies whose main priority is the well-being and advancement of the transnational religious community. This issue gained added significance following 9/11, as we shall see below.

Religion in contemporary world politics

Developments since the end of the Cold War are said to have generated a 'new agenda' for international relations. This agenda includes the environment, illegal drugs, AIDS, terrorism, migration, refugees, human rights, new conceptions of security, democratization and religious actors with political goals. Most of these issues are linked to cultural behaviour but they are also associated with religion as an aspect of cultural behaviour.

It is appropriate to make it clear at the outset what is meant by 'religion' (Box 9.1). It can be understood in two analytically distinct, yet related, ways. First, in a spiritual sense, religion provides a model of social and individual behaviour that helps believers to live their everyday lives. Religion is concerned with *transcendence* – that is, it relates to a supernatural reality; with *sacredness* – that is, to a system of language and practice that expresses the world in terms of what is deemed holy; and with *ultimacy* – that is, it relates people to the ultimate conditions of existence. In a second, more material, sense – the focus of this chapter – religion can defined by religious groups and movements. Several distinct kinds of religious groups and movements can be noted.

First, there are socially and politically conservative organizations like the

---

Box 9.1 Religion and politics

Religion is an important source of basic values. But it can have a powerful impact upon politics within a state or region, especially when it is linked to ethnicity and culture. Religious belief often reinforces both ethnic consciousness and inter-ethnic conflict, especially in the Third World (but not only there, think of Northern Ireland or the former Yugoslavia). Religious 'fundament-alism', denotes a 'set of strategies, by which beleaguered believers attempt to preserve their distinctive identity as a people or group' in response to a real or imagined attack from those who apparently threaten to draw them into a 'syncretistic, areligious, or irreligious cultural milieu' (Marty and Scott Appleby, 1993, p. 3). Sometimes such defensiveness may develop into a political offensive which seeks to alter the prevailing social, political and, on occasions, economic realities of state–society relations.

Roman Catholic body, Opus Dei, which have a global reach. Second, there are socially conservative religious groups, often regionally or nationally focused which, unlike Opus Dei, work to alter fundamentally the political scene, sometimes by resorting to terrorist tactics. Examples include India's Hindu chauvinist groups; American Christian fundamentalist organizations whose members have fire-bombed hundreds of abortion clinics and even murdered doctors who have performed abortions; and numerous Muslim bodies, including the Front Islamique de Salut (FIS of Algeria), the Islamic Party of Kenya, Balukta (Tanzania), Hamas (Palestine) and the Partai Islam (Malaysia).

A third category of religious groups is exemplified by the tens of thousands of Christian Base Communities (CBCs) that have formed in Latin America, the Caribbean (Haiti) and East Asia (the Philippines) with a combined membership of many millions of people. CBCs have a variety of religious and non-religious aims, but always with a strong developmental focus; they are almost entirely concerned with domestic issues and they do not have, or aspire to have, a global perspective. Finally, there are religious groups, such as the Association of Indonesian Muslim Intellectuals (Ikatan Cendekiawan Muslim se-Indonesia, known as ICMI), whose primary function, until the democratic changes in the country in the late 1990s, was to support the status quo by reinforcing the country's authoritarian political structure.

These examples demonstrate that religious groups have very diverse political and social aims in the contemporary world. The groups reflect not only their members' religious traditions and beliefs but also the complexities of their country's political culture(s) and system and, in some cases, external influences on the state. For example, Hamas has confronted Israel, in part because the political culture of the Palestinians in the Occupied Territories is rooted in decades of conflict with Israeli Jews.

To what extent are religious belief systems associated with political ideologies? The existence of a connection is not difficult to demonstrate. Close links exist, for example, between religion and nationalism in India, between Jewish and Christian fundamentalism and political conservatism, in Israel and the United States respectively, and between some of Thailand's new Buddhist movements and demands for a more just social, political and economic order. Religious groups now regularly express views on what constitute appropriate political and economic systems, on the nature of a country's inter-state relations, and on what social mores, customs and manners should prevail. Religio-political groups – religious groups with political aims – also endeavour sometimes to achieve their objectives by extending their field of operations from the domestic to the international field of action. An important example in this regard is Al Qaeda, a militant Islamic network with global interests and goals, which will be discussed in detail below (pp. 165–9).

Why has religion appeared as an issue on the world agenda?

The Gulf War of 1990–1 was the defining moment in the debate about the post-Cold War global order when Islamic militancy (or, pejoratively, 'fundamentalism') became widely perceived as perhaps the most significant new threat to Western security. Before the Gulf War, the US President, George Bush Snr, spoke confidently about the birth of a 'new world order' emerging from the collapse of the Soviet Union and its Communist empire. But the Gulf War dashed such optimism. Thereafter, it seemed that the West's aim was to build and maintain global stability rather than strive for a qualitatively *better* world order, as Bush had initially proclaimed. The aggression of Muslim Iraq against Kuwait, a strong ally of the West, crystallized for many the threat to the global order posed by Islam. For many the threat was made much more serious by the events of 9/11 and their aftermath.

The re-emergence of religion as an issue in world politics can be traced back to Iran's Islamic revolution in the late 1970s, a development which took many people by surprise. It went against the prevailing conventional wisdom that *all* societies would secularize as they modernized (see Box 9.2). Most analysts presupposed that over time religion would lose much of its social and political importance. 'Third World' or 'developing' countries – emerging in great numbers from colonial status in Africa and Asia in the 1950s and 1960s – were predicted to follow the path taken by the economically developed countries of North America and Europe, where religion had lost a great deal of public significance and clout (Haynes, 1998).

Such views have proved erroneous: the evidence is now clear that societies do not necessarily secularize as they modernize; some do, some do not. But

> ## Box 9.2 Modernization
>
> For over 50 years, one of the most resilient ideas about societal development has been that nations will inevitably secularize as they modernize. The idea of modernization has been strongly linked to urbanization, industrialization and the elimination of 'irrational' views associated with religion and ethnicity. Loss of religious faith and secularization dovetailed with the belief that technological development and the application of science would overcome the perennial social problems of poverty, environmental degradation, hunger and disease to bring about long-term human progress.

how do we explain the widespread 'unsecularization' identified by George Weigel? There is no simple, clear-cut reason for this turn of events; no single theoretical explanation covers every case. However, it is apparent that, as states have sought to develop by drawing on the processes of modernization, faith in the secular ideologies of change – such as socialism and communism – has declined, leaving many people with a sense of loss rather than achievement. This is because modernization undermines traditional value systems and yet at the same time allocates opportunities to people in highly unequal ways – both within and between nations. As a consequence, many people have begun to search for a new sense of identity, something to give their lives meaning and purpose during a period of historically unprecedented, diverse and massive change.

One consequence of the multiple political, social and economic upheavals that have occurred as the forces of modernization have swept so rapidly across the globe, affecting both developed and developing worlds, has been that large numbers of people now believe that they can most effectively pursue personal objectives by being part of a religiously-oriented group or movement. By the early 2000s, there was a wave of politically-oriented religiosity in the world – with serious implications for long-term social integration, political stability and international security. To complicate matters, politically-oriented religious groups and movements have not only attracted poor, marginalized segments of society. They cannot simply be thought of as contemporary manifestations of working class organizations using a religious ideology as a substitute for a secular one, such as socialism or communism. Many people with extensive education and high social status have also found religion to be attractive and fulfilling.

Are hostile religious and cultural actors a threat to the West's security?

Liberal democracy and capitalism have not been the only values projected after the Cold War. Several recent US presidents – including the triumphalist George Bush Snr, after the 1990–1 Gulf War and the self-satisfied Bill Clinton at the signing of the NAFTA in 1994 – sought to propagate the presumed virtues of liberalism. Several influential religious leaders and groups, however, including the late Ayatollah Khomeini and his conservative heirs in Iran, the globally influential Christian fundamentalist preachers, such as the Argentinian Luis Palau and the Nigerian Benson Idahosa, as well as the Hindu-chauvinists of the Rashtriya Swayamsevak Sangh and the BJP in India, and the Buddhist champions of socio-cultural renewal in Thailand, have all advanced fundamentally different values and conceptions of the future.

After the Cold War, two rival interpretations were put forward to account for the emerging trends appearing in world politics. An 'optimistic' view, propounded by writers such as Bartley (1993) argued that the dominant flow of historical forces in the twenty-first century could well lead to more widespread economic development and to growing demands for democracy and individual (or familial) autonomy which authoritarian governments will be forced to grant as a result of popular and international pressure. Instant worldwide communications will reduce the power of oppressive governments, while the growth in numbers of democratic countries will diminish any potential for inter-state conflict.

A second, probably more influential, view is much more pessimistic. Associated with the works of Samuel Huntington (1993, 1996) and Francis Fukuyama (1992), both conservative American commentators, the 'pessimistic' view identifies serious threats to global order from various non-Western religious and cultural sources. Huntington points to conflicting 'civilizations', based on religious and cultural distinctions between blocs of rival national groupings. He believes that a 'clash of civilizations' will be the primary source of conflict in the future. The main cleavage identified by Huntington establishes a 'West versus militant Islam' dichotomy, with the latter to pose a serious – and growing – threat to the West's security.

For Huntington, the West is identified in religious–cultural terms, coterminous with Christianity and a dominant democratic political culture emphasizing attributes of tolerance, moderation and consensus. Followers of militant Islam, on the other hand, are not seen to value such concepts and beliefs but, on the contrary, to hold a worldview that does not see virtue in such ideas. According to Huntington, the battle for global dominance is between the West (especially North America and Western Europe) and its rivals in the militant Islamic world, such as Iran, Sudan and, until recently, Afghanistan. Israel, with its dominant Jewish population, is considered to be a staunch ally of the West. For Huntington, the invasion of Kuwait in 1990 and the ensuing struggle between Iraq's armed forces and the diverse troops brought together under the UN flag was a highly significant event, a catalyst in the formation of battle lines between the (Muslim) Arab world and the (Christian) West. Even more significant for the future of global conflict, however, were the events of 9/11, identified by many commentator as a watershed in international relations.

Huntington's concerns were endorsed by Francis Fukuyama (1992). For him, the triumph of liberal democracy and capitalism over communism marked the end of the Cold War, and 'history', understood as a battle of ideologies, was over by 1989. No longer is there a plausible ideological alternative to the Western political–economic system. Henceforward, global political concerns (at least among Western states and emerging democracies elsewhere) will reflect shared political, security, economic and environmental goals. The 'fly in the ointment' is the mass of culturally different, non-Western countries – especially those espousing militant Islam – which not only fail to share the West's values but, worryingly, present alternatives of their own.

Fukuyama's earlier work (1989) exemplifies a shift from optimism to pessimism – from seeing 'the enemy' as the Soviet Union to seeing it as the culturally alien 'other'. In 1989, Fukuyama was the epitome of optimism: the 'end of history', he maintained, was marked by the ultimate and global triumph of liberal democracy and capitalism. For Fukuyama, the sudden collapse of East European communism indicated the passing of a particular phase of history, whereas the unequivocal victory of economic and political liberalism provided the final form of human government, and the arrival at the end-point of humankind's ideological evolution. The Western way of life represented for Fukuyama a pattern of universal validity, a ray of hope not only for the West but also for non-Western societies still struggling 'in history'.

In the developing world there would, no doubt, be 'minor' internal conflicts within states which remain 'in history' – because they are subject to 'archaic' conditions fostering nationalist, religious or ethnic disputes – but in the longer run they too will tread the path of economic and political liberalism. In sum, the post-Cold War global order was seen to be a liberal order, only mildly and intermittently troubled by tiresome, yet essentially irrelevant, disputes between peoples in the developing world who have not (yet) developed the same levels of tolerance, consensus and uniformity of value systems as those in the West.

In *The End of History and the Last Man*, published in 1992, Fukuyama is much more circumspect about the prospects for a liberal post-Cold War global order; in this book he becomes a global-order pessimist. In 1989, he assumed that economic and political liberalism would govern the world in the long run; but by 1992, liberal democracy had become only a transitory historical form, the process of whose dissolution was already proceeding. This is because the 'broad acceptance of liberalism, political or economic, by a large number of nations will not be sufficient to eliminate differences between them based on culture', differences which will 'undoubtedly become more pronounced as ideological cleavages are muted' (Fukuyama, 1992,

p. 233). 'Culture' is a contested term, taken here to mean people's feeling of separateness based on ethnicity, nationalism, religion and/or language. The spectre of 'clashing cultures' is also the theme of an article by John Mearsheimer, published in 1990. Mearsheimer argues that the end of the Cold War led to the revival of traditional state rivalries not only between countries in the developing world but also between the nation-states of Europe.

In sum, the chief post-Cold War threats to international stability, according to Huntington, Mearsheimer and Fukuyama, come from countries predominantly filled with non-Christian peoples, especially followers of militant Islam. Christianity, on the other hand, is deemed to be a religion that has spawned cultures that promote the growth of liberal democracy and, by extension, global peace and security. Fukuyama and others regard the collapse of dictatorships in southern Europe and Latin America in the 1970s and 1980s, followed by the development of liberal democratic political norms (rule of law, free elections, civic rights) as conclusive proof of the synergy between Christianity and liberal democracy, both foundations of global order. From this perspective, conflict between the West and various expressions of militant Islam is virtually certain, notwithstanding a trend towards the creation and consolidation of broadly democratic political systems in many areas of the world. Cultural and religious competition between such countries thus emerges as a key area of international antagonism.

But are such 'civilizations' as single-minded, undivided and uniform in the ways they act and perceive other civilizations as Huntington and others have asserted? Within most of the so-called great 'civilizations', Said observes that there is in fact a great deal of dispute (1995, p. 32). This is as true of the United States as it is of the Islamic world. As Said asks rhetorically, 'what is the real America?' Is it the mid-Western world of the moralistic Christian fundamentalists and televangelists? Or is it the gay communities of San Francisco and New York? Within 'civilizations', moreover, new political voices – often coming from the young and alienated – periodically emerge, demanding real changes, arguing that the dominant values and ideals of society are wrong. The point is that the main area of conflict is not necessarily *between* civilizations but could well be *within* them, as coreligionists present vying interpretations of what is 'the' correct way to live a 'proper' – that is, suitably religious – life. Some observers point to a generational element in contemporary religio-political struggles in some parts of the world. This is chiefly a question of relatively youthful people – often but not exclusively men – vying with older figures with higher levels of social, political and/or religious authority. The young pretenders employ differing religious interpretations in their struggle for recognition, status and socio-political domination over their older rivals. It is with these concerns in mind that we turn to what many regard as the most significant religious issue in international affairs in the early 2000s: the threat posed to global security by a militant Islamic organization, Al Qaeda.

Al Qaeda: anti-Western Islamic militancy

> In an age of despair the need for a hero who can inspire pan-Islamic
> victories becomes acute ... Despair can become a breeding ground for
> mavericks who believe in themselves and their version of the faith ...
> Osama bin Laden is in the tradition of another famous name from the
> eleventh century, Hasan i Sabbah, the Old Man of the Mountains, who
> has given the English language the word 'assassin'. (Akbar, 2002, p. 195)

Given that both 9/11 and many subsequent connected terrorist outrages
appear to have been perpetrated by Islamic radicals against Western targets,
the question can be asked whether these events mark the beginning of
Huntington's mooted 'civilizational' conflict between militant Islam and the
West. Some commentators, such as Akbar, allege that the 9/11 attacks and
the subsequent US response served to make Huntingtonian prophecies
about clashing civilizations appear far less abstract and far more plausible
than they had been when first made in the early 1990s.

Critics of Huntington's arguments have noted that it is one thing to argue
that various brands of political Islam have qualitatively different
perspectives on liberal democracy than some forms of Christianity, but
quite another to claim that Muslims *en masse* are poised to enter into a
period of conflict with the West. That is, there are actually many 'Islams'
and only the malevolent or misinformed would associate the terrorist
attacks with an apparently representative quality of a single idea of Islam.
Second, the 9/11 atrocities and subsequent bomb outrages in, *inter alia*,
Istanbul, Kenya, Madrid and Tanzania, do not appear to have been carried
out by a state or group of states or at their behest, but by Al Qaeda.

In addition, the idea of religious or civilizational conflict is problematic
because it is actually very difficult to identify clear territorial boundaries to
civilizations, and even more difficult to perceive them as acting as coherent
units. It has been suggested that Huntington's image of 'clashing
civilizations' focuses too closely on an essentially undifferentiated category
– 'a civilization' – and as a result places insufficient emphasis on various
trends, conflicts and disagreement that take place within all religious/
cultural traditions, whether Islam, Christianity or Judaism. The wider point
is that religions are not usefully seen as closed systems of essentialist values,
while it is implausible to understand the world to comprise a strictly limited
number of religious cultures, each with their own unique core sets of beliefs.
The influence of globalization in this regard is to be noted as it leads to an
expansion of channels, pressures and agents through which various norms
are diffused and interact.

Finally, the image of 'clashing civilizations' ignores the very important
sense in which both militant Islamic revolt and Al Qaeda terrorism are
aimed primarily at unrepresentative, corrupt and illegitimate – in short,
perceived 'un-Islamic' – governments within the Islamic world. Since the

1970s, the general rise of militant Islamic groups across much of the world can be seen as more a consequence of the failure of such governments, often supported by successive US administrations, than the result alone of Osama bin Laden's influence. That is, the contemporary resurgence of Islamic militancy – of which Al Qaeda is undeniably a component – carries within it both popular disillusionment at slow developmental progress as well as disgust with corrupt and unrepresentative governments in the Muslim world. Confronted by state power that seeks to destroy or control its communitarian structures and replace them with an idea of a national citizenry based on the link between state and individual, many militant Islamic organizations – such as Hamas in the Gaza Strip – are important vehicles of popular political aspirations.

While it is difficult to be sure about the level of support for bin Laden and Al Qaeda in the Muslim world, it is clear that there is, post-9/11, a high degree of anti-US resentment and a widespread belief among many Muslims that the West is opposed to Islam. After 9/11, support for the United States has generally dropped in much of the Muslim world. For example, in Morocco, public opinion surveys indicated support for the United States fell from 77 per cent in 2000 to 27 per cent in the spring of 2003; in Jordan, it fell from 25 per cent in 2002 to 1 per cent in May 2003; in Saudi Arabia, it fell from 63 per cent in May 2000 to 11 per cent in October 2003 (http://www.csmonitor.com/2004/0226/p03s02-usfp.html). This perception is fuelled by President Bush's move back towards rather uncritical support for Israel's Sharon government, including the assassination of the Hamas leader, Sheikh Yassin, in March 2004, and the invasion of Iraq and subsequent inability to rebuild a viable administration in the country. There are also influential voices in the United States that appear to play up the notion of civilizational conflict. For example, Democratic Congressman Tom Lantos stated in November 2001 that, 'unfortunately we have no option but to take on barbarism which is hell bent on destroying civilization ... You don't compromise with these people. This is not a bridge game. International terrorists have put themselves outside the bonds of protocols' (interview with Tom Lantos, BBC Radio 4 *Today* programme, 20 November 2001).

Such remarks appear to reflect a deep-rooted tradition in Western international thought that it is appropriate to set aside normal rules of international relations in certain circumstances. For example, during the centuries of Western imperialism, there were frequent debates about what rights non-Christian and non-European peoples should enjoy. In the centuries of competition and sometimes conflict between Christianity and Islam, the notion of 'holy war' emerged – that is, a special kind of conflict undertaken effectively outside any framework of shared rules and norms – and 'just war', carried out for the vindication of rights within a shared framework of values. There is also a further strand of conservative western thought that asserts that certain kinds of states and systems cannot be dealt with on normal terms, that the usual rules that govern international relations have to be set aside. For example, during 1980s the Reagan government in the United States averred that there was a basic lack of give-and-take when dealing with communist governments, which meant that it was appropriate that some basic notions of international law could be set aside in such contexts. This conservative tradition is also manifested in the remarks of Congressman Lantos noted above.

What links Al Qaeda's members and sympathisers is a belief in the correctness of 'holy war' (jihad) and an associated insistence that there is no place for political pluralism in a plausibly 'Islamic state'. Al Qaeda's ideology is sometimes referred to as 'jihadism', characterized by a willingness to kill 'apostate' Muslims and an emphasis on jihad. While it is clearly at odds with nearly all Islamic religious thought, its roots are found in the work of two Sunni Islamic thinkers: Mohammad ibn Abd al-Wahhab and Sayyid Qutb (Box 9.3).

Beyond the influences of Wahhabism and Qutb, the theology/ideology that bin Laden and fellow Al Qaeda ideologues advance is quite complicated. It contains a number of additions that do not have any basis in the Quran or in the Sunnah (teachings of the Prophet Mohammed). In addition, it is often described as a variation of the official version of Islam found in Saudi Arabia (which is itself a puritanical version) and one that most (Sunni) Muslims would probably not choose to follow. Finally, it is important to remember that the Al Qaeda version of Islam is a Sunni interpretation, with no appeal to Shi'a Muslims.

Box 9.3 Al Qaeda's ideological progenitors

Al-Wahhab was an eighteenth-century reformer who claimed that Islam had been corrupted a generation or so after the death of the prophet, Mohammed. He denounced any theology or customs developed after that as non-Islamic, including more than 1000 years of religious scholarship. He and his supporters took over what is now Saudi Arabia, where Wahhabism remains the dominant school of religious thought. Wahhabism emerged from the Arabian peninsula 200 years ago and over time took root in many parts of the Middle East, including Iraq. Wahhabism preaches against worship of 'false idols' that for its followers include: Sufism (Islamic mystics noted for saint worship), and the Shia, who revere the descendants of Ali, the prophet Mohammed's son-in-law.

Sayyid Qutb, a radical Egyptian scholar of the mid-twentieth century, declared Western civilization the enemy of Islam, denounced leaders of Muslim nations for not following Islam closely enough, and taught that jihad should be undertaken not just to defend Islam, but to purify it.

Three sets of beliefs are pivotal to the worldview of Al Qaeda, its followers and supporters:

- The West has subjugated the lands of Islam; and Western values have corrupted Islam internally.
- Only return to pure and authentic Islam as practised by the Prophet and his companions in seventh-century Medina will bring back glory and prominence to Muslims.
- These goals require the defeat of the West through various – including violent – means.

One way to comprehend the appeal of Al Qaeda for some Muslims is to focus upon what it rejects, including pluralism, relativism and radical individualism. Differences among groups affiliated or attracted to Al Qaeda are however influenced by political conditioning in different national contexts. It is problematic to analyze reasons for the appeal of Al Qaeda and its ideology in Muslim countries because there are specific causes within each country. However, it is possible to make several generalizations. First, Al Qaeda's brand of Islamic militancy is said to be a response to Western cultural, political and economic domination, the dangers of which were articulated most famously by the late Edward Said in his 1978 book, *Orientalism*. Said defined orientalism as a 'style of thought based upon an ontological and epistemological distinction made between the Orient and (most of the time) the Occident' (p. 2). Said claimed that many politicians and academics in the West had 'essentialised' Muslims and Islam into unchanging categories, and many of these assumptions were little more than generalizations with little foundation. He cited Lord Cromer, the British governor of Egypt between 1882 and 1907, who argued that 'the Oriental generally acts, speaks and thinks in a manner exactly opposite to the European'. While Cromer claimed that 'the European' is a 'close reasoner' and a 'natural logician', he believed 'the Oriental' to be 'singularly deficient in the logical faculty' (p. 39). Although Cromer was no doubt a product of his times, there is no obvious reason to believe that his prejudiced views are entirely extinct.

Second, Al Qaeda's militancy can be seen as a form of resistance to 'Western-style' modernization that is widely believed to bring traumatic social and economic dislocation, while embedded cultures can be significantly affected. As a result, some Muslims have sought comfort from such modernization in traditional patterns of behaviour found in their Islamic heritage. This heritage was downplayed by the secular – either military or nationalist – regimes of the Middle East that existed after the Second World War. These countries were considered weak *vis-à-vis* the West with few exceptions, and almost uniformly did not appear to meet the expectations of their citizens.

Third, many of the regimes in the Middle East have long suffered the effects of unequal development. That is, economic development was not matched by corresponding advancement in political participation, resulting in an educated class with no means to express its political sentiments, except through marginalized religious groups. Moreover, occasional economic downturns provided societal and political opportunities, exploited by various exponents of militant Islam, for a 'return to Islam'.

Conclusion

It is ironic that Al Qaeda ('the base') no longer appears to have a physical base, following the organization's expulsion from Afghanistan. Since 2001–2, the scattering of Al Qaeda has led to claims that it has been weakened, perhaps fatally. However, these assertions appear to be unfounded. Instead, Al Qaeda has transformed itself into a collection of autonomous militant Islamic terror groups that may, as a result, be even more dangerous.

There is a further irony in that the war in Iraq that began in March 2003 – presented by the US and UK governments as an unmissable opportunity to do away with Saddam's brutal, obnoxious regime – actually offered Al Qaeda and its followers a good chance to exploit the circumstances. The US government's claim was that Saddam's Iraq was a place where religious terrorists gathered; it appears that it wasn't then, but it certainly is now. George Tenet, who resigned as director of the CIA in June 2004, stated that, 'as we continue the battle against Al Qaeda, we must overcome a movement – a global movement infected by Al Qaeda's radical agenda' (http://www.csmonitor.com/2004/0226/p03s02-usfp.html). The inference is that Al Qaeda's extremist ideology is now attracting expanding networks and a new generation of supporters not only in Iraq but elsewhere in the Muslim world. Often, such people are young idealists who believe in the concept of global jihad to liberate Islam from foreign control. Al Qaeda strategists may not have hoped to defeat or even to weaken 'America' militarily, but to gain publicity, to reach out to further recruits; and this has been forthcoming. This amounts to a psychological victory, useful progress towards the achievement of Al Qaeda's three goals: to provoke a jihad against 'Christians' and 'Jews'; to get the Americans out of bin Laden's home country, Saudi Arabia; and to establish the puritanical rule of Wahhabism throughout the Sunni Muslim world.

Several of these objectives have already been achieved. Some of President Bush's responses to 9/11, especially the swift war in Afghanistan, were unavoidable given the state of public opinion after the attacks. However, the unfortunate crudeness and depth of response against what many Muslims believe is an assault not only on Al Qaeda but also on Islam itself, has done nothing either to defeat Al Qaeda or stop the spread of its ideology. President Bush quickly declared a 'crusade' both against the specific threat of bin Laden and Al Qaeda and terrorism in general. He sent the US fleet back to the Middle East, undermined the Saudi royal family, and removed US troops from the country. This led to two counterproductive outcomes: much free publicity for bin Laden and Al Qaeda, and the antagonism of many ordinary Muslims around the world because of various policies, including: 'racial profiling', draconian legislation, mass arrests, and detentions at Guantanamo Bay prison camp, Cuba.

I have suggested that Al Qaeda is now as much a religious ideology and a set of values as it is a single organization headed by Osama bin Laden. Al Qaeda has evolved into a brand name or a franchise, ineluctably linked with the various and complex manifestations of modern Islamic militancy. It may be that this is reflected in changing patterns of Al Qaeda terrorism. For example, the bombers in Madrid in March 2004 did not blow themselves up. Their earlier counterparts were people who saw their deaths as an essential aspect of their message, 'We love death as much as you love life'. Untypically, the Madrid bombings seem to have had a short-term, instrumental purpose: withdrawal of Spanish troops from Iraq.

Al Qaeda's religious terrorism also has universal themes. When we ask: 'What do they want?', we seek to apply a Western concept implying that the aim is achievement of certain *finite* goals. The question however can be posed differently: 'Why do Al Qaeda bombers believe that they *must* act in the ways they do?' It may well be that they literally believe they have no other choice. Such a presumption is underpinned by the timbre of militant statements from captured Al Qaeda personnel. They tend to emphasize both the general and the specific. For example, Imam Samudra, the Bali bomber, perceived Bali's nightclubs as an aspect of a general Western-directed cultural assault against Muslims. Such a conviction is a wider component of Islamic militant beliefs, wherever 'Muslim terrorism' is carried out or threatened, from Kashmir to Chechnya to France. In 2004, a previously unknown group threatened violence in France. It listed the banning of the veil from schools alongside continuing American support for Israel, the war in Iraq and the killing of civilians in Afghanistan as evidence that the West never abandoned the Crusades.

In short, a deeply held belief that an aggressive West seeks to humble, divide and ultimately take over the Islamic world lies at the core of modern Islamic militancy. Al Qaeda cadres may well believe that they are front-line troops engaged in a battle for the survival of their society, culture, religion and way of life, all undermined and attacked by an increasingly aggressive West. They appear to believe they are fighting in self-defence in a last-ditch stand; under such circumstances it is rational for them to justify the use of tactics that they believe are acceptable during conditions of 'holy war'.

The militants' perception of Western belligerence is underpinned by specific factors, especially the existentialist conditions for many ordinary Muslims both in the Middle East and elsewhere. Al Qaeda militants seek explanations for the economic, military, and political failures of many Muslim countries. Working from the presumption that Islam is the perfect social system they no doubt believe that something else – not Islam itself – *must* be to blame for the political, social and economic problems of their countries. The question they pose is: 'Why do self-serving, corrupt and unrepresentative governments rule nearly all Muslim countries?' The answer they prefer is that it is because both Western governments – especially that of the United States – allow them to, as do the mass of ordinary Muslims, many of whom fail to practise their religion with sufficient diligence. In this context, bomb attacks against Western targets are a potent way to try to: (1) restore Muslim pride, (2) weaken the Christian 'Crusaders', and (3) facilitate a return to Islam's golden age of a millennium ago, when Muslims comprised the world's leading power.

What can be done to counter the ideological appeal of Al Qaeda and, more generally, Islamic militancy with its rejection of Western political and social values? While the scale of the militants' aims make them very difficult to counter, there are practical policies that might help, such as, peace between Israel and the Palestinians. Although this unlikely event would almost certainly not end Islamic terrorism quickly, yet it would deny radical Islamists a key piece of 'evidence', and that would be a start. Pressurizing repressive governments of Muslim countries to reform politically might also help. However, the ultimate worry is not necessarily Al Qaeda but rather a diffuse, global militant Islamic ideology that predates Al Qaeda's creation, is locally organized, and constantly recruits new volunteers.

In sum, what does this chapter tell us about the nature of contemporary world politics? From the evidence presented, it is clear that the contemporary involvement of religion in world politics poses significant analytical problems. Chief among them is that political religion cannot easily be explained by factors of traditional analytical importance to political science, such as the economy or class. The end of the Cold War was followed by an eruption of religious conflicts within a large number of countries which raised serious doubts about the possibility of moving from an old order rooted in bipolarity, nuclear deterrence and ideological division to a new global order where the pursuit of peace, prosperity and cooperation would be paramount.

New threats to world order are widely traced to militant Islamic groups, especially the elusive Al Qaeda. It is difficult, however, to be certain to what extent militant Islam significantly threatens world order in a wider sense. It is clear that Al Qaeda does not enjoy anything like majority support among Muslims, almost all of whom express abhorrence at bomb outrages. This highlights more generally that, while contemporary religious movements with political goals may display a number of broadly similar features across cultural and state boundaries, there are also differences both *between* and *within* them. But this should not surprise us. The world religions have always functioned as 'terrains of meaning', subject to radically different interpretations and conflicts, often with profound social and political consequences. Not only Islam, but also Hinduism, Christianity and

Buddhism, all have long traditions of reformers, populists and 'protestants', seeking to give their religion contemporary meaning and social salience. The contemporary era is a period of wide religious reinterpretation, spurred by a plethora of changes at both the national and global levels, encapsulated by the amorphous yet ubiquitous term, 'globalization'. Those who neglect religion in analyses of world politics are sure to miss a highly dynamic feature of the global scene.

Guide to further reading

The literature on religion and politics in both domestic and international settings is vast and growing. It can be divided into three types, though there are overlaps between these categories. A first type examines the issues as a source of tension in regional and world politics, and includes Huntington (1993, 1996), Fukuyama (1992) and Mearsheimer (1990). In a second category, where authors conduct detailed studies of movements and their interactions with each other and with states, the following can be recommended: Beyer (1994), Haynes (1998), and Rudolph and Piscatori (1997). A third category of work analyzes religious militancy from comparative perspectives, while treating it as a global problem. Among the most useful sources are Marty and Scott Appleby (1993), Haynes (1998), Petito and Hatzopoulos (2003), and Carlson and Owens (2003).

Chapter 10

Migration and Refugees

SITA BALI

International migration is inextricably connected with a wide range of issues and dilemmas that confront governments and peoples across the globe today. Increasing racism and neo-Nazi violence in Germany, the re-emergence of the extreme right-wing British National Party in the United Kingdom, ethnic cleansing in former Yugoslavia and government complicity in the activities of the 'Arab' militia sparking the exodus of hundreds of thousands of 'Africans' from the Darfur region of Sudan, are all examples of problems that are linked to migration in one way or another. Migration, however, is as old as humanity itself, and has played a crucial role in shaping the world throughout history. But while it has been a constant feature of human history, the causes, characteristics, patterns and directions of migration have never remained constant; they have always influenced and been influenced by changing economic, social and political conditions within and between states The aim of this chapter is to chart the major developments in international migration and examine their implications.

Migration as an international issue

International migration involves the movement of people across state boundaries. In contrast to internal or intra-state migratory movements, international migrants leave the jurisdiction of one state and become subject to that of another. The migration can be either involuntary or voluntary depending on the underlying motivation of the migrant. Involuntary migration takes place as a consequence of natural disaster, war, civil war, ethnic, religious or political persecution, all creating situations where people are forced to flee their homes and countries. Involuntary migration, however, can also be coerced as with slavery, when people are compelled by force to leave their homes and are taken abroad for the purpose of exploitation. Although now illegal, slavery remains a worldwide and flourishing business. Millions of people, especially women and children, operate as slaves within their own societies, but there is also a huge traffic in slaves across state boundaries. For example, there are estimated to be 20 000 Burmese prostitutes in Thailand at any one time, some sold as slaves and others taken under false pretences (*Economist*, 21 September 1996).

The motivation underlying voluntary migration also takes different forms and can be divided into three subcategories. The first encompasses permanent settlers, such as the migrants who populated the United States or constituted the Asian and Afro-Caribbean minorities in Britain. The second subcategory identifies temporary settlers who account for the bulk of voluntary migrants. This category includes people who move to acquire education, promote business, or encourage tourism. In addition many temporary migrants take up specific jobs, such as the workers admitted to the Gulf States to service the oil-powered economic boom. Finally there is illegal migration, which can be temporary or permanent, but in either case is unauthorized by the receiving state. Once a migration pattern has been established, it can extend to embrace additional categories of migrants. For instance, Sikhs migrated voluntarily from the Punjab to Britain, but have been followed by Sikhs suffering political persecution at the hands of the Indian government because of their support for the Khalistan independence movement. Thus a stream of voluntary migrants can be joined by a stream of involuntary migrants. This intermingling of categories has led more and more states to refuse to discriminate between different types of migration.

The two main issues that arise from migration in the contemporary era are the regulation and control of international migration on the one hand, and the policies for dealing with ethnic migrant minorities, on the other. States, by virtue of their sovereignty, claim absolute authority to decide who is able to enter or leave their territorial jurisdiction. Although democratic states accept that citizens have an unconditional right to exit from the state, they invariably impose restrictions and conditions on the right of entry for foreigners. These restrictions are based on a variety of factors that include the demand for labour within the economy, considerations of public welfare and the preservation of the nature and integrity of society and its particular culture and way of life. However, most states officially support the international regime set up to deal with refugees in accordance with the Universal Declaration of Human Rights (1948) and the Convention Relating to the Status of Refugees (1951). Their response to involuntary or forced migration must, as a consequence, be consistent with these commitments. So categorization of international migration still has some relevance, even though the treatment of migrants by states is becoming increasingly undifferentiated.

In the long term, the most obvious effect of international migration is the creation of ethnic minorities in host countries. The existence of these communities has a substantial impact on social stability, economic prosperity and the internal politics of receiving states as well as on their relationship with the countries where these communities originate. Thus the establishment of the Indian community in Britain has had an impact on the nature of British society, economy and politics as well as on Britain's relationship with India.

International migration has become more prominent on the international agenda in recent years both because of its increasing scale and its growing impact on international affairs. Several factors account for these developments. First, the number of states in the international system has steadily increased since the end of the First World War. As the number of international boundaries containing the new states has increased, so too has the volume of international migrants. Second, there has also been a rapid increase in the world's population, and it continues to grow. The growth of population has led to overexploitation of regional resources, leading on occasions to catastrophic famine and population movement. Third, the revolution in communications and transportation has made people aware of conditions and opportunities in other parts of the world, as well as making travel to those areas easier. Finally, the turmoil and uncertainty of a turbulent and unstable world plays an important role in motivating people to search abroad for a better life (Teitelbaum, 1980, p. 21). However, care must be taken not to exaggerate the magnitude and importance of international migration as only a very small percentage of the world's population moves across borders. It is only in extremely rare cases that as much as 10 per cent of the population of a state emigrates.

People on the move

Migration is global in scope. There is no part of the world unaffected by migration, although the nature and intensity of its impact may vary from region to region, and over time. Colonialism provided the initial impetus for modern migration and it stimulated the movement of Europeans to Africa, Asia, South and North America, Australia and New Zealand. This initial pattern was then extended by the industrialization of Europe. The European demand for industrial labour first gave rise to internal migration from rural to urban areas, but this was soon followed by the mass international migration of Europeans to North America, with the British in the forefront. The United States became a country of immigrants who were indirectly responsible for the displacement and extermination of the indigenous population; 30 million people arrived between 1861 and 1920 (Castles and Miller, 1997, p. 55). The immigrants came mainly from Britain, Germany, Ireland, Italy and Eastern Europe (mostly Jews). Canada also saw a large influx of immigrants in this period. Table 10.1 shows the major migrations of the eighteenth and nineteenth centuries.

North America continued to be a favourite destination for migrants in the twentieth century, with 250 000–330 000 people arriving per year in the period 1951–70 (Castles and Miller, 1997, p. 74). Asian immigration to North America had begun in the early years of this century, but restrictions on racial grounds were soon put into place, and these lasted until after the Second World War. Immigrants to North America after 1945 continued to

Table 10.1   *Global migration patterns, 1760–1914*

Date	Type	Source	Destination	Number of migrants (million)
1760–1860	Slavery	West Africa	United States, Caribbean, South America	15
1845–80	Indenture	China	Southeast Asia, North America, Caribbean, Australia, New Zealand	5
1830–1920	Indenture	India	South and East Africa, Southeast Asia and Fiji, Caribbean	30 involved, 6 net migrations
1820–1914	Free	Europe	United States	25.5
			Canada	3–4
			Australia, New Zealand	2

Source: Compiled from Potts (1990); Castles and Miller (1997).

be predominantly European, but when the racial restrictions were finally eased in the late 1960s, substantial migration from South East Asia, and the Indian subcontinent, as well as Latin America began.

In Europe, the colonial era was marked not only by mass emigration to the new world and the colonies, but also by significant intra-European migration. Britain drew in vast quantities of labour to feed her rapidly-growing industrial sector. They came primarily from Ireland, particularly after the potato famines, but also included Jews fleeing the pogroms in the Russian pale. German industrialization was supported by workers from Poland and Italy, and French industry attracted workers from neighbouring countries. While French immigration to the new world was extremely limited, there was a significant movement of settlers to Algeria after its conquest in 1830. The long post-war economic boom saw Europe, particularly Northern Europe, draw in workers from peripheral countries of the Mediterranean and Southern Europe, as well as immigrants from former colonies, while transatlantic emigration also continued. Some countries saw the development of guest-worker systems, such as that which brought large numbers of Turks to Germany. France and Britain experienced substantial migrations, from North Africa in the case of the former, and the Caribbean, ex-colonies in Africa, such as Nigeria, and the Indian subcontinent in the case of the latter.

Like the United States, Australia was a recipient of mass migration and settlement by Europeans (with the British dominating), again at the expense of the indigenous population. But in contrast to the United States and other parts of the European empires, there was no movement of slaves or indentured labour to Australia. On the contrary, the government's White Australia policy, in place until the 1970s, ensured that the source of Australian immigrants was exclusively Europe, stretching to include large numbers of Southern Europeans after 1945. It was only with the victory of the Labour government in 1971 that entry criteria were changed, ending the discriminatory policy and promoting a substantial migration from South-east Asia and the Indian subcontinent. By the mid-1990s, Asian migration was the largest component of migration to Australia. Immigration levels in Australia have reflected the world economic climate, being considerably lower in recessions and higher in periods of recovery.

In conjunction with the mass movement of European labour and the creation of a global economy, there was also the forced migration of an estimated 15 million slaves from the West African coast to the Americas by 1850 (Appleyard, cited in Castles and Miller, 1997, p. 53). This trade was replaced by the movement of indentured labour from India and China after the abolition of slavery in 1834. The use of indentured labour became even more widespread than slavery, encompassing over 40 countries, between 12 and 37 million indentured labourers, and lasting until 1941 (Potts, 1990, pp. 63–104). The long-term political effects of some of these movements are only now, nearly a century on, beginning to make themselves felt.

New patterns of migration

The mid-1970s marked the end of the post-war economic boom in most of the advanced industrialized countries. This change in the economic climate and the more long-term structural economic adjustment it heralded had a substantial impact on migration patterns. More recent international migratory trends have been marked by a severe reduction in permanent settler migration opportunities. Permanent migrants can find a destination only in the traditional countries of immigration (United States, Canada, Australia), and potential migrants must now either be sponsored by family members already settled in the host country or possess skills and qualifications needed by the host country. The main areas of origin of immigrants to these countries lie in Asia and South America, not Europe. As the demand for labour in industrialized European countries has declined, legal permanent settler migration has also almost ceased except for family reunification. New areas have drawn in labour, and some of the largest migrations of workers in this period have been from Asia and the Middle East to the oil-producing states of the Persian Gulf. Israel has seen a dramatic increase in the number of Jews arriving from Eastern Europe and the former Soviet Union. With the collapse of the Soviet bloc, there has been an influx of ethnic Germans and others into Germany, and a movement of

Gypsies, Romanians and Albanians into Hungary and Western Europe. The countries of Southern Europe and the Mediterranean, traditionally countries of emigration, have become countries of immigration with movements of people from Eastern Europe, Turkey and North Africa affecting them. Some of the newly industrialized countries in Asia are becoming attractive to workers from other Asian countries, like China and Indonesia.

The end of the post-war boom did not lead to a decline in migration, quite the reverse According to the International Organisation for Migration, there were some 175 million international migrants in 2000, well over double the 84 million in 1975. The number of international migrants has steadily increased since the 1960s. Today, the migrant population represents some 2.9 per cent of the total world population. Put differently, 1 out of every 35 persons is an international migrant. If all international migrants lived in one place, it would be the world's fifth biggest country (World Migration 2003, on www.iom.int).

A refugee crisis

Also in the 1970s, a worldwide refugee crisis developed. This period saw the migrations of hundreds of thousands fleeing Vietnam, Cambodia and Laos to escape repression and civil war. Conflict in Lebanon created yet another dimension to the existing Palestinian refugee problem in the Middle East. The Soviet invasion of Afghanistan in December 1979 gave rise to a refugee flow of millions from that country to Pakistan and Iran. Conditions in Sudan, Uganda, Zaire and South Africa also created refugee movements, as did the repression of military dictatorships in Chile and Argentina. More recently, ethnic conflict in Sri Lanka and Rwanda, the collapse of the Soviet bloc and the disintegration of Yugoslavia have swelled refugee numbers.

It has been estimated by the United Nations High Commission for Refugees (UNHCR) that the total number of people of concern to them (including refugees, asylum seekers, returnees and some internally displaced people) was 8.2 million in 1980, had risen to 15 million by 1990, and was more than 27 million by 1995 (Castles and Miller, 1997, p. 87). However, according to the UNHCR that number had fallen back to 21.5 million by 1999 and by the beginning of 2004 was down still further at 17.1 million. This decrease is largely due to the increase in voluntary repatriation to Afghanistan since the removal of the Taliban government in 2001, as well as to several North African countries in recent years. It must be noted that the majority of refugees seek asylum in neighbouring countries, and the impact of refugee movements is felt by developing countries much more than it is by the developed world. UNHCR estimated that in 2003, while 3.1 million people had found refuge in Europe, the Americas and Oceania put together, Asia accommodated 3.6 million and Africa 3.3 million (UNHCR, 2003, p. 89).

New complexity

Contemporary international migration is more complex than migrations of the past because receiving countries are faced with various types of migration simultaneously. Thus immigration to Australia today is not only of the permanent settler kind, but will include refugees as well as seasonal migrations of labour from New Zealand. The migration of permanent settlers may turn into a stream of refugees if political conditions in the home state deteriorate. This differentiation of migration makes the task of governments devising policy regarding migration all the more complicated. Another change in migration in recent times is that increasing numbers of women are becoming immigrants and moving. Traditionally migration was a predominantly male phenomenon, with women migrating only to join their men in a process of family reunification. More recently, however, women from a range of countries have begun to migrate as workers and refugees in their own right, and Asian women are the fastest-growing category of foreign workers, increasing by 800 000 a year (*New Internationalist*, 1998). Sri Lankan and Filipino women who take up employment as domestic workers in the Gulf countries are perhaps the most obvious manifestation of this trend. This increasing feminization of migration also raises new issues for states' migration policies (Castles and Miller, 1997, p. 9).

In most host countries, and certainly in democracies, it has become clear that once migration takes place, for whatever reasons, and whether intended to be permanent or temporary, it almost inevitably results in at least some immigrants becoming citizens of the host country, and creating a cultural, linguistic, religious and possibly a racially distinct minority within the state. Further, immigration can affect political and social conditions, and even, in rare instances, fundamentally alter the nature of society in receiving countries, many years after the actual movement of people has ceased. An illustration of this can be seen in Fiji, where indenture migration created an Indian immigrant community over 70 years ago. In 1987 Fiji was racked by ethnic conflict and a coup d'état when an election brought an Indian-dominated political party to power, and gave Fiji its first Indian Prime Minister. In 2000 Fiji was confronted by ethnic conflict, for a second time, over the election victory of an Indian-dominated party and Indian-origin Prime Minister.

The pros and cons of migration

For a host state, the main economic concerns raised by international migration relate to the regulation of its flow, taking into consideration competing economic imperatives such as requiring more labour and avoiding increased unemployment rates. Home states need to strike a balance between economic reliance on the remittances from overseas workers and a concern about the loss of trained and qualified persons. Countries receiving migrants also need to maintain social stability and cohesion in the face of the multiculturalism produced by migration. States must also ensure that they meet their obligations under international treaties and protect the interests of those who are fleeing persecution. Restrictions placed upon the entry of immigrants will also have an impact on relations with the home state of the migrants. So migration impinges directly upon a state's economic, social and foreign policy. A comprehensive analysis of migration needs to incorporate the views of countries sending and receiving migrants.

The economic dimension

Economic or labour migration is affected by two structural factors. The first relates to 'wage zones' or 'wage differentials', because differential levels of wages and social benefits and thus standards of living, can have a major impact on migration between countries. The second factor relates to the demand for labour and the levels of unemployment. The combination of divergent wage and unemployment levels in different countries creates a powerful impetus for migration.

For a sending country, labour migration can relieve the problem of unemployment. But the extent of the relief depends on the percentage of the labour force that is able to emigrate. In countries like Algeria, Tunisia, Morocco and Mexico, where 10 per cent of the labour force have emigrated, the impact is certainly noticeable. However, given the large and rapidly expanding populations in most sending countries, labour migration would have to be much larger than is conceivable, given current economic and political realities, for states exporting labour to experience any substantial benefits. In most cases, migrant labour forms a small percentage of the sending country's work force, even though it may constitute a substantial addition to the work force in the receiving country.

Migration also reduces the pressure on facilities and consumption in the sending country. It lowers demand on schools, hospitals, transport and communication facilities. Labour migration can also relieve the tax-payer of the costs of social welfare. But, once again, it is the percentage of the work force engaged in migration that is important. Current labour migration has a very limited effect in this context. Emigration is also believed to lead to a boost in exports for the sending country, as emigrants settled abroad tend to purchase goods from the home country. A visit to Southall in London, the hub of the Punjabi community in Britain with its plethora of shops selling a variety of Indian goods, makes this point.

By far the most important effect of labour migration is the remittances emigrants send home. These rose from $40 billion in 1982, to $61 billion in 1989 (Collinson, 1995, p. 40) and to $71 billion by 1991 (*New*

Internationalist, 1998). For several developing countries, these sums are equivalent to a third or more of earnings from exports, as well as making up the deficit in the balance of payments. The importance of these factors to a Third World economy (as most of the sending countries are) cannot be overestimated. Remittances improve the standard of living of the receiving families, and can lead to productive investment, and better social facilities like education and health care. However remittances may be spent on non-essential 'luxury' goods, leading to inflation and the widening of societal inequality Furthermore, remittances signify dependence and their curtailment when migrants are forced home due to unfavourable economic circumstances in their host countries or due to war (as occurred in Kuwait in 1990), can have a detrimental effect on the economy of the sending country.

Figure 10.1   *Top 20 receiving countries of migrants' remittances in 2000*

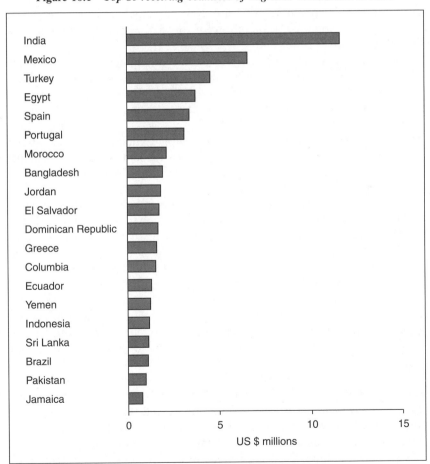

Source: Data from World Bank website.

The governments of sending countries used to prefer the migration of unskilled or semi-skilled labour because they were worried about the impact on the domestic economy of the departure of trained, educated and skilled workers. The emigration of Third World professionals like doctors and engineers is often depicted as a 'brain drain'. However, the educated sector of the population in many sending countries is now too large to be fully employed and governments encourage members of their educated middle classes to emigrate. Some countries now regard the emigration of educated personnel as 'brain overflow' rather than brain drain. It is recognized that the domestic economy does not have the capacity to absorb all the graduates and professionals produced by their education systems. Governments of sending countries are increasingly coming to appreciate the net gain of having their nationals employed abroad, acquiring skills and technologies, accumulating capital and sometimes influence in industrialized and prosperous countries. The importance of these effects for sending countries encourages their governments to use every diplomatic means available to them to ensure continued emigration for those of their nationals who wish to seek their fortunes abroad.

The main economic imperative for permitting immigration is a shortage of labour. However this is not a sufficient condition. States like Japan faced with labour shortages still resist importing labour because of concerns about the impact of large numbers of foreigners on their highly prized cultural homogeneity. Industries have to find other ways to deal with labour shortages, for example by adopting more capital-intensive and less labour-intensive technology, by incorporating new participants such as women into the labour market, or by moving outside the country to areas where labour is cheaper.

Nevertheless, in purely economic terms, imported labour can contribute to the prosperity of a host nation if economic growth has been impeded by the lack of human capital. Migrant labour can increase national productivity. It is no coincidence that large numbers of foreign workers were admitted to states during periods of rapid economic growth, such as that experienced by Europe after 1945. But although in some European countries imported labour came to make up approximately 9 per cent of the work force, this does not begin to compare with the Gulf states where imported labour forms an overwhelming majority of the work force: 70 per cent in Kuwait, 80 per cent in Quatar, and 85 per cent in the United Arab Emirates.

In recent years, increasing numbers of immigrants are highly skilled technical or managerial professionals. This development reflects the ever more globalized nature of the world economy and the importance of large international companies. But this increase does not appear to be of great concern to receiving countries, as this type of migration is easy to regulate, fills gaps in the skills of the indigenous work force, is generally temporary and is perceived to be beneficial.

But there are economic reasons for restricting migration, although there are various counter-arguments. Immigrant workers, it is asserted, displace local people in employment because they are prepared to work for lower wages. However studies in the United States suggest that this is not always the case. Immigrants often do jobs rejected by locals because of their unpleasant nature or low remuneration. Moreover, immigrants can often enhance the economies of their host countries by starting up businesses and creating employment. Nevertheless, critics of immigration assert that it overstretches housing and other welfare benefits in a receiving country. But, advocates claim, immigrant labour provides taxation revenue and at least part of the migrant's income is spent within the host economy. Critics in turn counter by arguing that importation of labour can delay structural change in developed economies by slowing down the move towards more capital intensive forms of production (Collinson, 1993, pp. 19–20).

The capitalist world economy, distinguished by the liberal Bretton Woods regime, permits and indeed encourages free movement of capital, goods and services. However there has been a shift away from liberal principles in the context of labour. There is universal agreement that the free flow of people, however beneficial for the world economy, should not be permitted. Restrictions on immigration became universal in the first decades of the twentieth century and today every country has restrictions, making immigration the only exception to liberal notions of free movement for all factors of production. This is because receiving countries see immigration not only in economic terms, but in terms of its wider effect upon their societies.

The social dimension

Admitting immigrant labour has long-lasting social effects on receiving countries. It can turn homogeneous societies into multicultural ones by the introduction of ethnically different people. Receiving societies are now having to evolve various ways of dealing with immigrants. These range from the acceptance of cultural diversity, with rapid naturalization of immigrants by granting full economic, social and political rights and formation of flourishing ethnic communities, to active discouragement of multicultural-ism by the denial of rights and the location of immigrants on the fringes of society. Most countries fall somewhere between these two extremes.

The traditional countries attracting migrants – Australia, Canada and the United States – are still the most open. Immigrants are quickly granted citizenship guaranteeing the security of their status and the permanence of their stay. Multiculturalism is accepted and even encouraged. Government help to preserve the language and culture of immigrant communities is the norm in Canada and Australia. It was not always so; all these countries have histories of excluding immigrants on purely racial grounds. But since the early 1970s, racially non-discriminatory policies have been in place. Some

European countries like Sweden have also followed similar policies, while others like Britain and France have granted citizenship and full rights only to immigrants from former colonies. Germany, Belgium and Switzerland have operated 'guest-worker' policies which granted only temporary admission to workers, and no rights to citizenship or permanent settlement. These differences should not be exaggerated. Countries like Britain and France amended their rules to put citizens of former colonies on a par with all other foreigners when they began to restrict immigration in the late 1960s, and many guest-workers were granted wider rights, including settlement, in Germany.

The Gulf states, with their authoritarian regimes and excessive reliance on an imported work force, have followed extremely harsh policies with regard to the status and rights granted to immigrant workers. The latter have to seek government permission before taking up a job, cannot change jobs without further approval, cannot form trades unions or hold public meetings, cannot usually own land, houses or businesses, are not granted the same social service facilities as citizens, cannot bring their families into the country unless their salaries are above a level specified by the state (which is high enough to exclude unskilled and semi-skilled workers) and cannot become citizens of the state. By placing such severe restrictions on the freedom of immigrant workers, and creating wide disparities between the indigenous population and immigrant labour, the Gulf states have been able to minimize both settlement and the social impact of the huge imported labour force in their countries.

Migrants raise social concerns because they potentially threaten to undermine the popularity and strength of the nation-state. At the moment nation-states remain the dominant unit of social organization across the globe with each state ostensibly forming a 'territorially based self-reproducing cultural and social system' (Zolberg, 1981, p. 6). Their members are seen to share a common history, language, religion and culture that binds them into a cohesive integrated unit with a shared sense of nationhood. As citizens of one state, moving to live and work in another, migrants clearly challenge traditional notions about membership of a state, the meaning of nationality and citizenship, and the rights and duties of citizens towards their state and *vice versa*. The fact that *very few* states fit the idealized picture of the homogenous nation-state, and that most states are cultural and social products of earlier movements of peoples, fails to register on the popular consciousness.

Societies are also seen to have a limited 'threshold of toleration' for immigration, and, if crossed, the flow of migrants will begin to undermine the social and political cohesion of the receiving country. The threshold is affected by economic, social and cultural circumstances in the receiving society as well as by the nature of the immigrants themselves, but it remains difficult to determine. In 1996, for example, facing an increasing level of Hispanic immigration, the US Congress voted in favour of the English

Language Empowerment Act, which declared English to be the official language of the United States. Anti-immigrant feeling and xenophobia also increases in times of recession and high unemployment and then abates in times of economic boom. Toleration levels are likely to be lower in countries without a tradition of immigration, and higher in those that have. Immigrants that are similar to the host population are also easier to accommodate and tolerate than if they are racially and culturally distinct. Often unrecognized is the fact that attitudes and responses of governments can themselves affect levels of toleration in societies.

The political dimension

Immigration is also perceived to have an impact on a nation's security. Immigrant communities tend to maintain a strong connection with their home countries, and turbulence or instability in those societies can find expression within the immigrant community as well, thereby bringing external problems into host societies. Instability in Algeria, for example, extends to the Algerian community in France and through to the wider French polity. This factor sometimes has to be taken into account in foreign policy decision-making by the host state. The stance of the Muslim communities in various European states, for example, affected the policies of those states during the Gulf War (Collinson, 1993, pp. 15–16).

The traumatic events of 9/11 have greatly exacerbated these concerns. The pilots and their accomplices who flew the aircrafts into the World Trade Center and other American landmarks were all immigrants to the United States, whether temporary or permanent, legal or illegal. Now, much greater attention is paid to the possible security threat posed by immigrants, particularly those from Muslim countries, in all Western/industrialized countries. All visitors to the United States from Islamic countries are rigorously checked, fingerprinted and quizzed. Immigrants from these countries are required to register with the US Immigration and Naturalisation Service, and far more stringent checks are applied before US citizenship is granted to such people. Similar measures are also in place in several other Western countries.

Immigrant communities often indulge in political activities, with considerable implications for home and host countries, when they try for instance to influence events directly in their home country. This can involve economic, political or military instruments, and may be used to promote or undermine their home government. Immigrant communities can also provide financial and military assistance to rebel groups, as the Irish Americans have done for the IRA. They also try to influence events in the home country by marshalling international public opinion through publicity campaigns, for example, aimed at the international community and more specifically at particular international organizations. The activities of Palestinian emigrants have certainly been successful in encouraging UN countries to embarrass Israel in that forum and elsewhere. Immigrant communities try to use their host government to influence events in their home country. Success depends on their own strength and the susceptibility of the host's political system. Jewish lobbying in the United States has long been recognized as an important factor in maintaining America's pro-Israel stance. The Greek community in the United States helped to get Congress to embargo military assistance to Turkey after the Turkish invasion of Cyprus. But an immigrant community can also be used by the government of the home country to pursue its own aims. The relationship between successive Israeli governments and American Jews illustrates this point. Host governments, too, will try to use their ethnic minority communities to achieve their own goals, particularly those in relation to events in the country of origin of that community, with Mafia leaders, for example, assisting the Allied invasion of Sicily during the Second World War.

Political activity by migrant groups can often become a source of conflict between the home government and host government. For instance, when the activities of a migrant community harm its home government, then the host government will be pressured to restrain the migrants. But, if the migrants are operating within the law, there may be little the host government can do. Relations between previously friendly countries can be strained as a consequence. The US government has been embarrassed by the activities of Irish Americans in assisting the IRA, and the activities of British Sikhs brought tension into generally amicable Anglo–Indian relations.

In the aftermath of 9/11, Muslim immigrant communities in industrialized countries have become the focus of security concerns. This is because the 9/11 hijackers, the Madrid Bombers, and various other terrorists have been drawn from amongst these communities and they are seen by many as supporters of Muslim terrorists. A sometimes hysterically Islamophobic Western media has aided in creating this perception. That such concerns are also taken seriously by governments is evidenced by the actions of the British government which has rushed through anti-terrorist legislation that allows indefinite detention without charge for non-nationals who are resident in the UK, and are considered to be a possible threat to security. It should be noted that these laws are currently being challenged in the Courts and the Law Lords ruled at the end of 2004 that the legislation is incompatible with European human rights laws. Governments have to tread a tight-rope balancing security concerns against the dangers of tarring the entire Muslim community with the brush of 'Islamic terrorism.'

The impact of large refugee flows has serious implications for sending and receiving countries, who are often neighbours. When a government becomes the unwilling host to a large refugee population, it is likely to take steps to ensure that the stay of the refugees is temporary. The movement of Afghans from their country to Pakistan in the 1980s, and Palestinians to a variety of Arab states after 1948 are examples of such situations. In both cases, the refugee influx played a decisive role in impelling the receiving governments to try to bring about a change of government in the sending state by arming the refugees.

Immigrant or ethnic minority communities, formed by labour or refugee migration, can play a significant independent political role in world politics. Their continued political involvement in states in which they no longer live, and whose rules they are not subject to, present a serious challenge to the sovereignty of that state. By the same token they challenge the ability of host states to exercise independent control over the direction of their own foreign and domestic policy.

Putting migration and refugees on the international agenda

Until recently, migration was not seen as a central political issue by most governments, who usually let the various government departments like Employment and Immigration deal with it. It was only in the 1980s, as the effects of past migrations began to be felt both domestically and internationally, and as immigration pressures on developed states increased, that migration rose to the top of the international political agenda and also became of increasing concern to students of world politics.

In the 1980s, many industrialized countries were in severe recession. As always, with a deterioration in the economic climate resulting in high levels of unemployment and social instability, attention started to focus on immigration. By this time, labour migration to most advanced countries had virtually ceased but, nevertheless, immigrant communities became the target of animosity from right-wing groups who blamed them for the high levels of unemployment and decline in general living standards. This period saw the rise of Le Pen in France, neo-Nazis in Germany and Austria and a renewal of extreme-right activity in Britain. Many immigrant communities, now in their second generation, responded with new confidence to this threat.

The rising tide of extremist opinion and associated violence focused the attention of governments on immigration. Many responded by hardening their stance, adopting, in modified form, the anti-immigrant agenda of the extreme right. The acceleration in immigration pressures, they claimed, had to be resisted, if only for the sake of better race relations and to integrate the established immigrant communities. Governments failed to realize that by taking a strongly anti-immigrant stance – reinterpreting their obligations towards refugees ever more strictly, legislating to deport immigrants found guilty of serious crimes and denying subsistence to asylum seekers – the message sent to society at large pandered to the worst instincts of the extreme right, and undermined the social stability that they sought.

As labour migration was reduced, asylum applications rose. Conditions that cause people to flee their homelands in search of a better life persisted and conflict continued to create refugee flows. But now more of these refugees than ever before could seek asylum in Europe and America rather than in neighbouring countries. The collapse of the Soviet bloc and the conflict in former Yugoslavia led to refugee flows into Europe, making it the second largest source of refugees after Africa. Asylum applications to OECD countries as a whole rose from 116 000 in 1981 (Castles and Miller, 1997, p. 88), reaching a peak of around 700 000 in 1992 before falling back to 550 000 in 1993 and to 330 000 in 1994 (Collinson, 1995, pp. 19–20). Table 10.2 charts the numbers of asylum applications in selected OECD countries through the 1990s. Compared to a total refugee population of approximately 15 million, these numbers may seem small, but their importance lies in the impact they have had on European policy.

Table 10.2   *Inflows of asylum seekers into selected OECD countries 1992–2001 (thousands)*

	1992	1996	2001
Australia	13.4	8.1	12.4
Austria	16.2	7.0	30.1
Belgium	17.5	12.4	24.5
Bulgaria	0.2	0.3	2.4
Canada	37.7	25.0	42.7
Czech Republic	0.9	2.2	18.0
Denmark	13.9	5.9	12.4
Finland	3.6	0.7	1.7
France	28.9	17.4	47.3
Germany	438.2	116.4	88.4
Greece	2.0	1.6	5.5
Hungary	0.9	0.7	9.6
Ireland	–	1.2	10.3
Italy	2.6	0.7	9.8
Japan	0.1	0.2	0.4
Luxembourg	0.1	0.3	0.7
Netherlands	20.3	22.9	32.6
New Zealand	0.8	1.3	1.7
Norway	5.2	1.8	14.8
Poland	0.6	3.2	4.5
Portugal	0.5	0.2	0.2
Romania	0.8	0.6	2.4
Slovak Republic	0.1	0.4	8.2
Spain	11.7	4.7	9.2
Sweden	84.0	5.8	23.5
Switzerland	18.0	18.0	20.8
United Kingdom	32.3	37.0	92.0
United States	145.5	150.0	86.4

Source: Data from OECD website extracted from *Trends in International Migration*, 2002 edition.

A further element that brought attention to migration, although far less easy to document by its very nature, has been the rise in unauthorized migration in Europe. This development brought home the inability of the state to implement fully any immigration policy or to police its borders. While this problem has long been acknowledged in the United States, where approximately a quarter of a million South Americans cross the Mexican–US border illegally each year, it had not been so widespread in Europe. With the opening up of the Eastern bloc, the war in the former Yugoslavia, and the ever-tightening restrictions on immigration into Europe, illegal migration, particularly into the Southern European states, has increased.

The loss of asylum

While the Universal Declaration on Human Rights grants everyone the right to exit from any country including their own, this right was and is denied by many states. 'Closing off free emigration is probably an essential policy for any regime that relies heavily on coercion' (Dowty, 1987, p. 60). A survey of countries that have had or continue to have total or limited restrictions on the right to exit shows that they included all the erstwhile communist states across the globe: Angola, Mozambique, Afghanistan, Laos, Mongolia, North Korea, Vietnam, Cuba and China; as well as other coercive regimes such as Iraq, Cameroon, Togo, Tanzania, Iran, Burma, Libya, Sudan and Syria. With the collapse of the Soviet bloc, and the unification of Germany, the restrictions on the right to exit in all East European countries and in many of the former republics of the Soviet Union were lifted. The less prosperous countries of Eastern Europe – Romania and Albania in particular – became a source of large numbers of immigrants for the first time leading to a substantial increase in East–West movements. Ethnic Germans, from all parts of the former Soviet bloc, took advantage of the German law that extends the right of return to them, and began to move to Germany. The war in Yugoslavia also contributed to the numbers trying to move from East to West. This influx put European countries under great pressure, at a time when their attitudes to asylum were hardening.

The collapse of communism has had a more deep-seated impact on Western governments' attitudes towards refugees. During the Cold War, when the Soviet Union and its allies restricted emigration, the West's willingness to offer asylum and refuge to those who did manage to escape the 'evil empire', was a weapon, albeit a small one, in its armoury. It reinforced the belief that communist repression was worth resisting, and that those escaping such repression were worth assisting. In the period 1952–80, a 'refugee' was defined in the United States by the McCarran-Walter Act (1952) as a person fleeing communist persecution (Teitelbaum, 1980, p. 24). With the removal of the threat which had dominated Western thinking for nearly half a century, and the lack of any equivalent substitute, the commitment of Western countries to the whole notion of asylum collapsed. Asylum depended upon the continued existence of a common enemy confronted simultaneously by the refugee and the West.

Institutional responses to migration and refugees

International institutional responses to deal with refugees have been in place since 1951 when countries signed up to the Convention Relating to the Status of Refugees. This Convention, designed to deal with large numbers of displaced persons in Europe at the end of the Second World War, obliges states to extend asylum and protection to those facing persecution, on grounds of religion, race, nationality or political opinion. Further, implicit in the meaning of refugee lies an assumption that the person concerned is worthy of being and ought to be assisted, and if necessary protected from the cause of flight (Goodwin-Gill, 1983, p. 1). In practice the Convention commits states to ensure that no refugee is sent back to any country where they are likely to face danger to life or liberty. Also relevant is the Universal Declaration of Human Rights (1948), which states in Article 14 that everyone has the right to seek and enjoy asylum from persecution in other countries.

Initial international efforts to deal with the problem of refugees began with the League of Nations, which defined refugees as those who were (1) outside their country of origin and (2) without the protection of the government of that state (Goodwin-Gill, 1983, p. 2). These were the criteria used to identify and assist Russians fleeing from the Soviet Union and later those fleeing Nazi persecution in Germany. Today, the UNHCR is the primary UN agency concerned with refugees, and the norms it follows are based on the 1948 Declaration and the 1951 Convention, as well as on customs and practices used in the field.

It must be noted that none of these agreements or practices actually guarantee anyone the right to asylum, only the right to seek it. This is because in practice there is total acceptance in the international community of the right of every sovereign state to decide for itself who should be allowed entry to its territory. Thus, the question of whether someone is a refugee and should be treated as such by a state is an issue to be decided by the government and the courts of the country in which refuge is sought. Nevertheless, these instruments form an important part of the international consensus on the treatment of refugees, and they lay down an important universal principle that most countries have come to endorse, namely that people with a well founded fear of persecution have a right to exit from their own country, cannot be returned to their country of origin, and have international status.

For a refugee to be recognized as such is a political decision, and depends to some extent on the relationship between the sending and receiving countries. For instance, in the 1980s the US government refused refugee status to Salvadoreans fleeing civil war because not to have done so would have acknowledged that a friendly government was indulging in human rights abuse. Nicaraguans, on the other hand, were readily identified as refugees because of American opposition to the Sandanista regime. Thus, states have considerable leeway in deciding whether or not people qualify for refugee status. The advanced industrial governments have adopted ever-stricter interpretations to enable them to minimize the number of people (mostly from Third World countries) eligible to enter their states. Some, like the British government, have enacted laws, like the Carriers' Liability Act (which imposes a fine of £2000 per person who arrives in the United Kingdom without proper documents on the airlines that carry them), which undermine the internationally established principle that 'everyone has the right to seek and enjoy asylum'.

EU countries, faced with increasing applications for asylum, have made moves towards a common set of policies for dealing with asylum seekers. For instance, when Germany, the country with the most unrestrictive asylum laws, tightened its policies in 1993, other European states followed suit, so that a decline in asylum applications to Germany would not result in a corresponding rise elsewhere. Further the Union agreed in the Dublin Convention, which came into force on 1 September 1997, that asylum seekers could only make one application for asylum in the Union, to the country first entered, and that asylum seekers arriving from safe third countries should be returned to those countries. The attention of governments has now shifted to restricting asylum applications, as many are seen to be 'bogus' and filed by economic migrants as a means of gaining entry to the Union. Further, once application has been made, it must go through the due process, which can be a long-drawn out and costly affair, and applicants have to be supported by the state while they wait for a decision on their case. Many European countries now have large backlogs of cases awaiting decision or under appeal, and asylum seekers can wait years to get a final decision. Examples of measures taken to discourage asylum seekers include visa restrictions, carrier-liability policies and voucher systems instead of cash benefits to those awaiting decisions on asylum applications. While a common European policy is still some distance away, its emerging form makes clear that it is unlikely to offer much hope to those suffering persecution. There is a danger that in the rush to protect themselves against unwanted immigration, states are creating a 'fortress Europe', failing to protect legitimate refugees and placing in jeopardy the existing albeit minimal international consensus.

No universal regime for the treatment of voluntary migrants exists, and states retain full powers to determine who shall enter their territory. In the absence of any universally agreed norm regarding immigration, all countries have set up their own restrictions, which they redefine as and when necessary, depending on their economic and social needs. However, EU members have embarked on what promises to be a fairly long-drawn-out process to create common immigration policies. Some have moved faster than others and in 1985 the Schengen Agreement, between Germany, France and the Benelux countries, established a common set of rules for entry to these countries. They were later joined by Austria, Italy, Greece, Spain, and Portugal, and the agreement came into effect in March 1995. It put in place a common list of countries whose nationals require a single visa to visit any 'Schengen' state and a common set of policies on visa restrictions. Sweden, Denmark and Finland are also moving towards signing the Schengen Agreement, but there is still a way to go before a comprehensive European immigration policy emerges.

Migration and contemporary world politics

Migration casts light upon both the nature of the state and inter-state relations in contemporary world politics. The traditional concept of a nation-state, consisting of a population unified by history, culture, language and religion, no longer stands up to scrutiny. Democracies are increasingly multicultural, and to maintain their democratic status, these states are having to learn to deal with cultural differences and to evolve policies that are inclusive and non-discriminatory. Ethnically distinct minorities within these states have heightened the awareness of the need to reconsider our understanding of fundamental concepts like citizenship. Citizens can no longer be identified by common historical, ethnic, cultural or religious ties. The inhabitants of the state must be identified and protected by laws that stress the rights of citizens.

The inability of states to maintain complete control of entry to their territory, or to prevent the formation of immigrant communities with extra-territorial connections and affiliations, points to an erosion of sovereignty. States are no longer able to exert control over their own destinies. The growth of non-indigenous ethnic minorities is helping to blur all distinctions between domestic and international boundaries. Migration also highlights the importance of economic issues in contemporary world politics, because of close association between economic pressures and the motivations for and responses to migration. Improved travel and communication not only facilitates global cultural exchange but also promotes international migration. Thus migration contributes to, illuminates and reinforces the interdependent nature of world politics.

The ability of immigrant communities to act as independent actors on the world stage undermines the traditional state-centred analysis of international relations. To understand contemporary world politics, we need to recognize the role played by non-state, non-governmental, even non-institutionalized actors, amongst which we must number politically active immigrant groups. Migration also casts light on the divided nature of the world in which we live, illuminating the vast gulf in living conditions between the developed, stable countries of the North and the unstable and underdeveloped South. It serves to reinforce the view that the turbulence created by Southern poverty and political uncertainty is not a phenomenon from which the North can easily insulate itself. It provides a forceful argument for constructive and supportive Northern assistance to the South.

Guide to further reading

The literature on migration is wide-ranging and interdisciplinary, reflecting the nature of the phenomenon itself. Explicitly political treatments of migration are increasing in number, and include Hammar (1985), Collinson (1993, 1995), Weiner (1995), Castles and Miller (1997), Castle and Davidson (2000), and Cesarani (1996), Cohen and Layton-Henry (1997) on Europe. Sheffer's (1986) edited volume on diaspora political activity is unique and insightful. Gordenker (1987), Goodwin-Gill (1983) and Zolberg *et al.* (1989) treat refugee issues comprehensively, while Dowty (1987) lucidly examines the political uses and implications of restrictions on emigration. Two edited volumes that present a useful interdisciplinary survey of migration issues are Jackson (1969) and Kritz *et al.* (1981). Potts (1990) provides a succinct study of the indenture system and Castles and Kosack (1985) an analysis of European guest-worker systems, while Cohen (1987) analyzes the role of immigrant labour in the world economy. Journals like *International Migration Review* and *Population and Development Review* and migration bulletins published by the OECD are also useful. Websites provide lots of useful and interesting material, statistical analysis and links to other migration related websites. See, for example, the United Nations High Commission for Refugees, http://www.unhcr.ch; the International Organization for Migration, http://www.iom.int; and the Immigration and Nationality Directorate of the UK government, http://www.ind.homeoffice. gov.uk/content/ind/en/home.html.

Chapter 11

Environment

JOHN VOGLER

Governments have been concluding agreements on matters relating to the conservation of the physical environment for over a century. Efforts to concert international action for the preservation of 'birds useful to agriculture' can be traced back to 1868 (Caldwell, 1990, pp. 17–18). A large number of international fisheries commissions were set up in the first half of the twentieth century and current international marine pollution law dates back to the 1950s. However, environmental issues were most definitely not considered to be part of the mainstream of world politics. Environmental politics were so 'low' as to be virtually invisible. In the most important textbook of the Cold War era, Hans J. Morgenthau's *Politics Among Nations* (1967), the only mention of the physical environment was as one element of national power (alongside decisive factors such as national character). Natural resources were in Morgenthau's words 'another relatively stable factor' (1967, p. 109). The environment, then, was simply regarded as the unchanging context of international politics and environmental issues the preserve of technical negotiations about fish stocks, wild life preservation and the design of oil tankers.

By contrast, it would be difficult today to write a textbook on world politics that did not contain a chapter on, or at least extensive reference to, environmental issues. The change – a rapid growth in the salience of environmental issues – started to occur in the 1960s. It grew from a public awareness of environmental degradation, the damage being done to the countryside by pesticides, the polluted state of rivers and beaches and the finite limits of a natural world confronted by the ever more voracious demands of developing industrial civilization. Concern was reflected in the emergence of pressure groups (mainly in the developed West) such as Friends of the Earth and Greenpeace and a distinctive brand of 'green' activism and political thought. Governments responded, not always very effectively, by creating departments of the environment and by passing legislation for the protection of habitats and endangered species and for the regulation of the discharge of effluents and preservation of air quality.

International awareness: from Stockholm to Rio

Pollution, whether atmospheric or marine, knows no boundaries. Neither do many endangered species. Their destruction also has an international

194

dimension because of the trade in animal products such as ivory. The first formal recognition of the international dimension of the new 'green' awareness occurred in 1972 with the calling of the UN Conference on the Human Environment (at Stockholm) to which 113 states sent representatives, though the Soviet bloc refused to participate on the grounds that the German Democratic Republic (GDR) had not been invited. The Conference drew up 26 Principles calling upon states to cooperate in the protection and improvement of the physical environment through the prevention of pollution, the fostering of education and the institution of rational planning. June 5 was chosen as World Environment Day and 109 specific recommendations for international action were made, including a 10-year moratorium on commercial whaling. At the same time the UN Environment Programme (UNEP) was created.

Reports of the Conference make it clear that many of the essential dilemmas and confrontations of subsequent international environmental politics were already emerging (UN, 1972, pp. 318–23). Several state representatives highlighted the role of capitalism, apartheid and nuclear proliferation in environmental degradation. The Americans and their allies responded by deploring the raising of such 'political' issues and asserting the sanctity of free trade and the GATT system. Most important were fundamental divisions of opinion about development and the environment and about the allocation of responsibility. Could continued economic growth and industrialization be channelled to allow the preservation of the natural environment or were there, as a famous report of the period argued, *Limits to Growth* (Meadows *et al.*, 1972)? Was the main problem unbridled population growth in the developing countries (something that continues to be an extraordinarily sensitive and controversial subject in international gatherings) or was there a clear duty on the developed countries which had both created and benefited from the environmental 'mess' to pay for clearing it up?

In the following 20 years, leading up to the 1992 Rio 'Earth Summit', interest in environmental issues among American and developed world publics waxed and waned. Occasionally, it reached peaks of intensity stimulated by disasters such as the lethal radioactive discharge that blew across Europe from the crippled Soviet reactor at Chernobyl in 1986, the 1989 *Exxon Valdez* oil spill or the dramatic discovery of the Antarctic 'ozone hole' in the mid-1980s. At other times concern with economic recession seemed to exert a contrary pull. Nonetheless, the scientific effort to comprehend the mechanics of global environmental change gathered pace, as did the policy response in terms of the development of international environmental law. In 1987, the World Commission on Environment and Development headed by the then Prime Minister of Norway, Gro Harlem Brundtland, published *Our Common Future*, providing an influential warning and call to action. Most significantly, it coined the phrase 'sustainable development' – an attempt to reconcile the conflict between growth and environmental conservation that had dogged international discussion since Stockholm. Some would say that this was merely a highly political attempt to 'square the circle', but it provided a major cue for the subsequent Rio 'Earth Summit' attended by most heads of government and an additional cast of thousands.

Before Rio, there had already been some landmark international agreements, notably the 1985 Vienna Convention and 1987 Montreal Protocol on restoring the stratospheric ozone layer through action to ban ozone-depleting chemical substances. At Rio, which was preceded by several years of intense preparatory negotiations, the participants agreed not only a declaration of principles but Agenda 21. Painstakingly negotiated, Agenda 21 was remarkable not only for its scale but also for its reach which explicitly extended below the level of government action to communities and local authorities. Its recommendations continue to be discussed and monitored by the UN's Commission for Sustainable Development (CSD).

Elsewhere at Rio there was no agreement on an issue which had given rise to increasing alarm – the systematic and accelerating destruction of tropical rain forests. Agreement was reached, however, on a Convention on Biological Diversity (CBD). Because this appeared to provide developing countries with a means of asserting their sovereignty over and claiming payment for genetic resources located within their territory, the United States at first refused to join. Later, under the Clinton Presidency, the United States signed the Convention and was involved with the other Parties in the difficult task of negotiating a Biosafety Protocol. This covered the contentious area of the rights of governments to protect their territory from the environmental damage that might be inflicted by the release of genetically modified (GM) organisms imported from abroad. Because of heavy investment in the new biotechnology industry and GM seeds, the Protocol had major commercial implications for the United States and other agricultural exporters. Nevertheless, it was concluded in early 2000.

The other Rio outcome was the creation of a Framework Convention on Climate Change (FCCC). This was significant in that it marked the beginnings of a systematic international attempt to grapple with the problem of 'global warming'. With the recession of fears of nuclear war, many of those who have looked at the scientific evidence consider that this represents the gravest threat to the long-term survival of human civilization. It took until the end of 1997 to agree measures to control emissions of the greenhouse gases held to be responsible for the projected rise in mean global temperature. The 1997 Kyoto Protocol to the FCCC required that the developed countries cut their emissions by an average of 5 per cent by the period 2008–12. It also contained 'mechanisms' to assist the process such as emissions trading and 'joint implementation' with developing countries. The process of developing this climate change regime to ward off the alterations in climate and associated disasters that are predicted if nothing is done looks set to continue for many years to come. Thus, environmental questions became part of the regular agenda of world politics, a process nicely described in a book by a British Foreign Office participant as *The Greening of Machiavelli* (Brenton, 1994).

The rising profile of environmental issues

The sources of environmental change and degradation are various, interconnected and sometimes highly controversial. The simplest cases involve emissions of particular chemicals or pollutants (pesticides, heavy metals, sewage) which are readily identified and can be avoided or regulated without excessive costs. Much more difficult to cope with are the inevitable environmental consequences of 'normal' human activities, of economic growth and industrialization and associated population growth and pressure upon resources.

The scale of the problem

Environmental damage may be localized with the effects of pollution incidents confined to a particular area. It may be regional with transboundary phenomena, such as acid rain deposition spanning national frontiers, or it may occur on a truly global scale as with stratospheric ozone layer depletion. A very significant trend in the interval between the Stockholm and Rio conferences was a broadening awareness of the scope of environmental problems. In the 1970s, the dominant concern was with issues such as long-range transboundary air pollution or the pressing need to 'save' the Mediterranean from being abused as a sewer. The solution of such problems required intensive international cooperation because the sources of pollution were frequently located far away from their impact. A well known case is provided by the emissions of UK coal-burning power stations which without expensive 'scrubbing' equipment emitted sulphur dioxide which was then carried eastward by the prevailing winds and deposited on German and Scandinavian forests as highly toxic 'acid rain'. Effluents in the North Sea, which are deposited by the prevailing currents many miles away from their source, provide another example.

By the end of the 1970s, indications of degradation on a global scale began to emerge. The most important case was provided by a new scientific understanding of the destructive impact of certain man-made chemicals, such as chlorofluorocarbons (CFCs) and halons, on the earth's stratospheric ozone layer. Such supposedly benign and inert gases had been manufactured since the 1930s and used for a variety of purposes in refrigerators, air conditioners, fire extinguishers and most famously as propellants in aerosol cans and for the production of the polystyrene boxes in which burgers were sold. Although there was then no indisputable evidence that the ozone layer was being harmed, US environmental groups pressed Congress to legislate a 1977 ban on the use of CFCs. They made the point that risks should not be taken with the health of the ozone layer because of its fundamental significance in protecting human beings, animals and plants from the harmful effects of UV/B radiation from the sun. This was known to increase the risk of skin cancer and to cause other genetic mutations. By the mid-1980s dramatic evidence was found that very serious damage had in fact already occurred to the stratospheric ozone layer and the first systematic attempts to organize a solution to a global environmental problem were made – the Vienna Convention 1985 and Montreal Protocol 1987.

The most comprehensive of global environmental issues is 'global warming' and associated climate change. Unlike the scientific understanding of ozone depletion, hypotheses concerning global warming have long been propounded. To be precise, we are dealing here with the 'enhanced greenhouse effect'. The 'greenhouse effect' refers to the way in which the temperature of the earth is maintained by certain gaseous components of the atmosphere – carbon dioxide, methane, nitrous oxide (to which may be added the CFCs). The presence of these gases in the atmosphere ensures that the warmth from solar radiation is retained at the earth's surface – hence the 'greenhouse' analogy. Without this effect, life on earth as we know it would be impossible.

However, what has occurred since the industrial revolution is a gradually increasing concentration of greenhouse gases – notably carbon dioxide from the burning of fossil fuels but also methane from agriculture. This, according to the majority of scientific opinion, leads to an 'enhanced greenhouse effect' where, instead of the maintenance of a stable temperature, there is a slow but inexorable increase. There is evidence that this has been occurring (the 1980s was the hottest decade on record) but there is still uncertainty and some dispute as to the likely future magnitude of change and, most crucially, as to the consequences over the next hundred years. An understanding of these rests upon predictions made by climate modelling which cannot provide exact answers. The worldwide consensus among climate modellers has been presented in the assessments of the Intergovernmental Panel on Climate Change (IPCC). One global impact is likely to be a rise in mean sea levels through a process of thermal expansion and the melting of the polar ice caps. Another is greater climatic turbulence and shifts in the climate of various regions of the world – although there is, as yet, little precision in the prediction of such effects.

When considering these phenomena it is now commonplace to speak of Global Environmental Change (GEC) or in US usage simply 'global change'. This is because in dealing with greenhouse gas concentrations and the 'drivers' of the world's climate we are confronted with a single, yet extraordinarily complex, global system. Awareness of this has been one of the defining characteristics of environmental discourse since the 1980s. To give one example, Antarctica, once regarded as a frozen wilderness of no great significance, is now seen to be intimately connected to global change in a number of ways. The drilling of its ice cores provide the best record of atmospheric chemical concentrations in previous centuries; it is an integral part of the climate system in terms of its role in establishing thermal gradients; it provides an enormous store of ice which, once melted, would increase sea levels. There is no exaggeration in saying that what occurs in Antarctica is related to, for example, increasing desertification in Sub Saharan Africa. There are also global connections between the destruction of tropical rain forests, the emissions of carbon dioxide from industrialized areas and long-range shifts in agriculture (where temperate zones will become arid) and rising sea levels.

Evaluating the threat

Those who seek to ameliorate or retard global environmental change face real problems of urgency, intensity and visibility. Some environmental issues exhibit all three characteristics. Examples would include 'disasters' when supertankers spill oil, volcanoes erupt or when environmental damage occurs in the context of military action. Saddam Hussein's release of oil into the Persian Gulf and subsequent torching of the Kuwaiti oil wells as a last desperate response to military defeat in 1991 provides a dramatic instance. It is much easier for issues to appear on political agendas and for national and international action to be concerted if environmental effects are tangible and immediate. Unfortunately the effects of polluting activities may not always be known until it is too late to prevent damage, or there may be endless scientific uncertainty which serves as an excuse for political inaction.

It is for this reason that the 'precautionary principle' has become so significant in environmental policy. This states that it is prudent to assume the worst in dealing with potential hazards and not to wait until there is full scientific consensus. Stratospheric ozone depletion provides a perfect example of how an issue moved from the level of scientific uncertainty and public ignorance to one of high visibility and urgency which impelled the chemical industry and governments to take concerted action. Under-pinning this process through the 1970s and mid-1980s was growing scientific certainty as to the nature of the problem and the effects of CFCs that had previously been considered benign. It took some time, however, for any sense of urgency to be instilled into governments.

In the United States, there were bizarre suggestions from the Secretary of the Interior that the solution was to be found, not through regulating industry to restore the ozone layer, but in the wearing of sunglasses and hats. *A New York Times* cartoon appeared depicting a flock of sheep protecting themselves from genetic mutations by following the Secretary's advice! Eventually US policy was reversed – and it was not without significance that President Reagan himself suffered from a skin cancer at this time. The event that gave real impetus to the ozone negotiations and established a sense of urgency, however, was the discovery in mid-1985 of what had only been inadequately predicted – a very large 'hole' in the stratospheric ozone layer over the Antarctic. This thinning of the ozone layer was of much greater severity than had been expected. In fact data from a US Nimbus satellite had previously been rejected as spurious because they were so far beyond the expected values. It took a British Antarctic Survey balloon to confirm the alarming magnitude of the damage that had already been done to the ozone layer.

The problem with other global change phenomena is that they are much more insidious and uncertain even though, in the longer run, they may potentially pose an even greater threat than ozone layer depletion. The full impact of increasing concentrations of greenhouse gases in the atmosphere will only be visited on the earth towards the end of the twenty-first century – IPCC predictions offer a range of scenarios. For the period 1990–2100 estimated mean temperature increase is in the range 1.4–5.8°C, with an associated sea-level rise of 0.09 to 0.88 metres (Houghton *et al.*, 2001, pp. 15–16). These figures may seem small and they depend upon what can be achieved in restraining climate change in the next decades. However, even small increases can have radical effects upon agricultural production, diseases and the habitability of land. They are also sufficient to inundate many low-lying areas, including not only the small island states of the Pacific but also many of the major world cities which are built at sea level. This has already alarmed some of the most immediately vulnerable like the Alliance of Small Island States (AOSIS) who have been very active in international negotiations on climate change. The first Conference of the Parties to the FCCC in 1995 demonstrated some of the different perspectives on interest and threat in international environmental politics. The Group of 77 – a UN-based caucus of developing states – found itself divided on the issue. The oil-producing states, unlike other members, refused to accept international restrictions on the use of fossil fuels. One can only speculate as to the kind of private disagreements that must have occurred between, say, Bangladesh with its miserably poor population located at sea level and oil-rich Saudi Arabia.

For many countries the threat, although potentially catastrophic, is hardly urgent or immediate. Thus, in the climate-change negotiations some developed countries, including the United States and Australia, have opposed stringent measures to control greenhouse gas (GHG) emissions, concerned about the effects upon their economic performance. The EU has taken a more progressive stance and before Kyoto offered a collective reduction in its GHG emissions – although its collective 'burden sharing' agreement allowed some Member States actually to increase their emissions. The United States, while agreeing to, but not ratifying, the Kyoto Protocol began to urge that any future action be dependent upon emissions reductions by developing as well as industrialized countries. The advent of the Bush Administration in 2001 led to a new and potentially fatal development in which even the United States' signature of the protocol was 'denounced' as inimical to national energy interests.

A reluctance to be involved with making immediate economic and political sacrifices in order to confront an uncertain long-range threat is understandable. Politicians notoriously tend to discuss issues within a time frame that does not extend very much further then the next election. Corporate executives are often longer-sighted, having an horizon that is bounded by the life cycle of a product, a process, or an investment. Thus for example, discussions under the Montreal Protocol about the point at which HCFCs (the relatively less damaging substitutes for CFCs) will be phased out tend to converge upon the date, 25 years hence, when the current generation of air conditioners will have reached the end of their useful life.

In dealing with long-range threats one critical determinant will be the extent, to use economists' language, to which we discount the future. Are we concerned enough about what will happen to our great-grandchildren to induce us to make inconvenient changes in present consumption patterns or lifestyles? Very much to the point in discussions of sustainable development is the difference between the way in which the affluent and the poor discount the future. For the poor who worry about whether they will be able to survive tomorrow, contemplating the impact of their actions upon conditions 100 or even 30 years hence must seem an irrelevant luxury. Cutting down and burning trees or other non-sustainable activities may seem the only way to ensure immediate survival regardless of the long-run damage inflicted upon the biosphere.

The problem of lack of immediacy is compounded by uncertainty. It cannot be overstressed that at present potential climate change is still challenged as an hypothesis, although supported by the overwhelming weight of scientific opinion and although confirmatory evidence is becoming available, including for many analysts the record summer temperatures experienced in Europe in 2003. Even less clear and dependent upon complex modelling are the precise impacts of temperature changes. As has often been said, the fateful irony is that by the time we acquire absolutely certain evidence that the enhanced greenhouse effect hypothesis is correct, temperature rise will have become irreversible and there will be no possibility of taking effective remedial action to prevent its more disastrous impacts. High levels of scientific uncertainty and public scepticism militate against political action and there are always those who will argue that no action is needed unless – as in the case of stratospheric ozone – there is tangible evidence and an obvious threat to life.

This has been counteracted by the extensive organization of international scientific cooperation on environmental matters since Stockholm. At the centre is the IPCC itself, which has institutionalized a process in which governments are continually warned as to the nature and gravity of the threat on the basis of a general scientific consensus which is difficult for sceptics to challenge. However, generating the political momentum to make the required economic sacrifices in terms, for example, of energy taxes to limit carbon dioxide emissions remains exceedingly difficult. In Britain, the attempt to double the VAT on domestic fuel in the early 1990s (ostensibly to assist in meeting Rio commitments) proved so unpopular as to be politically unsustainable. While high-profile events such as Chernobyl, the discovery of the ozone hole or Earth Summit itself may increase the short-run saliency of environmental issues, tax and economic welfare questions tend to dominate the domestic political agenda. Environmentalists often hope, therefore, for a run of hot summers in the United States which would put some urgency and immediacy back into the discussion of global environmental change.

Defining the problem

At the most profound level the imperative of sustaining the physical environment has to be reconciled with a range of other human aspirations, most notably those relating to economic growth. Ever since the industrial revolution, key indicators of production – resource use, emissions of carbon dioxide and so on – have shown an exponential growth pattern which accelerates rather than maintains a steady linear increase. The increase in the human population provides the most awesome illustration. In 1700 world population was 615 million, in 1800 900 million and by 1900 it had reached 1.625 billion. By 1965, despite two world wars, population had more than doubled to 3.33 billion, in 1999 it reached 6 billion and is projected to rise to 8.89 billion by the year 2030 (World Bank, 1999, p. 196).

Most people continue to exist in relative poverty and have legitimate aspirations to achieve the living standards of affluent 'developed' sections of the world's population. In absolute terms, levels of human development have improved since the 1960s; but in relative terms, there have been sharp increases in inequality. Thus, the ratio of the GNP *per capita* of the richest 20 per cent of world population to that of the poorest 20 per cent rose from 30:1 in 1960 to 74:1 in 1997 (UNDP, 1999, pp. 104–5; see also Table 5.3). At the same time, however, the contribution of this richest 20 per cent to environmental degradation, as measured for instance in carbon dioxide emissions *per capita*, is incomparably greater. Yet the consequences of environmental change are likely to be visited first and with the greatest severity upon the poor. It is they, for example, who are forced to migrate through increasing desertification or who live in the midst of unregulated and life-threatening pollution of air and water. Most at risk are the populations of 'damage-prone areas of the developing world that do not have the resources to cope with impacts' (Watson *et al.*, 1996, p. 11). Yet as Figure 11.1 graphically illustrates they are hardly responsible for the problem – the 35 countries with the lowest level of human development producing a mere 0.7 of global emissions of carbon dioxide.

It is important to grasp the point that the 'problem' here is not really environmental but socio-economic. From the very first international discussions of the environmental crisis at Stockholm it has been impossible to separate environmental issues from questions of development and North–

Figure 11.1   *National carbon dioxide emissions and population, 1996*

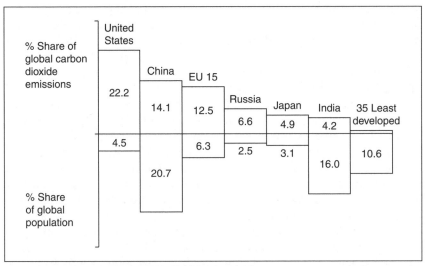

Source: Data from UNDP (1999), Tables 16 and 18.

South inequality (see also Chapter 5). The 2002 World Summit on Sustainable Development, held at Johannesburg a decade after Rio, served to re-emphasize the point for its discussions were dominated by demands for poverty reduction in developing countries as the indispensable counterpart to environmental improvement. At issue is the question of whether Brundtland's objective of 'sustainable development' can be achieved. Will the attempts by developing countries to engage fully in the global trade and production system mean that they are bound to follow the growth trajectory of the current industrialized countries? Will not the attainment of levels of consumption for the majority of earth's population that even approach those of the currently developed countries in terms of resource exploitation inevitably mean the collapse of the physical environment and the realization of the worst fears of those who study climate change? There is no clear consensus on this most contentious of questions. Optimists argue that there are 'win–win' solutions and that new technologies and a more prudent and efficient use of resources can, if implemented in time, produce a sustainable future that satisfies development aspirations (Meadows *et al.*, 1992).

The role of international cooperation

Sustainable development

As was most evident at Rio, the international political system now provides a forum in which such questions are frequently aired. The UN has established the Commission for Sustainable Development and holds special

General Assembly sessions and conferences. The multilateral institutions like the World Bank and the WTO now have sustainable development as a permanent feature on their agendas. The conventional wisdom, both among practitioners and most academics involved with the international relations of the environment, is that however hypocritical and self-interested governments may be, their involvement in finding solutions to the problem of sustainable development is unavoidable

The argument proceeds as follows. Because there is no overarching political authority at the global level and the authority to regulate lies with around 200 sovereign states, the solutions to transboundary and global environmental problems have to be sought through inter-state cooperation. This is particularly so in the global commons – the oceans, Antarctica, outer space and the atmosphere (Vogler, 2000). Their defining feature is that they do not come under any national jurisdiction but are nevertheless critical to human welfare. Without some form of regulation there is an inevitable short-term temptation for users to exploit common resources, bringing about their long-term degradation and collapse. The fate of the great whales, virtually wiped out by the voracious whaling fleets of the late nineteenth and early twentieth centuries, provides a graphic illustration and it is worth noting that the whaling industry itself (with a few isolated exceptions) soon followed its prey into extinction. The problem has been most famously described by Hardin (1968) as the 'tragedy of the commons'. International cooperation is needed to prevent such tragedies to ensure, for example, that common fish stocks are not overexploited. There will need to be agreed 'sustainable' catch limits and some form of policing to prevent cheating by fishermen.

In this sense the problem of international cooperation is the same one that is encountered in other issue areas – developing arms control measures or managing international trade and monetary relations. In fact they are all related anyway, not just in terms of the common problem of cooperation but in very substantive ways. Environmental change in relation to, say, forests cannot be isolated from the trade and monetary systems which set the context within which trees are either logged to extinction or sustained. A major difficulty is that the UN and other bodies continue to treat the problems separately and even schizophrenically. For instance, the WTO considers environmental issues in a rather limited way within its Committee on Trade and the Environment, concentrating on potential conflicts between trade and environmental regimes. The existing trade rules forbid import restrictions on goods that have been unsustainably produced and little progress has been made on this issue during recent WTO rounds.

Radical alternatives

Although most International Relations scholars (Young, 1989; Haas *et al.*, 1994) conceptualize the problem in terms of the imperative of international cooperation, other activists and writers disagree, arguing that this is a narrow and ultimately fruitless representation of the issue of global environmental change. An insight into this very different perspective can be gained from the following commentary on Rio by *The Ecologist*.

> Unwilling to question the desirability of economic growth, the market economy or the development process itself, [the Rio Summit] never had a chance of addressing the real problems of 'environment and develop- ment'. Its secretariat provided delegates with materials for a convention on biodiversity but not on free trade; on forests but not on logging; on climate but not on automobiles. Agenda 21 – the Summit's action plan – featured clauses on 'enabling the poor to achieve sustainable livelihoods' but none on enabling the rich to do so; a section on women but none on men. By such deliberate evasion of the central issues which economic expansion poses for human societies, UNCED condemned itself to irrelevance even before the first preparatory meeting got under way. (*Ecologist*, 1993, pp. 1–2)

For more radical commentators such as Saurin (1996), Paterson (2001) and Lipschutz (2004) international cooperation between states can never fully address the problems of environmental degradation. The modern state is deeply compromised and often regarded as powerless in the face of those globalizing forces that also drive environmental change. Intimately connected with corporate capitalism and imbued with authoritarian 'managerialist' conceptions, the inter-state system is itself very much part of the problem rather than the solution. Thus political answers are sought not through international cooperation but through generating resistance and self reliance at local and transnational levels.

Getting on the international agenda

The exact way in which particular issues appear and disappear in the public consciousness and become salient for governments continues to puzzle and intrigue political scientists. Certainly, as we have seen, environmental issues have moved rather dramatically on to the international political agenda but their salience appears to have a cyclical character, rising to a peak in the period 1988–92, but then falling away. Certain critical events have clearly helped to stimulate public awareness and political responses. At the same time there has been insistent pressure from transnational scientific and expert communities on particular issues which have kept them alive and influenced the policies of governments.

No discussion of environmental politics would be complete without mention of a vast range of NGOs that have made environmental issues peculiarly their own. Greenpeace and other campaigning NGOs 'cut their teeth' by generating public protest against whaling and have gone on to deal with radioactive and oil pollution and the whole range of global commons issues, often taking direct action in order to generate public interest. More 'establishment' groups like World Wildlife Fund (WWF) or the International Institute for Environment and Development (IIED) routinely advise governments, and NGOs are now granted observer rights at UN conferences and some of their members even appear within national delegations. The 'Global Forum' at Rio demonstrated the full range and diversity of NGOs and some have even begun to talk of the emergence, alongside the states system, of a 'global civil society'.

There is little doubt that NGOs have made a very major impact upon international environmental politics and that their public campaigning has virtually created a number of issues – for example the early public opposition to ozone-depleting chemicals, the moratorium on whaling and the need for a more environmentally stringent regime in Antarctica. In comparison to many state governments, well-financed NGOs deploy far greater research resources and can, therefore, enjoy a serious position of influence if invited to advise. However, a note of caution is in order. In the final analysis they will always lack legitimacy alongside an elected government and they, like other actors, will have their own organizational interests to pursue and will not, on occasion, be above misrepresenting scientific evidence (as Greenpeace was honest enough to admit in the case of the Brent Spar oil platform). Their function is pre-eminently to create and publicize issues, and it is here that they have played their most significant role in recent environmental politics.

Environmental issues after the Cold War

The end of the Cold War coincided with the rise of environmental issues in the period before Rio. Was there a connection? It might be argued that a slackening of Cold War tension gave the 'space' for environmental issues to assume a greater prominence. Indeed, Thomas explicitly links together the end of the Cold War with the influence of NGOs:

> the current diplomatic profile of environmental issues derives largely from the activities of NGOs who took advantage of the political space provided by the fortuitous ending of the Cold War. (Thomas, 1992, p. 14)

Politicians, including President Clinton, argued that the common threat of environmental destruction had replaced the threat of mutual nuclear annihilation that had characterized Superpower relations during the Cold War. There were also some suggestions that redundant military establishments should be given a new role as protectors of the environment. Consideration of the environment as a national security issue is one aspect of the wider debate on the redefinition of security that will be discussed in the conclusion to this chapter. In the aftermath of the Cold War some activists attempted, often in a rather grandiose way, to suggest that the problems of GEC were so daunting that only the kind of persistent mobilization of resources that had sustained the Cold War confrontation would be adequate. Hence, national security and environmental security were uneasily yoked together in an attempt both to generate extra attention and funds for environmental projects and, on occasion, to provide new missions for military establishments facing an uncertain future.

During the Cold War, some environmental and global commons issues provided one of the few areas on which the Superpowers *could* agree – for example the Long-Range Transboundary Air Pollution Convention of 1979 and its Helsinki and Sofia Protocols of 1985 and 1988. Another important example is provided by the Antarctic Treaty, signed in 1959 in the depths of the first Cold War. This placed territorial claims in abeyance and initiated a regime that demilitarized Antarctica and committed participants to peaceful scientific research. Since then the scope of the Antarctic Treaty System has greatly expanded to include a wide range of provisions protecting the environment of this last great wilderness on earth.

Although Cold War concerns sometimes interfered with environmental negotiations (as in the Soviet bloc's refusal to participate in the Stockholm Conference) the key disagreements were not East–West but North–South. This arose from the nature of the issues at stake: population, development and the responsibility for funding environmentally sound policies. This remains the case in the early years of the twenty-first century despite the replacement of Cold War antagonism by the amorphous 'war on terror' .

Managing environmental problems

International cooperation to 'manage' environmental and global commons problems does not enjoy universal approval but it remains the dominant approach. There may be no international government to regulate and enforce but there are forms of international *governance* that can fulfil similar functions. These forms of governance can be described as *regimes*. This is an all-encompassing term that includes the principles, norms, rules and decision-making procedures that serve to coordinate international action.

Thus, if we were to speak of the marine-pollution regime we would include shared understandings on the dangers of certain forms of pollution (oil, radioactive material, sewage and so on) and on the legitimacy of controlling the activities of governments, ship owners and operators, industrial plant and so forth. There would be general norms of behaviour concerning what could and could not be thrown into the oceans and very specific sets of rules deriving from the various legal Conventions and Protocols like the 1972 London Convention on dumping, the 1973–8 Convention for the Prevention of Pollution from Ships (often known as

MARPOL) and specific regional rules for the Mediterranean and North Sea. These are supported by 'guidelines' for good environmental behaviour developed by UNEP. UNEP itself and the International Maritime Organization are also key parts of the regime because they organize the monitoring of compliance, the conduct of research and the taking of collective decisions about how the regime will develop. A major problem with such regimes is that they tend to be partial – in the sense that they are designed to deal with certain sources of pollution from ships or through industrial dumping, but not well developed when it comes to regulating the major land-based sources of marine degradation.

At the heart of international environmental regimes are multilateral treaties – usually referred to as Conventions. These constitute sets of binding legal rules and they may be regional or global in scope. There are well over 100 such environmental agreements, most of which have been created since the 1972 Stockholm Conference. Some of the major Conventions and Protocols are listed in Box 11.1.

One problem with the development of international environmental law is that the growth of scientific understanding often outpaces the more cumbrous procedures of negotiation and ratification of international conventions. When negotiators identify a problem they may wish to commence remedial action but they may not be fully aware of its extent or the precise measures that will be required. To meet this problem the ozone negotiations started with a 'framework' Convention (Vienna 1985) and then proceeded to draw up detailed control measures in the Montreal Protocol 1987 and subsequent London and Copenhagen agreements – which reflected a growing scientific and political consensus on the dimensions and causes of stratospheric ozone depletion. The Framework Convention on Climate Change (1992) followed a similar pattern. Its parties recognized that a serious problem existed and that the developed countries had a particular responsibility to curb the sources of greenhouse gases and to preserve sinks, but largely owing to American objections it did not contain any binding commitments to national reductions in GHG emissions. The 1997 Kyoto Protocol, the product of much hard negotiation in the context of increasing scientific certainty as to the reality of 'global warming', rectified this omission and points the way to further action (see Box 11.2). It is important to note that the mechanisms were merely outlined in principle in the Protocol and that it took until the Marrakech Conference of 2001 to negotiate the details of an agreement that was fit for ratification. This was achieved in the teeth of US hostility and provides a testament to the important leading role now played by the EU. The latter made another contribution by developing the world's first fully-fledged emissions trading system, beginning in 2005. Entry into force of the Protocol in February 2005 was delayed until Russian ratification had been achieved and even then it was generally acknowledged that the promised emissions reductions were merely a beginning.

Box 11.1 Key multilateral environmental agreements

1946 **International Convention for the Regulation of Whaling**
Eventually provided framework for 1985 moratorium on commercial whaling and subsequent whale sanctuaries.

1959 **Antarctic Treaty**
Allowed development of environmental recommendations and the 1980 Convention on the Conservation of Antarctic Living Marine Resources plus the 1991 Madrid Protocol which introduces strict environmental impact assessment.

1973 **International Convention for the Prevention of Pollution from Ships and 1978 Protocol**
Usually known as MARPOL, this Convention sets up rules to prevent the operational discharge of oil and other harmful substances from ships and to minimize accidents. It is one of a large number of regional and world marine environmental agreements.

1973 **Convention on International Trade in Endangered Species of Wild Fauna and Flora (CITES)**
Signatories ban trade in wild-caught specimens of species threatened with extinction.

1979 **Convention on Long-Range Transboundary Air Pollution (LRTAP)**
Aims to limit and reduce air pollution in the area of North America and Europe. Subsequent protocols have dealt with national emissions of sulphur, nitrogen oxides and volatile organic compounds.

1985 **Vienna Convention for the Protection of the Ozone Layer and 1987 Montreal Protocol on Substances that Deplete the Ozone Layer**
The Protocol ensured the phasing-out of production of CFCs, mainly responsible for the depletion of the stratospheric ozone layer by 1996 (for the developed countries). It has gone on to tackle other ozone-destroying chemicals.

1992 **United Nations Framework Convention on Climate Change (FCCC) and 1997 Kyoto Protocol**
The Convention recognized the special responsibilities of developed countries for human-induced climate change, the need for research and the obligation of all countries to report their emissions of GHGs. The Kyoto Protocol set up binding reduction targets for developed countries and instituted 'mechanisms' (such as emissions trading) to assist the process.

1992 **United Nations Convention on Biological Diversity (CBD) and 2000 Cartagena Biosafety Protocol**
The Convention aims to conserve and allow sustainable use of and equitable sharing of benefits from the earth's biodiversity. It has been developed in the form of a Biosafety Protocol which allows governments to control the import of, GM organisms on the grounds that they may endanger health and the environment.

Box 11.2 The Kyoto Mechanisms

The 1997 Kyoto Protocol to the UN FCCC commits the developed countries to making actual cuts in their GHG emissions by 2008–12. Commitments vary, but they average 5 per cent from a 1990 baseline. In order to provide 'flexible' ways of achieving such reductions and to make agreement possible, three mechanisms were also agreed:

1. *Emissions trading.* Under this mechanism Parties may trade their emissions allowances with each other, for example buying extra permits to emit if they are unwilling to reduce their own fossil fuel use. Such systems, long discussed, are supposed to improve flexibility and economic efficiency by creating a market in rights to pollute.

2. *Joint implementation (JI).* Here a developed country can receive additional emissions units for itself by financing projects that reduce emissions in another developed country. Experiments have already been conducted and an essential justification is that spending the same amount of money in a relatively energy-inefficient foreign country yields greater net emissions reductions than could have been achieved at home.

3. *The clean development mechanism (CDM).* Applies the same principle to the relations between developed and developing parties, whereby the former gain credit for financing emissions-avoiding projects in the latter.

Another approach to the problem of negotiating binding rules that reflect current scientific understanding is reflected in the growth of what lawyers term 'soft law' – that is to say guidelines for good environmental behaviour which do not have the full force of international treaty law but can as a consequence be produced and revised much more speedily. UNEP has pioneered a mass of 'soft law' in, for example, its Regional Seas Programme. The whole of Agenda 21, which provides guidelines on almost every environmental topic imaginable at every level – see, for instance, the special role of women and the responsibilities of local authorities – constitutes an exercise in 'soft law'-making.

There are a number of international organizations, like the World Meteorological Organization (WMO) or the International Council for the Exploration of the Seas (ICES), whose primary remit has always been the conduct of research relevant to environmental questions. They, together with UNEP, have actively sponsored the development of environmental regimes. UNEP has also been involved in monitoring compliance with international rules (in the ozone regime) and it has been described as having a 'catalytic and coordinating' role (Imber, 1993). This is certainly needed in the UN system where not always successful attempts have been made to persuade all its component parts, from the World Bank to the Food and Agriculture Organization (FAO), to take environmental issues seriously. At the apex of the system the Commission for Sustainable Development attempts to continue the work of Rio and receives periodic reports from members and from the EU and other organizations on how they have responded to Agenda 21.

The ultimate and much-disputed question is whether such management efforts have been effective in arresting environmental degradation and whether they stand any chance of coping with the new agenda of GEC issues. For radical commentators the answer, almost by definition, is a resounding 'no'. Even those who hope for effective international cooperation make the point that it is very difficult in a world of sovereign states not only to persuade governments to agree to environmentally sound policies which may be contrary to their short-run economic interests, but also to enforce those to which they have agreed. The record is extremely patchy. There have been disasters such as the near-extinction of the great whales before the 1985 International Whaling Commission moratorium and the current worldwide collapse of fish stocks – where international regulation has been fragmented and inadequate. On the other hand, there are regimes where rules have been adequate and well-respected and where threatened environments have been preserved. With some reservations, Antarctica and Mediterranean pollution control could be placed in this category. The air-pollution regime in Europe has also proved to be a success. The ozone regime has attracted most attention because it addressed a dramatic global problem. The indications here are good because strong measures have been taken to eliminate CFCs. Even though the ozone layer will not return to its former health until some point beyond the middle of the present century, the signs are encouraging because current readings show a reduction in atmospheric concentrations of ozone-depleting chemicals. Thus there are physical indications that the ozone regime is 'working'.

The environment and contemporary world politics

Arguably, the recent treatment of environmental issues reveals a shift in the subject matter of international politics or at least some re-ordering of the priority afforded to them. It also, at the same time, involves new participants. Diplomats at the UN in New York have been required to deal with environmental specialists and foreign offices have had to contend with subject matter, such as the content of Agenda 21, which was previously well beyond their remit. What this demonstrates is that the distinction between the high politics of 'state-to-state' diplomacy and the low politics of areas such as environmental protection is exceedingly blurred and has probably ceased to exist. Summit meetings between the leaders of the G7 nations now make declarations about forests and pollution as well as their more traditional preoccupations with domestic interest rates and 'political' and security matters.

The erosion of the boundary between high and low politics is nowhere more evident than in considerations of the changing meaning of the concept of security. Traditionally security was construed as 'national security' and involved the construction of military defences and alliances against potential external armed threats. Such thinking dominated the Cold War period. Yet, after the Cold War the question was legitimately asked – do such threats still constitute the essential security problem? One answer was provided in the immediate aftermath of the events of 11 September 2001. The new threat in the global system was defined by the United States and its allies in terms of the unholy trinity of terrorism, failed states and weapons of mass destruction.

Yet it can be argued that global environmental change and a complex of inter-related issues involving poverty, population growth and inequality constitute a new security problem of greater profundity that should be treated with the same urgency as national defence. After all, if the definition of security is absence of threat then some of the gravest, if not the gravest threats, to the survival of societies are environmental. Thus Sir David King, the UK Government's Chief Scientific Advisor, was able to make the controversial claim that, in terms of the actual and potential deaths involved, climate change represented a far greater threat than terrorism (*Science*, 9 January 2004, vol. 303, pp. 176–7). This idea has some attractions in terms of seizing the attention of governments but it also has serious drawbacks. Environmental issues are very different from traditional security issues. There is usually no identifiable enemy and degradation is the result of 'business as usual'. In national defence the threats are usually readily understandable and military measures can be taken to counter them – this is not the case with long-run environmental threats. Even if we reject the attempt to re-define traditional concepts of security, there is still a sense in which environmental issues are entangled with the security preoccupations of international relations. Environmental degradation is not just the consequence of war as in Laos and Cambodia in the 1960s or more recently in the Gulf, but it is increasingly likely to be among the causes as well. As natural resources are destroyed conflict between those who depend upon them is likely to become sharper while desertification and ecological collapse will produce social and economic disruption and population movements, the consequences of which are likely to pose security threats of the most traditional kind. At the same time, it would appear that the avoidance of further degradation and the reduction in the extent of future climate change may point us in the same policy direction as the need for the developed nations to reduce their geopolitical dependence on volatile oil-producing regions in the Middle East and elsewhere. Finding efficient substitutes for fossil fuels may thus hold the key to future security.

The discussion so far has centred upon the relationship between environmental issues and the international political system, primarily composed of sovereign state governments. We have noted that most of the academic writing about the environment and world politics focuses upon how states can be induced to cooperate in the solution of common problems. Yet it is also the case that environmental change is increasingly viewed as a truly global phenomenon which has given rise to forms of activism that transcend the nation-state. The role of NGOs has been particularly important in this area and, although they attempt to influence state policy, many of those involved in 'green' politics are increasingly irritated by the hypocrisies and delays of inter-state cooperation. In philosophical and practical terms, they often regard the nation-state as part of the problem and urge community action in response to world environmental problems in accord with the famous slogan 'think globally act locally'.

One of the most interesting questions about post-Cold War politics is whether this kind of activity, particularly when it is linked together across frontiers by such powerful tools as the internet, presages the emergence of a global polity that may ultimately subvert the international political system. This is a question for the future, but events such as the Rio summit and much of the environmental politics of the 1980s and 1990s certainly demonstrate the coexistence and interaction between the inter-state system and a bewildering range of transnational – and even, perhaps, global – political action. This is not to say that in environmental policy-making and the generation of scientific knowledge, state governments do not remain at centre stage. For example the FCCC is an *international* treaty and the authoritative scientific body is significantly named the *Intergovernmental* Panel on Climate Change (IPCC). Nonetheless, responsibility for the emergence of environmental issues on the international agenda certainly lies elsewhere.

Guide to further reading

The increasing significance of environmental issues in world politics is demonstrated by the availability of good recent textbooks. Of these Porter and Brown (2000), Elliott (2004) and Lipschutz (2004) stand out. Vogler (2000) provides a comparative analysis of global commons regimes, while Barnett (2001) is a stimulating introduction to the environment and security debate. An older but very extensive and influential treatment is to be found in Caldwell (1990). Hurrell and Kingsbury (1992) provide a significant set of essays on many aspects of the subject to which may be added the collection in Vogler and Imber (1996) which provides some indication of the range of theoretical debate. For a liberal and institutional approach the work of Young (1989) is indispensible. An angry, radical and readable alternative is to be found in *The Ecologist* (1993) while the specifics of Rio and the various agreements are well covered in Grubb *et al.* (1993). For up-to-date material on international environmental agreements and organisations consult the *Yearbook of International Co-operation on Environment and Development* published annually by the Fridtjof Nansen Institute and Earthscan.

Amongst the journals, *Environmental Politics* (London: Frank Cass) is always worth consulting alongside *Global Environmental Politics* (Cambridge, Mass: MIT Press)

Those with an interest in current international environmental politics are very well served by the internet. A first port of call should be the UNEP website, http://www.unep.org, which provides updates on the activities of UNEP alongside details of the key conventions. The secretariats of the conventions, such as the FCCC also have their own sites, accessible via UNEP, which can provide documents and conference papers. Also not to be missed are the numerous other sources on the web – see, for example, the World Resources Institute, http://www.wri.org, and the sites which provide detailed reporting of negotiations – for example, *Earth Negotiations Bulletin*, http://www.iisd.ca.

Chapter 12

Media and Communications Technology

SUSAN CARRUTHERS

Once or twice daily, invariably at the least convenient moment, my life at home in New Jersey is interrupted by a phone call from India. I have never visited that country, nor do I have friends or family there. My anonymous callers, however, don't know me, nor do they want to chat. Their typical business is to entice me to buy financial services from a US company on whose behalf they are soliciting. However resistant I remain, and however improbable the pretence that these calls emanate from somewhere local, this now-familiar scenario is emblematic of the way in which communications technology functions as a vector of 'globalization': enabling a whole variety of cross-border transactions, traffic and trade, but, in so doing, animating an array of discrepant responses. In the United States, the outsourcing of jobs to distant, poorer countries, has become an emotive issue for unemployed Americans who see themselves disadvantaged by corporations' restless search for cheaper labour. In India, meanwhile, the burgeoning call-centre industry (at least as US press reports tell it) inspires, on the one hand, enthusiasm for free enterprise among young Indians eager to accept not only these comparatively well-remunerated jobs but also the trappings of consumer lifestyle that accompany them. And their enthusiastic embrace of 'Westernization', in turn, disturbs those concerned with the preservation of local culture, languages, and customs in the face of a new foreign incursion. After all, it's worth remembering that these particular jobs are outsourced to India – as opposed to, say, Guatemala or Indonesia – on account of its vast reservoir of English-speakers. Had it not been for the British Raj, then, the US-owned call-centres would be elsewhere: a salutary reminder that cross-currents of global interconnectedness have a history several centuries old.

As this example suggests, a consideration of media and communications technology as the connective – but abrasive – thread that links people, places and products while throwing ideas and values into disarray takes us into multiple domains of academic study and human activity. Economics, politics, sociology, and anthropology all come into play in determining what media are and what communicative functions they fulfil. It is, after all, impossible to study media and communications technologies without some consideration of global political economy, since the media landscape – global, regional, and within many states – is increasingly monopolized by giant conglomerates. Thanks to mergers between companies and 'convergence' of media and communications technology, the same corporation (SONY, for example) may at once provide consumers with the equipment they need to watch television or play and burn DVDs and CDs, while also providing at least some of the actual content (X studio). This level of horizontal and vertical integration – monopolization by any other name – does not simply happen by magic: by the sheer steamrollering momentum generated by huge media megaliths, although it's often imagined that MNCs resist restraint by any more old-fashioned source of territorialized power (like governments or international governmental organizations). The terms of economic life are, however, subject to regulation. Political decisions taken at the state and supranational levels establish the regulatory framework within which media and communications companies operate. So any consideration of how media technologies and products flow across borders is necessarily 'political' in this narrow sense.

At the same time, the functions fulfilled by media are nothing if not political – or ideological – in the far broader sense that our channels of communication, forms of entertainment and sources of news alike, help to naturalize (or sometimes to contest) particular understandings of how the world works, and the justice (or injustice) of the order that currently prevails within and between states. Media thus occupy crucial terrain in the cultural life of technologized communities. In this capacity, media play a constitutive role in shaping micro-communities of those, scattered across geographical space, sharing the same passionate involvement in, for example, *Star Trek*. But at the same time channels of communication also help bind communities anchored by very specific territorial attachments, even when diasporic members may be dispersed. Permitting the instantaneous dispatch and receipt of text and image alike, today's electronic media and digital communications technologies thus encourage a whole array of transnational communities, whether of shared interest or common descent.

> As Turkish guest workers in Germany watch Turkish films in their German flats, as Koreans in Philadelphia watch the 1988 Olympics in Seoul through satellite feeds from Korea, and as Pakistani cabdrivers in Chicago listen to cassettes of sermons recorded in mosques in Pakistan or Iran, we see moving images meet deterritorialized viewers. (Appadurai, 1996, p. 4)

Media and communications technologies function in multiple different, and sometimes seemingly quite discrepant, ways. Similarly, what comprises 'the medium' and who delivers its 'message' ranges from giant MNCs to expressly national (sometimes state-funded) broadcasting networks, and from small independent companies to lone individuals who run radio stations from their backrooms or post a personal 'blog' on the web. Given this diversity of form and function, how does one even begin to make some generalized observations about 'the media' and global politics? This chapter approaches its task by considering the media as the connective tissue of international processes in three distinct domains, all of which have generated a good deal of recent discussion within public and academic circles alike. The first part thus considers media and *state* power: in other words, the ways in which states attempt to coopt, or circumvent and supplant, mass media as vehicles for opinion-massaging efforts aimed at foreign audiences. The second considers how far we might regard the media as *actors* in the foreign policy process in their own right, focusing on a debate surrounding the role of 'real-time' images and 'intervention' that elicited much scrutiny during the 1990s. And the third section explores questions of media *imperialism* that have received fresh invigoration following 9/11, as Americans (and others) repeatedly enquire what it is about the United States that causes others to resent, envy and/or hate the world's pre-eminent power to the point of launching a retaliatory strike against so loaded a symbolic target as the Twin Towers, at such cost to human life. Since this discussion in mainstream US outlets generally devotes rather less attention to what it is about the exertion of US *power* globally that might animate such fury, much commentary invokes either timeless American values ('they hate us for what we are') and/or the ubiquity of US products around the world, which are commonly held to excite the envy of those who can't afford them, and the resentful rage of those who can, but can't consume guiltlessly without a sense that their identity is jeopardized, their heritage indicted, in succumbing to the temptation of 'Americanization'. It seems timely, then, to consider both the cohesive and disintegrative properties so commonly imputed to media and communications technologies.

Media and state power

Communications as 'soft power'

Pick up any textbook on world politics or international relations written before the 1990s (or even during that decade) and you will probably find very few references to the media. If communications received consideration at all within the academic discipline of International Relations, it was usually under the subheading of 'propaganda', with mass media understood as potential (or actual) tools of state power (see Box 12.1). Under this interpretation, the media's significance to world politics flows from their function as channels through which politicians, diplomats and allied opinion-formers seek to reach audiences beyond their own boundaries. The media, if suitably pliable to state purposes, duly form an instrument of 'soft power': a potent means of winning friends and influencing people abroad – at least if persuasive strategies succeed. This idea is not new. As early as 1939, on the very eve of the Second World War, the renowned historian and theorist of international relations, E. H. Carr, observed that 'Power over opinion is not less essential for purposes of government than military and economic power' (Carr, 1939, p. 3). And having observed the use that industrialized states were currently making of radio broadcasting and film export across international borders – whether to promote particular ideologies or demoralize putative enemies – Carr was equally convinced that the search for control over public attitudes was not just a domestic function of the modern state but a vital weapon in the arsenal of statecraft.

The rise of 'mass society' appeared to herald a new era in both domestic and international politics, rendering politicians and diplomats ever more responsive to the force of popular opinion, and accordingly eager to massage sentiment both at home and abroad. However narrow the stratum of society formally involved in foreign policy decision-making, it had begun to matter what 'ordinary people' thought about their own state's actions beyond its borders, and how favourably or otherwise they regarded foreign competitors, allies or enemies. Today, although public opinion is sometimes disregarded – as majority disapproval for the UK's participation in the war on, and occupation of, Iraq suggests – it is never a matter of outright indifference to political leaders.

'Public diplomacy': influencing the media

Elite efforts at manipulation assume distinct forms, with differing degrees of intervention into processes of mass mediation. These range from day-to-day 'media management' to more heavy-handed forms of control (such as censorship) and outright appropriation or creation of media outlets. At the lower level of this spectrum (and taking the United States as a prolific practitioner), the daily, routinized business of briefings, press releases and news conferences staged in the White House, State Department and Pentagon offer opportunities to 'spin' certain messages about US foreign policy to a domestic audience while simultaneously influencing perceptions about American dispositions, intentions and capabilities among foreign audiences.

Public diplomacy refers to (often fairly low-level) initiatives to manage a state's mediated self-image abroad. These efforts may be enacted on a country's own soil or abroad, in tandem with more conventional diplomatic activity. Increasingly, governments and state agencies additionally use the web to advertise their activities and promote benign responses to them, Israel being an early pioneer of the internet for such ends. Paradoxically, even 'secret services' (such as the CIA) are now using websites for purposes of self-advertisement, where previously their very existence was sometimes officially 'secret', however implausible this pretence. Where states lack systematic access to global media, or are wanting in the expertise required to 'massage' the media proficiently, they may also resort to hiring the services

Box 12.1 The propaganda model

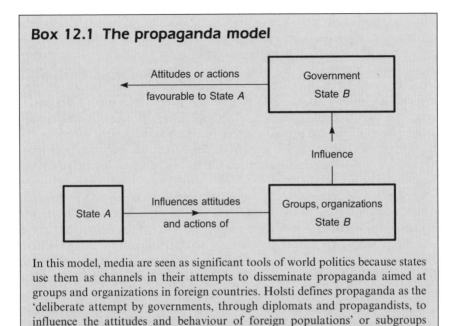

In this model, media are seen as significant tools of world politics because states use them as channels in their attempts to disseminate propaganda aimed at groups and organizations in foreign countries. Holsti defines propaganda as the 'deliberate attempt by governments, through diplomats and propagandists, to influence the attitudes and behaviour of foreign populations' or subgroups thereof.

Source: Compiled from Holsti (1992), pp. 158–60.

of professional public relations (PR) firms, onto whom the task of burnishing a tarnished international image is devolved. Strikingly, after Iraq invaded Kuwait in August 1990, the exiled Kuwaiti royal family did not rely solely on Saddam Hussein's blatant breach of international law to rally the UN into action to recoup Kuwait. Impatient with the slow pace of General Assembly debates and Security Council resolutions, it hired the services of the American-based PR company, Hill and Knowlton (H&K). For the handsome sum of $10.8 million, H&K set about the somewhat delicate task of presenting Kuwait as a deserving victim of sympathy and support: a country sufficiently 'Westernized' (where women could drive, even if they couldn't vote) that Westerners should eagerly seek its liberation from the evil dictator, Saddam Hussein, whose forces had engaged in such monstrosities as throwing Kuwaiti babies from their hospital incubators (MacArthur, 1993, pp. 57–9)

Controlling the media: war as a special case?

Democratic theory takes 'freedom of speech' to be a central value and virtue of liberal polities. Democracies are sustained by affording citizens access to information and commentary on important matters of state, so that they can discharge their civic responsibilities (including informed criticism of government) with due deliberation. Many liberal states accordingly enshrine guarantees of press freedom in their constitutions, with the media conceived as a 'fourth estate' or watchdog on the state. In closed regimes, press freedom may be non-existent: with media production, personnel and content all closely supervised. But in *all* states, freedom of speech is tempered by the need to protect other rights and to offer citizens certain safeguards (of personal privacy, say, or of freedom from 'hate speech'). The boundaries of the expressible vary from place to place, and shift over time, shaped by the values that determine the hierarchy of rights in any given polity. Accordingly, material deemed 'blasphemous' and banned in one society might be acceptable for widespread public consumption in another, which may not even recognize 'blasphemy' as an offence. So, while the Italian government in 2004 sought to prohibit sales of the best-selling novel *The Da Vinci Code* – for its apostasy to Catholicism – many western European governments, a decade earlier, were entirely unsympathetic to Muslim calls for the banning of Salman Rushdie's *The Satanic Verses*, as an offence against Islamic belief.

But however much states protect or violate freedom of expression in peacetime, war presents them with a perceived need (and usually with particular opportunities) to exercise greater control over media. The centrality of media to war-waging has long been recognized – whether as channels of (mis)information, or providers of morale-boosting entertainment. Sometimes media may also play significant *preparatory* roles before war begins, mobilizing certain communities – to a heightened degree of ethnic or national antagonism against particular 'outgroups' – in readiness for conflict. Nazi Germany, perhaps most notoriously, harnessed newspapers, radio and cinema to the task of thoroughly imbuing Germans with Nazi ideology, encouraging hatred of the Third Reich's proclaimed enemies (Jewish and Slavic *untermenschen* most particularly) whether they lay outside the Reich or within (Welch, 1993). In Rwanda, radio broadcasts in the months preceding the 1994 genocide emitted a constant stream of vitriol. Demagogic broadcasters persuaded Hutu to regard themselves as beleaguered by Tutsis, who were branded *inyenzi* ('cockroaches'), to be stamped on before they overran Rwanda and returned the Hutu to a colonial state of servitude. So virulent was this propaganda, and so direct its incitement to slaughter, that radio broadcasters were among those later indicted by the UN Commission on Human Rights as responsible for the genocide (African Rights, 1994, pp. 127–8).

During wartime itself, since the rise of mass media in the late nineteenth century, states of all kinds have employed – and continue to use – various measures to control media based within their borders, and to influence allied, neutral and enemy populations beyond. During both world wars the combatant states' surveillance over, and intervention in, their media's operations was at its most invasive (Carruthers, 2000, pp. 54–107). Where 'national security' appears decisively at stake, it is relatively easy for states to persuade reporters, photographers and filmmakers (and the organizations to which they belong) that their freedom of manoeuvre must necessarily be curtailed in the interests of military victory and survival. It is no surprise, then, that the White House since September 2001 repeatedly announced the United States' 'war on terror' as a new form of unlimited war. Presidential rhetoric has constantly framed this war-without-end as analogous to the 'good war': when the 'free world' again confronts a threat as existential as that posed by Hitler's search for world domination – a gauntlet thrown down by history to test the martial mettle of the babyboom generation.

Invariably states justify censorship (or 'news management' as they may prefer to term it) on the grounds that military security must take precedence over freedom of expression. In other words, the public's 'right to know' (to the extent that these same states acknowledge it in peacetime) ranks below the military's need to protect operational secrecy and soldiers' lives. The release and reporting of news must duly be scrutinized to ensure that nothing of possible benefit to the enemy inadvertently slips out. However, states can abuse 'operational security' to rationalize illiberal measures in wartime. And constraints over the media are apt to become most controversial when the status of 'wartime' itself is indeterminate. Whether *counter-terrorist campaigns* constitute a state of war or not has long formed a vexed issue – for national and international law, and for state–media relations, since governments are often minded to insist that terrorism mandates particularly stringent forms of censorship in order to starve illegitimate actors of what Mrs Thatcher famously termed the 'oxygen of publicity' (Paletz and Schmid, 1992). In such circumstances, states are vulnerable to charges of employing censorship less for purposes of military necessity than political expediency: to rally citizens behind military operations – only questionably just or necessary – by denying public access to fuller and more balanced information and imagery.

Following the Vietnam War, it became almost axiomatic within military circles that America's own media destroyed home-front morale, turning the public against a war that television represented as both unjust and unwinnable. Many media scholars fiercely refute the claim that media – television in particular – effectively 'lost the war' in Vietnam, pointing out that it was only after the American policy-making elite itself revealed fissures that news routinely included more oppositional viewpoints (Hallin, 1989). But military thinking about the media in wartime remains profoundly influenced by an unshakeable belief in the power of news-media, *visual* media most especially, to undermine civilian tolerance for casualties. Hence the Pentagon's extensive efforts during the 1991 Gulf War not only to regulate the flow of news but to curtail the very access of photographers, reporters and camera operators to the battlefield and personnel by confining journalists to 'media-reporting teams' invasively monitored by military 'minders'. Far from being designed merely to preserve the secrecy of the UN coalition's battle plan, the overarching intention of such 'media management', critics such as Douglas Kellner and Bruce Cumings insist, was the sanitization of war itself. Television became 'Pentavision' for the duration, fetishizing the astonishing accuracy with which smart weapons ostensibly found their targets (Cumings, 1992; Kellner, 1992). Twelve years later, as 'Operation Iraqi Freedom' was unleashed in March 2003, the Pentagon employed similar – but yet more intrusive – measures to curb the freedom of manoeuvre of US journalists who were firmly 'embedded' with combat units, many of them seemingly rather willing hostages to this particular exercise in patriotic cheerleading (Hess and Kalb, 2003; Katovsky and Carlson, 2003).

Creating media

Although journalists may, then, sometimes appear as accomplices in the act of public opinion-management, states nevertheless often seem reluctant to rely on commercial media alone to further their interests. Policy-makers and militaries sometimes accordingly supplement *mass* media with narrower channels of their own devising, but whose provenance is frequently masked. During the 1991 Gulf War, for example, the US-led coalition established radio stations in support of *psychological operations* aimed at enemy troops, who were also bombarded with leaflets encouraging them to surrender, and reassuring them of the fair treatment they would receive in Coalition hands. These 'psyops' drew on a long history of such stratagems. During the Second World War, for example, propagandists working for the Allied Psychological Warfare Executive and its predecessors created 'black' radio stations. These were largely aimed at enemy soldiers and operated under the fiction that disaffected Germans ran them. Programming combined music, news (both casualty statistics which the Reich suppressed and items of wilful disinformation), and scurrilous commentary on the Nazi leadership's peccadilloes (Howe, 1982).

Radio, however old-fashioned it might now seem, continues to be a potent medium that reaches 'invisibly' across borders. In recent conflicts and to considerably different ends, the UN has explored the potential of radio broadcasting to assist peacekeeping operations. In the former Yugoslavia, for example, UN radio transmissions sought to restore communication between embattled Serb, Croat and Bosnian communities, and to bolster confidence in the UN's own efficacy and impartiality as 'peace-keeper' (Taylor, 1997, pp. 188–9).

The invention and subvention of media outlets is not a wartime expedient alone: and besides, policy-makers often manage to find new uses for enterprises that originated as weapons of war. Since the 1930s, radio has been a favoured vehicle for various forms of what might politely be labelled as 'cultural diplomacy' or, undiplomatically, as propaganda. The USSR's Radio Moscow was the first large-scale overseas broadcasting network. For its part, the BBC World Service – originally the BBC's external services – has long been heavily subsidized by the Foreign Office. By the 1930s, the Foreign Office recognized that overseas listeners' esteem for the BBC could readily translate into emulation of Westminster-style parliamentary proceedings, and confidence in Britain's fairness abroad. But, of course, preserving a news provider's reputation for impartiality and accuracy usually requires that state subsidies remain shadowy. The very qualities which gain a respectful audience abroad are likely to be compromised if that broadcaster appears too obviously a foreign state's tool. State-funded overseas radio networks which fail to mystify their origins or funding can accordingly suffer a relative lack of trust among listeners. During the Cold War, the Voice of America (VOA) network (run by the US Information Agency and funded by the State Department) tended to be less highly regarded in Eastern bloc countries than Radio Free Europe (RFE) and Radio Liberty. The latter stations, in contrast, were established with CIA funds but staffed primarily with émigrés from Eastern Europe, whose motives appeared less questionable to listeners (Short, 1986).

Of course, listeners were not mistaken in detecting a less than entirely altruistic ambition behind such stations. The US government's purpose in funding such services behind the Iron Curtain – grandly launched as a 'Campaign of Truth' – was profoundly self-interested. In supplying news and commentary, US cold war strategists intended to promote Eastern bloc citizens' long-term dissatisfaction with their politico-economic situation. Exposed to more informative and entertaining 'outside' sources, Eastern Europeans (and Soviet citizens when they could pick up transmissions through their regime's efforts at 'jamming') would more intensely mistrust their own media and the states that controlled them, clamouring instead for the freedoms of the West. When the Cold War ended, the strategic character of Washington's investment was exposed by the rapidity with which funds were withdrawn from RFE – a state of affairs loudly bemoaned by some Eastern Europeans. Following 9/11, however, many *American* politicians began to bemoan the underfunding of VOA, whose budget was swiftly expanded to equip it for a new role in the 'war on terror'. This reinvigoration of radio broadcasting – particularly angled at Muslim audiences to woo them away from 'extremists' and persuade them of the United States' benign purposes in the world – was accompanied by other new initiatives in the sphere of television broadcasting. Washington has duly underwritten an Arabic language satellite network, *al-Hurrah* ('The Free One'), launched to draw viewers away from the Qatar-based channel, *al-Jazeera*: a particular source of concern to the State Department and Pentagon on account of its purportedly anti-American bias, and a target of both physical and verbal attack by the US during Operation Iraqi Freedom in 2003 (Allan and Zelizer, 2004).

Media as 'actors' in world politics

The 'CNN effect' debated

Since the start of the 1990s, television viewers – particularly with access to satellite- or cable-delivered 24-hour news channels – have become used to watching 'real-time' footage: pictures beamed to audiences almost simultaneously with their filming. In the wake of this development, spearheaded by Atlanta-based CNN, a number of observers have claimed that the old relationship between media and states – understood to be one in which the latter essentially led the former – has been reversed. Now, the emotive power of instantaneous images of victims of violence or catastrophe results in insurmountable pressure on politicians to 'do something'. Foreign policy-making, previously the isolated preserve of diplomats and states-persons, is exposed to unprecedented levels of public pressure – for better or worse. Far from passively holding a mirror to the world 'out there', media now (or so it is often argued) *instigate* policy decisions.

This topic has animated a good deal of disagreement – among journalists, policy elites, and scholars alike. Some enthusiasts for 'humanitarian intervention' welcome the media's role in constituting global 'macropublics of hundreds of millions of citizens' moved to regard human suffering anywhere as a matter of concern to all (Keane, 1996, pp. 172–3). But a number of policy-makers have voiced alarm that media now overstep the conventional bounds of the 'fourth estate' and drive foreign policy with negative consequences. Television stands accused of fickleness, of 'touching the heart without reaching the brain': mobilizing public compassion and then recklessly puncturing it (Seib, 1998, pp. 44–5). Where television images galvanize action, they rarely sustain a commitment to humanitarianism that expends 'our' lives in the interests of saving 'theirs'. Events in Somalia (see Box 12.2), graphically dramatized in Ridley Scott's *Black Hawk Down*, are often cast as the paradigm case of this alleged 'push-me-pull-me' effect of real-time images.

What sparked debate about the 'CNN effect'? Anxiety about the emotive power of images has a long pedigree. Throughout the twentieth century, wartime censorship generally rationed photographic or televisual imagery more stringently than other forms of information. Images – especially of human suffering – are often held to have an inescapably emotive effect on those exposed to them. To many observers, the correlation between Vietnam as America's first 'living-room war' and the first war America lost is all too apparent. Television, the new ingredient in the equation, must explain defeat. Many militaries derived the lesson from Vietnam that pictures attesting the human costs of war must be curtailed if future wars were to be fought and won. Accepting similar understandings of media power but driven by different imperatives, anti-war activists and civil libertarians often stake their claim for press freedom in wartime: citizens must be fully

Box 12.2 Somalia: the paradigmatic case of a 'CNN effect'?

- The US-led intervention in Somalia: (Operation 'Restore Hope', 1992–3) is often taken as the paradigmatic case of the CNN effect in operation (though arguably it was also present during the Kurdish uprising after the Gulf War, in Bosnia and in Rwanda).

- In this instance, those bemoaning the deleterious effects of media reporting suggest that television pictures of starving Somalis mobilized the American public to demand that President Bush 'do something', bypassing normal diplomatic channels and foreclosing the deliberation that effective policy formulation requires.

- Under emotional public pressure, a US-led UN mission was assembled, rapidly finding itself engaged in the attempt to disarm warlords in a 'failed state' where the delivery of food was complicated by the absence of civic order.

- As the mission expanded, however, the American public's charitable impulses were as quick to evaporate as they had been to emerge. When CNN screened pictures of a dead US Ranger being dragged through the streets of Mogadishu in September 1993, public pressure on the White House to quit Somalia without further casualties brought the Operation to a premature end.

- But, those less persuaded by notions of a CNN effect point out that branches of the Bush's administration themselves worked hard to encourage US and international media to take an interest in the Somali famine throughout the latter months of 1991 and early 1992. In other words, NGOs and state agencies continue to play an active role in directing media attention to 'big stories' which news agencies are neglecting. This attention in turn puts pressure on the presidency – or wider 'international community' – to mount a more forceful response. In short, media still derive their lead from elements of the establishment, rather than short-circuiting usual policy-making channels.

- The pictures alleged to have prematurely ended the mission were not in fact filmed or relayed in 'real-time'. By the time they were broadcast, most US and international news teams had left, Somalia having become too dangerous an assignment. The images in question were filmed by the Somali driver of the Reuters team, who became video cameraman when the other Western journalists quit.

- Although President Clinton did indeed claim to have been deeply affected by the images of the dead US Ranger – 'the worst day of my life' – some analysts argue that the White House/Pentagon decision to wind down the mission had already been taken. The pictures may thus have offered a pretext for announcing the end of 'Restore Hope' (but US troops in fact remained in Somalia until March 1994).

- Rather than a case of media 'fickleness' destroying an operation, Somalia may then represent an instance of policy-makers failing to calculate the costs of their policy exaggerating the public's unwillingness to sustain casualties; and failing to provide the kind of leadership that would have generated ongoing civilian support for the operation.

Sources: Livingston and Eachus (1995); Minear *et al.* (1996); Natsios in Rotberg and Weiss (1996).

exposed to military action and its consequences (for soldiers and civilians on both sides) if they are to make informed choices about supporting wars waged in their name. Pictures may, in this view, destroy support for a war but where wars fail to merit public support media fulfil a vital democratic function.

None of this, however, explains the particular eruption of the 'CNN effect' debate in the 1990s. Its specificity derives from a context of post-Cold War 'humanitarian interventions' coupled with growing elite concern over the impact of 'globalized' media. With the advent of corporations like BBC World and CNN International – a household brand following the 1991 Gulf War – policy-makers fretted that these global players, broadcasting to myriad publics, no longer conceived themselves as owing allegiance to any particular state. As a result, 'global media' would be less easily bridled should the need for reporting restrictions arise during future military conflicts; a problem increased by the rapid miniaturization of satellite broadcasting and video-editing equipment, and the growing use of scrambling and decrypting technology, enabling journalists to make their own communications more secure and the state's less so.

In an era of rapid technological change, policy-makers frequently represent their autonomy and efficacy as challenged by a combination of seemingly new factors: de-territorialized electronic media on whose 'patriotism' the state cannot rely in wartime; communications technology ever less susceptible to censorship by civil or military authorities; and the constitution of an enlarged audience cued by instantaneously transmitted images of human suffering to demand quick-fix humanitarian responses.

News values, sources and the construction of an agenda

It is as well to recall that these 'global media' are less universal than commonly supposed. One commentator suggests that CNN is better understood as 'the office intercom of global elites' than a ubiquitous presence in everyday life (Parker, 1995, p. 440). Such media are less widespread than often imagined, and more regionally inflected where they do reach (thus CNN's broadcasts in Latin America are in Spanish and also differ in content from the North American service). Television's impact on viewers may also be less drastic than represented in many impressionistic accounts of media effects. As the Somali case study suggests, we should be sceptical of certain claims made about 'real-time' television, both by those eager to hail it as an agent of cosmopolitan consciousness and those who regret its undermining of policy-makers' prerogatives. A number of more nuanced studies of the media's role in situations of grave humanitarian crisis temper any sense that media automatically galvanize states – or the 'international community' – into precipitate action. The wars in the former Yugoslavia, for example, represent a case where media offered 'blanket coverage', but statespersons nevertheless largely resisted engagement in the kind of militarized response that some journalists promoted (Minear *et al.*, 1996, p. 57). Journalistic calls for a ground war as the logical extension of NATO's aerial bombardment of Serbia – waged in the name of Kosovo's endangered Albanian population – fell on similarly deaf ears.

Satellite television may have 'compressed response times' for policy-makers, as journalist Nik Gowing suggests, but we should no more rely on 'global media' to alert us to *all* instances of human suffering on an epic scale than we should expect media coverage invariably to instigate action (Gowing, 1996, p. 83). Most Western media failed, for example, to provide even minimal coverage of a famine in the Sudan which claimed more lives in the early 1990s than its Somali counterpart. Yet throughout the course of 1992, American evening news programmes carried six stories about the Sudanese famine as against 468 relating to Somalia (Seib, 1998, p. 44). Similarly, reporting of the Rwandan genocide in 1994 was extremely thin as the killing actually occurred, despite many warning signals that mass slaughter could erupt. Only during its aftermath, once Rwanda was less a story of genocide than a story of stricken refugees, displacement and disease – with Westerners again coming to the rescue – did international media descend on central Africa *en masse*.

There are a number of important prohibitions on media assuming the role of 'lamplighter' to injustice, in Martin Bell's phrase. Where conflict-riven states obstructively withhold entry visas, relentless bombardment denies foreign journalists safe passage, or inaccessible terrain curtails television crews' mobility, few stories – if any – are likely to reach distant viewers' screens. Other factors additionally determine which stories become news and why only *some* cases of distant war, killing and starvation receive magnification as 'global crises'. In determining the agenda, journalists draw on 'news values' – considerations of 'timeliness', 'topicality', 'proximity' and so on – which help them evaluate which events merit attention. Although journalists often talk about these selection criteria as natural (a story's newsworthiness as somehow self-evident) news values mirror broader social, economic and ideological structures in which media organizations are enmeshed. What passes muster as news, and how particular events are then emplotted as stories, invariably reflects culturally-specific notions of what knowledge is significant to a certain audience and why. Where the bottom-line of news production is commercial, such decisions also, often more obviously, flow from considerations of profitability. In many Western polities, short-term, dramatic events – emphasizing the episodic and calamitous dimensions of life – receive priority over less visible forces and phenomena (the long-term causes and effects of poverty, for example) which fail to present themselves as the usable stuff of news stories.

Often, television news remains premised on a notion that one of its primary functions is to explicate (or predict) policy decisions within the particular country or region to which it is broadcasting. News – perhaps most notably in the United States – accordingly remains very much attuned to the actions of policy elites, who retain considerable power to shape its agenda. Occasionally there may be instances of media highlighting situations to which governments were seemingly inattentive, or certainly inactive. More frequently, cameras and reporters are not ubiquitously where 'the story' is (as they like to maintain) but rather go where powerful sources lead them, as a closer reading of the Somali case suggests.

Similarly, news organizations still tend to assume that their audience (regionally, nationally or locally conceived) is not 'naturally' interested in distant events and people so much as in those closer to them, and more closely resembling them. Thus a CNN executive is alleged to have informed an NGO officer that the network did not immediately dispatch a crew to Rwanda when killing began there in April 1994 because available personnel were tied up covering the inauguration of Nelson Mandela as first President of post-apartheid South Africa. Simultaneous good and bad news from Africa would have 'confused their audience' (Gassman in Girardet, 1995, p. 157). A number of media critics also point out that news organizations, calculating a low threshold of viewer interest in matters international, frequently refuse to carry too many foreign stories which appear to replicate one another. So, if one 'ethnic conflict' is receiving attention in former Yugoslavia, then another in Tadzhikstan becomes superfluous to requirements. By the late 1990s, news organizations had recourse to a new coinage, 'compassion fatigue', to rationalize their rationing of distressing foreign news. Repeated calls upon viewers for their empathetic engagement with distant suffering had reached saturation point – or so certain news organizations insisted (Moeller, 1999).

Media imperialism

Recently rather less has been heard of notions such as 'compassion fatigue', the 'CNN effect', or a notion much in vogue following NATO's Kosovo campaign, 'spectator sport war' (Ignatieff, 2000; McInnes, 2002). If a liberal consensus briefly crystallized in the late 1990s over the desirability of waging what was billed as humanitarian war against violators of human rights, the post-9/11 campaigns in Afghanistan and Iraq have, in at least some quarters, made 'intervention' appear rather less compelling a cause. Greater scepticism certainly prevails (in the United Kingdom to a greater extent than the United States, admittedly) over wars waged in the name of the extension of rights and freedom. And for all Washington's squeamishness about acknowledging Iraqi or Afghan victims, few critics would insist that the mode in which media report these débâcles presents a thrilling spectacle of war as 'spectator sport': a criticism made of the way in which much coverage of Kosovo (mis)represented airpower as capable of achieving political ends without damage to human flesh. In the altered geo-political landscape, discussion of humanitarian intervention has lost ground to critiques of *imperialism*.

Our purpose here, however, is not to review the resurrection of imperialism as the prevailing rubric under which popular and academic discussion of US hegemony proceeds. Rather, the sudden resurgence of interest in empire forms a segue to our consideration of long-running debates about information imbalances, technological asymmetries, and cultural exchanges that unfold under the banner of *media imperialism*.

Global information imbalance

News media construct maps of the globe in which some countries feature with exaggerated prominence while others are omitted altogether. Similarly, only particular issues are presented as meriting urgent or sustained attention, and only some responses appear within the range of imaginable possibilities. News media, in short, fulfil an *ideological function*. Johan Galtung and Richard Vincent (quoted in Alleyne, 1997) suggest that international news (in North America and Western Europe) embodies an 'occidental cosmology'. Its embedded assumptions predispose media towards reporting just that news from 'peripheral' countries (in the South) which confirms certain stereotypes of life there: that it is, for example, plagued by coups, corruption, earthquakes and famines. Stories failing to fit the guiding frames are simply ignored. Meanwhile, the implication of the North in creating and reproducing global patterns of inequality and poverty is written out of the account.

As already noted, Western or global news media display a marked tendency to privilege stories from close at hand. The South duly makes only sporadic appearances in newscasts and press columns. More surprisingly, perhaps, in the news media of the developing world this bias to the North often reappears. Because the most powerful international news services are European and North American – and long have been, since the early days of telegraphic 'wire services' like Reuters and Associated Press – the South has enjoyed few resources to challenge the prevailing global information flows, and so suffers a glut of data, pictures and footage from the North (Figure 12.1).

During the 1970s and 1980s, developing states attempted to lodge the issue of global information imbalance on the international agenda, with calls in the UN for a New World Information and Communication Order (NWICO). Protests against inequality prompted an International Commission for the Study of Communication Problems (the MacBride Commission). Its subsequent report, however, did little more than highlight issues with which the protesters were all too familiar, while exhorting wealthier states and MNCs to effect structural change in international communications and intensify export of information technology to the South. Of course the most powerful communications corporations and the information-rich states of the North exhibit little interest in any such costly restructurings. In response to the report, those with a vested interest in the status quo

Figure 12.1   *The structure of global news*

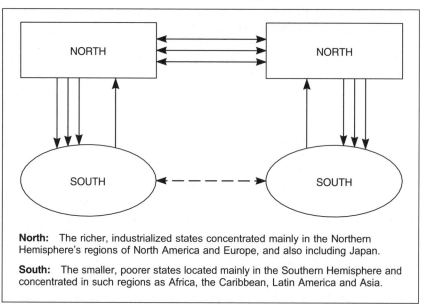

North: The richer, industrialized states concentrated mainly in the Northern Hemisphere's regions of North America and Europe, and also including Japan.

South: The smaller, poorer states located mainly in the Southern Hemisphere and concentrated in such regions as Africa, the Caribbean, Latin America and Asia.

Source: Alleyne (1997), p. 12.

deployed the ideologically powerful notion of a 'free press' to legitimate opposition to any state interventionism in media provision, and to decry international interference in the supposedly free flow of global information. The UK and US governments even withdrew from UNESCO in 1985 to signal their deep displeasure with an agency that had lent tentative support to the NWICO (Herman and McChesney, 1997, pp. 24–5).

A global culture?

Many information-poor states conceive the problem of global information imbalance as not simply one of technology (lack of hardware and software taken for granted in the North) but of *cultural autonomy*. Local habits, mores, traditions, languages, dialects and distinct forms of cultural expression are commonly seen as submerged by the incoming wave of foreign cultural and consumer products as 'Coca-Colonization' sweeps the world. Fears that globalization is eroding cultural difference and producing a monocultured 'McWorld' exist in information-rich societies too (Barber, 1996). Consider, for example, the French Academy's attempts to ban imported linguistic pollutants like 'le weekend' and 'le parking', or the protests which periodically greet the construction of McDonald's restaurants in more affluent English towns.

Unease about global sameness, and the political and cultural consequences of international communication, reaches deep. In some states, where 'Western values' are unwelcome invaders, governing elites and custodians of national culture ponder how – and if – they can make territorial boundaries more impregnable. States in which political change along 'Western' lines is feared show particular anxiety about foreign media intrusion, lest they catalyze local democracy movements and human rights activism. The People's Republic of China, for example, engaged in long negotiations with Rupert Murdoch's corporation over the contents of his Star Asia satellite service. More recently, Beijing has attempted to limit the material China's 9 million internet users can transmit, making it an offence to disclose (altogether undefined) 'state secrets' (*Guardian*, 27 January 2000).

Doubtless the fate of the USSR bulks large in the minds of policy elites seeking to seal themselves from global informational and commercial flows. For despite the best efforts of the USSR to render its citizens immune to the appeals of consumer culture, and to news broadcasts emanating from the Western side of the Iron Curtain, all such attempts ultimately proved fruitless. Of course, the claims made of behalf of Western broadcasting by some of its practitioners and admirers may be overstated: the USSR didn't collapse because of Western propaganda alone; by the 1980s, irresolvable structural problems with the Soviet economy could no longer be plausibly concealed. But the failure of the system to deliver the 'good life' which citizens of the Eastern bloc imagined their West European neighbours to be enjoying – thanks to ever-increasing media penetration of the bloc (and availability of photocopiers within the USSR to circulate *samizdat* literature) – surely did not alleviate Gorbachev's problems. Indeed, his own moves to expose the Soviet press to greater freedom under the banner of *glasnost* may only have hastened the regime's demise (Scott, 1994).

But it is not just conservative regimes, eager to secure their own longevity, that fear the cultural consequences of globalization. Ordinary citizens, too, may feel themselves victims of what its critics term '*cultural imperialism*', or sometimes (perhaps not wholly accurately) '*Americanization*'. Such concepts require nuance. A number of cultural theorists point out that homogenization can be exaggerated, and that 'Americanization' often serves as shorthand for modernizing processes that accompany the spread of global capitalism: a phenomenon which exceeds the arena of purely *American* corporate power (Tomlinson, 1991). Furthermore, local resistance – some commentators insist – manifests itself. American products sometimes fail to find receptive markets. Certain countries and regions show a marked preference for locally based provision of television programming and film entertainment. In Latin America, for example, Brazil and Mexico serve as major regional providers of television soap operas. The Indian film industry similarly enjoys an expansive market in the vast diasporic Indian community worldwide, and other cultures (Sinclair *et al.*, 1996). Although both Brazilian soaps and 'Bollywood' films may owe *something* to the modes of American popular culture, they remain distinctive rather than merely derivative. What we observe, then, is a process of 'creolization', whereby cultures exposed to powerful outside influences are not simply swept away but appropriate certain 'foreign' elements, transmuting them in ways which mesh with local traditions and preferences (Hannerz, 1996). After all, 'pure' cultures rooted in one particular geography – and unsullied by any alien input – are as mythical a conception as pure races undiluted by miscegenation (Morley and Robins, 1995, p. 7). Throughout history, cultures, along with people, have constantly diffused and re-fused in new settings and forms.

That said, however, not everyone remains convinced that hybridity and cross-cultural fertilization of this kind are entirely welcome developments, nor that such international exchanges occur freely and fairly. Westerners may more eagerly savour a piquant infusion of exoticism in their cultural melting pot than do those from whom the borrowings occur. At the other end of the process, communities increasingly surrounded by consumer and cultural products that function as Western lifestyle advertisements are more likely to fear that imported 'genes' will overwhelm less potent indigenous strands in a competition which is anything but free and fair, given the unequal commercial power of international and local media. Whatever 'transgressive' uses and readings local audiences may make of imported fare, it surely tells us something about Hollywood's hegemony that in countries as diverse as Argentina, Brazil, Chile, Japan, Malaysia and Mexico, *Terminator 2* was the top-grossing film of 1991; or that during one weekend in Moscow in 1993, Muscovite cinema-goers had the choice of only six Russian films as against 111 American offerings (Barber, 1996, p. 308; Wagnleitner, 1999, p. 512).

Indeed, global imbalances between rich and poor nations, and between rich and poor citizens within the same state, are if anything *more* marked now than when developing states first attempted to draw the UN's attention to information inequality in the 1970s. This observation is true both in absolute terms – of the widening gulf between the world's super-wealthy and the growing proportion of global citizens whose conditions are more wretched, and expected life-spans dramatically shorter, than they were in some thirty years ago – and of a technology-gap between haves and have-nots in particular. In the face of repeated invocations of the global village in which we're commonly imagined to dwell, it is sobering to be reminded that New York City (populated by some 7.3 million) contains more telephones than all of Sub Saharan Africa (whose 650 million inhabitants – 12 per cent of the world's population – own only 2 per cent of its telephones). Meanwhile, Britain possesses more televisions than the whole of Africa, while Japan houses more sets than South America in its entirety; 95 per cent of all computers can be found in the 29 wealthiest OECD countries, although the OECD accounts for only 20 per cent of the world's population; and 85 per cent of all human beings lack a telephone, and well over half have never made a phone call (Sussman, 1999, p. 44). Bearing in mind also that an estimated third of the poorest countries' populations is illiterate, 'wired world' looks decidedly less global.

Conclusion

Positive and negative assessments of electronic media and their international implications contend with one another. For those who see television images of human suffering as summoning a global humanitarian consciousness, there are others who point to the growing parochialism and inattentiveness of much televised news to 'the international'. Those hailing the internet as enabler of cross-border activism are countered by others pointing out that electronic communications technology can 'be used just as much to violate human rights as to promote them', by states that keep invasive track of their citizens, and manipulate the data so gathered for illiberal ends (Metzl, 1996, p. 713). And, in Benjamin Barber's (1996) formulation, for every manifestation of homogenized 'McWorld' there exists copious evidence of fissiparous 'jihad' – sharpened particularities in dispute with one another, and at war with Westernization. In the face of this seeming paradox, a number of commentators suggest that we understand 'fragmentation' not as contradictory to globalization but rather as its concomitant: contemporary processes perhaps more aptly termed 'glocalization' (Holton, 1998). So, while some beneficiaries of the electronic revolution fondly imagine themselves as members of on-line communities inhabiting 'no-place' and 'every-place', many people's identities remain firmly rooted in particular localities, and perhaps more stubbornly to where globalization is experienced as culturally corrosive.

Electronic communications undoubtedly influence the character of international exchanges. However, some claims made about their 'revolutionary' nature are profoundly ahistorical, frequently predicated on an assumption that technologies themselves determine their own applications, not the humans who devise, use and regulate them. In the face of technological flux, it seems sensible to remember that sweeping assertions – both optimistic and pessimistic – have been made of many new technologies whose impact has turned out to be less, or slower, than expected. When Alexander Graham Bell's telephone was displayed in 1876, some worried that telephones would spread germs through the wires, destroy local accents or give authoritarian governments a listening box in their subjects' homes. Enthusiasts, on the other hand, predicted a greater 'kinship of humanity' and 'nothing less than a new organization of society' (RosenZweig, 1999, p. 160). In some ways, both were right – but neither prediction was wholly warranted nor rapidly realized. With regard to current technology, ringing endorsements and dire forewarnings alike will doubtless require modification as electronic communications evolve, and as the world in which they are employed also changes.

Guide to further reading

No single volume deals with the issues raised in this chapter in their totality. Taylor (1997) provides a useful survey, but is focused largely on the operations of media in wartime and their deployment in psychological operations. The following books pursue particular areas in more detail (presented in the same order that topics are covered in this chapter). On theories of propaganda, a comprehensive introduction can be found in Jowett and O'Donnell (1992). For an overview of the uses and functions of media in wartime, Carruthers (2000) offers a synopsis of the field as a whole. Readers seeking to understand the way in which the American media's role in Vietnam has been consistently misrepresented should refer to Hallin (1989). A brief but thoughtful assessment of the media's role in the 'humanitarian interventions' of the 1990s is provided by Minear *et al.* (1996), and in the Rotberg and Weiss collection of essays (1996). As an antidote to liberal enthusiasm for global media, readers are referred to Herman and McChesney (1997) and Sussman (1999). John Tomlinson (1991) offers a nuanced discussion of 'Americanization', and offers a wide-ranging survey of culture and globalization in his latest work (1999). A further account of globalization's intertwined fragmentary and homogenizing effects ('glocalization') is provided by Robert Holton (1998).

Chapter 13

Transnational Crime and Corruption

PHIL WILLIAMS

The rise of transnational organized crime in the last decades of the twentieth century was as unexpected as the end of the Cold War, if far less dramatic and abrupt. In some respects, however, the challenges posed to national and international governance and international security by transnational criminal organizations could prove more enduring, more complex and, in some respects, more difficult to manage than the US–Soviet nuclear relationship. Obviously, the consequences of a failure to manage the transnational organized crime challenge will be much less horrendous than the consequences of a mis-managed Superpower crisis would have been. Yet, in looking back at the Cold War, what is most striking is its ultimate stability. Nuclear deterrence, in spite of its detractors, compelled both the United States and the Soviet Union to behave with a degree of prudence and care that belied the aggressive rhetoric on both sides. Part of the stability stemmed from simplicity – it was powerful state against powerful state. The challenge posed by transnational organized crime to states in the post-Cold War era is more complex: the enemy is novel and unfamiliar, the battle-lines are blurred and confused, the stakes are often obscured until it is too late, and the definition of success is likely to prove much more elusive.

Moreover, the consequences of failure, while not sudden and dramatic, would certainly not be negligible. If the problem in the past has been the anarchy of the state system, the lack of a central over-riding authority to impose order, the problem in a world in which transnational organized crime is not contained will be anarchy in a more fundamental sense – chaos, disorder and lawlessness as some states at least become little more than fronts for criminal enterprises. The issue will be not simply rogue states that do not observe the conventions and norms of inter-state relations, but criminal states that pursue profits in ways that fundamentally challenge the rule of law. In some cases 'rogue' policies and criminal activities will go together. As North Korea has already demonstrated by its extensive criminal activities, ranging from methamphetamine production and heroin trafficking, to the smuggling of endangered species and counterfeiting, states will not only challenge global norms and agreements such as the non-proliferation regime, but do so by using criminal activity to raise funds for their disruptive policies (Kaplan, 1999). In such cases, the problem is not that organized crime has taken over the state but that the state has taken over organized crime. In both cases, however, the challenge to international order is very real. States that are deeply penetrated by organized crime and states that raise funds through criminal activities both promote disorder and anarchy in the international system.

Avoiding this new variant of anarchy will require that major powers give the challenge posed by transnational criminal organizations a high priority in terms of both resource allocation and the development of appropriate strategies. And even then, the prospects for success – for reasons outlined below – are limited. Part of the problem is that the Westphalian state is in a long-term secular decline, which is already reflected in a crisis of governance in many countries and regions. The emergence of organized crime, both domestic and transnational, is not only a symptom of this underlying crisis of governance but also a development that is intensifying this crisis, not least because in some areas – the favelas of Rio de Janeiro and Sao Paolo are good examples – organized crime provides an alternative form of governance to that of the state. Ironically, organized crime is simultaneously a force of disorder and a form of organic or bottom up governance that challenges the traditional top-down governance of the state. Consequently, pessimism might be justified.

Since September 2001, the challenge to security and stability posed by transnational organized crime has been greatly overshadowed by the threat from Islamic terrorism. This is not surprising. The threat from organized crime is long-term, subtle and insidious whereas the threat from terrorism is immediate, dramatic and obvious. It is the difference between the long-term threat of HIV/AIDS and the immediacy of an outbreak of smallpox. Nevertheless, to ignore the threat from organized crime would be a mistake for several reasons, not the least of which is that organized crime exploits weak states and 'lawless areas' where the state is absent to develop sanctuaries or safe havens from which they can operate with a high degree of impunity. Moreover, terrorist organizations are increasingly using organized crime activities to fund their campaigns of terror. In a few cases close cooperation has even taken place between organized crime and terrorists. Although this is not the norm – and the two kinds of groups have very different objectives – it does pose increased problems for national and international efforts to combat terrorism and its financing.

Against this backdrop, this chapter sets out to do several things. In the first place, it highlights the transformation of organized crime from a domestic law-and-order problem to a global phenomenon that not only poses problems for global governance but also challenges key components of both the realist and neo-liberal conceptions of world politics. Second, it outlines the major concepts associated with transnational organized crime and corruption, and suggests that corruption needs to be understood as an extremely important weapon for transnational criminal organizations.

Third, and drawing out some of the implications of the conceptual analysis, the analysis offers a 'net assessment' of the relationship between states and transnational criminal organizations. It contends that there are several distinctive features of this relationship that will make the transnational organized crime problem a particularly challenging and intractable one for some states. It also acknowledges, however, that at least some states have been successful in containing and even reducing the power of organized crime. The international community has also taken considerable strides in developing measures to combat organized crime. Moreover, some of the steps that have been taken to combat terrorism and especially its finances are likely to have a significant impact on the ability of organized crime to launder money through the financial system.

Transnational crime and corruption as an issue in world politics

Like the end of the Cold War, the rise of transnational organized crime as an issue in world politics poses serious challenges to much International Relations theory. Indeed, neither Hobbesian realism (and its derivative neo-realism) on the one side, nor liberal institutionalism or neo-liberalism on the other, readily and comfortably accommodate – at either a conceptual or a practical level – transnational criminal organizations. For the realists these organizations are irrelevant to the perennial struggle between states seeking power and security; for the institutionalists, they are unwelcome – a form of discord in a world of growing cooperation and harmony.

The problem for the realists is that their state-centric view of the world ignores what is, in effect, a new breed of powerful actors who in so many respects fit the Hobbesian paradigm of behaviour but are, in Rosenau's apt phrase, 'sovereignty-free' (Rosenau, 1989). Although they lack the attributes of statehood, in other respects criminal organizations operate in the classic anarchical environment so familiar to realism and neo-realism: there are no formal rules governing their behaviour, they compete with one another, they resort to violence against their adversaries (whether rival criminal groups, law enforcement personnel, government officials unwilling to support them, or recalcitrant businessmen who refuse to cooperate) and they focus their attention primarily on maximizing profits, and secondarily on obtaining the power necessary to protect and promote their profit-seeking behaviour. Their violence is small-scale rather than large-scale and much more narrowly focused than that typically used by states. Nevertheless, the willingness to use force is one of their most distinctive features and poses a challenge to the notion of state monopoly on the use of force. It suggests that the realist paradigm needs to be extended to accommodate a wider range of non-state and transnational actors who, in many other respects, fit the mould of behaviour typical of states operating amid anarchy.

The other dimension of the challenge to realist conceptions is that, in an increasing number of cases, state structures will be subverted, neutralized, or penetrated by criminal organizations intent on the creation of safe havens from which they can operate with relative impunity. Realists have traditionally categorized states according to their location within the hierarchy of power and their orientation towards the existing distribution of power – status quo, revisionist, or revolutionary. In the future, however, one of the determining characteristics of a state's position, standing and credibility in the international system will be its relationship to criminal organizations, and where it is on a continuum that can range from criminally collusive at one extreme to confrontational at the other. Moreover, this determinant will cut across the power category: it is possible that some large, powerful states and many small states will be so penetrated by organized crime that it will be impossible to see where the state apparatus ends and criminal organizations begin. Although the international community has little experience with states deeply penetrated by organized crime, learning how to respond to these states and to the criminal groups with which they are linked is likely to be one of the major security imperatives of the twenty-first century.

Indeed, it is not inconceivable – although admittedly less likely after 9/11 – that the major global divide will be caused not by competing ideologies, the struggle for power, or the 'clash of civilizations' (Huntington, 1996) but more prosaically by a clash between those states that uphold law and order and those that are dominated by criminal interests and criminal authorities. It is a vision of the future that is as chilling as it is conceivable. The battle-space in this world will not only encompass the relations among nations but also the space within them as émigré criminal groups seek to subvert the political and legal institutions of their host society. At its worst, it could be a merger of Thomas Hobbes and Al Capone, the Chicago of the Prohibition era elevated to the global level where the defining conflict of the international system becomes that between criminal states on the one side and law-abiding states on the other. Although states will still play a central role in this system, the capacity of criminal groups to penetrate and manipulate states will give global politics a very distinctive character.

The challenge to neo-liberalism is, in some respects at least, even more fundamental than that posed to realism. Liberal institutionalists, implicitly or explicitly, have almost invariably held up the vision of a new nirvana, of progress towards an international system that is more peaceful and harmonious than that portrayed in conceptions of anarchy (in either sense). Economic interdependence and globalization, it was believed, would fundamentally transform the international system, transcending the security dilemmas and arms races of an anarchical environment, encouraging, if not compelling, inter-state cooperation, and creating a new breed of global citizens and NGOs which would promote peace, harmony and disarmament. Private aid organizations, charitable foundations and the imperatives of business cooperation, it was assumed, would bring civility to the international system, facilitating new forms of global governance that would be supported at the nation-state level by free-market economies and democratic polities.

This vision cannot be dismissed out of hand. Globalization has certainly brought with it many benefits, including the rise of global citizens and transnational non-profit organizations seeking to improve the global environment, alleviate poverty, reduce conflict, and create a more harmonious world in which there is an equitable distribution of resources. Yet this is only part of the whole – and the other part of the picture is far less palatable. Globalization has a dark side, which has been ignored or dismissed by liberal institutionalists intent only on extolling the virtues of interdependence and globalization. One of the main beneficiaries of globalization has been organized crime, which has extended its reach across national boundaries and, in some jurisdictions, achieved a position of considerable power. The key dimensions of globalization – the compression of time and distance, the emergence of a global trade system, the development of a global financial system and the communications and information revolutions – have all benefited organized crime as much as they have benefited legitimate business. And while some proponents of globalization look forward to a global civil society, this could well be outweighed by the development of an uncivil global society that is already evident in large parts of the world.

Problems of crime and corruption

Organized crime in the 1980s and 1990s created or exploited huge markets for products that are either taxed differentially in different jurisdictions, are regulated, or are prohibited. Indeed, criminal enterprises found that they were able to move illegal products relatively easily within the vast and complex flows of legal commodities, able to move the proceeds of crime quickly and anonymously around a global financial system based on 'megabyte money' (Kurtzman, 1993) and able to exploit new information and communication technologies to enhance efficiency and effectiveness. Moreover, in several so-called 'states in transition' the economy is based not so much on the free market as on the informal and the illegal markets. In Russia, the privatization process, which was intended to facilitate the transition and to energize the market economy, was subjected to little oversight and much abuse. Government resources and private capital, rather than being separated, became intermixed with a criminal economy. Rather than the emergence of a new entrepreneurial class, there is a seamless web of criminal groups, corrupt politicians and officials and ruthless businessmen. Liberal democratic norms, far from taking root, have been overwhelmed by deep and pervasive corruption. And although not analytically useful, notions such as 'kleptocracy' or 'mafiocracy' are appropriately vivid descriptions of many of the states in the former Soviet Union. In Uzbekistan, for example, the country's leading criminal and the country's leading entrepreneur are embodied in the same person.

Another consequence of globalization has been to sharpen the divisions in some societies between the wealthy and the poor, between those with access to legitimate avenues of advancement and those who are compelled to operate in the illegal economy as the only source of advancement. In the final analysis, globalization has assisted the rise of transnational organized crime in several ways (see Box 13.1).

In short, globalization has provided new opportunities for transnational organized crime, additional incentives and pressures for the creation and operation of criminal enterprises and criminal markets, and novel resources that make organized crime a more formidable challenge for domestic law enforcement. Organized crime has become the dark underside of

Box 13.1 Globalization and organized crime

- The growth of global communications and information systems, the development of a global financial system in which money can be moved rapidly and easily and often anonymously, and the upsurge of global trade have provided new opportunities that organized crime has been quick to exploit.
- The strains on societies and economies resulting from globalization and economic and political transitions (with their attendant forms of economic and social dislocation) have marginalized significant portions of the population, thereby providing both incentives and pressures for large cadres of recruits to join criminal enterprises that might allow them to escape poverty.
- Significant population movements have been facilitated by the transportation and communications revolutions and, in turn, have resulted in large émigré populations being transplanted into societies where they provide an important resource for criminal enterprises that can increasingly be understood as network forms of organization. Many organized crime groups function effectively across borders because they are able to exploit diasporas and ethnic networks that are difficult for domestic law enforcement agencies to infiltrate. Whether the focus is on Nigerian criminals in the United Kingdom and South Africa, Chinese criminal networks in the United States and Western Europe, Russian émigré criminals in the United States and Israel, Turks and Kurdish criminals in the Netherlands, or Albanian drug traffickers operating throughout Eastern and Western Europe, it is clear that ethnicity provides an important bonding mechanism for organized crime groups, that ethnic communities provide both cover and recruitment, and that transnational ethnic networks are an important, if often unwitting, support mechanism for criminal enterprises.

globalization, an underside that liberal institutionalists and proponents of globalization not only failed to foresee but have subsequently been reluctant to acknowledge – even though transnational criminal organizations might prove to be one of the most enduring and powerful of the new breed of non-governmental transnational actors.

The implication of all this is that neither realism nor neo-liberalism adequately captures the complexity of a world in which transnational organized crime is a major player in both domestic and international relations. Far more appropriate and compelling is Rosenau's conception of a future in which there are two worlds of world politics – the state-centric and the multi-centric. The former embodies the traditional state-centric view of international relations and focuses on the relationship among states themselves, and the latter concentrates on the various non-state actors that have emerged. Rosenau also argues that the relationship between these 'two worlds of world politics' will be a critical determinant of the future (see Rosenau, 1989). The interactions between states and transnational criminal organizations can be understood as a particularly important manifestation of this relationship. Before looking at the underlying logic and rationale for this argument, however, it is necessary to elucidate more fully the main concepts and terms being used.

Crime and corruption on the international agenda: key concepts

Organized crime

Definitions of organized crime abound in the criminology literature. Although there is considerable controversy over the meaning and implications of the term 'organized', it is possible to identify three main types of definition – simple lists of characteristics (the set menu); sophisticated lists which identify some essential characteristics and some à la carte characteristics; and definitions which try to capture the essence of organized crime. The first two approaches usually define organized crime in terms of the presence of such characteristics as membership of three or more people, hierarchical structure, specialization of roles within the organization, continuity of criminal operations and activities, the use of violence and corruption, the supply of illicit goods and services and the use of rituals and secrecy. If the essence approach is adopted, then organized crime very simply is the systematic pursuit of profit through illicit means by criminal groups. In Clausewitzian terms, organized crime is the continuation of business by criminal means. Implicit in this definition is the notion of organized crime as a form of enterprise, located on a continuum with licit enterprises on the one end and illicit enterprises on the other.

In terms of the relationship between organized crime and the state, however, there are three different dimensions of organized crime that are particularly important: organized crime structures, organized crime activities, and organized crime efforts to protect themselves. Organized crime structures embody a concentration of illegal power in society and challenge state authority; they also act as a substitute for the state where state capacity is low. Criminal organizations are also inherently violent, challenging the state monopoly of coercive power. Contract killings are used to remove competitors and obstacles to criminal businesses as well as investigators and judges. Indeed, organized crime uses violence and intimidation against those resisting the penetration of the state or the trans-shipment of illicit commodities. Criminal violence is a frontal attack on the rule of law and, at the very least, creates higher levels of violence in societies. Organized crime activities provide enormous profits that are used in part to facilitate and protect the criminal organizations. Many of these activities involve trafficking of illegal goods across national borders which undermines a critical component of sovereignty – territorial control. Organized crime risk management strategies often involve the use of corruption in an effort to neutralize or undermine the power and authority of the state. Indeed, organized crime–corruption networks can be understood as the AIDS of the modern state, circumventing and breaking down the natural defences of the body politic.

In addition to its impact on individual states, organized crime has a major impact not only on regional and global security, but also on human security. Trafficking in arms, drugs, and nuclear materials, for example, undermines international peace and security, while trafficking in people, especially women and children, involves violations of human rights that, at their most egregious, constitute a new form of slavery. Organized crime also contributes to the outbreak of – and often perpetuates – armed conflicts. Warring factions or insurgencies adopt organized crime methods and sometimes link with criminal enterprises, selling them drugs or exchanging drugs for arms. Criminal enterprises led by people such as Viktor Bout and Leonid Minin also sell arms to belligerents in violation of Security Council resolutions, thereby perpetuating conflicts. Moreover, criminal networks that exploit wartime conditions generally continue after hostilities have ceased, complicating efforts to create a sustained peace and engage in effective state-building. In other words, transnational criminal networks pose distributed, dynamic and mobile threats that are based in safe havens, operate across multiple jurisdictions, and engage in jurisdictional arbitrage to protect themselves.

Transnational organized crime

Standard definitions of transnational activity, stemming from the work of Huntington (1973) and Keohane and Nye (1972), delineate transnational activity in terms of the movements of information, money, physical objects, people, or other tangible or intangible items across state boundaries, when at least one of the actors involved in this movement is non-governmental. It is hardly surprising, therefore, that a great deal of organized criminal activity has become transnational in form and scope. And from this perspective, transnational organized crime can be understood, very simply, as organized crime which involves, in one way or another, the crossing of borders or national jurisdictions. Although this might seem a very simple notion, however, it is more complex than initially appears since border crossing is effectively multi-dimensional. Indeed, there are five separate components or categories of border-crossing that can give organized crime a transnational dimension (see Box 13.2).

Organized crime can become transnational in any one or more of the ways in Box 13.2. In some cases, such as Colombian drug trafficking organizations, the bulk of the criminal activities will involve the crossing of borders and criminal operations in multiple markets and therefore multiple jurisdictions. In other cases, criminal organizations will be primarily domestic but might engage in transnational money laundering in an attempt to protect their profits from law enforcement. Whatever the case, however, it is clear that the transnational nature of organized crime is not purely incidental. Not only does it reflect the globalization processes discussed above, but also rational decisions by criminal organizations related to both risk and profit. Indeed, there are several reasons why criminal organizations and activities will cross borders. These can be understood largely in terms of seeking the most profitable markets – which are generally in advanced post-industrial states with populations with considerable disposable income. It is in these countries that illicit goods and services generally fetch the highest price. Smuggling cocaine across the border from Mexico to the United States, for example, increases the price that can be obtained for the cocaine by at least six hundred per cent.

Criminal organizations generally seek to maximize profits within the constraints of acceptable risks. Indeed, the risk–profit equation is one that all criminal organizations face. Yet they do not all respond the same way. Some criminal organizations, for example, will try to avoid risk and confine their operations to low-risk jurisdictions, while others will seek the large profits that are to be obtained in countries such as the United States – where there is considerable disposable income and a correspondingly large market for illicit goods and services – even though the risks from law enforcement are rather higher. In the case of illicit products such as drugs, the producers are usually developing countries, while the major markets are in advanced industrialized and post-industrial societies. To get from the former to the latter it is often necessary to cross the borders of other states which then become – unwittingly and often unwillingly – trans-shipment states for criminal organizations. Having obtained their profits, criminal organizations will also move them back to the home state or to states – such as

Box 13.2 The transnational dimensions of organized crime

- The *actual or potential perpetrators of crime* who cross borders in the course of their activities or in efforts to evade law enforcement and seek a safe haven. Russian hit-men who have engaged in contract killings in several West European countries fit into this category.
- Either *illicit products* such as drugs or *licit products* that are stolen and smuggled out of the country (cars) or taken out of the country in violation of export restrictions (art and antiquities) or imported to another country in violation of import restrictions or international embargoes (arms to Yugoslavia). The list here is a long one and includes drugs, arms, nuclear materials, counterfeit goods, intellectual property, fauna and flora, art and antiquities and cars.
- *Illegal aliens* who enter countries (either clandestinely or using false documentation) in violation of immigration restrictions and women and children who are trafficked across borders to fulfil demand in the global sex trade. In effect, the people in this category are treated as human commodities.
- The *proceeds of illicit activity*. Criminal enterprises, whether transnational or domestic in scope, are primarily engaged in the pursuit of profit. In many jurisdictions, however, money obtained through criminal activities such as drug trafficking is subject to seizure and forfeiture. Consequently, this money is often moved through a variety of foreign jurisdictions in order to obfuscate the trail. It often ends up in an offshore financial centre or bank secrecy jurisdiction which is not readily amenable to efforts to seize the funds by national authorities in the country in which the initial crimes were committed.
- The *transmission, of digital signals* or what is, in effect, a 'virtual', as opposed to a physical, border crossing. These signals can take the form of child pornography, malicious code that is designed to attack or destroy computer and information systems or electronic bank robberies that move funds illegally from legitimate accounts to a location where they are available to the perpetrators. Because of the global nature of information space, much digital crime is inherently transnational in character.

offshore financial centres and bank secrecy jurisdictions – where they are unlikely to be seized. In addition, criminals will often use weak laws and the absence of extradition laws in/ some jurisdictions to find additional safe havens. Moreover, the crossing of borders, whether for criminals themselves or their proceeds, complicates the tasks of national law enforcement agencies. While safe havens for criminal organizations are often found in the home base, where the state is generally weak, organized crime will seek to perpetuate and increase that weakness. In this connection its major instrument is corruption.

Corruption

Definitions and discussions of corruption are many and varied. They range from simple notions that corruption is the exercise of public power for private gain to more complex econometric analyses that try to measure the impact of corruption. Corruption has been attributed to a variety of factors ranging from cultural mores, particularly those based on patron–client relations and family and kinship networks, on the one side and individual greed on the other. Yet other observers have seen corruption as an inevitable consequence of particular kinds of political and administrative arrangements. Robert Klitgaard (1998), for example, has suggested that corruption stems from arrangements in which there is a monopoly of power, considerable discretion in how that power is used, and a lack of accountability about its use. In terms of the impact of corruption, assessments range from those who believe it is purely negative to those who view it as a form of income re-distribution or a means of rewarding public servants who are not adequately recompensed by the state.

What became distinctive about corruption in the late 1990s, however, was the intensity of concern and the growing sense that the problem was almost becoming contagious. In response to what one observer termed the 'global corruption epidemic', the international community began to address the problem with a new urgency (Leiken, 1996–7). Spurred on by a series of scandals ranging from President Mobutu's siphoning of American aid money for his personal wealth, to concerns about the fate of aid money to Russia and other states of the Former Soviet Union (FSU), and encouraged by various NGOs such as Transparency International – which developed and disseminated corruption indices that ranked states from most to least corrupt – governments and international donor agencies began to give anti-corruption initiatives greater visibility on their agendas. The Clinton Administration, for example, with Vice-President Gore in the forefront, held a major international workshop in Washington dealing with corruption, and what could be done about it, while the OECD adopted a convention making bribery by transnational companies illegal. The OECD convention, in particular, was hailed as a major advance in preventing and combating corruption. In fact, it deals with only one aspect of it – companies paying corrupt officials – and does not really touch on the organized crime aspect which, arguably, is the most pernicious form of corruption. Moreover, by dealing only with the supply side of the equation (that is, the supply of bribes) the focus on business could well have all sorts of inadvertent consequences. If the demand for bribery continues, and transnational business is no longer meeting this demand, then transnational organized crime could well fill the breach. This is likely to occur in Africa and elsewhere in the developing world, offering organized crime new opportunities to embed itself in state structures and making the task of combating transnational criminal organizations even more difficult.

Perhaps the most important aspect of corruption, but one that is being ignored in too much of the current debate, is its increasingly widespread use as an instrument of organized crime. Corruption is treated merely as a condition when it also needs to be understood as an instrument. The real questions then become who is trying to corrupt whom for what purposes using what means. This is not to suggest that all corruption is organized crime-related; nor is it to conflate corruption and organized crime. It is merely to argue that organized crime uses corruption as a major instrument – and that, therefore, the focus of attention, at least in part, needs to be on the exchange relationships. The purposes of corruption strategies adopted by transnational criminal organizations – as well as the targets of corruption – are discussed more fully below.

Crime and corruption after the Cold War

In considering the relationship between transnational criminal organizations and states, there are several trends that need to be considered – many of which appear to work in favour of the former. Perhaps the most striking change in the 1990s was that transnational criminal organizations became both more pervasive and more diverse. Traditional organized crime groups (such as the Cosa Nostra in the United States, the Sicilian Mafia, Chinese Triads, and the Japanese Yakuza) with a long – if not illustrious – pedigree have been joined by criminal parvenus such as Russian criminal networks, Turkish and Albanian clans, Nigerian organizations involved in drug trafficking and financial fraud, Mexican drug traffickers and a host of subsidiary criminal players. The diversity of these groups is also striking. They vary considerably, for example, in their portfolio of activities: Colombian and Mexican groups are involved primarily, if not exclusively, in drug trafficking and everything else, such as money laundering, has a direct connection to the trafficking business; Russian and Chinese groups engage in much more diverse activities ranging from financial fraud and extortion to car theft, alien smuggling, antiquities trafficking and trafficking in women for commercial sex.

Another important trend in the criminal world has been the development of cooperative linkages among criminal organizations. These linkages take a variety of forms and fulfil a variety of purposes. At the most advanced level they involve what can be termed long-term strategic alliances among criminal organizations; at the most basic level there are one-off supplier connections. Other types of relationship include short-term tactical alliances and contract and service relationships. As with licit firms, these relationships are helpful in entering new markets, sharing risks, compensating for weaknesses or lack of resources in a particular area by mobilizing complementary expertise, and coopting potential competitors and adversaries. Among the most important developments in this area has been the emergence of a triangular relationship involving Russian criminal networks, Italian Mafia families and Colombian drug traffickers. The triangle has been characterized by arms for drugs exchanges, mutual assistance in money-laundering, and the development of new drug markets in the FSU. Although such relationships can prove volatile, their significance is difficult to overestimate – they enormously complicate the task of governments in their efforts to combat transnational criminal organizations.

Another important trend is towards greater sophistication, whether in the armaments that are available to criminal organizations, the techniques and mechanisms utilized for money laundering, the methods for concealment of illegal products, or the exploitation of information technologies not only as channels for both new and familiar forms of criminal activity but also as both weapons and targets. One development that is likely to benefit transnational organized crime enormously is the diffusion of strong forms of encryption. This will make it very difficult for law enforcement effectively to intercept communications, a tool that the Federal Bureau of Investigation (FBI) used very effectively against Cosa Nostra in the United States.

Managing crime and corruption: criminal organizations versus states

All the trends described in the last section help transnational organized crime. They also help to ensure that the low-key but intense competition between transnational criminal organizations on the one side and states on the other will endure through much of the twenty-first century. While this competition is only one example of the interplay between the state-centric and the multi-centric worlds, several distinctive features of this issue area will ensure an enduring competition rather than a rapid triumph for states.

This is not to suggest that states are oblivious to the challenge. Indeed, more and more states are developing legal frameworks that include provisions for attacking criminal organizations as organizations and that permit electronic surveillance techniques, the seizure and forfeiture of the proceeds of crime, and witness protection. In many respects, the US model for combating organized crime – Racketeering Influenced and Corrupt Organizations Statutes which allow law enforcement agencies to go after criminal 'kingpins' as well as the foot soldiers, wiretapping, infiltration, provision for witness protection for informants, and anti-money laundering legal provisions – has become the new global standard. Countries such as South Africa, for example, have adopted several aspects of the US approach to combating organized crime. There has also been widespread adoption of measures to combat money laundering. The key development here was the creation of the Financial Action Task Force (FATF) by the G7 in 1989. Based in Paris, the FATF, in April 1990, issued a set of 40 recommendations on anti-money laundering provisions that have been widely adopted by a range of states, going well beyond the initial 26 members. These provisions included the need for due diligence and know-your-customer requirements, reporting of cash transactions over $10 000 or its equivalent, suspicious activity reporting, and the creation of Financial Intelligence Units to analyze the reports. The FATF developed procedures for self-assessment and mutual evaluation that institutionalized the pressure on members to adopt the recommendations. In 1999 the FATF went considerably further and initiated a name-and-shame campaign against states and jurisdictions which were not taking effective measures to combat money laundering. The black list that was announced annually for the next several years became an important stimulus for reform both in small countries such as the Bahamas (which required greater transparency of ownership in companies registered in the islands) and in countries anxious to join the EU. In October 2001, the FATF extended its mandate to cover terrorist financing, urging its members to freeze and confiscate terrorist assets, impose anti-money laundering requirements on alternative remittance systems such as hawala, and generally make it more difficult for terrorists to use the global financial system. The difficulty with such measures is that terrorist networks can carry out attacks with relatively little money.

Perhaps the most important single measure against transnational organized crime, however, was the United Nations Convention against Transnational Organized Crime unveiled in December 2000 in Palermo – a highly symbolic venue given the city had long been dominated by the Sicilian Mafia. The UN Convention was designed 'to promote cooperation to prevent and combat transnational organized crime more effectively' (article 1). The Convention identifies four specific crimes – participation in organized criminal groups (article 5), money laundering (article 6), use of corruption (article 8), and obstruction of justice (article 23) – which provide a basis for extradition and mutual legal assistance. In addition, the Convention creates a framework for joint investigations (article 19) and other forms of cooperation among law enforcement agencies. In effect, the Convention encourages states to develop legal systems that are compatible with one another even if not fully harmonized. The main provisions of the Convention are intended to ensure that 'the approaches taken by different states under their domestic legislative and law enforcement regimes are as coordinated as possible to make collective international measures both efficient and effective'. The Convention also has attached Protocols against Trafficking in Persons, Smuggling of Migrants, and Illicit Trafficking in Firearms. The Protocol on Trafficking in Persons creates obligations on the signatories to attack the traffickers, but also to offer protection and support to the victims of trafficking.

Overall, the Convention can be understood as a major step forward in the effort to combat transnational organized crime. It establishes a set of norms and standards for signatories to meet, while the emphasis on international cooperation is an appropriate response to the inability of even very powerful states acting alone to combat transnational organized crime. Although of major importance, the Convention against Transnational Organized Crime is only one of several initiatives that the international community has taken in recent years to combat the challenge posed by organized crime in an era of globalization. A new organization – Europol – has been set up in the EU to facilitate efforts to combat organized crime, while at the global level efforts have been made to reinvigorate Interpol which is an important mechanism for international exchange of information.

In short, from the late 1980s onwards, states have been moving ahead on several fronts to establish global governance regimes to combat transnational organized crime and money laundering. Yet, these governance efforts have been – and are likely to continue to be – sporadic, incomplete, ineffective, and ultimately futile. The reasons for this can be found partly in the shortcomings of states and partly in the advantages of transnational criminal organizations. The relevant characteristics of each type of actor are summarized in Table 13.1

One of the most important asymmetries favouring criminal organizations is that they operate, offensively at least, in what for their purposes has become virtually a borderless world. States, in contrast, are still constrained by national sovereignty, hampered by different legal systems and stymied by the complexity of cases involving multiple jurisdictions. As suggested above, the crossing of national borders by criminals, their illicit commodities, or the proceeds of their activities, is central to transnational organized crime. And because criminal activities are embedded in a myriad of legal transactions, involving trade, finance, or travel, it is inordinately difficult for governments and law enforcement agencies to identify these activities. As a result, efforts to prevent and control transnational organized crime are easily circumvented.

Table 13.1   *States and transnational criminal organizations*

States	*Transnational criminal organizations*
Sovereign-bound, territorial entities in bordered world	Sovereign-free transnational entities in borderless world
Hierarchical	Predominantly network-based
Cooperation inhibited by sovereignty	Extensive cooperation developing
Rule-bound	Rule-free
Limited institutional memory	Adaptable learning organizations
Fragmented approach	Systematic risk-management strategies
Susceptible to corruption	Vulnerable to infiltration
Problem of defection of 'captured' or 'criminal' states	Problem of defection of members

There is an additional wrinkle to this that provides yet another advantage to transnational criminal organizations – their willingness and ability to use national borders and concepts of national sovereignty for defensive purposes. In Colombia, for example, periodic efforts to extradite drug traffickers to the United States have resulted not only in violence but also in a public vilification of such agreements as a violation of sovereignty and an affront to Colombian nationalism. This should not be surprising. Criminal organizations flourish where the state is weak and do their utmost to ensure that the state remains weak. This provides them with a sanctuary or safe haven from where they can direct their transnational criminal networks and business enterprises. Nor are criminal organizations reluctant to use the sovereignty of others for their own purposes. Jack Blum, a Washington attorney, who has been a key figure in the fight against transnational organized crime, has suggested that criminal organizations rent the sovereignty of offshore financial centres and bank secrecy jurisdictions for the safe keeping of the proceeds of crime. Money placed in these jurisdictions is difficult to trace and even more difficult to seize.

A second advantage of criminal enterprises is that they are for the most part network-based organizations. Networks are very sophisticated organizational forms, offering enormous flexibility, adaptability, redundancy and resilience. Network-based organizations are excellent at acquiring and disseminating intelligence and counter-intelligence, necessary both for effective marketing of illicit products and for evading or neutralizing efforts to put them out of business. They can cross national borders and extend from the illicit to the licit sector with considerable ease, neutralizing or coopting key individuals and sometimes even institutions. At the same time, by ensuring that there is both loose coupling (Perrow, 1984) among key components of the network and considerable redundancy in network structures and functions, they can limit the damage incurred as a result of the efforts of governments and law enforcement agencies. Even if some parts of the network are removed, other components remain intact so that the network can either continue to function with minimal disruption or, in the event that the damage is more serious, can reconstitute itself in a relatively short time. Governments, in contrast, are still organized according to hierarchical and bureaucratic principles that make it difficult for them to match transnational criminal organizations in speed of decision-making and implementation, let alone in inventiveness and flexibility. Law enforcement efforts are often hindered by inter-agency rivalry, concerns over the distribution of benefits from successful initiatives, and zealous adherence to standard operational procedures. The need for overt success measured through seizures and arrests also leads law enforcement agencies to focus on interdiction efforts and the arrest of peripheral members of the network, rather than devising more complex strategies that can seriously degrade the operations of the network.

A third asymmetry is that criminal organizations, for the most part, are rule-free organizations whereas governments are rule-bound. Although criminal organizations often observe 'rules of prudence', preferring for the most part to use corruption and cooption rather than to initiate a frontal and violent assault on governments and law enforcement agencies, they have the advantage of operating outside the law and, therefore, are far less constrained than governments. Law enforcement agencies, for the most part, have to wait until crimes are committed to act; criminal organizations can take initiatives whenever and wherever they want; law enforcement agencies have to obtain permission to use electronic eavesdropping; criminal organizations can simply purchase such capabilities; law enforcement can buy information and people but cannot offer nearly as much as criminal organizations. Moreover, it is not only in terms of resources that the criminals have the advantage, the penalties they can impose on traitors, defectors or infiltrators are generally greater than those imposed by governments.

A fourth asymmetry is that criminal organizations, very importantly, are learning organizations that adapt to their environment very successfully and avoid mistakes of the past (Kenney, 1999). As a result of setbacks in the late 1980s and the first half of the 1990s, for example, Colombian drug trafficking organizations realized that vertically integrated operations 'from leaf to nose' made them vulnerable to US law enforcement efforts. As a result, they subsequently truncated their operations, relying on Mexican traffickers to cross the southwest border into the United States and Dominican and Puerto Rican smugglers to move cocaine and heroin through the Caribbean to New York. Although this meant that some of the profits went to their partners, this sacrifice was deemed acceptable because of the accompanying and very significant reduction in risks to Colombian traffickers. Governments, in contrast, are not good at developing and maintaining institutional memory or adapting to failures. For them the stakes are less important, the constraints on innovation and adaptability are much greater, and continuity is interrupted by changes in government that are generally accompanied by shifting priorities. Not only does government have to re-learn lessons, but the shifting level of commitment can degrade the morale and effectiveness of law enforcement agencies.

A fifth consideration is that criminal organizations have become very adept at managing the risks they face from governments and law enforcement agencies, developing elaborate strategies not only to prevent and control risks but also to mitigate the consequences of costs imposed by law enforcement. Government efforts, in contrast, are generally more diffuse and fragmented. Few governments have developed comprehensive and effective strategies for combating organized crime. This is not to deny that governments have had successes; it is to argue, however, that few governments have defined the end game in the struggle against transnational organized crime, few have elucidated measures of success, and few have attacked criminal organizations in a comprehensive fashion that simultaneously targets key nodes and connections in networks, the profits from criminal enterprises, and the connections to government and business.

A key part of the effort to manage risks is the use of corruption by criminal networks. As suggested above, corruption is a crucial instrument of organized crime. It can be used for specific operational purposes and as a systemic weapon to penetrate the state. Among the specific objectives of organized crime-related corruption is the neutralization of border control authorities in the home state, in trans-shipment states and in destination or market states. Operational corruption of this kind is designed to ensure that cross-border trafficking – whatever the product – is subjected to as little interference, interdiction, and damage as possible. Corruption is also employed to coopt financial institutions and ensure that they can be used to move and hide the proceeds of drug trafficking and other criminal activities. In effect, corrupting bank officials is a means of circumventing the impact of regulations relating to suspicious transactions. In Russia and other states in the FSU, organized crime has infiltrated the banking system using a potent mixture of coercion and corruption, violence and bribery. In the early and mid-1990s banking was a high-risk profession and bankers who resisted the blandishments of organized crime were killed.

Corruption is also used to neutralize the punitive powers of the state. Criminal organizations want to maintain a highly congenial low-risk environment as a safe haven. Consequently, they have many targets for corruption, including the police and the military (to undermine control and enforcement efforts), the judiciary (to ensure favourable verdicts or, at the very least, lenient penalties), the legislature (to inhibit the passage of effective and stringent laws) and the executive branch (to obtain protection and support). In some cases, the use of corruption penetrates the state to such an extent that it results in the development of what Roy Godson has termed the 'political–criminal nexus' (Godson, 1997). In 'penetrated' states there is a symbiosis between politicians and criminals. The criminals provide money and help to mobilize political support for the politicians; the politicians provide protection, information and support for the criminals. Italy under successive Christian Democrat governments provided an excellent example of the protection for votes deal, although one that fell apart in the 1980s. Another classic example of high-level political support for criminal organizations occurred in Mexico where Raoul Salinas, brother of President Salinas, was alleged to have been the protector of drug trafficking organizations, and to have, as a result, been able to deposit well over US $100 million in Swiss bank accounts. The other striking thing about Mexico, however, is the alleged pervasiveness of corruption at every level of government. Although the ending of the PRI's monopoly of political power and the reform measures of the Fox government have gone some way to alleviate the situation, the problems posed by organized crime and drug trafficking remain immense.

If Mexico can be considered a penetrated state so, too, can Russia, where the 'iron triangle' of politicians, businessmen and criminals has become one of the dominating features of the post-communist system. With a seamless web between these three groups, capital flight and money laundering are – not surprisingly – virtually indistinguishable from one another. One astute observer has even suggested that in Russia, the transition from communism has led not to the democracy and free market eagerly anticipated by most Westerners but to a 'new authoritarianism' of organized crime (Shelley, 1997). Extensive corruption has been buttressed by violence, with contract killings targeted at anyone – investigative journalist, political reformer, businessman – who in any way threatens organized crime. Under Putin, the situation seems to have improved somewhat, although whether organized crime has been significantly weakened or has simply become more consolidated and less visible remains uncertain.

Another example of organized crime becoming a threat to the state apparatus – and the penetration of the state becoming a distinct possibility – is South Africa. Although the state is fighting back and has adopted legislation based on the United States' Racketeering Influences and Corrupt Organizations Act (RICO) that allows it to attack organizations exhibiting a pattern of criminal behaviour, the task is an uphill one in a country where the challenge comes from both indigenous criminal organizations and transnational groups including Russians, Chinese, Italians and Nigerians (Gastrow, 1998). The transition to the post-apartheid state has brought a government to power with much greater legitimacy than its predecessors, but law enforcement agencies still have a low status and limited resources. Consequently, policemen are often tempted by bribery and on occasion have even formed criminal gangs of their own. Limited economic opportunities for the majority black population, and the disparities of wealth and power, also ensure that organized crime groups and less sophisticated gangs such as those in the Western Cape always have plenty of recruits. The high level of violence in both organized and random crime has given South Africa a very high homicide rate and recent reports suggest that the activities of Nigerian criminals – who control both the drug trade and prostitution in significant parts of Johannesburg and other cities – are increasingly characterized by violence (Gastrow, 2000). South Africa also attracts outside groups because of its well developed infrastructure, its connections to the rest of the world (which make it an ideal trans-shipment country for all sorts of illicit goods) and its sophisticated financial system. Opportunities are readily available for both domestic and transnational organized crime groups, and the state is still weak enough that the risks do nothing to outweigh the incentives and gains from criminal enterprise. In South Africa, as in the FSU, organized crime will do all it can to ensure that the state remains weak and that the country continues to provide a safe haven. Without a systematic and sustained campaign against organized crime, therefore, South Africa could well end up as another penetrated state.

In states that are penetrated by organized crime, the state will still carry out many of its functions in international relations, while ensuring that organized crime functions unhindered and uninhibited in its pursuit of wealth. In a penetrated state, members of government and representatives of the state benefit directly from criminal activities, if only in the form of bribes and pay-offs. There is another category of state, however, where the process has gone beyond this and the state leaders do not simply benefit from organized crime but actually control much of it. The two prime examples of this are Nigeria and North Korea. In the case of Nigeria, the military government essentially ran criminal enterprises under the guise of the state apparatus. Revelations that the Swiss Federal Police have discovered $654 million in various Swiss banks accounts belonging to former President Abacha and members of his family suggest that defrauding the state and using the state as a cover for crime can be very lucrative. In a similar vein, North Korea is alleged to have used organized crime activities – often carried out by its diplomats – as a major source of revenue in the face of its international isolation.

There is yet another category in which the state is neither criminal nor penetrated so much as it is contested. Yet, even in these cases, criminal activities are often used by the competing factions to finance the struggle for power. Internal conflict and instability not only encourages indigenous criminal activities for political purposes, but – unless it is particularly dangerous and uncontrollable – also invites external criminal intervention. States in turmoil are an easy target and established criminal networks from a variety of countries will often try to exploit the unrest to engage in various kinds of profitable activities, whether supplying arms to the combatants, removing diamonds, or trafficking in endangered species. Indeed, criminal organizations excel at identifying new opportunities and positioning themselves to maximize the benefits. Where the state is contested, therefore, not only do the combatants use crime themselves but they are also willing to forge relationships with criminal networks from elsewhere. Significantly, however, the state often remains the prize of the contest.

The implication of all this for the continued contest between states and transnational organized crime is profound. It means that states have to contend with defections that will seriously hinder multilateral efforts to combat transnational organized crime. In many cases, the issue will simply be one of gaps in state capacity – a significant number of developing states and states in transition simply lack the resources required for the operation of an effective criminal justice system and the provision of adequate law enforcement capabilities. Such states provide sanctuaries for criminal organizations, whether they like it or not. In other cases, the issue will not necessarily be capacity so much as a matter of will. The corollary is that the defections themselves will take various forms. At one level there will be tacit defections, where there is nominal adherence to global regimes and multilateral efforts against transnational organized crime, but the pretence of cooperation will not be accompanied by substantive action. Other defections will be much more explicit and overt, reflecting the emergence of penetrated and criminal states. These defections will also have serious consequences. Perhaps most significantly, they will increase the number of safe havens from which transnational organized crime operates. They will also ensure that regimes aimed at transnational organized crime will be seriously incomplete, allowing geographic and jurisdictional loopholes that provide ample opportunities for criminal groups to adapt to the challenge and find ways around the obstacles. The overall effect will be not the containment of criminal activity but its displacement – geographical and methodological. In short, multilateral efforts by states to combat transnational organized crime will continue to exhibit serious deficiencies.

Crime, corruption and world politics

The implication of the preceding analysis is that the international system throughout much of the twenty-first century will be divided between those states that adopt a confrontational attitude towards transnational organized crime and those that either tacitly or overtly support criminal organizations. In such a world, claims to extra-territorial jurisdiction will be both enormously important and enormously controversial. Similarly, the use of military intervention to deal with the most egregious offenders also becomes an option – and, of course, already has a precedent in the US intervention in Panama in 1989 to remove President Noriega – although one whose attraction is likely to be tempered in a world where penetrated or criminal states wield considerable military power.

It is tempting to suggest that much of this analysis reinforces the contention of some observers that the state is in retreat. On reflection, however, a world divided between those states that uphold the rule of law and those that are captured by criminal organizations or are themselves criminal states is one in which the state is very robust. Some states will be the prize for transnational organized crime, but that is, in part, because states, as such, remain the most important defining units of world politics. The discussion here suggests that it is necessary to take a more differentiated approach to the notion of state decline. Some states are in retreat – and are likely to become fronts for criminal organizations – and some are not. Criminal organizations will not supersede the state – but in many cases they will target both home and host states, subvert them, neutralize their social control capabilities and even act as substitute providers for both state authority and state provision. The result will be not a new form of warlordism and the decline of the Westphalian system (although these characteristics will exist in parts of Africa and in Central Asia) but a new divide in global politics between those who uphold law and order and those for whom the state is both a sanctuary and the best of all possible fronts for transnational criminal activities. And ironically, for those who uphold the rule of law, multilateral cooperation (one of the basic tenets of liberal institutionalism) will be an imperative. Although transnational organized crime has emerged in ways that liberal institutionalists and proponents of global governance did not foresee, the challenge to stability, security and governance makes efforts to establish effective governance and multilateral cooperation even more urgent. In effect, the aspirations of the liberal institutionalists become the new imperatives. Whether aspirations or imperatives, however, the efforts to establish global governance are likely to be overwhelmed by an alliance of state and sovereign-free actors whose intellectual roots are in Hobbesian realism and whose *modus operandi* was delineated by Al Capone.

Guide to further reading

For background on organized crime and the debate in the United States as well as much useful contemporary material, see the collection edited by Ryan and Rush (1997). On the pervasiveness and impact of transnational organized crime groups, see Robinson (1999). This book is an excellent introduction and an exciting read, with much good detail. More academic treatments can be found in Williams (1994) and Shelley (1995). Most of these analyses emphasize the seriousness of the threat. An excellent critique and an alternative view can be found in Naylor (1995). For an excellent attempt to portray the issue in terms of criminal markets, see the collection edited by Friman and Andreas (1999). Useful journals are *Law, Crime and Social Change* which is not exclusively focused on organized crime but contains many good articles on the subject, *Trends in Organized Crime*, and *Global Crime* which supersedes *Transnational Organized Crime*.

Chapter 14

Terrorism

TIM DUNNE*

In September 1901 President Theodore Roosevelt led a campaign to eliminate terrorism after an anarchist had assassinated President McKinley. The same month, the same year, one hundred years later, it was evident for all to see that terrorism had not been eliminated. Quite the opposite. Enemies of the United States had turned civilian aircraft into deadly guided missiles with sufficient force to bring down the Twin Towers in Manhattan and to destroy a section of the Pentagon building in Washington DC.

Today we continue to live in an age of terror. The word – or its cousin terror*ism* – can be read in newspapers and heard in news bulletins on a daily basis. Routine aspects of twenty-first century life have changed their meaning: taking the subway or boarding an aircraft are perceived to be risky in a manner unthinkable a generation ago. It is not just the habits of ordinary citizens that have been transformed: across the world, governments have redefined their national security policies to respond to the perceived threat posed by terrorist groups. This is a profound change in the business of statecraft. What used to be thought of as a purely domestic issue has become internationalized. What used to be dealt with through the law courts is increasingly the business of the armed forces. What Americans call 'homeland' security is now a matter of international security.

It is a truism to state that when the world changes, the theories and concepts we use change with it. The academic study of world politics is no exception. Research and teaching on terrorism used to be limited to a sub-field of scholars with a largely empirical focus on particular terrorist groups, their motivations and techniques, and the responses these engendered on the part of particular governments on international institutions. Today, undergraduate and graduate programmes on International Relations (IR) include modules on terrorism and the evolving structures and processes of world order.

Two digits mark the moment when this transformation occurred: 9/11. Between the hours of 8.46 and 10.03, four airliners had been hijacked and

* I would like to acknowledge my debt to a friend and mentor, Ken Booth. We collaborated in putting together a collection of post-9/11 essays (Booth and Dunne, 2002) – an experience which shaped my thinking when drafting this chapter. His work exemplifies the kind of contribution IR can make to understanding the problems and possibilities of our colliding worlds.

crashed, two bringing down the North and South Towers of the World Trade Center, a third into the western side of the Pentagon, and a fourth in a field in Pennsylvania. 2600 people died at Ground Zero, 125 died in the Pentagon inferno, and 256 died on the four planes. Such 'immeasurable pain', to use the words of the 9-11 Commission Report 'was inflicted by 19 young Arabs acting at the behest of Islamist extremists headquartered in distant Afghanistan' (2004, p. 2).

It was not the attacks themselves that altered the landscape of world politics and put terrorism at the top of the international agenda. What brought the nameless post-Cold War era to a certain end was the response of the United States and its allies. The so-called 'war on terror' has profoundly challenged a number of analytical and normative assumptions about world politics. It has challenged the prevailing assumption that terrorism only constitutes a 'local' threat rather than a global threat. It has challenged the claim made by modern sovereign states that war is a rational instrument used for political purposes within a framework that regulates both the cause and the conduct of warfare: 9/11 showed that war *is* the goal of certain political groups, and at the same time, it showed that distinctions fundamental to the inter-state legal order, such as the separation between combatants and non-combatants, were not universally shared. It has challenged the assumption that the inter-state order was built on secular principles rather than ideological and religious rivalry. It has challenged the previously held assumption that terrorists ought to be treated as criminals rather than enemies. Lastly, and indirectly, 9/11 transformed America's view of its security and in the process transformed the global security agenda.

This brief sketch of the context within which we understand terrorism is a prelude to a wider discussion of different dimensions to the issue. These broadly converge on the typology set out by the editors in the opening chapter. Specifically, the chapter will consider the following questions. It opens with a discussion about the definition and scope of terrorism, then moves on to consider the significance of terrorism both to the real world agenda of international politics and to academic analysis. What follows is a discussion of the problem that 'new terrorism' poses for state leaders. This leads into an analysis of the spectrum of possible responses to the threat posed by terrorism, from intelligence gathering and police action to all-out war. The chapter ends with a reflection on the impact of state-based forms of terror, and non-state terrorist groups, on contemporary world politics.

Terrorism: scope and definition

There is no generally accepted definition of terrorism. It is possible to find over 100 usages of the term in UN documentation. Even the UN resolutions of September 2001, condemning the terror attacks on the United States, avoided an explicit statement about what kinds of action constituted terrorism. While the reasons for the lack of an agreed definition are largely conceptual – as discussed below – it should also be noted that definitional disputes have a real-world dimension in terms of the problems of agreeing terms for the extradition of suspected terrorists.

Why does the term terrorism have no settled meaning? There are three answers to this dilemma. First, the meaning of terrorism has changed historically. In the 1940s and 1950s it was commonly used to describe the violent struggles by nationalist or anti-colonial movements in Africa, Asia and the Middle East. With the completion of decolonization, terrorism became attached to the actions of dissatisfied national and ethnic groups within states such as the United Kingdom (by the Irish Republican Army (IRA)), Spain (by ETA, the front for the Freedom of the Basque Homeland), and Canada (the FLQ or Front de Libération du Québec). From the 1980s to the present, successive US administrations have applied the word to states who allegedly 'sponsor' or 'harbour' terrorists. Post-9/11, the term has been almost become a synonym for anyone or anything that is evil: in a televised debate about natural disasters, an Oxford philosopher was moved to say that their existence proved that, if there is a God, s/he must be a terrorist.

While we do not need to reflect on the theology of terrorism, the serious point which needs further elaboration is the question of *who* produces terror? Here we find a second reason why terrorism is almost impossible to define. It is a term that is applied to a diverse set of organizations pursuing different (often multiple) goals. Chechens seek independence from Russia as well as religious goals. Supporters of militant Islamic groups seek revenge against the Infidel West *and* want to violently overthrow the leadership of 'apostates' – the rulers of Islamic states such as Pakistan and Saudi Arabia who have compromised their strict interpretation of the Islamic faith. Others seek the narrower political goal of liberation, as is the case with pro-Palestinian organisations such as Hamas, and also the Liberation Tigers of Tamil Eelam in Sri Lanka. These diverse groups and networks favour different tactics: some target infrastructure with the aim of raising the costs to the 'enemy' of continuing the struggle. Others target civilians, as in the case of the Lockerbie bombing in 1988, and more recently, in cases where pro-Palestinian supporters wrap themselves in plastic explosives and commit suicide while killing and maiming as many Israeli civilians as possible.

The issue of agency – who is a terrorist and what kinds of violence are perpetrated – leads to a third complication in trying to arrive at a stable definition of terrorism. The US State Department's definition limits the capacity to generate terror to 'sub-national' groups only. This belief that governments cannot perpetrate acts of terrorism is a long-standing one. It is rooted in the Weberian idea that the state has a monopoly on the *legitimate* means of violence: by implication, violence committed by non-state actors is illegitimate. States can mobilize force domestically to uphold the law, and states can fight wars internationally in accordance with the laws of war. There are no permissive conditions for violence to be used by non-state groups.

The claim that sovereign states are an exception to the modern idea that force is no longer a legitimate instrument for securing political ends is highly contentious. Looking back at the twentieth century, the most abhorrent acts of terror against civilian populations were committed by agents acting on behalf of the state. Examples here would include the actions of secret police in the Soviet Union whose activities induced fear in order to deter dissent. More directly, governments have commissioned death squads to kill and spread terror (a particular pattern that has afflicted many Latin American states in recent times). Governments can also be complicit in using violence to eliminate or disperse a target ethnic group, such as the use of chemical weapons by Iraq against the Kurds in March 1998.

Western states are no strangers to wielding the weapon of terror. Civilians have frequently born the brunt of Israeli incursions into Lebanon (with the support of the US government). In Latin America, the United States has engaged in numerous covert military operations to effect political change. Similarly, the conduct of the US-led 'war on terror' has been such that at times it has begun to resemble the forces of darkness it set out to banish. It is noteworthy that, three weeks into the bombing of Afghanistan in late 2001, the chief of the UK Defence Staff said that US–UK attacks would continue 'until the people of the country themselves recognise that this is going to go on until they get the leadership changed' (Chomsky in Booth and Dunne, 2002, p. 133).

What the preceding discussion has established is the simple fact that terrorism is a contested concept. While Western governments try to restrict the definition either to the actions of sub-state groups, or non-democratic states who harbour terrorists, even a cursory history of violence in the modern era tells us that acts of terror have been perpetrated by non-state actors *and* states. Moreover, Western states have not been immune to the temptation to use coercive means to generate fear in the minds of a target population. The double standard at the core of traditional definitions of terrorism is nicely exposed by Noam Chomsky who argues, 'we have to qualify the definition of terrorism given in official sources: the term applies only to terrorism against *us,* not the terrorism we carry out against *them.*' (2002, p. 131).

Although students of IR no doubt feel frustrated by the fact that there are no widely accepted definitions of key terms, it is also important to remember that many key concepts in the fields of politics and IR are 'essentially contested'. Such a term denotes not only a plurality of interpretations but also the fact that there is no neutral position from which one could arbitrate among them. As a consequence, political actors contest meanings. Notice how, post-9/11, the leadership in Russia and Israel has been able to convincingly portray its enemies (the Chechens and pro-Palestinians respectively) as terrorists. Interestingly, however, the meaning of terrorism is not entirely malleable. When the Zimbabwean leader Robert Mugabe tried to portray British journalists as 'terrorists', such an interpretation received no support outside his narrow band of political allies.

In other words, while the term terrorism is broad and in large measure context-dependent, it is possible to apply it incorrectly. Such an observation forces us to come up with a definition and a set of parameters so we can at least distinguish terrorism from other kinds of violence (such as inter-state war or civil war). The most persuasive definition of political terrorism is:

> The use, or the threat of use, of violence by an individual or a group, whether acting for or in opposition to established authority, when such an act is designed to create extreme anxiety and/or fear-inducing effects in a target group larger than the immediate victims with the purpose of coercing that group into acceding to the political demands of the perpetrators (Wardlaw, cited in Rogers, 2002, p. 215).

Points to highlight in respect of this definition include the following. Terrorism requires the threat or use of force – this sets such actions apart from other instruments of political change such as demonstration or passive resistance. Terrorism requires an impact beyond those immediately affected by a violent event: assassinations are terrorist acts if they are intended to send a signal to other members of a target group (as opposed to simply removing one leader so that a rival can succeed her). Terrorism is political – violence is not undertaken for reasons of personal ambition or financial gain.

While there is no escaping the contestability of terrorism, it is useful to elaborate some basic distinctions that can provide greater analytical clarity. In the extensive literature on the subject, it has become commonplace to refer to sub-state activity as terror*ism,* and state (and state-sponsored) activity as terror. Similarly, while eschewing the distinction between domestic and international terrorism – almost all terrorist organisations have a transnational dimension – the chapter will nonetheless make use of the label 'new terrorism' to describe the various radical Islamist movements dedicated to waging war on the West.

The significance of terrorism

Consider the following two empirical statements. In 2003, the total number of lives lost in UK road accidents was 3508, vastly greater than the total fatalities estimated by the US State Department to have been caused by terrorism. The attacks on the United States in 2001 killed around 3000 people: this is a comparable figure to the number of children who die *every day* of preventable diseases in the poorest parts of the world. Do these statements imply that terrorism is not *really* important when we consider it in relation to other tragedies? Such a question begs two different answers that are mutually inconsistent but at the same time reveal important aspects of our perception of the threat posed by terrorism.

If we return to the definition above, we see that the purpose of terrorism is to create fear and anxiety. One of the reasons why terrorist groups have been successful is that they manage to generate a level of fear and anxiety that is disproportionate to the security threat they represent. 9/11 directly affected thousands of families. Yet hundreds of millions of people around the world were drawn into this spectacle, shocked by the fact that ordinary citizens simply getting on with their daily routine became instruments in a wider struggle between Islamist factions and Western governments. In the aftermath of the attacks, families began to re-evaluate daily decisions about where and when to travel, how long to spend away from home, and what to make of strangers who could be monsters. The political theorist Jean Bethke Elshtain recalled how her grandchildren responded to the spectacle by drawing planes flying into skyscrapers. They also asked questions about what would happen if their Grandma's plane was hijacked. This curiosity elicited the following response: 'we reassure them, knowing that the correct answer cannot be spoken aloud to children' (2002, p. 268). Neither was the correct answer given in 2004 to school children from Beslan in North Ossetia, who would have been asking their parents what the new school year was likely to bring, only to be herded into a gym at gunpoint for 53 hours of torment ending in carnage.

Cleaning office blocks in New York, partying in Bali, commuting in Madrid, going to school in Beslan, dealing with migration issues in Nairobi, having a drink in a café in Tel Aviv. Each activity is part of daily life in which the individuals concerned anticipate will occur without incident. Yet instead of participating in the banality of normality, those involved became witnesses to the nihilism of evil. This capacity to turn sanity into madness, familial dependence into despair, and spectators into sympathisers, is what enables the actions of terrorists to assume an importance that is far greater than a simple body-bag count would suggest.

One reason why terror attacks have become more significant is that terrorist groups have increasingly shown themselves to be capable of striking at distant targets: the hijacking of civilian airliners since the late 1960s is evidence of the transnational character of terrorist activities. While it might be useful to examine the differences between those terrorist groups seeking to affect political change *inside* the boundaries of their sovereign state as opposed to those fighting a jihad against an entire civilization, it is important to note that the definition of terrorism cited above does not rely on a specific geographic referent. Such a distinction between domestic and international terrorist activity is also problematic for the reason that there was always a transnational element to the former: the IRA, for example, has for many decades received finance from the United States and military hardware from other terrorist organizations.

The growing importance of terrorism is due in part to the audacity of the spectacle, and the fact that images of despair and destruction are instantly replayed on screens around the world. Furthermore, terrorist groups are skilled at using the media for their political ends: a message from Osama bin Laden filmed in an Afghan cave on a simple camcorder is instantly played and replayed in the global media. So effective is Al Qaeda's communications strategy that it prompted Richard Holbrooke (former Under-Secretary of State in the Clinton Administration) to ask: 'How can a man in a cave outcommunicate the world's leading communications society?' (9-11 Commission, 2004, p. 337).

Insurgents in Iraq who oppose the US-led war and subsequent occupation use the internet as an outlet to relay macabre images of their victims being beheaded. The symbolic power of such acts of violence is an example of terror theatre *par excellence*: it is designed to undermine support for the war in the United States, while striking fear into the minds of all the potential hostages in Iraq. Most significantly of all, it is an example of asymmetric violence in which the powerless proclaim victory over the powerful.

There is strong empirical evidence to suggest that public opinion in Western states regards terrorism as a major threat. Much of the political analysis of the 2004 US Presidential election claimed that the Republican party's emphasis on deeply conservative 'values' was the reason for their success. Exit poll data showed that 22 per cent of the electorate regarded moral values as the most significant issue, while 15 per cent believed it to be Iraq and 19 per cent believed it to be the war on terror. Given the skilful way in which the Bush campaign succeeded in arguing that Iraq was the new fault-line in the war on terror, it logically follows that many American citizens believed that terrorism and the threat posed by states who harbour them should be a highly significant determinant of the election result.

From the election result in Spain (in March 2004), following former President Aznar's hapless attempt to blame Basque terrorists for the Madrid bombings, to the re-election of George W. Bush in the same year, it is not difficult to make a case for the political importance of terrorism as an issue in domestic and international politics. Can the same be said for the study of world politics? To what extent is terrorism now on the agenda of the discipline? Before addressing this question, it is useful to reflect for a moment on certain features of the approach to terrorism pre-9/11. It is almost impossible to find serious treatments of terrorism in IR textbooks in the 1980s and 1990s – not even in works on the sub-field of security studies (Croft and Terriff, 2000). Even key introductory textbooks that sought to survey the field as a whole, such as the first edition of this book and the first two editions of Baylis and Smith, *Globalization of World Politics* (1997, 2000), neglected the issue.

Part of the explanation for this silence about terrorism in academic writing on world politics is due to the issue being domiciled in a separate sub-field of 'terrorism studies'. Scholars working in this area were drawn from a variety of disciplines, including psychology, criminology, and area or country specialists. Valuable work was produced by this interdisciplinarity (for example, Lutz and Lutz, 2004), albeit at a cost of influencing agendas inside the various overarching disciplines of history, politics and law. One marked feature of a great deal of work in terrorism is the obsession to categorize various terrorist groups in the hope of capturing the essence of domestic terrorism versus international terrorism, or terrorism versus paramilitarism. The flaw with such a method is neatly exposed by M. R. L. Smith and Alan O'Day. Why should, they ask, the Red Army Faction in West Germany in the 1970s – ostensibly the product of leftist student radicalism – have anything in common with Irish nationalist violence? They go on to argue:

> [T]he study of terrorism often draws together these varied low-level wars by trying to make theoretical generalisations primarily on the basis of tactical modality. Individual wars are thus disconnected from their historical and cultural backgrounds. Clearly this is an unsatisfactory way to analyse what are usually complex and highly divergent conflicts. The damage caused to the decent study of low intensity wars by the decontextualisation of conflicts as a result of terrorist studies methodology, seen in the superficiality of some works in the area, has been vast. (Smith and O'Day in Whittaker, 2001, p. 239).

For its part, the study of world politics has for too long been wedded to a state-centric view of the world such that terrorism was easily dismissed as a sub-state phenomenon. The only violence thought to be significant, at least for the realist tradition, is the threat or use of force by sovereign states. War, by definition, is something that only sovereign states can do. Events in the world have challenged such narrow minded scholarship: even if academic IR is not interested in terrorism, terrorism is interested in the 'international'.

'New terrorism' on the international agenda

Beneath the surface of the disciplinary debate about terrorism studies lies a series of fundamentally important questions about the nature of world politics. As Paul Wilkinson rightly argues, 'prior to 9/11 the conventional wisdom was that the use of terrorism was endemic in low-intensity conflict around the world but that it rarely, if ever, posed a strategic threat to the security of a major power or the international community' (2003, p. 32). The growth of 'new terrorism' (Lacqueur, 2001) in the form of Al Qaeda has changed all that. What is new about Al Qaeda is the breadth of its organisation, the capacity to plan 'spectactulars' that cause immense harm, and the ability to use late-modern technologies – satellite TV networks, cell phones, laptops, the internet and so on – in the confrontation with 'infidel' and 'apostate' peoples.

The movement that became Al Qaeda al-Sulbha (The Solid Base) grew out of the anti-Soviet struggle in Afghanistan between 1979 and 1989. Osama bin Laden, from the richest non-royal Saudi family, became its leader at about the time that the humiliated Soviet army divisions were withdrawn from Afghan territory. The hub of the Al Qaeda network has been in states where lawlessness is the norm (Sudan until 1996 and then Afghanistan until shortly after the 9/11 attacks) – outside of the hub, location is fluid and depends on how vigorously the organization is being pursued. One of the striking characteristics of the network is its organizational reach. Al Qaeda's Emir General Osama bin Laden refers to the organization as a family, and members are referred to as brothers. One expert described the breadth of the extended family in the following terms: 'Al-Qaeda's families included Egyptians, Algerians, Moroccans, Libyans, Tunisians, Turks, Kurds, UAEs, Jordanians, Syrians, Palestinians, Lebanese, Somalis, Sudanese, Saudis, Yemeni, Kenyans, Tanzanians, Maurithenians, Chechen, Uigurs (Xingjiang, China), Uzbeks, Tajiks, Turkmens, Kryrgyz, Kazakhs, Pakistanis, Kashmirs, Bangladeshis, Moros (Mindanao, Philippines), Singaporeans, and Rohingiyas (Myanmar)' (Gunaratna, 2003, p. 39). In addition, membership is drawn from Muslims in Europe and North America.

It was the Egyptian family that organised the 9/11 attacks under the operations command of Mohammad Atta. This event marked a watershed in that it ensured Al Qaeda became known worldwide where previously its activities had been the subject of scrutiny by a relatively narrow group of experts in various intelligence agencies. Why did they do it? Al Qaeda understands itself to be fighting a religious war against enemies of Islam (the religious motivation is thought to be a defining characteristic of 'new terrorism'). The year he sought refuge from the Taliban-dominated Afghan government, bin Laden issued a fatwa, or religious ruling, calling for the murder of any American: it was the 'individual duty for every Muslim who can do it in any country in which it is possible to do it' (9-11 Commission, 2004, p. 47). He put this into practice two years later with the bombing of the American embassies in Nairobi and Dar es Saleem. Such attacks on US infrastructure are meant to punish and weaken the Infidel.

How much support is there for Al Qaeda in the Muslim world? The theology underpinning 'the solid base' is unintelligible within the mainstream interpretation of Islam. The vast majority of ordinary Muslims do not support the vision of a transnational Islamic order let alone the use of violence and terror as instruments in support of this goal. Yet there is widespread sympathy for the charge that the United States and its allies are hypocritical imperialists. Hypocritical in that they used overwhelming force to expel Iraq from Kuwait while allowing Israel's continued occupation of Palestinian territory. Imperialist in that the United States is blind to the virtues of other belief systems. Instead of allowing other cultural values to flourish – a cardinal assumption of the non-intervention principle in IR – the United States believes *its* values are *universal*. Moreover, not content with its feelings of cultural superiority, the United States ruthlessly exploits its power and the power of international institutions to impose liberal values on others.

The psychological processes by which these widely held beliefs are transmuted into active support for terrorism is complex. Mohammed Atta's testament, found in a bag which never went on board his final flight, revealed disturbing levels of 'psychological indoctrination' (Gunaratna, 2003, p. 43). As a reward for their sacrifice, Atta promised his accomplices that 'the gardens of paradise are waiting for you in all their beauty'. The women in paradise call out to them 'dressed in only their most beautiful clothing' (Amanat, 2001, p. 45). Such contradictory narratives, interwoven from Koranic verses and images of worldly hedonism, shows the manipulation that is required in order to win the hearts and minds of recruits.

Following a raid on a suspected Al Qaeda cell in Manchester (in May 2000), a 'manual' was recovered. It included a 'Declaration of Jihad Against the Country's Tyrants (quoted in Kiras, 2004, p. 489). The following passage illustrates the intensity of the ideological calling:

> The confrontation that Islam calls for with these godless and apostate regimes, does not know Socratic debates, Platonic ideals, nor Aristotelian diplomacy. But it knows the dialogue of bullets, the ideals of assassination, bombing, and destruction, and the diplomacy of the cannon and machine-gun.

The violence and hatred contained in such messages further reinforces the claim that 'new terrorism' is more radical and difficult to deter. If martyrdom is the ultimate way to spiritual purity, then force is not an appropriate instrument with which to respond (Kiras, 2004, p. 249).

One of the striking contradictions in the representation of Al Qaeda in the West is the claim that the movement is either pre-modern or anti-modern. Behind speeches by Prime Minister Blair and President Bush lurks an image of bin Laden and his followers as something that stands in opposition to modern ideas of toleration and progress. For his part, bin Laden feeds this caricature by playing the role of a pre-modern crusader wearing long robes with nothing but the Koran under his arm and a rifle on his back. Both versions of this representation are flawed. From the West's point of view, there is an inability to recognize that there are multiple ways of being modern 'some of them monstrous' (Gray, 2003, p. 2). As Chris Brown neatly puts it: 'Osama bin Laden is as modern a figure as Tony Blair, but represents a different *kind* of modernity' (Brown, 2002, p. 298). Even a cursory history of the twentieth century tells us that there have been other monstrous attempts at modernization, specifically the Nazis in the first half of the century and authoritarian socialists in the second. For his part, the fact that bin Laden *has* a public relations strategy, including the successful manipulation of a global satellite television network, suggests that he is every bit as aware of the technological possibilities offered to political actors by our late modern age. Despite the messianic mantras, the Al Qaeda leadership is dominated by educated men who are capable of employing advanced models of business administration to invest in markets, recruit volunteers, communicate with cells in distant places, coordinate military activity, and integrate other strands of militant Islamist activity into the movement.

As noted earlier, Al Qaeda was known to pose a significant threat to US interests well before 9/11. Following the attacks on US embassies in Africa, President Clinton ordered retaliatory strikes in the hope of killing bin Laden. He has been on the CIA's 'most wanted' list since then. What changed after 9/11 is that the entire US national security strategy shifted towards recognising that Islamic holy warriors constituted *the* most significant security threat. Later security strategy documents by the UK Government and the EU echo the same realization (Dunne, 2004). It is hard to understate the significance of this move to students of world politics: the most powerful states in the world no longer view other states as the primary threat. Instead, at the top of their security agenda, is an elusive transnational network of terrorists who are said to be outside the traditional parameters of international order. Acting beyond the sovereign-state system, they are consequently beyond the laws of war. More controversially, Western state leaders portray Al Qaeda followers as barbarians with pathological mindsets whose actions cannot be predicted or deterred.

Institutional responses to terrorism

Given the diversity of terrorist organizations and tactics, it is not surprising that a variety of techniques to combat terrorist threats have been deployed by governments and international institutions. Such measures are usefully covered by the term 'counter-terrorism'. At one end of the spectrum are political measures, including negotiation, reform and diplomacy. At the other are punitive measures, including sanctions, detention, torture, punishment and all-out war. To illustrate two distinct strategies at either end of the spectrum, the following discussion will briefly analyze the UK Government's response to the activities of the IRA in Northern Ireland, and the US-led response to the threat posed by 'new terrorist' groups such as Al Qaeda.

The 'troubles' in Northern Ireland go back to the 1960s. The costs of the conflict have been prohibitively high: 3500 civilians lost their lives, 30 000 were injured, and the damage to property takes the total cost of the 'troubles' to billions of pounds a year. Given that the total population is only 1.6 million, no one was untouched by the conflict between nationalists and unionists. At its core, the conflict is one of national identity. Catholics see themselves as Irish and aspire to a united Ireland: they believe themselves to be a victim of illegitimate British rule. 'Nationalists', as they are more accurately referred to, are represented politically by Sinn Fein and associated with various paramilitary organisations including the IRA and the Provisional IRA (or PIRA). Protestants are fiercely loyal to the United Kingdom. 'Unionists' are led by two political parties (the Democratic Unionist Party and the Ulster Unionists) and have links to several paramilitary organisations, including the Ulster Freedom Fighters (UFF). Since the Good Friday Agreement in 1998 regarding the necessity of constitutional reform by consensus (by communities on both sides of the border) there has been an uneasy peace between the protagonists, with the IRA declaring an end to the armed struggle.

What is particularly relevant to this discussion is the nature of the 'armed struggle' engaged in by the unofficial PIRA and the counter-terrorist measures taken by the UK Government. The aim of the armed struggle was to protect nationalists from intimidation by Unionists and the mainly Protestant security services. Such a strategy had widespread support among the nationalist community, particularly as it resurrected a historical struggle that the Irish had waged against the British for centuries. The military targets of the PIRA were wide-ranging. Soldiers serving in the British Army were targets, members of the police force (on- or off-duty), and local businesses in Unionist areas. Car bombs were a favoured method of attack as they were inexpensive, hard to prevent, and caused mayhem in the vicinity (not to mention killing and maiming civilians who were not employed by the British security services). The IRA and its military offshoots also took their campaign of violence abroad, attacking British military targets in England, Germany and Gibraltar. Violence was not limited to military installations: pubs and shopping centres were bombed, as was the city of London. MPs were assassinated, and most famously, the Grand Hotel in Brighton, where the Conservative Party was holding its annual conference, was bombed on 12 October 1984.

The counter-terrorist strategy of the UK Government centred upon militarized containment. Aside from having a heavy British Army presence in Northern Ireland, the UK Government used the Special Air Services Regiment (SAS) to pre-empt terror attacks, as well as the intelligence agencies to close in on suspected terrorists and gather information on possible future targets. In addition to high-profile military 'policing' in Belfast and across other fault-lines in the six counties, the UK government used a variety of authoritarian measures to contain and punish terrorists. When it became increasingly difficult to convict suspected terrorists – due both to the legitimacy of the armed struggle in the minds of many ordinary nationalist citizens and also due to a degree of intimidation of witnesses and jurors – the British government resorted to so-called Diplock Courts where

IRA defendants were put on trial in front of a judge but without a jury. Such measures ran counter to the principles of the British judicial system, a result that was seized upon by nationalists for propaganda purposes.

The question of how far democratic states are willing to suspend civil liberties is a dilemma in which many countries have found themselves after 9/11. Tightening up 'homeland security' has been a growing preoccupation of domestic legal authorities in the United States and the United Kingdom. Such measures as the Patriot Act in the United States and the UK Government's Anti-Terrorism, Crime and Security Act, are important components of the counter-terrorist strategy. It is worth noting in this context that the FBI were allegedly in possession of a laptop belonging to one of the 9/11 assassins but were not authorized to access it. On the other side of the ledger, opponents of such illiberal measures worry where the process will end. If basic rights are denied to suspected terrorists today, will they be denied to political opponents of the state tomorrow? The appalling treatment of suspected terrorists detained in Guantanamo Bay illustrates the depravity to which a liberal state can sink. By referring to captured persons as 'enemy combatants' rather than 'prisoners of war', the US government sought to place the detainees in a legal black hole.

The justification for these actions is provided by the 'war on terror', the phrase first used by President George W. Bush in his address to Congress on 20 September 2001. Within days of the attacks on New York and Washington, the Bush Administration made it clear that the only response to such an act of war was war itself. Was there an alternative? The eminent historian Sir Michael Howard suggested at the time that those responsible should be hunted down and brought before an international tribunal in much the same way that the former President of Yugoslavia, Slobodan Milosevic, is standing trial in The Hague. The principal attraction to such a strategy is that it distances the victims of the crime and their political leaders from the legal process of judging the accused. Set against this, there were many practical barriers to the pursuit of international police action. How were the accused to be found and apprehended when they were being protected inside a sovereign state? And would a guilty verdict from an international tribunal be seen as legitimate in the Muslim world?

Such possibilities soon became irrelevant. On 8 October 2001, 'Operation Enduring Freedom' began as USAF planes struck at suspected Al Qaeda targets. By early 2003, the United States and its allies opened up a new front in the 'war on terror': Iraq. Strategy and tactics in these two theatres suggest that the most powerful states in the world believe that terrorism is a new kind of war which, if allowed to go unchecked, will lead to death and destruction on a scale not seen since the dropping of nuclear bombs on Hiroshima and Nagasaki. Pentagon planners are haunted by the possibility that one of the jets that ploughed into the World Trade Center could have been carrying a 'dirty' nuclear bomb. As President Bush put it, the United States must act before the mushroom cloud billows into the sky. The question in the minds of neo-conservatives in the White House is one that Prime Minister Tony Blair has been prompted to ask: Do these new threats demand a change in the way the West thinks about what is an appropriate response?

Albeit with a different tone, the United States and the United Kingdom both justified the 2003 war against Saddam Hussein's Iraq using the same language: Iraq had links with Al Qaeda, Iraq already had the potential to inflict harm on its neighbours and the region and, if left unchecked, Iraq would develop a WMD capability that would threaten the West. These themes formed the backdrop to UN Security Council resolution 1799 that demanded that Iraq disarm its existing WMD and put a halt to the development of all WMD programmes.

The diplomatic debacle that ensued in early 2003 illustrated how far international institutions had become marginalized in the war on terror. In the absence of an agreement to use force within the UN Security Council, the United States led a coalition of states which were prepared to act outside the Council. In terms of the implications for how the international community deals with future instances of counter-terrorism, there are two possible readings of this case. The view of neo-conservatives in the Bush administration is that terrorism, and the threat posed by Islamist warriors, is too important to be left to the UN. In a unipolar world, the United States is not going to seek anyone's permission for defending its population and securing its vital interests. If needs must, the United States will act pre-emptively even if this is at odds with the UN's use of force rules (see US Government, *National Security Strategy*, 2002). It is interesting to note in this respect that even the very measured 9-11 Commission Report sees no significant role for multilateral international institutions in defending the United States from any future threats. Outside of contemporary US politics different lessons are being drawn from 9/11 and the Iraq war. Many sympathetic to the UN argue that Security Council reform holds the key to responding effectively to Al Qaeda and other terrorist organizations who pose a significant threat to international peace and security.

The cases of the IRA and Al Qaeda illustrate two very different counter-terrorist strategies. At the same time it is important to recognize that both are 'punitive' and reactive. In terms of prevention, a different set of tools may be required. A strategy favoured by many European leaders is often labelled 'draining the swamp', in other words, providing economic and social regeneration to those parts of the world which appear to believe that acts of suicidal terror hold the key to salvation. An alternative – and complementary approach – is to take more seriously the need to engage in dialogue with those of the Islamic faith who feel deeply aggrieved about the current state of world politics. Such an account ought to begin with a desire to understand different forms of life and how mutual respect among them can be achieved (Linklater, 2002; Parekh, 2002).

The high-level panel reporting to the UN Secretary-General has sought to bridge these two responses in its report *A More Secure World – Our Shared Responsibility* (UN, 2004). The main elements of the strategy centre around 5 Ds: first, to dissuade groups from wielding the weapon of terror in order to achieve their goals; second, to deny terrorists the capability to carry out their attacks; third, to deter states from supporting terrorists; fourth to develop states' preventative capacity; fifth, to defend human rights in the struggle against terrorism.

Conclusions and implications

There will be many new challenges to international peace and security in the twenty-first century. Pollution and the degradation of the environment will trigger effects that are threatening to peoples in many parts of the world. The increasing inequality of wealth and power between the 'haves' and the 'have-nots' will sow the seeds of mass migrations leading to endless conflicts. Epidemics that will threaten entire populations will be increasingly hard to contain. To this list of new security problems must be added terrorism.

The spectre that haunts leaders and citizens in the West is the explosive combination of WMD harnessed to the pathology of terrorism. There will soon be laboratories around the world producing germs with the potential to spread lethal infectious diseases in a matter of days. Given the complex issue of 'dual use' (that is, civil and military) in this case, it is hard to see how an effective inspections regime can come into being. The spectre that haunts leaders and citizens in the Middle East is the fear that the West will continue to wage wars of aggression in which tens of thousands of civilians will be killed – and many more will die because essential services are disrupted and water supplies are either interrupted or contaminated. Defenders of liberal interventionism will continue to claim that wars for regime change are not acts of terrorism as civilian casualties are unintentional: to critics of interventionism, such an evasion implies that decision-makers have forgotten General Sherman's dictum that 'war is hell'. Moreover, the imposition of Western values looks like a continuation of an imperial strategy that European great powers practised for many centuries.

Wherever acts of terror are perpetrated, ordinary citizens caught up in them have long understood how such practices brutalize everyday life. Today the threat posed by terrorism is one which is being recognized by international institutions and leading states in the world, evident in a variety of key documents on national and international security (UK – *International Priorities*, 2003; *National Security Strategy of the United States of America*, 2002; *European Security Strategy*, 2003; UN – *A More Secure World*, 2004). Despite the increasing prominence of counter-terrorism as a military and political priority, the preceding discussion has given us reasons to be pessimistic about the prospects for international society's ability to contain and eradicate the threat.

Heading the list of reasons to be pessimistic is the on-going disagreement about the meaning of terrorism. This has, in the words of the UN Secretary-General, 'weakened' the 'moral authority of the UN in dealing with the problem' (Annan, 2005, p. 2). The principal problems identified in the chapter can be characterized as ones of bias and selectivity. Bias in the sense that states refuse to admit that they have been perpetrators of acts of terror on a massive scale. Selectivity in the sense that, in key regions of the world such as the Middle East, the term 'terrorism' is often ascribed to the actions of pro-Arab militias but not to the Israeli security forces.

When it comes to the threat posed by new terrorism, the response has engendered many difficulties. The victory of war-fighting over policing as the dominant strategy – as least in the armoury of the United Kingdom and the United States – has blurred the boundaries between the methods used by the terrorists and those used by the self-proclaimed enemies of terrorism. This miscalculation is mirrored in the domestic realm of many liberal states as they struggle to deliver security to their population without significantly eroding the human rights of individuals.

Four years after the Twin Towers were demolished, the war on terror has engendered an escalation of fear and enmity in many parts of the world. Rather than letting terrorism win, 'terrorism can be defeated today (if not eradicated) by employing the means, however imperfectly, that are the moral equivalent of the ends we seek' (Booth and Dunne, 2002, p. 21). The challenge facing all of us as students of world politics is to reflect critically on the dynamics of terrorism and counter-terrorism: such a position enables us to see how the words of bin Laden and George W. Bush can be viewed as the embodiment of truth and virtue in their own backyards while thought to be just as depraved in the minds of distant others. Critical thinking must also be guided by the need to strengthen the power of legitimacy in international society. An agreement between states and peoples as to the nature of the terrorist threat and the appropriate action to take is unlikely to stop terrorists in their tracks, but in the long run such a strategy has a better chance of persuading the dispossessed from turning to terror. Where this fails, any remedial action must be consistent with the rules of international law thereby driving a wedge between terrorism and the actions of those who oppose it.

Guide to further reading

For a general analysis of terrorism see Laqueur (1977), and Lutz and Lutz (2004). Paul Wilkinson (2000) usefully counterposes the narratives of terrorism and liberalism. Since 9/11 writings on terrorism have focused on the war on terror, see Booth and Dunne (2002); Buckley and Fawn (2003); Lacqueur (2001).

In addition to reading academic texts, readers are strongly advised to consult policy documents which highlight the priority accorded to terrorism in contemporary security thinking. See especially: US, *National Security Strategy Document* (2002), UK, *International Priorities* (2003), *European Security Strategy* (2003); UN Secretary-General's High Level Panel report (2004) and the 9-11 Commission Report (2004).

Chapter 15

Issues in World Politics Reviewed

BRIAN WHITE, RICHARD LITTLE AND
MICHAEL SMITH

The first edition of this book was prepared in 1996, half a decade after the demise of the Soviet Union and the call from the United States for a 'New World Order'; the second was published in 2001, in the months before the attacks on the United States that took place on 11 September of that year. Much of the initial optimism accompanying the end of the Cold War had already evaporated by 1996, and by 2001 it was clear that new challenges and new forms of global tension had emerged. Few doubted as the twentieth century drew to a close and the twenty-first began that the unanticipated collapse of communism across Eastern Europe and the former Soviet Union (FSU) represented a development of staggering significance with consequences that would continue to reverberate well into the twenty-first century. But it is clear that the removal of the Soviet threat in the early 1990s had not paved the way in any straightforward fashion to a new and more benign world order.

Key issues on the global agenda, such as development and inequality or the environment were largely unaffected by the termination of the Soviet empire and, unsurprisingly, the problems surrounding these issues did not seem any easier to solve in the new post-Cold War era. Other issues that could have been more directly affected by the elimination of Soviet power, such as arms and arms control or peacekeeping and humanitarian intervention, also failed to give rise to any substantial new developments that would self-evidently create a safer and more ordered world. More disturbingly, long-standing issues such as nationalism and ethnic conflict as well as migration and refugees were seen to pose a greater threat to world order than they had during the Cold War, with the consequence that they were now located in a more prominent position on the international agenda.

In this edition, we can now look back at the twentieth century from the vantage point of a new century and, indeed, a new millennium. But even with the benefit of this additional hindsight, our starting point has not changed. We accept that future generations will probably continue to see the end of the Cold War as representing a turning point in history. Certainly this assessment has not been affected by the many significant events that hit the headlines and rocked international diplomacy in the final years of the twentieth century and the dawn of the twenty-first century, even before 11 September 2001 – from the war in Kosovo in Europe and the testing of the 'Hindu' and 'Muslim' nuclear weapons in South Asia, through to the 'collapse' of the Asian economies in 1998–99, the attempts by black war veterans to wrest land from the white farmers in Zimbabwe and the large-scale protests about the effects of economic globalization directed at meetings of the WTO in Seattle and the World Bank in Washington. Since 9/11 there has been a tendency in some analyses to argue that everything changed at that time, but it is equally possible to argue that the attacks on New York and Washington crystallized trends that had been under way for years if not decades. What is clear is that by the time this third edition of the book has been published there may well have been other earth-shattering events amplified by the global communications network; indeed, as the text was being finalized, the Asian tsunami of December 2004 provided just such an example.

Our focus is not on specific events, even those dramatic events like the ending of communism, the events of 9/11 or the Asian tsunami that might be claimed to have changed the course of history. We are concerned with broader and more enduring global issues and the changing position of these issues on the international agenda. In the first edition, we acknowledged that a wide range of issues had played an important role in the evolution of world politics during the latter part of the twentieth century and in the second edition we presupposed that most of these issues would continue to be of significance in the twenty-first century. We have made the same broad assumption in this third edition. What we have aimed to do in all three editions is to extract some of these issues from the complex web of world politics and to examine, among other things, whether or not they have been affected by the ending of the Cold War and the course of the post-Cold War era; what factors have influenced their salience in world politics; how these issues have been managed at the level of world politics; and what an analysis of the issues tells us about the nature of world politics.

The selection of issues

The issues that were investigated in the first and second editions were chosen, of course, because we regarded them as important and representative features of world politics at the end of the twentieth century. In aggregate, we thought that they provided an interesting cross-section of what was happening in the international system at that time. But we readily acknowledged that the issues covered in the first edition did not add up to a comprehensive picture of world politics, and thus we expanded the range for the second edition. So, for example, although we focused on the development and global impact of Islamic fundamentalism, we also noted that Muslims only represent 20 per cent of the world's population. The study of Islamic fundamentalism, therefore, does not begin to exhaust the impact of religion on world politics. We stressed that it is important not to overlook the impact of other religions on world politics and to keep in mind that the overall importance of religion has all too often been underestimated in the study of world politics. In the second edition it seemed helpful to have a more comprehensive assessment of religion as an issue in world politics.

Crime and corruption was also acknowledged in the first edition as an international issue that had been excluded from discussion. Yet it cannot be denied that crime in particular represents an international issue of crucial importance in the contemporary world. There is, for example, widespread concern about the global trafficking in drugs. Yet the drug trade is just one aspect of the very much broader issue of international crime and the range of issues considered in the second edition was extended in order to take it on board.

International crime has been facilitated in part, of course, by the incredible developments in international communications at the end of the twentieth century. But then there is virtually no aspect of world politics that has not been dramatically affected by this revolution in communications. The impact of the internet alongside 'real-time' reporting of events around the world is seen to have transformed the texture of international politics. This development was signalled as an issue of central importance in the first edition and it provided the focus of a third new chapter in the second edition.

The single additional chapter in the third edition is that on terrorism; an addition that in light of 9/11 and related events might seem to need no further justification. But it must be remembered that international terrorism has occupied an important position on the international agenda ever since the 1970s (and, as Tim Dunne points out in Chapter 14, arguably since the early twentieth century). Most attention has been focused on the use of terror by non-state actors that are endeavouring to put pressure on an established government by attacking civilians across international borders; thus for many in the 1970s, international terrorism was epitomized by the incident at the Olympic Games in Munich in 1972 when a faction of the Palestinians infiltrated the Olympic Village, took Israeli athletes hostage and eventually killed them before being killed themselves. There was, of course, a very good reason for choosing to attack the Olympic Village. Terrorists not only aim to intimidate civilians but to do so in circumstances that will give their cause international publicity. There were echoes of this earlier incident when a bomb was planted in a public arena at the 1996 Olympics in Atlanta. The emergence of a worldwide media has undoubtedly made international terrorism an increasingly attractive option for terrorist groups, and thus the phenomenon intersects with a number of the other issues covered in this volume. It has also been touched upon in the context of religion. Islamic and Christian fundamentalists have felt perfectly entitled to use violence to promote their goals. In plural democratic societies, of course, the use of violence is abhorred. But there have always been religious and indeed political fundamentalists who have been willing to resort to terrorism and violence in order to promote their beliefs.

Of course, the range of issues covered in the book could not be extended indefinitely and there remain many issues that, while central to the study of world politics, are still not directly covered. Perhaps most significantly, the issue of gender has been overlooked, although there are references to gender in Chapters 5 and 10 and there is no doubt that the issue of gender is absolutely central to understanding issues such as migration and development. International sport is another interesting feature of contemporary world politics that is not dealt with in this book, although the antecedents can be traced back to ancient Greece where the first Olympic Games were held. As with crime, for example, this is an issue that has tended to be ignored in traditional discussions of IR. We hope that the approach adopted in the book will enable the reader to pursue and evaluate the significance of such issues and generate a range of questions to guide further study.

Links between issues

As the connection between religion and terrorism illustrates, issues in world politics are, in fact, inextricably linked to each other and attention is frequently drawn to this characteristic feature of world politics in earlier chapters. An important link is observed, for example, between migration and development. Although, tragically, there are still people being sold into slavery, the vast majority of migrants in the contemporary world are motivated to move for economic gain. They leave their own country voluntarily and settle in another in order to improve their standard of living. But as we have seen, migration not only assists the individual migrant and the receiving country; there are also many economic side-payments associated with migration that accrue to the benefit of the sending country. There is, therefore, an important link between migration and economic development.

A more complex link can also be established between economic development and ethnicity. There are, of course, many factors that account for the growth of ethnic tensions in contemporary world politics, but the problems associated with economic development are certainly an important element. In the case of the genocidal conflict that escalated between the Hutus and the Tutsis in Rwanda during 1994, for example, one source of the conflict related to the lack of economic development and the Hutu resentment of the economic advantages putatively enjoyed by the Tutsis.

A direct consequence of this conflict was the migration of thousands of Hutus into refugee camps in neighbouring Zaire because, in the aftermath of the conflict, they feared Tutsi reprisals. In similar fashion, the conflict in Sudan during the early years of the new millennium led to forced movements of people from the province of Darfur into neighbouring territories. There have been, in fact, many cases of enforced migration taking place because of national and ethnic conflict. At the time of the partition between India and Pakistan, in 1947, for example, between 12 and 14 million people moved across the frontier because they believed that it was unsafe to remain in their homes, with Hindus moving out of Pakistan into India and Muslims moving out of India into Pakistan.

It would not be difficult to multiply these examples of issues that become inter-related at the level of world politics. All of the issues discussed in the previous chapters can be shown to be interlinked together in one way or another to form a complex matrix of inter-related issues. But this does not diminish the utility of treating them separately in the first instance for analytical purposes. The task of the analyst is to identify the central features of any issue and then to explore how these features are affected by links with other related issues.

Practitioners proceed in a similar fashion. Analysts who fail to reveal how issues are inter-related inevitably produce a distorted picture of world politics. By the same token, if practitioners fail to take account of these inter-relationships, then they can often end up by implementing policies that are, even from their own perspective, counter-productive or self-defeating. States in the Middle East, for example, have been required by the World Bank to introduce structural adjustment strategies that have had the effect of eliminating state-sponsored welfare programmes. This development, however, has created a 'political space' that has been filled by organizations sponsored by political Islamist groups. Contrary to the intentions of the World Bank, therefore, as the result of the SAPs, the political support for the Islamist groups has increased whereas support for the governments has often diminished.

Governments, however, are frequently well aware of the interlinkage between issues and they have developed a variety of strategies to cope with them. In the United States, for example, it has been noted that there is a substantial gap between the rhetoric and practice surrounding immigration. The stated policy associated with immigration suggests that immigrants are subject to very severe restrictions – and this has been re-emphasized after the attacks of 9/11 in the context of 'homeland security'. In practice, however, the policy has long been to maintain a half-open door, and even some of the post-9/11 restrictions have not been sustained. In this way, the government can use the stated policy to contend with the hostility to migration (on security or economic grounds) frequently expressed by the indigenous population, while using the actual policy to regulate the flow of immigrants dictated by the needs of the economy.

Issues and contemporary world politics

Although it was never intended in this book to offer a comprehensive assessment of the issues that emerge in world politics, it is hoped that the issues examined here provide a representative picture of contemporary world politics. Having acknowledged that there are important issues that have not been investigated, and accepted that although issues can be isolated for analytical purposes, in practice they are all interlinked, we will now go on to examine the picture of world politics that emerges from a survey of the issues that have been presented in this text.

It is appropriate to start with the state and statehood. Throughout the first half of the twentieth century it was widely taken for granted that the state was, and would remain for the foreseeable future, the primary unit of organization in world politics. For many theorists and practitioners it was considered axiomatic that world politics was about the relations between states. The growth of nationalism in the nineteenth century, however, had also encouraged the belief that states should coincide with nations. This belief had a substantial impact on events throughout most of the twentieth century. Attempts were made after the First World War, for example, to carve up the Ottoman and Austro-Hungarian multinational empires into their constituent national units. Then in the era after the Second World War, the European colonial empires, established over the previous 400 years, were also dissolved to form a host of new states. By the end of the Cold War, colonization was a thing of the past and the entire globe was ostensibly divided into independent states and it did not now seem out of place to identify these basic building-blocks of world politics as nation-states. This was the term habitually used in textbooks on world politics.

But the label was and had always been a fiction, as subsequent events were to demonstrate. During the final decade of the twentieth century, at one end of the spectrum, the last but one of the Eurasian multinational empires collapsed, demonstrating the failure of the Soviet Union to weld the people on its territory into a nation or even a cohesive multinational unit. The start of what has been identified as the 'short twentieth century', therefore, was marked by the final collapse of two major multinational empires: the Ottoman and Austro-Hungarian empires, and it closed with the collapse of a third: the Soviet Union. There has been much discussion subsequently about whether China, the last remaining Eurasian multinational empire, can survive in a post-imperial era.

At the other end of the spectrum, Czechoslovakia, ostensibly established as a nation-state after the First World War, divided into two new states, Czechland (the Czech Republic) and Slovakia, because of long-running ethnic tensions. Developments of this kind have raised the spectre of world politics in the future taking place in an arena made up of many hundreds of states. But, as Chapter 2 makes clear, this is not the only possible outcome. Large tracts of Africa have been rendered ungovernable because of persistent violence between groups fighting for self-determination. A similar phenomenon occurred for a time following the collapse of Yugoslavia, while in central Asia there were challenges to a number of states emerging from the collapse of the Soviet empire and in Southwest Asia Afghanistan provided a stark example of what might happen to 'failed states'. During the last decade of the twentieth century, therefore, some credence was given to the assertion that the whole notion of statehood was coming under threat as a growing sector of the globe was falling prey to anarchy. But no one is suggesting that there is any virtue to living under conditions of civil war and so this development, far from undermining the relevance of statehood, has served to reinforce the importance of this dimension of world politics.

Attention, however, is also drawn in Chapter 2 to the argument that statehood started to be drained of much of its significance during the second half of the twentieth century. As the end of the century approached there were increasing references to the idea of the 'hollow' state emerging as the result of processes either by design or by default reducing the power and role of the state. In part, this development was the consequence of the triumph of liberalism and the widespread belief that the state had become bloated during the Cold War era and needed to be 'down-sized'. Privatization, deregulation and SAPs are obvious examples of processes set in motion across the globe in the 1980s and 1990s that were intended to transfer power from the state to the market. But paradoxically, some of the most vociferous advocates of these processes were simultaneously demanding, certainly in Britain, that the sovereignty of the state – statehood – must be protected and they were vehemently opposed, as a consequence, to the establishment of a common European currency, among other things. The role of the state, therefore, remains of crucial significance. Throughout the subsequent chapters, there are persistent references to the issue of statehood and the changing status of the state in contemporary world politics.

Nowhere is this more true than in the discussion of the world economy in Chapter 3. Ever since the 1970s, increasing attention has been paid to economic issues in the study of world politics. This represented a substantial shift in the discipline. In the years after the Second World War, there was a tendency to assume that economic issues fell within the arena of 'low politics' (see Chapter 1). Attention was concentrated in the study of IR on the military and political implications of the confrontation between the United States and the Soviet Union. By the 1970s, however, there was a growing realization that the world economy had become much more politicized than had previously been acknowledged. In the early days of the Cold War, an economic division between East and West had mirrored the ideological split. During this period, the United States had been able to use its overwhelming economic strength to isolate the Soviet bloc and to ensure that the rest of the world was locked into the capitalist world economy. By the 1970s, however, the United States no longer had the economic muscle to regulate this global economy. As a consequence, during this period there was increasing reference to the fact that states were operating under conditions of economic interdependence.

The implications of economic interdependence had been left largely unexamined during the first 20 years of the Cold War because it was an era of extraordinary economic recovery. But by the 1970s, and as a consequence of this recovery, it was impossible to ignore either the economic potential of Japan and the members of the EEC or the fact that these countries had their own views on the nature of the mechanisms and rules that should regulate the world economy. From this point on, the world economy became more overtly political, although the United States continued to dominate economic discussions, not only because it still possessed the largest economy, but also because it was impossible to ignore the impact of issue linkage brought about by the continued reliance of every state in the West on the security guarantee provided by the United States.

During the 1970s and 1980s, the assumption still prevailed that it made sense to talk about the state as an economic unit. Since the start of the 1990s, however, particularly after the demise of the Soviet Union, this assumption has been seriously questioned. The idea of economic interdependence has given way in large part to the concept of globalization. In conjunction with the assumption that the state is being 'hollowed out' from the inside has emerged the idea that it is also losing the ability to hold the external economic environment at bay. The 'outer shell' of the state is seen to be ever more porous. This development can be observed in the areas of investment, trade and finance. From the 1970s onwards attention has been drawn to the ability of MNCs to engage in FDI, whereby these firms set up production operations outside of their home economies. But even in the 1970s, this development simply meant that companies that were clearly associated with the United States were extending their production abroad. Now this has become a global phenomenon and MNCs have become transnational organizations which not only operate in more than one country, but engage in a high volume of intra-firm trade which now constitutes more than three-quarters of all trade. A final illustration of the porous nature of the state's 'outer shell' is growth in foreign exchange dealing. The volume is now so great that it is beyond the capacity of any state to defend its own currency if it comes under attack on the foreign exchange market, and many national governments have effectively given up the attempt to do this. All of these developments support the conclusion that states are not even 'empty shells' any longer. From the perspective of the world economy, there is apparently no longer a role for states to play.

Although the argument has sometimes been pushed this far, there are good reasons for pulling back. It is an illusion to imagine that economic markets operate in a political vacuum. Foreign trade, investment and exchange markets may appear to be completely unfettered, but in fact they operate within a complex framework of rules, established and supported by states. The same is true for trade and investment. It is simply not the case that states have handed, or even could hand over, all their power to markets. Nor is it true to suggest that states are now 'hollowed out' and very porous 'shells'. Some states may have privatized major industries, but they continue to support these industries in the global market. The state, it could be argued, has simply changed the traditional instruments which they have used to regulate the economy. In place of an increasingly permeable 'shell', they have established a porous but very much stronger 'steel mesh' to protect their domestic economies.

An important illustration of the new ways of coping with interdependence in economic and other areas of state activity is provided in Chapter 4. Regions defined as geographical areas in which states have a 'common historical experience and sense of shared problems' provide an opportunity through what is called 'regionalism' for states to cooperate together to solve common problems. At one extreme, European countries through the EU have a highly developed sense of regionalism and have constructed over the last 50 years a close integrating network of relationships that extends across an ever-widening range of issue areas. At the other end of the spectrum is a large number of regional agreements in many areas of the world that focus on a much smaller range of states and a limited number of issue areas.

While there are considerable variations, one of the most important developments in regionalism in the 1990s, with implications for the role of states and the structure of world politics, was the growth of economic integration in a number of regions creating powerful new blocs. Apart from the EU, other important examples include NAFTA and APEC. Para-doxically, such developments can be interpreted as both strengthening and weakening states. On the one hand, governments regard these organizations as a way of improving their chances of securing national policy objectives, particularly in the areas of wealth and welfare. Such blocs can also provide a means of extending and consolidating influence and a useful defence against the vagaries of global economic and financial systems. But, from a different perspective, regionalism can also be seen as providing a challenge at best and a threat at worst to states and statehood to the extent that key functions hitherto performed by states are being transferred to regional organizations. This apparent loss of independence or 'sovereignty' is itself a highly controversial issue which can most clearly be seen in contemporary political debates in Western Europe.

The universal ability of the Western economies to industrialize during the nineteenth century and the speed with which the European economies recovered after the Second World War encouraged economists to believe that it would be possible for the European colonies to achieve similar success once they had been given their independence. By the 1970s, however, it was clear that these hopes had been overoptimistic. And by the 1990s, the assessment had become even more pessimistic as it was acknowledged that poverty and hunger were as much features of the inner cities in the so-called 'developed world' as they were in the so-called 'developing world'. The traditional assumption of modernization theorists that development was a linear process and that once an economy had taken off, standards of living would steadily improve across the board is now seriously questioned. By the same token, the idea that the Third World would be given a helping hand by the developed world has proved to be sadly mistaken. Even the hope that wealth over time would 'trickle down' to the poor has proved false. On the contrary, as the figures given in Chapter 5 illustrate, income inequality increased during the second half of the twentieth century.

It would be simplistic to suggest, however, that the problems confronted by the Third World are simply the consequence of exploitation by the rich states. The economies of many of these developing countries have been generating higher rates of growth than those found in the developed world. But the anticipated benefits to be accrued from economic growth have failed to materialize because the population has been increasing at an even faster rate in these developing countries. It is also the case that wealth in some of these countries has been concentrated in the hands of too few people. There is a growing recognition, moreover, that it may not be helpful to think purely in terms of a North–South divide. Taking a broader perspective, it becomes possible to see that the problems confronted in the Third World have some obvious counterparts in the developed world. It has been noted, for example, that every First World city contains a Third World *city* in which unemployment, overcrowding, hunger and disease are the norm. But by the same token, every Third World city contains a First World city characterized by international fashion, high technology, global communication and transnational corporations. This has led analysts to talk in terms of the 'global North' and the 'global South' to capture some of these complexities.

But, of course, there is also some truth to the idea of a North–South split. In particular, many of the poor in Third World countries live in rural conditions. Developmental economists have taken too little account of this fact. There is, therefore, growing attention being paid to the work of Muhammad Yunus. Trained in the United States, he soon found the economics he was teaching when he returned to South Asia in 1972 to be utterly irrelevant to the circumstances of his own country. There were terrible man-made famines in 1974 in the newly formed state of Bangladesh and according to some estimates, as many as 1.5 million people died. The attempts by Western economists and institutions to alleviate the poverty in countries like Bangladesh were not working. Muhammad Yunus attempted to identify more effective remedies. In place of large-scale aid programmes, he concluded that attention should be focused on the people who were endeavouring to escape the poverty trap. What they almost invariably lacked was the necessary capital, often very small amounts, to create their own small businesses. He set up the Grameen Bank ('rural bank' in Bengali) staffed, initially, by his own graduate students and with the objective of providing micro-loans to the destitute. The clients were mainly women and it was found that women were more careful about managing debt and ensuring that the entire family benefited from the loan. It is too early to be sure about the long-term consequences of this experiment. But Yunus has been consulted by the World Bank and his ideas have been seen to provide a model for relieving poverty in inner-city areas in the United States. What this experiment illustrates is that some development issues may be dealt with most effectively at the local level, and this is a lesson that needs to be taken on board by those operating in the sphere of world politics.

If some issues can be dealt with effectively at local or regional levels, there are other issues that do need to be dealt with primarily at the level of world politics. The discussion of the spread and control of weapons in Chapter 6 provides a good illustration. During the Cold War most attention in the West was focused on WMD and nuclear weapons, in particular, although the dangers of CBW were also widely recognized. Very little progress was made to eradicate these weapons during the Cold War. Indeed, the doctrine of deterrence did much to legitimate the decision to maintain these weapons. Throughout the Cold War the emphasis was on arms control rather than disarmament. The intention was not to eliminate these WMD but to make possession of them safer.

After the Cold War was over, it was argued by opponents of these weapons that a window of opportunity had opened up through which it might be possible to push some substantial disarmament measures. Ironically, however, with the Cold War over and the communist threat eliminated, it proved impossible for proponents of disarmament to engender any sense of urgency about the need to eliminate weapons of mass destruction. Hopes for a new world order where weapons of mass destruction would be eliminated quickly faded. Even more depressing for advocates of disarmament have been developments in the area of conventional weapons. It is made very clear in Chapter 6 that, whereas the sale of conventional weapons was justified during the Cold War era in terms of security considerations, arms sales are now justified on economic grounds and these sales remain a crucial element of world trade. Hopes that conflict on the periphery of the international system would diminish in the absence of the fuel provided by the ideological competition between the United States and the Soviet Union quickly faded. The pattern of conflict established during the Cold War, with an uneasy peace maintained at the centre of the system and persistent outbreaks of violence on the periphery remains unchanged, states are as unwilling as ever to curb the arms industries that enable these conflicts to continue unabated.

Growing despair at the inability to transform the nature of world politics has also been very evident among advocates of peacekeeping measures. It was believed that in the wake of the Cold War it would be easier for the international community to take concerted action to stem violence within and between states. The vigorous response orchestrated by the United States after the invasion of Kuwait by Iraq in 1990 seemed to suggest that it really was possible for the international community under the auspices of the UN to stand up to international aggression. As Chapter 7 makes clear, the number of peacekeeping missions established by the United Nations mushroomed in the early 1990s. It began to seem possible that the UN could in fact start to police the international system. Such optimism, however, proved to be misplaced and failed to take account of the very real constraints under which the UN operates. At the end of the day, the UN is not a supranational organization with an autonomous executive and independent sources of finance. It is an international organization made up of states that fund the organization and need to reach a consensus before any major police actions can be undertaken. The response in 1990–1 to Saddam Hussein in Kuwait was possible only because the United States was prepared to take military action and, as a consequence, provide the very considerable diplomatic and economic support needed to establish a coalition of states that would legitimize the action. The contrast between the 1991 Gulf War and the US-led attack on Iraq in 2003 seemed to many to sum up the increasingly difficult position occupied by the UN, which could apparently be bypassed by powerful states in pursuit of their interests, and it led to an agonized debate about the future of the UN in the area of international peace and security.

There is, in fact, no great incentive for wealthy states to expend resources on peacekeeping action unless their own interests are directly or indirectly involved. At a time when even the most wealthy states are finding it difficult to fund basic welfare programmes and are looking for ways to divest themselves of the responsibility, there is a very great reluctance to divert scarce resources to fund ventures in places which their electorate could not even locate on the map. At the same time, for the United States as the most powerful state in the world arena, the UN has often appeared to be a needless obstacle to the realization of its plans for a new world order. Nevertheless, the UN can still appeal to broader interests and ideals. As is apparent from Chapter 8 (and Chapter 12), there are occasions when images projected by the world's media of the misery caused by conflict has periodically galvanized public opinion. During the Cold War there was a widespread assumption that conflict anywhere around the world related to the ideological conflict between the Superpowers. In the early days of the Cold War, there was widespread support in the West for the strategy of providing military support for the opponents of communism. The rationale for this support, however, was based on a distorted picture of world politics. It encouraged the image of leaders on the periphery as puppets on strings that were pulled from Moscow. The disastrous intervention by the United States in Vietnam complicated the task of responding to conflict on the global periphery. But there was always an assumption during the Cold War that the explanation of any conflict could be traced back to the ideological bipolar confrontation. Now that easy equation has been eliminated, but it was replaced initially in the 1990s by two alternative and equally facile explanations.

In the first of these, conflicts were seen to be the result of ethnic tensions which arose from primordial roots. The conflict between Serbs, Croats and Bosnians in the former Yugoslavia or between the Tutsis and Hutus in Rwanda, for example, were accounted for in terms of hostility that traces back to the beginning of time. There is nothing that can be done about such atavistic conflict, it was suggested, and so we are absolved of any responsibility to take any action. The reference to ethnicity, however, does not so much explain conflict, as explain it away. And it conveniently justifies the reluctance to make judgements about the conflict, or to become involved. A closer investigation of the conflicts in former Yugoslavia and Rwanda, however, fails to support the idea that the sources of the conflict were primordial. The conflict between the Hutus and the Tutsis can be traced back to policies pursued by the West during the colonial era and the conflict in Yugoslavia was fostered, albeit inadvertently, by policies implemented during the communist era. A better understanding of these conflicts does not necessarily make them any easier to solve. But, as Chapter 8 makes clear, it should encourage the international community to promote a greater tolerance of pluralism when demands for self-determination are raised.

The second salient approach to treatment of post-Cold War conflicts has been closely associated with the dominance of the United States – and within the United States, of groups often termed 'neo-conservative'. These groups, particularly influential in the administrations of George W. Bush from 2000 onwards, based their analysis of international conflict squarely on the absence of democracy in many key areas of the global arena, and argued that the primary purpose of US power was to confront and overthrow tyranny wherever it occurred. The establishment of democracy through the use of US power would lead almost inevitably to a more peaceful world, since it was argued that democracies rarely fought among themselves. Such analysis and prescription was turned into action in the aftermath of 9/11, especially in Afghanistan and then on a grander scale in Iraq. At the time of writing this chapter, it is clear that democracy in Iraq is a fragile flower at best, and that US power will continue to be engaged there for the foreseeable future. Some would draw from this the conclusion – as in the case of ethnic conflicts – that effective policy must be prepared to accept a more plural world than that envisaged by the 'neo-cons' and their allies.

Securing a plural world, however, will not be easy. As the discussion of religion in Chapter 9 makes clear, there are potentially very wide cultural divisions opening up in the contemporary international system. Far from a common global culture emerging, the globe is becoming 'unsecularized'. Islamists, for example, have a vision of social order which is very much at odds with the vision projected in the West, and which has been strengthened if anything by the ways in which it has been confronted by the United States and others. When the Islamists took control in Iran in 1979, for example, although they made some concessions to the indigenous Jews, Catholics and Zoroastrians, these were not extended to other indigenous minority groups that have been systematically persecuted ever since. Similarly in Afghanistan, the Taliban militia which started as a movement of Islamic seminary students, and eventually took control of the entire country, capturing the capital Kabul in September 1996, imposed a very strict Islamic order. As in Iran, it was women who were most affected. Schools for girls were closed, women were banned from most jobs and females were not allowed to go shopping without being accompanied by a male. The identification of this regime with a faithful interpretation of the Koran, however, also served an important strategic goal, because it justified the Taliban claim to transcend the ethnic divisions within the country. In practice, however, the Taliban had recruited very heavily from among the Pathan clans in the South and central regions of the country. The Taliban regime, therefore, not only opened up the potential for future ethnic confrontation, but also generated unease among the minority Shia community because of the strict interpretation of the Koran. This fragmentation became painfully apparent when the United States and its allies invaded Afghanistan in the aftermath of 9/11, since it meant that at least initially there was no basis on which to build democratic institutions and practices. In like fashion, the US-led invasion of Iraq could overthrow an existing and oppressive regime, but could not avoid the consequences of releasing the ethnic and other divisions within the country.

Moreover, the issue is more complex than the advocates of pluralism allow. Globalization is seen to be a product of Western capitalism which, far from tolerating cultural diversity, is having the effect of eroding cultural differences. But much worse, it is seen to be locking many sectors of the Third World into a subordinate economic position. Islamic societies, seeing the effect of globalization, have perhaps inevitably started to retreat and shelter behind the walls of a very strict interpretation of Islam. But this assessment of globalization can be questioned. It is an oversimplification to suggest that globalization can be equated with Westernization. As the 'economic tigers' of East Asia have demonstrated, it is possible for non-Western cultures to flourish in the global economy. As Chapter 9 concludes, the image advanced by Huntington of 'the West versus the rest' fails to take account of the growing cultural diversity that is occurring within all his putative 'civilizations'. It is much more likely, as a consequence, that globalization will be associated with multiculturalism than Westernization.

Some support for this assessment can be found in the discussion of refugees and migration in Chapter 10. The evidence reveals very clearly that neither migrants nor refugees disperse in a random fashion. Very clear patterns emerge. Individuals move to where contacts have already been established. As a consequence, although the link may initially have been economic, with migrants moving to improve their standard of living, they may be followed, later, by refugees seeking political asylum. Strong links are maintained, therefore, between individuals in the receiving and sending states. Migrants not only bring their labour but also their culture. Of course, this is not a new phenomenon. It is a characteristic feature of world history. But it is one which does not square easily with the recent concept of the nation-state. The concept is, of course, a myth. But it is a powerful myth which many wish to defend.

The fear of imported culture has led defenders of the nation-state in the United States to worry about the 'decay of our civilization' rather than to celebrate the diversification of culture. But the evidence suggests that such fears are wildly exaggerated. Although it is true that there are 329 languages spoken in the United States, out of a population of 230 million Americans, 198 million speak English. Only the 17 million Spanish speakers pose any threat to the dominance of English. Moreover, studies show that 90 per cent of the children of migrants speak English. But culture involves a great deal more than language and certainly in cities there is increasing evidence of cultural diversification. More than a third of London's population, for example, now comes from non-British stock. This is an important dimension of globalization. There is a tendency to focus on the homogenization of culture as the result of the ubiquitous signs for McDonald's and Coca-Cola. But this underestimates the significance of multiculturalism fostered, at least in part, by migration.

The diversification and the homogenization of culture appear, in practice, to be two processes going on simultaneously in world politics. It is impossible to predict what the outcome of these competing forces will be in the twenty-first century. What will become increasingly apparent, however, is that human beings, whatever their cultural differences, are operating within a common global environment which is much more fragile than previous generations realized. The image of the earth swimming in space is now almost a cliché, but it remains an important dimension of globalization. Whatever the differences that separate human beings, it has become impossible to ignore the fact that the accumulation of apparently insignificant individual acts across the globe, like spraying a deodorant, can collectively have devastating effects. As the Cold War drew to a close in the 1980s, for example, scientific evidence began to mount that the ozone layer in the earth's stratosphere, and protecting the globe from the sun's ultraviolet light, was being slowly but surely destroyed. Despite attempts to alleviate the causes, by 1995, the evidence indicated that the hole over the Antarctic, already three times the size of continental North America, was larger than ever and expanding faster than ever. Even if full cooperation is secured across the globe, the ozone hole is not expected to close before the middle of the twenty-first century.

As noted in Chapter 11, the environment was an issue that scarcely registered on the international agenda at the onset of the Cold War, but it is now a major source of concern. Nevertheless, states have proved reluctant to take decisive action. The reluctance stems in part from the fact that the scientific evidence about the nature and scale of many environmental problems remains controversial. But it is also a product of the conflicts of interest that continue to divide states despite the existence of common environmental problems. For example, Third World states are of the opinion that since there are substantial costs associated with the measures that will have to be put in place in order to protect the environment, these costs should primarily be borne by the developed states. Most states in the developed world remain unwilling to accept this line of argument and endeavour to justify policies that permit them to escape any significant responsibility for Third World states. Most significantly, the United States has not committed itself to the most significant efforts at international action, for example through the Kyoto Protocol designed to regulate carbon emissions.

But, as discussed in Chapter 12, there is a powerful school of thought that maintains that it is going to become increasingly difficult for governments to turn a blind eye to unpleasant events that happen beyond their own borders. We are now moving into an era when we can observe what is happening in any part of the world in 'real time' by means of the global media. The 'CNN effect' is seen to have helped to promote the rash of humanitarian interventions that took place at the end of the twentieth century. Images of human suffering beamed into our homes are seen to have precipitated some significant international political responses – nowhere more spectacularly than with the impact of the Asian tsunami in December 2004 and January 2005. But perhaps even more important, in the long run, ordinary citizens using the internet can now begin to communicate instantaneously with large and complex networks of people operating across the globe. Individuals, therefore, can start to mobilize political responses on an international rather than a local or national basis. This growth in electronic communications represents another crucial dimension of globalization and some analysts insist that it is starting to transform the nature of the international system because it is helping to precipitate the emergence of an international civil society. From this perspective, as individuals across the world establish links from one corner of the globe to another, the image of the 'global village' is starting to become a reality.

Not everyone, however, accepts this benign view of the communications revolution. In the first place, it is argued in Chapter 12 that it underestimates how the impact of the communications revolution is skewed in favour of some groups and against the interests of others. In the excitement about all that has been accomplished in the world of electronic communications, it is often overlooked that most people do not even possess a telephone and that, staggering for a Western audience, half of the world's population has never even used a phone. But even if we focus on that part of the world where the communications revolution has penetrated to the greatest depth, it is still possible to argue that its impact has been exaggerated. As the Somalian case study in Chapter 12 (Box 12.2) illustrates, despite the conventional view that the Clinton Administration was forced by public opinion to withdraw from Somalia, some analysts believe that the administration had decided to withdraw before the image of a dead American soldier was shown on the world's media.

Even more to the point, it is, perhaps, naive to imagine that the communications revolution is working only in favour of the formation of a global civil society. There is a darker side to the communications revolution that is brought out very clearly in Chapter 13 where it is shown how global communications have undoubtedly helped to promote the growth of transnational organized crime. Nowhere is this more apparent than in the case of the drug trade.

Trafficking in drugs is not, of course, a new phenomenon. And indeed it has not always been illegal. Ever since the end of the nineteenth century, however, there has been increasing concern about the use of drugs. Cocaine was first produced from the coca leaf in the 1860s, and then in 1898 heroin was manufactured from morphine, itself a derivative of opium. Both drugs proved to be highly addictive. During the course of the twentieth century, the production and distribution of illicit drugs processed from natural plant products in conjunction with synthetically produced drugs, such as amphetamines, has escalated in an astonishing fashion. Figures produced by the UN suggest that the annual turnover now exceeds $500 billion. This illegal traffic is estimated to represent one-tenth of total international trade and both production and distribution are worldwide. The sale of drugs is now larger than the sale of either oil or food. The supply, of course, is primarily from the Third World, but the high return on the sale of drugs is a consequence of the demand from Europe and the United States which still represents the economic centre of the developed world. There are many ironies associated with the drug trade. For example, Afghanistan, despite the influence of Islamic fundamentalists, was the largest exporter of opium and heroin in the final years of the Taliban regime, and after the US-led invasion during 2001–2, the trade rapidly resumed despite the efforts of the occupying forces.

No country is completely free of the international consequences of the drug trade. But drug trafficking is only one dimension of the issue of transnational organized crime discussed in Chapter 13. At the heart of this chapter is the recognition of just how serious is the threat posed by international crime to the system of states. It is also noted that states in the contemporary international system are divided between those that have adopted a confrontational approach to international crime and those that either tacitly or overtly underwrite transnational criminal organizations. It is unlikely that this situation will persist during the twenty-first century because deviant states will be strongly encouraged by other members of the international society of states to break their links with organized crime.

Defeating transnational organized crime, on the other hand, will prove to be much more difficult; indeed, it is probably an impossible task.

The points made above about the impact of organized crime on world politics can in many respects be repeated and reinforced by reference to the arguments about terrorism put forward in Chapter 14. As the chapter makes clear, concern with terrorism as a challenge to statehood – both in general and in specific instances where states have been subverted or overthrown – is not a product just of the past decade, and the fluctuating attention paid to terrorism over the past century and a half has been reflected also in the ways in which it has affected international political analysis. During the Cold War, it could be argued that terrorism should be relegated to a rather peripheral role, compared with the central conflicts and confrontations among the Superpowers. Even where terrorism did occur, as in the Middle East, it was often very closely related to the East–West tensions between the United States and the Soviet Union, and analyzed in terms of its effect on the overall Cold War balance.

The end of the Cold War, as in so many of the other issue areas studied in this book, had effects in the case of terrorism rather like those of taking the lid off a pressure-cooker. With the challenges to existing states and the collapse of some (including most obviously the Soviet Union), the proliferation of weak and 'failed' state structures seemed to produce new opportunities for the use of violence by non-state actors, sometimes inspired by ethnic loyalties, sometimes by religious affiliation, sometimes by criminal intent or the search for economic gain. Not only this, but the multiplication of so-called 'asymmetric' conflicts, where the power in conventional terms was heavily on one side but the power in unconventional terms was by no means so unbalanced, gave new chances for the de-stabilization and the erosion of state power. This can be seen as a challenge to the state system as a whole, and was defined by a number of national leaders as such: the use of terror thus became subject to a variety of sanctions and punishments, but was very difficult to counter by traditional uses of state power.

This is what accounts for the phenomenon assessed in more detail in Chapter 14: the uncertainties for both analysis and policy created by the 'new terrorism' of the post-Cold War era. As Chapter 14 shows, the linkages between the 'new terrorism' and state power, or technological change, or economic globalization, are close but highly fluid and unpredictable. The 'de-territorialized' qualities of terrorist networks such as Al Qaeda can be overstated, but there is no doubt that they intersect with a number of other trends and tendencies to produce new perceptions of insecurity and uncontrollability. Because of this, those attempting to confront terrorism in the 'war on terror' themselves had to devise new methods and approaches, and in turn, some of these could be seen as challenges to either the independence of states or the rights of individuals on a global basis. The dramatic impact of terrorist incidents such as those of 9/11 or the later Bali and Madrid bombings also throws into strong relief the ways in which communications media and other resources can be used by those responsible to promote their message – a lesson brought home with additional force by the televising of video recordings of hostages and their execution in Iraq after the war of 2003. Terrorism thus – in common with a number of the issues analyzed in this book – has a kind of catalytic effect both on the study and on the practice of world politics.

Conclusion

A survey of the chapters in this book fails to reveal a dominant picture or image of world politics. During the Cold War, there was a tendency to portray world politics in terms of two major fault-lines, one running East–West and the other running North–South. Even during that era, this characterization was problematic and it has become even more so in the post-Cold War era. There is, of course, still some mileage to be obtained by thinking of world politics in these terms. If there were no East–West division, then it becomes possible to think of Europe extending across Eurasia to the Pacific. In practice, the Europeans are unwilling to think in these terms, but there is no agreement about where the longitudinal line separating East from West lies. And the connotations of this line now embrace cultural factors as well as economic and security ones. No one doubts that the Czechs and the Poles are European. But some see it as problematic to identify the Turks or the Russians as European. Others wonder why it should matter. As with the East–West division, although there still remains some substance to a metaphorical latitudinal line dividing the developed from the developing states, attention is now frequently being drawn to the evidence of the 'South' in the 'North', and *vice versa*. So, all round, world politics appears more complex since the end of the Cold War.

The survey also suggests that while some kind of transformation is taking place, the changes are cumulative; they coincided with the ending of the Cold War rather than having been brought about by the end of the Cold War just as they were later crystallized by 9/11 rather than being caused by it. The Cold War has been thought of metaphorically in terms of an overlay, placed on the top of world politics, influencing state practice but also dominating the analyses of world politics throughout that era. Once removed, while there has been considerable readjustment in world politics, it has also become easier to see clearly what has been going on beneath the overlay. Ethnicity, for example, was a feature of world politics throughout the Cold War. But, with the ending of the Cold War, it became easier to observe this feature. By contrast, the greater salience of environmental issues in the 1990s was unrelated to the ending of the Cold War. In similar fashion, as noted above, the impact of 9/11 was in laying bare the growing influence of certain types of terrorist groups and their association with religious, ethnic or other factors, and in confronting policy-makers with problems they might have wanted to ignore.

The tentative conclusion that can be reached at the end of this survey is that at the onset of a new century, world politics has developed the potential to become truly globalized politics. The concept of 'globalization' has become seriously overworked over the last few years and its use often conveys *very* little of significance. It provides a rhetorical flourish to suggest that we are living in momentous times. In attempting to justify the flourish, the rather dramatic idea is sometimes advanced that the nation-state is now a 'hollow state' and that we are witnessing the demise of this mode of political organization. More frequently the term suggests no more than that there is a lot of activity going on in the international arena, with British firms, for example, setting up factories in China to produce plastic bags that are then shipped back to Britain to be sold to supermarkets to hold our weekly shopping.

What has emerged from the analysis offered in this book, however, is that we are entering an era where citizens and states are having to come to terms with the fact that we are living in a global system where states remain the only viable mode of political organization. To a very large extent, however, the foundations for this view of world politics were laid down during the Cold War. During that era, the implications of what it means to live in a global system were fully assimilated for the first time. No one who thought about world politics could doubt that if a nuclear war escalated, it would have catastrophic consequences for the entire globe. But as the Cold War persisted, states developed a range of mechanisms for managing this global problem. When the global implications of the environment became apparent, therefore, it is unsurprising that states quite quickly began to design measures to bring the problems under control. And when confronted with the dramatic events of 9/11, states and their political leaderships all over the world were quick to respond, often in unsure and contradictory ways but with no less affirmation of the continuing vitality of state power in a globalizing world. No doubt the measures to regulate nuclear weapons, conserve the environment or to confront terrorism have been inadequate, but it seems clear that the solutions to the problems associated with these and other issues are more likely to be provided by means of inter-state collaboration than by any other route.

Bibliography

Books and articles

Adams, N. (1993) *Worlds Apart: The North–South Divide and the International System*, London, Zed.

AfricaFocus (2004) 'Africa: Mobile Renaissance?', in *AfricaFocus Bulletin*, 6 May (040506) from www.africafocus.org.

African Rights (1994) *Rwanda: Death, Despair and Defiance*, London, African Rights.

Agence France-Presse International News (1995) 'Russia Probes Alleged Cyprus Chechenya Arms Link', 12 January.

Aggarwal, V. and Fogarty, E. (eds) (2004) *EU Trade Strategies: Between Regionalism and Globalism*, Basingstoke, Palgrave.

Akbar, M.J. (2002) *The Shade of Swords. Jihad and the Conflict between Islam & Christianity*, London and New York, Routledge.

Ali, T. (ed.) (2000) *Masters of the Universe? NATO's Balkan Crusade*, London, Verso.

Allan, S. and Zelizer, B (2004) *Reporting War: Journalism in Wartime*, London, Routledge.

Alleyne, M. (1997) *News Revolution: Political and Economic Decisions about Global Information*, London, Macmillan.

Amanat, A. (2001) 'Empowered through Violence: The Reinventing of Islamic Extremism', in S. Talbott and N. Chanda (eds), *The Age of Terror: America and the World After September 11*, London, Perseus Press, pp. 23–52.

Ambrosio, T. (2001) *Irredentism: Ethnic Conflict and International Politics*, Westport, Col., Praeger.

Anderson, K. and Blackhurst, R. (eds) (1993) *Regional Integration and the Global Trading System*, London, Harvester-Wheatsheaf.

Annan, K. (2005) 'A Global Strategy for Fighting Terrorism'. Keynote address to the International Summit on Democracy, Terrorism and Security, Madrid, Spain, 10 March, pp. 1–6 at http://www.un.org.

Appadurai, A. (1996) *Modernity at Large: Cultural Dimensions of Globalisation*, Minneapolis, University of Minnesota Press.

APSA Task Force (2004) 'American Democracy in an Age of Rising Inequality', public report of task force chaired by Theda Skocpol, June, http://www.apsanet. org/section_256.cfm/taskforcereport.pdf.

Badaracco, J. (1991) *The Knowledge Link*, Boston, Mass, Harvard Business School Press.

Balaam, D. N. and Veseth, M. (2000) *Introduction to International Political Economy*, 2nd edn, Upper Saddle River, NJ, Prentice Hall.

Barber, B. (1996) *Jihad vs. McWorld: How Globalism and Tribalism are Reshaping the World*, New York, Ballantine Books.

Barkin, J. S. and Cronin, B. (1994) 'The State and the Nation: Changing Norms and Rules of Sovereignty in International Relations', *International Organization*, 48(1), pp. 107–30.

Barnett, J. (2001) *The Meaning of Environmental Security: Ecological Politics in the New Security Era*, London, Zed Books.

Bartley, R. (1993) 'The Case For Optimism', *Foreign Affairs*, 72(4), pp. 15–18.

Baylis, J. and Smith, S. (eds) (1st edn 1997, 2nd edn 2000) *Globalization of World Politics*, Oxford, Oxford University Press.

Bellamy, A. J. and Williams, P. (eds) (2004) *Peace Operations and Global Order*, London, Cass.

Bellamy, A. J., Williams, P. and Griffin, S. (2004) *Understanding Peacekeeping*, Cambridge, Polity.

Berdal, M. R. (1993) *Whither UN Peacekeeping*, Adelphi Paper, 281, London, IISS.

Berdal, M. R. (1995) 'Reforming the UN's Organisational Capacity for Peacekeeping', in R. Thakur and C. A. Thayer (eds), *A Crisis of Expectations: UN Peacekeeping in the 1990s*, Adelphi Paper, Boulder, Col., Westview Press.

Berdal, M. (2003) 'Ten Years of *International Peacekeeping*', *International Peacekeeping*, 10(4), pp. 5–11.

Berridge, G. (1992) *International Politics. States, Power and Conflict since 1945*, 2nd edn, New York, Harvester Wheatsheaf.

Best, G. (1994) *War and Law Since 1945*, Oxford, Clarendon Press.

Beyer, P. (1994) *Religion and Globalization*, London, Sage.

BIS (Bank for International Settlements) (1999) Press Release, 10 May, Bank for International Settlements.

BIS (Bank for International Settlements) (2002) *Triennial Central Bank Survey: Foreign exchange and derivatives market activity in 2001*, Bank for International Settlements.

Black, R. M. and Pearson, G. S. (1993) 'Unequivocal Evidence', *Chemistry in Britain*, July, pp. 584–7.

Bono, G. and Ulriksen, S. (eds) (2004) 'The EU, Crisis Management and Peace Support Operations', special issue of *International Peacekeeping*, 11(3).

Booth, K. (1991) 'Introduction: The Interregnum: World Politics in Transition', in K. Booth (ed.), *New Thinking about Strategy and International Security*, London, HarperCollins, pp. 1–28.

Booth K, and Dunne, T. (eds) (2002) 'Worlds in Collision', in K. Booth and T. Dunne (eds), *Worlds in Collision: Terror and the Future of World Order*, Basingstoke, Palgrave, pp. 1–23.

Boutros-Ghali, B. (1992) *An Agenda for Peace*, New York, United Nations.

Boutros-Ghali, B. (1995) 'Report of the Secretary-General on the Work of the Organization. Supplement to an Agenda for Peace', UN Doc. A/50/60, 3 January.

Bowen, W. Q. and Dunn, D. H. (1996) *American Security Policy in the 1990s: Beyond Containment*, Aldershot, Darmouth.

Brahimi Report (2000) *Report of the Panel on United Nations Peace Operations*, New York, UN Document A/55/305 S/2000/809, 21 August.

Bremner, I. and Bailes, A. (1998) 'Sub-regionalism in the Newly Independent States', *International Affairs*, 74(1), pp. 131–48.

Brenton, T. (1994) *The Greening of Machiavelli: The Evolution of International Environmental Politics*, London, Earthscan/RIIA.

Breslin, S., Hughes, C., Phillips, N. and Rosamond, B. (eds) (2002) *New Regionalisms in the Global Political Economy: Theories and Cases*, London, Routledge.

Broad, R. and Landi, C. M. (1996) 'Whither the North–South Gap?', *Third World Quarterly*, 17(1), pp. 7–17.

Brown, C. (2002) 'Narratives of Religion, Civilization and Modernity', in K. Booth and T. Dunne (eds), *Worlds in Collision: Terror and the Future of World Order*, Basingstoke, Palgrave, pp. 293–302.

Brown, S. (1995) *New Forces, Old Forces and the Future of World Politics*, New York, HarperCollins.

Buckley, M. and Fawn, R. (2003) *Global Responses to Terrorism 9/11, Afghanistan and Beyond*, London, Routledge.

Bull, H. (1977) *The Anarchical Society: A Study of Order in World Politics*, London, Macmillan.

Burton, J. W. (1997) *Violence Explained*, Manchester, Manchester University Press.

Buzan, B. (1991) *People, States, and Fear: An Agenda for International Security Studies in the Post-Cold War Era*, 2nd edn, London, Harvester-Wheatsheaf.

Buzan, B. (1995) 'Focus On: The Present as a Historic Turning Point', *Journal of Peace Research*, 30(4), pp. 385–98.

Buzan, B. and Rizvi, G. (1986) *South Asian Insecurity and the Great Powers*, London, Macmillan.

CAAT (Campaign Against the Arms Trade) (1996) *Campaign Against the Arms Trade News*, 136, March, p. 6.

Cable, V. and Henderson, D. (eds) (1994) *Trade Blocks? The Future of Regional Integration*, London, RIIA.

Caldwell, L. K. (1990) *International Environmental Policy: Emergence and Dimensions*, 2nd edn, Durham, Md and London, Duke University Press.

Camilleri, J. A. and Falk, J. (1992) *The End of Sovereignty? The Politics of a Shrinking and Fragmenting World*, Aldershot, Edward Elgar.

Cantori, L. and Spiegel, S. (1970) *The International Politics of Regions: A Comparative Approach*, Englewood Cliffs, NJ, Prentice-Hall.

Caporaso, J. (1996) 'The European Union and Forms of State: Westphalian, Regulatory or Post-Modern?', *Journal of Common Market Studies*, 34(1), pp. 29–52.

Carlson, J. and Owens, E. (eds) (2003) *The Sacred and the Sovereign*, Washington, DC: Georgetown University Press.

Carpenter, T. G (1992) 'A New Proliferation Policy', *The National Interest*, Summer. pp. 63–72.

Carr, E. H. (1939) *Propaganda in World Politics*, Pamphlets on World Affairs 16, New York, Farrar & Rinehart.

Carruthers, S. (2000) *The Media at War: Communication and Conflict in the Twentieth Century*, London, Macmillan.

Castles, S. and Davidson, A. (2000) *Citizenship and Migration*, Basingstoke, Macmillan.

Castles, S. and Kosack, G. (1985) *Immigrant Workers and the Class Structure in Western Europe*, 2nd edn, Oxford, Oxford University Press.

Castles, S. and Miller, M. (1997) *The Age of Migration: International Population Movements in the Modern World*, 2nd edn, London, Macmillan.

Cavanagh, J., Wysham, D. and Arruda, M. (1994) *Beyond Bretton Woods: Alternatives to the Global Economic Order*, London, Pluto Press.

Center for Global Development (2004) *On the Brink: Weak States and US National Security*, Washington, DC, May.

Cesarani, D. (1996) *Citizenship, Nationality and Migration in Europe*, London, Routledge.

Chalmers, M. and Greene, O. (1995) *Taking Stock: The UN Register After Two Years*, Bradford Arms Register Studies, 5, Bradford, Westview Press.

Chandler, D. (2004) 'The Responsibility to Protect? Imposing the Liberal Peace: A Critique', in A. Bellamy and P. Williams (eds), *Peace Operations and Global Order*, London, Cass, pp. 59–81.

Chatterjee, P. and Finger, M. (1994) *The Earth Brokers*, London, Routledge.

Chayes, A. and Chayes, A. (eds) (1996) *Preventing Conflict in the Post-Communist World: Mobilizing International and Regional Organizations*, Washington, DC, Brookings Institution.

Chesterman, S. (2004) *You, The People: The United Nations, Transitional Administration, and State Building*, Oxford, Oxford University Press.

Chomsky, N. (1999) *The New Military Humanism: Lessons from Kosovo*, London, Pluto.

Chomsky, N. (2002) 'Who are the Global Terrorists?', in K. Booth and T. Dunne (eds), *Worlds in Collision: Terror and the Future of World Order*, Basingstoke: Palgrave, pp. 128–40.

Chopra, J. (2000) 'Building State Failure in East Timor', *Development and Change*, 33(5), pp. 979–1000.

Chua, A. (2002) *World on Fire: How Exporting Free-Market Democracy Breeds Ethnic Hatred and Global Instability*, New York, Doubleday.

CIA (Central Intelligence Agency) (2004) World Factbook, Central Intelligence Agency, http://www.cia.gov/cia/publications/factbook/rankorder/2001rank.html.

Cirincione, J. (ed.) (2000) *Repairing the Regime: Preventing the Spread of WMD* Washington, DC, Carnegie Endowment for International Peace.

Cirincione, J. (2004) 'Two Terrifying Reports: The U.S. Senate and the 9/11 Commission on Intelligence Failures Before September 11 and the Iraq War', *Disarmament Diplomacy*, no 78, July/August, pp. 3–10.

Cirincione, J., Wolfsthal, J. B. and Rajkumar, M. (2002) *Deadly Arsenals: Tracking Weapons of Mass Destruction*, Washington, DC, Carnegie Endowment for International Peace.

Clancy, T. (1994) *Debt of Honour*, London, HarperCollins.

Clark, I. (1998) 'Beyond the Great Divide: Globalization and the Theory of International Relations', *Review of International Studies*, 24(4), pp. 479–98.

Clary, C. (2004) 'A.Q. Khan and the Limits of the Non-proliferation Regime', *Disarmament Forum*, No 4, Geneva, United Nations Institute for Disarmament Research, 2004, pp. 33–42.

Claude, I. L. (1955) *National Minorities: An International Problem*, Cambridge, Mass, Harvard University Press.

Cohen, R. (1987) *The New Helots: Migrants in the International Division of Labour*, Aldershot, Avebury Press.

Cohen, R. and Layton-Henry, Z. (1997) *The Politics of Migration*, London, Edward Elgar.

Coleman, W. and Underhill, G. (eds) (1998) *Regionalism and Global Economic Integration*, London, Routledge.

Collinson, S. (1993) *Beyond Borders: Western European Migration Policy towards the 21st Century*, London, RIIA and Wyndham Place Trust.

Collinson, S. (1995) *Migration, Visa and Asylum Policies in Europe*, Wilton Park Paper, 107, London, HMSO.

Cox, R. (1986) 'State, Social Forces and World Orders: Beyond International Relations Theory', in R. Keohane (ed.) *Neorealism and Its Critics*, New York, Columbia University Press, pp. 204–54.

Cox, R. (1987) *Production, Power and World Order*, New York, Columbia University Press.

Croft, S. and Terriff, T. (eds) (2000) *Critical Reflections on Security and Change*, London, Frank Cass.

Cumings, B. (1992) *War and Television*, London, Verso.

Davis, Z. S. (1996) 'The Spread of Nuclear-Weapon-Free Zones: Building A New Nuclear Bargain', *Arms Control Today*, 26(1), February. pp. 15–19.

De Flers, N. and Regelsberger, E. (2005) 'The EU, New Regionalism and Inter-regional Relations', in C. Hill and M. Smith (eds), *International Relations and the European Union*, Oxford, Oxford University Press.

Del Rosso Jr, S. J. (1995) 'The Insecure State: Reflections on "the State" and "Security" in a Changing World', *Daedalus*, 124(2), pp. 175–208.

Development Initiatives (1997) *The Reality of Aid 1997/8*, London, Earthscan.

Dicken, P. (2003) *Global Shift*, 4th edn, London, Sage.

Dollar, D. and Kraay, A. (2000) *Growth is Good for the Poor*, Washington DC, World Bank, March, http://www.worldbank.org/research/growth/pdfiles/growthgoodforpoor.pdf.

Dowty, A. (1987) *Closed Borders*, New Haven and London, Yale University Press.

Duffield, M. (2001) *Global Governance and the New Wars: The Merging of Development and Security*, London, Zed Books.

Dunne, T. (2004) 'When the Shooting Starts: Atlanticism in British Security Strategy, *International Affairs*, 80(5), pp. 893–909.

Dunning, J. (1993) *The Globalization of Business*, London, Routledge.

Durch, W. (ed.) (1994) *The Evolution of United Nations Peacekeeping: Case Studies and Comparative Analysis*, London, Macmillan.

Dyson, K. (1980) *The State Tradition in Western Europe*, Oxford, Martin Robertson.

Ecologist, The (1993) 'Whose Common Future? Reclaiming the Commons', London, Earthscan.

Economist, The (1995) 'Who's in the Driving Seat?: A Survey of the World Economy', 7 October.

Economist, The (1996) 21 September.

Economist, The (1999) 'Time for a Redesign: A Survey of Global Finance', 30 January.

Economist, The (2003) 'A Cruel Sea of Capital: A Survey of Global Finance', 3 May.

Economist, The (2004a) 'Perpetual Motion: A Survey of the Car Industry', 4 September.

Economist, The (2004b) 'Exclusive: Not All Trade Agreements are Good', 20 November, p. 94.

Edwards, G. and Regelsberger, E. (eds) (1990) *Europe's Global Links: The European Community and Inter-Regional Cooperation*, London, Pinter.

Elliott, L. (2004) *The Global Politics of the Environment*, 2nd edn, Basingstoke, Palgrave Macmillan.

Elshtain, J. B. (2002) 'How to Fight a Just War', in K. Booth and T. Dunne (eds), *Worlds in Collision: Terror and the Future of World Order*, Basingstoke, Palgrave, pp. 263–9.

Esman, M. J. and Herring, R. J. (eds) (2001) *Carrots, Sticks and Ethnic Conflict: Rethinking Development Assistance*, Ann Arbor, University of Michigan Press.

EU Study Group (2004) *A Human Security Doctrine for Europe*, Barcelona, September.

European Security Strategy (2003) 'A Secure Europe in a Better World' at http://ue.eu.int/uedocs/cms_upload/78367.pdf.

Evans, G (2004) 'When is it Right to Fight?', *Survival*, 46(3), pp. 59–82.

Falk, R. (1995) *On Human Governance. Toward a New Global Politics*, Cambridge, Polity Press.

Fawcett, L. (2003) 'The Evolving Architecture of Regionalization', in M. Pugh and W. P. S. Sidhu (eds), *The United Nations and Regional Security: Europe and Beyond*, Boulder, Col., Lynne Rienner, pp. 11–30.

Fawcett, L. (2004) 'Exploring Regional Domains: a Comparative History of Regionalism', *International Affairs*, 80(3), pp. 429–46.

Fawcett, L. and Hurrell, A. (eds) (1995) *Regionalism in World Politics: Regional Organization and International Order*, Oxford, Oxford University Press.

Finn, P. (2004) 'Putin: Russia to Deploy Missiles "Unlikely to Exist" Elsewhere', *Washington Post*, 18 November, p. A25.

Fleitz, F. H. (2002) *Peacekeeping Fiascoes of the 1990s: Causes, Solutions, and U.S. Interests*, New York, Praeger.

Friman, H. R. and Andreas, P. (1999) *The Illicit Global Economy and State Power*, Lanham, Md, Rowman & Littlefield.

Frost, M. (1991) 'What Ought to be Done about the Condition of States?', in C. Navari (ed.), *The Condition of States. A Study in International Political Theory*, Milton Keynes, Open University Press, pp. 183–96.

Fukuyama, F. (1989) 'The End of History', *The National Interest*, 16, pp. 3–18.

Fukuyama, F. (1992) *The End of History and the Last Man*, Harmondsworth, Penguin.

Gamble, A. and Payne, T. (eds) (1996) *Regionalism and World Order*, London, Macmillan.

Gastrow, P. (1998) *Organised Crime in South Africa*, Johannesburg, Institute for Security Studies.

Gastrow, P. (2000) 'An International Link to Organised Crime', *Business Day*, South Africa, 21 January.

Gellner, E. (1983) *Nations and Nationalism*, Oxford, Blackwell.

Gibb, R. and Michalak, W. (eds) (1994) *Continental Trading Blocs: The Growth of Regionalism in the World Economy*, Chichester, Wiley.

Gill, S. and Law, D. (1988) *The Global Political Economy*, London, Harvester Wheatsheaf.

Gilpin, R. (1987) *The Political Economy of International Relations*, Princeton, Princeton University Press.

Gilpin, R. (2001) *Global Political Economy*, Princeton, Princeton University Press.

Girardet, E. (1995) *Somalia, Rwanda and Beyond: The Role of International Media in Wars and Humanitarian Crisis*, Dublin, Crosslines Global Report.

Godson, R. (1997) 'Political–Criminal Nexus: Overview', *Trends in Organised Crime*, 3(1), pp. 4–7.

Goodwin-Gill, G. (1983) *The Refugee in International Law*, Oxford, Oxford University Press/Clarendon.

Goose, S. D. and Smyth, S. (1994) 'Arming Genocide in Rwanda', *Foreign Affairs*, 73(5), pp. 86–96.

Gordenker, L. (1987) *Refugees in International Politics*, New York, Columbia University Press.

Gottemoeller, R. (2003) 'Beyond Arms Control: How to Deal With Nuclear Weapons', *Policy Brief No. 23*, Washington, DC, Carnegie Endowment for International Peace,

Goulding, M. (1996) 'The Use of Force by the United Nations', *International Peacekeeping*, 3(1), pp. 1–18.

Goulding, M. (2002) *Peacemonger*, London, John Murray.

Gow, J., Paterson, R. and Preston, A. (eds) (1996) *Bosnia by Television*, London, BFI Publishing.

Gowing, N. (1996) 'Real-Time TV Coverage from War: Does it Make or Break Government Policy', in J. Gow *et al.* (eds), *Bosnia by Television*, London, BFI Publishing.

Gray, J. (2003) *Al Qaeda and What it Means to be Modern*, London, Faber.

Grieco, J. (1988) 'Anarchy and the Limits of Co-operation: A Realist Critique of the Newest Liberal Institutionalism', *International Organisation*, 42(3), pp. 485–507.

Grubb, M. *et al.* (1993) *The Earth Summit Agreements: A Guide and Assessment*, London, RIIA/Earthscan.

Gunaratna, R. (2003) 'Al-Qaeda Organization and Operations', in M. Buckley and R. Fawn (eds), *Global Responses to Terrorism: 9/11, Afghanistan and Beyond*, London, Routledge, pp. 37–51.

Gurr, T. R. (1993) *Minorities at Risk: A Global View of Ethnopolitical Conflict*, Washington, DC, United States Institute of Peace.

Gurr, T R. (2000) *People Versus States: Minorities at Risk in the New Century*, Washington: United States Institute of Peace Press.

Haas, P. M., Keohane, R. O. and Levy, M. (eds) (1994) *Institutions for the Earth: Sources of Effective Environmental Protection*, Cambridge Mass, MIT Press.

Hallin, D. (1989) *The Uncensored War: The Media and Vietnam*, New York, Oxford University Press.

Hammar, T. (ed.) (1985) *European Immigration Policy: A Comparative Study*, Cambridge, Cambridge University Press.

Hannerz, U. (1996) *Transnational Connections; Culture, People, Places*, London, Routledge.

Hannum, H. (1990) *Autonomy, Sovereignty and Self-Determination*, Philadelphia, University of Pennsylvania Press.

Hardin, G. (1968) 'The Tragedy of the Commons' reprinted in G. Hardin and J. Baden (eds), *Managing the Commons*, San Francisco, W.H. Freeman and Co. (1977) pp. 16–30.

Harff, B. (1992) 'Recognizing Genocides and Politicides', in H. Fein (ed.) *Genocide Watch*, New Haven, Yale University Press, pp. 27–41.

Harff, B. and Gurr, T. R. (2004) *Ethnic Conflict in World Politics*, 2nd edn, Boulder, Col., Westview.

Hartung, W. D. (1995) 'US Conventional Arms Transfers: Promoting Stability or Fueling Conflict?', *Arms Control Today*, 25(9), pp. 9–13.

Haynes, J. (1993) *Religion in Third World Politics*, Buckingham, Open University Press.

Haynes, J. (1998) *Religion in Global Politics*, London, Longman.

Held, D. (1993) 'Democracy From City-States to a Cosmopolitan Order?', in D. Held (ed.), *Prospects For Democracy*, Cambridge, Polity Press, pp. 13–52.

Held, D., McGrew, A., Goldblatt, D. and Perraton, J. (1999) *Global Transformations: Politics, Economics and Culture*, Cambridge, Polity Press.

Helman, G. B. and Ratner, S. R. (1992–3) 'Saving Failed States', *Foreign Policy*, 89, pp. 3–20.

Henrard, K. (2004) 'Relating Human Rights, Minority Rights and Self-determination to Minority Protection', in U. Schneckener and S. Wolff (eds), *Managing and Settling Ethnic Conflicts*, London, Hurst and Company.

Herman, E. and McChesney, R. (1997) *The Global Media: The New Missionaries of Global Capitalism*, London, Cassell.

Hess, S. and Kalb, M. (2003) *The Media and the War on Terrorism*, Washington DC, Brookings Institution Press.

Hettne, B., Inotai, A. and Sunkel, O. (eds) (1999) *Globalism and the New Regionalism*, Basingstoke, Palgrave.

Hill, C. (ed.) (1983) *National Foreign Policies and European Political Cooperation*, London, Allen & Unwin.

Hill, C. (ed.) (1996) *The Actors in Europe's Foreign Policy*, London, Routledge.

Hobsbawm, E. (1995) *Age of Extremes: The Short Twentieth Century, 1914–1991*, London, Abacus.

Hobson, J. M. (2000) *The State and International Relations*, Cambridge, Cambridge University Press.

Hocking, B. and McGuire, S. (eds) (2004) *Trade Politics*, 2nd edn, London, Routledge.

Hocking, B. and Smith, M. (1995) *World Politics. An Introduction to International Relations*, 2nd edn, Hemel Hempstead, Prentice-Hall/Harvester Wheatsheaf.

Hoffmann, S. (1995–6) 'The Politics and Ethics of Military Intervention', *Survival*, 3(4), pp. 29–51.

Hoffmann, S. (1998) *World Disorders: Troubled Peace in the Post-Cold War World*, Lanham, Md, Rowman & Littlefield.

Hogan, M. J. (ed.) (1992) *The End of the Cold War: Its Meaning and Implications*, Cambridge, Cambridge University Press.

Holm, T. T. and Eide, E. B. (eds) (2000) *Peacebuilding and Police Reform*, London, Cass.

Holsti, K. (1992) *International Politics: A Framework For Analysis*, Englewood Cliffs, NJ, Prentice Hall.

Holton, R. (1998) *Globalization and the Nation-State*, London, Macmillan.

Horowitz, D. L. (2000) *Ethnic Groups in Conflict*, 2nd edn, Berkeley, University of California Press.

Horsman, M. and Marshall, A. (1995) *After the Nation-State: Citizens, Tribalism and the New World Disorder*, London, HarperCollins.

Houghton, J. T. *et al.* (eds) (1996) *Climate Change 2001: The Science of Climate Change, Contribution of Working Group I to the Second Assessment Report of the Intergovernmental Panel on Climate Change*, Cambridge, Cambridge University Press.

Howard, M. (1989–90) 'The Springtime of Nations', *Foreign Affairs*, 69(1), pp. 17–32.

Howe, E. (1982) *The Black Game: British Subversive Operations Against the Germans during the Second World War*, London, Futura.

HRW (Human Rights Watch)/Arms Project and Physicians for Human Rights (1993) *Landmines: A Deadly Legacy*, New York.

HRW (2004) Human Rights Watch Report, *Failure to Protect: Anti-minority Violence in Kosovo*, March, 16(6)(D), available at: www.hrw.org/reports/2004/kosovo0704.

Huntington, S. (1973) 'Transnational Organisations in World Politics', *World Politics*, 25(3), pp. 333–68.

Huntington, S. P. (1993) 'The Clash of Civilizations', *Foreign Affairs*, 71(3), pp. 22–49.

Huntington, S. P. (1996) *The Clash of Civilisations and the New World Order*, New York, Simon & Schuster.

Hurrell, A. (1992) 'Latin America in the New World Order: A Regional Bloc of the Americas?', *International Affairs*, 68(1), pp. 121–39.

Hurrell, A. (1995) 'Explaining the Resurgence of Regionalism in World Politics', *Review of International Studies*, 21(4), pp. 331–58.

Hurrell, A. and Kingsbury, B. (eds) (1992) *The International Politics of the Environment*, Oxford, Clarendon.

Hutchinson, J. and Smith, A. D. (eds) (1994) *Nationalism*, Oxford, Oxford University Press.

Hutchinson, J. and Smith, A. D. (eds) (1996) *Ethnicity*, Oxford, Oxford University Press.

Hymer, S. (1972) 'The Multinational Corporation and the Law of Uneven Development', in J. Bhagwati (ed.) *Economics and World Order*, London, Collier-Macmillan, pp. 113–40.

ICISS (International Commission on Intervention and State Sovereignty) (2001) *The Responsibility to Protect*, Ottawa, International Development Research Centre.

Ignatieff, M. (1998) *The Warrior's Honor: Ethnic War and the Modern Conscience*, London, Chatto & Windus.

Ignatieff, M. (2000) *Virtual War: Kosovo and Beyond*, London, Chatto & Windus.

Imber, M. (1993) 'Too Many Cooks? The Post-Rio Reform of the UN', *International Affairs*, 69(1), pp. 150–66.

IMF (International Monetary Fund) (2000) 'Recovery from the Asian Crisis and the Role of the IMF', IMF, June.

IMF (International Monetary Fund) (2003) 'IMF Surveillance', A factsheet, April.

InterAction (2003) American Council for Voluntary International Action, Natsios at 'Forum 2003, The Challenge of Global Commitments: Advancing Relief and Development Goals through Advocacy and Action', 19–21 May (available at www.interaction.org/forum2003/panels.html).

Ishizuka, K. (2005) 'Japan's Policy Towards UN Peacekeeping Operations', in M. Caballero-Anthony and A. Acharya (eds), 'UN Peace Operations and Asian–Pacific Security', special issue of *International Peacekeeping*, 12(1).

Jackson, B. (1990) *Poverty and the Planet*, Harmondsworth, Penguin.

Jackson, J. A. (1969) *Migration*, Cambridge, Cambridge University Press.

Jackson, R. H. (1990) *Quasi-States: Sovereignty, International Relations and the Third World*, Cambridge, Cambridge University Press.

Jackson, R. H. and James, A. (1993) 'The Character of Independent Statehood', in R. H. Jackson and A. James (eds), *States in a Changing World*, Oxford, Oxford University Press, pp. 3–25.

Jacques, M. (2004) 'Face It: No One Cares', *The Guardian*, 29 July.

Jakobsen, P. V. (1998) *Western Uses of Coercive Diplomacy after the Cold War: A Challenge for Theory and Practice*, London, Macmillan.

James, A. (1987) *Sovereign Statehood: The Basis of International Society*, London, Allen & Unwin.

James, A. (1994) 'Problems of Internal Peacekeeping', *Diplomacy and Statecraft*, 5(1).

Jervis, R. (1978) 'Cooperation Under the Security Dilemma' *World Politics*, 30(2), pp. 167–214.

Jones, R. J. B. (2000) *The World Turned Upside Down*, Manchester, Manchester University Press.

Jowett, G. and O'Donnell, V. (1992) *Propaganda and Persuasion*, London, Sage.

Kaldor, M. (1999) *New and Old Wars: Organized Violence in a Global Era*, Cambridge, Polity Press.

Kaldor, M. (ed.) (2000) *Global Insecurity: Restructuring the Global Military Sector*, London, Continuum.

Kaplan, D. E. (1999) 'The Wiseguy Regime: North Korea Has Embarked on a Global Crime Spree' *US News and World Report*, 15 February, pp. 36–9.

Katovsky, B. and Carlson, T. (2003) *Embedded: the Media at War in Iraq*, Guilford, Conn., Lyons Press.

Katzenstein, P. (1993) 'Regions in competition: comparative advantages of America, Europe, and Asia', in H. Haftendorn and C. Tuschhoff (eds), *America and Europe in an Era of Change*, Boulder, Col., Westview Press, pp. 105–26.

Kay, D. (1994) 'The IAEA: How Can it be Strengthened?', in M. Reiss and R. S. Litwak (eds), *Nuclear Proliferation After the Cold War*, Washington, DC, Johns Hopkins University Press, pp. 309–33.

Keane, J. (1996) *Reflections on Violence*, London, Verso.

Keating, M. (1998) *The New Regionalism in Western Europe: Territorial Restructuring and Political Change*, Cheltenham, Edward Elgar.

Kegley, C. W. and Wittkopf, E. R. (1993) *World Politics: Trend and Transformation*, 4th edn, London, Macmillan.

Kellner, D. (1992) *The Persian Gulf TV War*, Boulder, Col., Westview Press.

Kenney, M. (1999) 'When Criminals Out-smart the State: Understanding the Learning Capacity of Colombian Drug Trafficking Organizations', *Transnational Organized Crime*, 5 (1) (Spring), pp. 97–119.

Keohane, R. O. and Anderson, L. (1995) 'The Promise of Institutionalist Theory', *International Security*, 20(1), pp. 39–51.

Keohane R. O. and Nye, J. S. (eds) (1972) *Transnational Relations and World Politics*, Cambridge, Mass, Harvard University Press.

Keohane, R. and Nye, J. S. (1977) *Power and Interdependence*, Boston, Little, Brown & Co.

Khiddu-Makubuya, E. (1994) 'Violence and Conflict Resolution in Uganda', in K. Rupesinghe (ed.), *The Culture of Violence*, Tokyo, United Nations University Press, pp. 144–77.

Kiernan, B. (2003) 'The Demography of Genocide in South East Asia', *Critical Asian Studies*, 34(4), pp. 585–97.

Kinloch Pichat, S. (2004) *A UN 'Legion': Between Utopia and Reality*, London, Cass.

Kiras, J. (2004) 'Terrorism', in J. Baylis and S. Smith (eds), *The Globalization of World Politics*, Oxford, Oxford University Press.

Klitgaard, R. (1998) 'International Cooperation Against Corruption', *Finance and Development*, 35(1), pp. 3–7.

Korten, D. C. (1990) *Getting to the 21st Century: Voluntary Action and the Global Agenda*, New Haven, Conn., Kumarian Press.

Krasner, S. (1995) 'Power-Politics, Institutions and Transnational Relations', in T. Risse-Kappen (ed.), *Bringing Transnational Relations Back In*, Cambridge, Cambridge University Press, pp. 257–79.

Krasner, S. (1995–6) 'Compromising Westphalia', *International Security*, 20(3), pp. 115–51.

Krasner, S. (1999) *Sovereignty: Organized Hypocrisy*, Princeton, Princeton University Press.

Kritz, K., Keely, C. B. and Tomasci, S. M. (eds) (1981) *Global Trends in Migration: Theory and Research on International Population Movements*, New York, Center for Migration Studies.

Kumar, K. (ed.) (2001) *Women and Civil Wars*, Boulder, Col., Lynne Rienner.

Kuper, L. (1985) *The Prevention of Genocide*, New Haven, Yale University Press.

Kurtzman, J. (1993) *The Death of Money*, New York, Simon & Schuster.

Lacqueur, W. (1977) *Terrorism*. London, Weidenfeld & Nicholson.

Lacqueur, W. (2001) *The New Terrorism*, London, Phoenix Press.

Laffan, B., O'Donnell, R. and Smith, M. (2000) *Europe's Experimental Union: Rethinking Integration*, London, Routledge.

Lake, D. A. and Rothchild, D. S. (eds) (1999) *The International Spread of Ethnic Conflict: Fear, Diffusion, and Escalation*, Princeton, Princeton University Press.

Laurance, E. J. (1993) 'The UN Register of Conventional Arms: Rationales and Prospects for Compliance and Effectiveness', *The Washington Quarterly*, 16(2).

Leahy, P. (1995) 'The CCW Review Conference: An Opportunity for US Leadership', *Arms Control Today*, 25(7), pp. 20–4.

Leiken, R. S. (1996–7) 'The Global Corruption Epidemic', *Foreign Policy*, 105.

Leyton-Brown, D. (2000) 'The Political Economy of North American Free Trade', in R. Stubbs and G. Underhill (eds), *Political Economy and the Changing Global Order*, 2nd edn, Toronto, Oxford University Press, pp. 352–65.

Lijphart, A. (1977) *Democracy and Plural Societies*, New Haven, Yale University Press.

Linklater, A. (2002) 'Unnecessary Suffering', in K. Booth and T. Dunne (eds), *Worlds in Collision: Terror and the Future of World Order*, Basingstoke, Palgrave, pp. 303–12.

Lipschutz, R. D. (2004) *Global Environmental Politics: Power Perspectives and Practice*, Washington DC, CQ Press.

Livingston, S. and Eachus, T. (1995) 'Humanitarian Crises and US Foreign Policy: Somalia and the CNN Effect Reconsidered', *Political Communication*, 12(4), pp. 413–29.

Lombard, B. (2000) 'Small Arms and Light Weapons: A Neglected Issue, A Renewed Focus', *Disarmament Diplomacy*, no. 49, August, p. 29.

Luard, E. (1990) *The Globalization of Politics*, London, Macmillan.

Lutz, J. M. and Lutz, B. (2004) *Global Terrorism*, London, Routledge.

MacArthur, J. (1993) *Second Front: Censorship and Propaganda in the Gulf War*, Berkeley, Cal., University of California Press.

Machel, G. (2001) *The Impact of War on Children*, London, Hurst.

Madeley, J. (1999) *Big Business Poor Peoples: the Impact of Transnational Corporations on the World's Poor*, London, Zed Books

Mann, M. (1993) 'Nation-States in Europe and Other Continents: Diversifying, Developing, Not Dying', *Daedalus*, 122(3), pp. 115–40.

Manners, I. and Whitman, R. (eds) (2000) *The Foreign Policies of European Union Member States*, Manchester, Manchester University Press.

Marty, M. E. and Scott Appleby, R. (1993) 'Introduction', in M. Marty and R. Scott Appleby (eds), *Fundamentalism and the State: Remaking Politics, Economies and Militance*, Chicago, University of Chicago Press, pp. 1–9.

Mattli, W. (1999) *The Logic of Regional Integration: Europe and Beyond*, Cambridge, Cambridge University Press.

May, R. and Cleaver, G. (1997) 'African Peacekeeping: Still Dependent?', *International Peacekeeping*, 4(2), pp. 1–21.

Mayall, J. (1990) *Nationalism and International Society*, Cambridge, Cambridge University Press.

Maynard, K. (1999) *Healing Communities in Conflict: International Assistance in Complex Emergencies*, New York, Colombia University Press.

McGarry, J. and O'Leary, B. (1993) *The Politics of Ethnic Conflict Regulation*, London, Routledge.

McGrew, A. (1992) 'Conceptualizing Global Politics', in A. McGrew and P. Lewis (eds), *Global Politics*, Cambridge, Polity Press.

McInnes, C. (2002) *Spectator-sport War: The West and Contemporary Conflict* Boulder, Col., Lynne Rienner.

Meadows, D. H. *et al.* (1972) *The Limits to Growth: A Report for the Club of Rome's Project on the Predicament of Mankind*, London, Pan.

Meadows, D. H. *et al.* (1992) *Beyond the Limits: Global Collapse or a Sustainable Future?*, London, Earthscan.

Mearsheimer, J. J. (1990) 'Why We Will Soon Miss the Cold War', *The Atlantic Monthly*, 166(2), pp. 35–50.

Mearsheimer, J. J. (1994–5) 'The False Promise of International Institutions', *International Security*, 19(3), pp. 5–49.

Metzl, J. (1996) 'Information Technology and Human Rights', *Human Rights Quarterly*, 18(4), pp. 705–46.

Miall, H., Ramsbotham, O. and Woodhouse, T. (1999) *Contemporary Conflict Resolution*, Cambridge, Polity Press.

Milanovic, B. (2003) 'The Two Faces of Globalization: Against Globalization we Know It', *World Development*, 31(4), pp. 667–83.

Miller, J. D. B. (1986) 'Sovereignty as a Source of Vitality for the State', *Review of International Studies*, 12(2), pp. 79–89.

Minear, L., Scott, C. and Weiss, T. (1996) *The News Media, Civil War and Humanitarian Action*, Boulder, Col., Lynne Rienner.

Mingst, K. (2003) 'The US–UN Relationship', *International Peacekeeping*, 10(4), pp.82–93.

Moeller, S. (1999) *Compassion Fatigue: How the Media Sell Disease, Famine, Death and War*, New York, Routledge.

Morgenthau, H. J. (1967) *Politics Among Nations: The Struggle for Power and Peace*, 4th edn, New York, A.A. Knopf.

Morley, D. and Robins, K. (1995) *Spaces of Identity: Global Media, Electronic Landscapes and Cultural Boundaries*, London, Routledge.

Murphy, A. B. (1994) 'International Law and the Sovereign State: Challenges to the Status Quo', in G. J. Demko and W. B. Wood (eds), *Reordering the World. Geopolitical Perspectives on the 21st Century*, Boulder, Col., Westview Press, pp. 209–24.

NATO (2004) *Financial and Economic Data Relating to NATO Defence: Defence Expenditures of NASTO Countries (1980–2003)* at http://www.nato.int/docu/pr/2003/p03–146e.htm.

Navari, C. (1991) 'Introduction: The State as a Contested Concept in International Relations', in C. Navari (ed.), *The Condition of States. A Study in International Political Theory*, Milton Keynes, Open University Press, pp. 1–18.

Naylor, R. T. (1995) 'From Cold War to Crime War: The Search for a New National Security Threat', *Transnational Organised Crime*, 1(4).

New Internationalist (1998) 305, September.

Newsweek (1995) 26 June.

9-11 Commission Report (2004) Final Report of the National Commission on Terrorist Attacks Upon the United States, Official Government Edition, at http://www.9-11commission.gov/.

Nye, J. Jr (1971) *Peace in Parts: Integration and Conflict in Regional Organisation*, Boston, Little Brown.

Olsson, L. and Tryggestad, T. L. (eds) (2001) *Women and International Peacekeeping*, London, Cass.

Orton, A. and Cirincione, J. (2004) 'WMD in Iraq: Evidence and Implications', *Disarmament Diplomacy*, no. 75, Jan/Feb., pp. 31–4.

Ozkirimli, U. (2000) *Theories of Nationalism: A Critical Introduction*, Basingstoke, Macmillan.

Paletz, D and Schmid, A. (1992) *Terrorism and the Media: How Researchers, Terrorist, Government, Press, Public, Victims View and Use the Media*, Newbury Park, Calif., Sage.

Parekh, B. (2002) 'Terrorism and Intercultural Dialogue', in K. Booth and T. Dunne (eds), *Worlds in Collision: Terror and the Future of World Order*, Basingstoke, Palgrave, pp. 270–83.

Paris, R. (2004) *At War's End: Building Peace After Civil Conflict*, Cambridge, Cambridge University Press.

Parker, R. (1995) 'The Future of Global Television News: An Economic Perspective', *Political Communication*, 12(4), pp. 431–46.

Paterson, M. (2001) *Understanding Global Environmental Politics: Domination, Accumulation, Resistance*, Basingstoke, Palgrave.

Pearson, G. S. (1993) 'Prospects for Chemical and Biological Arms Control: The Web of Deterrence', *The Washington Quarterly*, 16(2), pp. 145–62.

Perrow, C. (1984) *Normal Accidents*, New York, Basic Books.

Petito, F. and Hatzopoulos, P. (eds) (2003) *Religion in International Relations. The Return from Exile*, New York, Palgrave.

Porter, G. and Brown, J. W. (2000) *Global Environmental Politics*, 3rd edn, Boulder, Col., Westview Press.

Potter, W. C. (1995) 'Before the Deluge? Assessing the Threat of Nuclear Leakage From the Post-Soviet States', *Arms Control Today*, 25(8), pp. 9–16.

Potts, L. (1990) *The World Labour Market: A History of Migration*, London, Zed Books.

Power, S. (2003). *A Problem from Hell: America and the Age of Genocide*, London, Flamingo.

Premdas, R. (1991) 'The Internationalization of Ethnic Conflict: Some Theoretical Explorations', in K. M. de Silva and R. J. May (eds), *The Internationalization of Ethnic Strife*, London, Pinter, pp. 10–25.

Pugh, M. (2003) 'The World Order Politics of Regionalization', in M. Pugh and W. P. S. Sidhu (eds), *The United Nations and Regional Security: Europe and Beyond*, Boulder, Col., Lynne Rienner.

Pugh, M. (2004) 'Peacekeeping and Critical Theory', in A. J. Bellamy, and P. Williams (eds), *Peace Operations and Global Order*, London, Cass.

Pugh, M. and N. Cooper with J. Goodhand (2004), *War Economies in a Regional Context: Challenges of Transformation*, Boulder CO: Lynne Rienner.

Pullinger, S. (2004) 'Lord Butler's Report on UK Intelligence and the Iraq War', *Disarmament Diplomacy*, No 78, July/August, pp. 10–17.

Rafferty, K. (1996) 'US Key to Keeping Japan Non-Nuclear', *The Guardian*, 1 March, p. 11.

Rahnema, M. and Bawtree, V. (eds) (1997) *The Post Developmental Reader*, London, Zed Books.

Ramsbotham, O. (1997) 'Humanitarian Intervention, 1990–95: A Need to Reconceptualize?', *Review of International Studies*, 23(4), pp. 445–68.

Ramsbotham, O. and Woodhouse, T. (1996) *Humanitarian Intervention in Contemporary Conflict*, Cambridge, Polity Press.

Reich, R. (1990) 'Who is US?', *Harvard Business Review*, 68(1), pp. 53–64.

Rieff, D. (2002) *A Bed for the Night: Humanitarianism in Crisis*, London, Vintage.

Roberts, A. (1995–6) 'From San Francisco to Sarajevo: The UN and the Use of Force', *Survival*, 37(4), pp. 7–28.

Roberts, A. (1999) 'NATO's Humanitarian War' over Kosovo', *Survival*, 41(3), pp. 102–23.

Robinson, J. (1999) *The Merger: How Organized Crime in Taking over the World*, London, Simon & Schuster.

Rogers, P. (2002) 'Political Violence and Global Order', K. Booth and T. Dunne (eds), *Worlds in Collision: Terror and the Future of World Order*, Basingstoke, Palgrave, pp. 215–25.

Rome Statute of the International Criminal Court (1998) at http://www.un.org/law/icc/statute/romefra.htm.

Rosecrance, R. (1991) 'Regionalism and the post-Cold War Era', *International Journal*, 46, pp. 373–93.

Rosenau, J. (1989) *Turbulence in World Politics*, Princeton, Princeton University Press.

RosenZweig, R. (1999) 'Live Free or Die? Death, Life, Survival and Sobreity on the Information Superhighway', *American Quarterly*, 51(i), pp. 160–74.

Rotberg, R. and Weiss, T. (eds) (1996) *From Massacres to Genocide: The Media, Public Policy and Humanitarian Crises*, Washington, DC, Brookings Institution.

Rudolph, S. H. and Piscatori, J. (eds) (1997) *Transnational Religion and Fading States*, Boulder, Col., Westview Press.

Ruggie, J. G. (1996) 'The United Nations and the Collective Use of Force: Wither or Whether?', in M. Pugh (ed.), *The UN, Peace and Force*, London, Frank Cass, pp. 1–20.

Rupesinghe, K. (1990) 'The Disappearing Boundaries between Internal and External Conflicts', paper presented to International Peace Research Association Conference, Groningen.

Rupesinghe, K. (1998) *Civil War, Civil Peace*, London, Pluto Press.

Russett, B. (1967) *International Regions and the International System*, Chicago, Rand McNally.

Ryan, P. J. and Rush, G. E. (1997) *Understanding Organised Crime in Global Perspective*, London, Sage.

Sagan, S. and Waltz, K. N. (2003) *The Spread of Nuclear Weapons: A Debate Renewed*, 2nd edn, New York, W.W. Norton.

Sahn, D. and Stifel, D. (2003) 'Progress Toward the Millennium Development Goals in Africa' *World Development*, 31(1), pp. 23–52.

Said, E. (1978) *Orientalism*, London, Penguin.

Said, E. (1995) 'What is Islam?', *New Statesman and Society*, 10 February, pp. 32–4.

Sakamoto, Y. (ed.) (1995) *Global Transformation: Challenge to the State System*, Tokyo, United Nations University Press.

Saurin, J. (1996) 'International Relations, Social Ecology and the Globalisation of Environmental Change', in J. Vogler, and W. M. F. Imber (eds), *The Environment and International Relations*, London, Routledge, pp. 77–96.

Scherrer, C. P. (2003) *Ethnicity, Nationalism and Violence*, Aldershot: Ashgate.

Schimmelfennig, F. (2003) *The EU, NATO and the Integration of Europe*, Cambridge, Cambridge University Press.

Schneckener, U. and Wolff, S. (eds) (2004) *Managing and Settling Ethnic Conflicts*, London, Hurst.

Schwartz, H. (2000) *States versus Markets*, 2nd edn, Basingstoke, Palgrave.

Scott, S. (1994) *Dismantling Utopia: How Information Ended the Soviet Union*, Chicago, Ivan R Dee.

Seib, P. (1998) *Headline Diplomacy: How News Coverage Affects Foreign Policy*, Westport, Col., Praeger.

Shaw, M. (1994) *Global Society and International Relations*, Cambridge, Polity Press.

Shea D. A. (2004) 'Terrorism: Background on Chemical, Biological, and Toxin weapons and Options for Lessening Their Impact', *CRS Report for Congress*, Washington, DC, Congressional Research Service.

Sheffer, G. (ed.) (1986) *Modern Diasporas in International Politics*, London, Croom Helm.

Shelley, L. (1995) 'Transnational Organized Crime: An Imminent Threat to the Nation-State?', *Journal of International Affairs*, 45(2), pp. 463–89.

Shelley, L. I. (1997) 'Post-Soviet Organized Crime: A New Form of Authoritarianism', in P. Williams (ed.), *Russian Organized Crime: The New Threat?*, London, Cass.

Short, K. (1986) *Western Broadcasting Over the Iron Curtain*, London, Croom Helm.

Simpson, J. (1995) 'The Birth of an Era? The 1995 NPT Conference and the Politics of Nuclear Disarmament', *Security Dialogue*, 26(3).

Sinclair, J., Jacka, E. and Cunningham, S. (1996) *New Patterns in Global Television: Peripheral Vision*, Oxford, Oxford University Press.

SIPRI (Stockholm International Peace Research Institute) (1996) *SIPRI Yearbook 1996*, Oxford, Oxford University Press.

SIPRI (Stockholm International Peace Research Institute) (2004) *Armaments, Disarmament and International Security*, Oxford, Oxford University Press.

Sisk, T. D. (1996) *Power Sharing and International Mediation in Ethnic Conflicts*, Washington, DC, United States Institute of Peace.

Sklair, L. (2001) *The Transnational Capitalist Class*, Oxford, Blackwell.

Sköns, E. *et al.* (2004) in SIPRI, *Armaments, Disarmament and International Security*, Oxford, Oxford University Press.

Slocombe, W. B. (2003) 'Force, Pre-emption and Legitimacy', *Survival*, 45(1), pp. 117–30.

Small Arms Survey (2004) *Small Arms Survey 2004: Rights at Risk*, Oxford, Oxford University Press.

Smith, A. D. (1991) *National Identity*, Harmondsworth, Penguin.

Smith, A. D. (1995) *Nations and Nationalism in a Global Era*, Cambridge, Polity Press.

Smith, M. (1993) 'Beyond the Stable State? Foreign Policy Challenges and Opportunities in the New Europe', in W. Carlsnaes and S. Smith (eds), *European Foreign Policy: The EC and Changing Perspectives in Europe*, London, Sage, pp. 21–44.

Sorensen, G. (1998) 'IR Theory after the Cold War', *Review of International Studies*, 24 (Special Issue), pp. 83–100.

Sorensen, G. (2001) *Changes in Statehood: The Transformation of International Relations* Basingstoke, Palgrave.

Sorensen, G. (2004) *The Transformation of the State: Beyond the Myth of Retreat*, Basingstoke, Palgrave.

South Commission (1990) *The Challenge to the South*, Oxford, Oxford University Press.

Spear, J. (1996) 'Arms Limitations, Confidence Building Measures, and Internal Conflict', in M. Brown (ed.), *The International Dimensions of Internal Conflict*, Cambridge Mass, MIT Press, pp. 377–410.

Spear, J. (2003) 'Organizing for International Counterproliferation: NATO and U.S. Nonproliferation Policy', in J. E. Nolan, B. I. Finel and B. D. Finley (eds), *Combating Weapons of Mass Destruction: Ultimate Security*, New York, The Century Foundation.

Spear, J. (2004) 'Africa, Latin America Act on Small Arms', *Trust and Verify*, Issue 114, May–June, 1–8.

Spero, J. and Hart, J. (2003) *The Politics of International Economic Relations*, 6th edn, Belmont, Wadsworth.

Stavenhagen, R. (1996) *Ethnic Conflicts and the Nation-State*, Basingstoke, Macmillan.

Stein, A. A. (1990) *Why Nations Cooperate: Circumstance and Choice in International Relations*, Ithaca and London, Cornell University Press.

Stopford, J. and Strange, S. (1991) *Rival States, Rival Firms: The Global Competition for Market Shares*, Cambridge, Cambridge University Press.

Strange, S. (1994) *States and Markets*, 2nd edn, London, Pinter.

Strange, S. (1996) *The Retreat of the State: The Diffusion of Power in the Global Economy*, Cambridge, Cambridge University Press.

Strange, S. (1998) *Mad Money*, Manchester, Manchester University Press.

Stubbs, R. and Underhill, G. (2000) *Political Economy and the Changing Global Order*, 2nd edn, Toronto, Oxford University Press.

Suhrke, A. (2001) 'Peacekeepers as Nation-Builders: Dilemmas of the UN in East Timor', *International Peacekeeping*, 8(4), pp. 1–20.

Sussman, G. (1999) 'Urban Congregations of Capital and Communications: Redesigning Social and Spatial Boundaries', *Social Text*, 17(3), pp. 35–51.

Taras, R.C. and Ganguly, R. (2002) *Understanding Ethnic Conflict: The International Dimensions*, 2nd edn, New York, Longman.

Tardy, T. (ed.) (2004) *Peace Operations after 11 September 2001*, London, Cass.

Taylor, P. (1997) *Global Communications, International Affairs and the Media Since 1945*, London, Routledge.

Teitelbaum, M. S. (1980) 'Right vs. Right: Immigration and Refugee Policy in the United States', *Foreign Affairs*, 59(1), pp. 21–59.

Teló, M. (ed.) (2001) *European Union and New Regionalism: Regional Actors and Global Governance in a Post-hegemonic Era*, Aldershot, Ashgate.

Thomas, C. (1992) *The Environment in International Relations*, London, RIIA.

Thomas, C. (2004) 'Poverty, Development and Hunger', in J. Bayliss and S. Smith (eds) *The Globalization of World Politics*, 3rd edn, Oxford, Oxford University Press.

Todaro, M. P. (1989) *Economic Development in the Third World*, New York and London, Longman.

Tomlinson, J. (1991) *Cultural Imperialism: A Critical Introduction*, London, Pinter.

Tomlinson, J. (1999) *Globalization and Culture*, Cambridge, Polity Press.

Traynor, I. (2004), 'Battle groups aim for speed in a crisis', *The Guardian*, 8 October, p. 4.

UK Government (2003) *International Priorties: A Strategy for the FCO* at http://www.fco.gov.uk.

UN (1972) *UN Yearbook 1972*, New York, United Nations.

UNAIDS (2004) *2004 Report on the Global Aids Epidemic* http://www.unaids.org/bangkok2004/report.html.

UNCTAD (United Nations Conference on Trade and Development) (2004) *World Investment Report: The Shift Towards Services, Overview*, United Nations, New York and Geneva.

UNDP (United Nations Development Programme) (1994) *Human Development Report, 1994*, Oxford, Oxford University Press.

UNDP (United Nations Development Programme) (1999) *Human Development Report, 1999*, Oxford, Oxford University Press.

UNDP (United Nations Development Programme) (2002) *Human Development Report 2002*, http://www.undp.org.

UNDP (United Nations Development Programme) (2003) *Human Development Report 2003*, http://www.undp.org.

UNHCR (United Nations High Commission for Refugees) (2003) *Global Refugee Trends*.

UN Secretary-General High Level Panel (2004) *A More Secure World: Our Shared Responsibility*, http://www.un.org/secureworld.

US Government (2002) *National Security Strategy of the United States of America*, at http://www.whitehouse.gov.

US Senate Government Affairs Permanent Subcommittee on Investigations (1995) 'The Global Proliferation of Weapons of Mass Destruction: A Case Study on the Aum Shinrikyo', Staff Report, October 3, Section IV, 'The Operation of the Aum'. Available at http://www.globalsecurity.org/security/library/Congress/1995_r/aum/part04.htm, accessed February 2005.

Vallely, P. (1990) *Bad Samaritans: First World Ethics and Third World Debt*, London, Hodder & Stoughton.

van Ham, P. (1994) *Managing Non-Proliferation Regimes in the 1990s: Power, Politics and Policies*, London, RIIA.

Vaux, T. (2001) *The Selfish Altruist – relief work in famine and war*, London, Earthscan.

Vernon, R. (1971) *Sovereignty at Bay*, London, Longman.

Vogler, J. (2000) *The Global Commons: Environmental and Technological Governance*, Chichester, John Wiley.

Vogler, J. and Imber, M. F. (eds) (1996) *The Environment in International Relations*, London, Routledge.

Wade, R. (2001) 'Winners and Losers', *The Economist*, 26 April.

Waever, O. *et al.* (1993) *Migration, Identity and the New European Security Order*, London, Pinter.

Wagnleitner, R. (1999) 'The Empire of Fun, or Talkin' Soviet Union Blues: The Sound of Freedom and US Cultural Hegemony in Europe', *Diplomatic History*, 23(3), pp. 499–524.

Walker, W. (1998) 'International Nuclear Relations After the Indian and Pakistani Test Explosions', *International Affairs*, 74(3), July, pp. 505–28.

Wallace, W. (1990) *The Transformation of Western Europe*, London, Pinter/RIIA.

Wallensteen, P. and Sollenberg, M. (1999) 'Armed Conflict, 1989–98', *Journal of Peace Research*, 36(5), pp. 593–606.

Washington Post (2004) 'Report: Land Mine Pact Cuts Global Casualties', 18 November, p. A28.

Watson, R. T. *et al.* (1996) *Climate Change 1995 – Impacts, Adaptation and Mitigation of Climate Change Scientific-Technical Analysis, Contribution of Working Group II to the Second Assessment Report of the Intergovernmental Panel on Climate Change*, Cambridge, Cambridge University Press.

WCED (World Commission on Environment and Development) (1987) *Our Common Future*, Oxford, Oxford University Press.

Welch, D. (1993) *The Third Reich: Propaganda and Politics*, London, Routledge.

Wheeler, N. J. (2001) *Saving Strangers: Humanitarian Intervention in International Society*, Oxford, Oxford University Press.

Whittaker, D. (ed.) (2001) *The Terrorism Reader*, London, Routledge.

Wilkinson, P. (2000) *Terrorism versus Democracy: The Liberal State Response*, London, Frank Cass).

Wilkinson, P. (2003) 'Implications of the Attacks of 9/11 for the Future of Terrorism', in M. Buckley and R. Fawn (eds), *Global Responses to Terrorism: 9/11, Afghanistan and Beyond*, London, Routledge, pp. 25–36.

Williams, M. (1994) *International Economic Institutions and the Third World*, London, Harvester Wheatsheaf.

Woodhouse, T. and Ramsbotham, O. (eds) (2000) *Peacekeeping and Conflict Resolution*, London, Frank Cass.

Woods, N. (2000) *The Political Economy of Globalization*, Basingstoke, Macmillan.

Woollacott, M. (1996) 'How the World Grew to Love the' Bomb' *Guardian Weekly*, 11 February, p. 10.

World Bank (1995) *Mainstreaming the Environment: The World Bank Group and the Environment Since the Rio Earth Summit*, Washington, DC, World Bank.

World Bank (1999) *World Development Report 1999: Development and the Environment*, Oxford, Oxford University Press.

World Bank (2003) *World Development Indicators* http://www.worldbank.org/data/wdi2003.worldview.pdf.

WTO (World Trade Organization) (1995) *Regionalism and the World Trading System*, London, World Trade Organisation.

WTO (World Trade Organization) (1999) 'World Trade Growth Slower in 1998 After Unusually Strong Growth in 1997', Press Release, 16 April.

WTO (World Trade Organization) (2004), 'World Trade 2003, Prospects for 2004', Press release, 5 April.

Young, O. R. (1989) *International Cooperation: Building Regimes for Natural Resources and the Environment*, Ithaca, Cornell University Press.

Zimmerman, P. (1994) 'Proliferation: Bronze Medal Technology is Enough', *Orbis*, 38 (1), pp. 67–82.

Zolberg, A. (1981) 'International Migrations in Political Perspective', in K. Kritz and S. M. Tomasci (eds), *Global Trends in Migration: Theory and Research on International Population Movements*, New York, The Center for Migration Studies, p. 6.

Zolberg, A., Suhrke, A. and Aguayo, S. (1989) *Escape from Violence*, New York, Oxford University Press.

Internet sources

Regions and regionalism

< http://europa.eu.int/index-en.htm > The European Commission.

< http://www.wto.org > The World Trade Organisation.

< http://www.nato.int > NATO.

< http://www.weu.int > The Western European Union.

< http://www.osce.org > OSCE.

< http://www.nafta-sec-alena.org > The NAFTA Secretariat.

< http://www.apecsec.org.sg > APEC.

Peacekeeping and humanitarian intervention

< http://www.un.org > United Nations.

< http://www.unfoundation.org > UN Foundation.

< http://www.jha.ac.uk > Journal of Humanitarian Assistance.

< http://www.crisisgroup.org > International Crisis Group.

< http://www.un.org/Depts/DPKO/dpkomap.html > List of UN peacekeeping operations.

Nationalism and ethnic conflict

< http://www.un.org/peace/Kosovo/pages/Kosovo1.html > UN Mission in Kosovo.
< http://www.cidcm.umd.edu/inscr/mar/ > Minorities at Risk.
< http://www.incore.ulst.ac.uk > Web Sites related to ethnic conflict.

Migration and refugees

< http://www.unhcr.ch > UNHCR Website.
< http://www.iom.ch > International Organisation for Migration.
< http://www.ind.homeoffice.gov.uk/content/ind/ > Immigration and Nationality Directorate of the UK government.

Environment

< http://www.unep.org > UNEP Website.
< http://www.wri.org > World Resources Institute.
< http://www.iisd.ca > Earth Negotiations Bulletin.

Index

United States (US) (*cont.*)
  immigration 175–6, 183, 185, 278
  intra-regional relations 65–6
  languages 288
  media imperialism 217
  media management 221–2
  Muslim anti-Americanism 166
  and NAFTA 68
  neo-conservative groups 286
  organized crime 247
  outsourcing of call centres 215
  overseas radio networks 223
  peacekeeping 124, 132–3, 285; and
       UN control of operations 130–1;
       in US interests 129
  Presidential election 2004 263
  Racketeering Influences and Corrupt
       Organizations Act (RICO) 247,
       253
  refugee status 191
  religion 156
  shift in security strategy 267
  trade conflicts with Japan 46
  Vietnam War 73, 221, 224, 285
  war on terror 32, 221, 258, 269–70,
       272
Universal Declaration of Human
     Rights 174, 189, 190
UNMIK 135, 141
Uruguay Round agreement 55

van Ham, P. 113
verification 115
Versailles settlement 137
vertical proliferation 98
Vienna Convention 196, 198, 208, 209
Vietnam Veterans of America
     Foundation 111
Vietnam War 73, 221, 224, 285
violence, crime and 242
Voice of America (VOA) 223
voluntary migration 174, 191–2

Wahhabism 167
war 242, 285–6
  and controlling the media 219–22
  holy war 166, 167
  just war 119, 166
  see also ethnic conflict; peacekeeping
       and humanitarian intervention
war on terror 32, 221, 258, 269–70, 272
Washington consensus 78–9, 82–3

Wassenaar Arrangement on Export
     Controls for Conventional Arms and
     Dual-Use Goods and
     Technologies 109, 113
weapons of mass destruction (WMD) 32,
     96–7, 97–104, 270, 271, 284
  ballistic missiles as delivery systems for
       WMD payloads 106
  international control mechanisms 113,
       114–15, 116
Weigel, George 155
Western European Union (WEU) 61
Western worldview 146
Westphalia, Treaty of 21, 141, 157
whales 204, 211
Wilkinson, P. 264
Windhoek Declaration on Mainstreaming
     Gender 130
women 130, 179, 283–4
World Bank 39, 90, 204, 278
  development 78, 79, 82, 84–6;
       SAPs 85–6
  economic interdependence 53
World Commission on Environment and
     Development (WCED) 91, 195–6
world economy *see* economic
     interdependence
World Meteorological Organization
     (WMO) 210
World Summit on Social
     Development 90, 91–2
World Summit on Sustainable
     Development 203
World Trade Organization (WTO) 14,
     15, 39, 46, 55, 69
  Cancun ministerial meeting 94
  Doha Round 55
  environment 204
  meeting in Seattle 1999 55, 94
World Wildlife Fund 206

Yugoslavia
  classification by religion 8–9
  collapse of 18, 123
  conflicts in former Yugoslavia 73,
       226–7, 286; *see also* Bosnia;
       Kosovo
Yunus, Muhammad 283–4

Zaire/Democratic Republic of
     Congo 10–11, 31, 143